This book examines the income di........ ....experience of fifteen developed economies – representing a wide range of social and economic strategies – over the past two decades. Experts from each of the countries have carefully documented the pattern of distributional change in individual earnings and household income in their countries and analysed the driving forces behind these changes. Separate chapters are devoted to the experiences of Australia, Canada, the Czech Republic, Finland, France, West and former East Germany, Greece, Hungary, Ireland, Israel, Japan, the Netherlands, Sweden, the United Kingdom and the United States. The authors examine the effects on the inequality of household income of the development of individual earnings, unemployment, inflation, public sector transfers and taxes, and demographic changes. Several of the authors also examine the development of and underlying causes for changes in poverty in their countries.

The individual country essays view the changes in inequality against the backdrop of structural macroeconomic repercussions following two oil crises and political tides moving towards the right and decentralisation. The diversity of backgrounds also provides an opportunity to pursue the influence on the income distributions of traditionally centralised and decentralised labour markets and to examine the comparative performance of the traditional welfare states. The experiences of a cross-section of countries are compared and analysed in comparative studies of the United Kingdom and the United States. In a separate introductory study, the threads of the individual essays are woven together into a general picture of the development and causes of change in inequality over the past two decades.

Changing patterns in the distribution of economic welfare

Changing patterns in the distribution of economic welfare
An international perspective

edited by

PETER GOTTSCHALK
Boston College

BJÖRN GUSTAFSSON
Gothenburg University

and

EDWARD PALMER
Uppsala University

CAMBRIDGE
UNIVERSITY PRESS

CAMBRIDGE UNIVERSITY PRESS
Cambridge, New York, Melbourne, Madrid, Cape Town, Singapore,
São Paulo, Delhi, Dubai, Tokyo

Cambridge University Press
The Edinburgh Building, Cambridge CB2 8RU, UK

Published in the United States of America by Cambridge University Press, New York

www.cambridge.org
Information on this title: www.cambridge.org/9780521142694

First published 1997
This digitally printed version 2010

A catalogue record for this publication is available from the British Library

Library of Congress Cataloguing in Publication data

Changing patterns in the distribution of economic welfare:
an economic perspective / edited by Peter Gottschalk, Björn Gustafsson,
and Edward Palmer,
p. cm.
ISBN 0-521-56262-7 (hardcover)
1. Income distribution – Case studies. 2. Transfer payments – Case
studies. I. Gottschalk, Peter, 1942– . II. Gustafsson, Bjorn, 1948
III. Palmer, Edward E., 1945– .
HC79.I5D528 1997
339.2′2–dc20   96–13019
                                                                 CIP

ISBN 978-0-521-56262-1 Hardback
ISBN 978-0-521-14269-4 Paperback

Contents

Contributors

LEA ACHDUT Administration of Research and Planning, National Insurance Institute, Jerusalem

IRENE BECKER Johann Wolfgang Goethe-Universität

TIM CALLAN Economic and Social Research Institute, Republic of Ireland

PIERRE CONCIALDI Centre d'Etude des Revenus et des Coûts, Paris

ÖDÖN ÉLTETÖ Hungarian Central Statistical Office

SADETTIN ERKSOY Department of Economics, Dalhousie University

KAREN GARDINER Ministry of Finance and Economic Planning, Uganda

PETER GOTTSCHALK Boston College and the Institute for Research on Poverty

BJÖRN GUSTAFFSSON Department of Social Work, University of Gothenburg

RICHARD HAUSER Johann Wolfgang Goethe-Universität

MARKUS JÄNTTI Åbo University, Finland

RUUD MUFFELS Tilburg Institute for Social Security Research (TISSER)

JAN NELISSEN Tilburg Institute for Social Security Research (TISSER)

BRIAN NOLAN Economic and Social Research Institute, Republic of Ireland

LARS OSBERG Department of Economics, Dalhousie University

EDWARD PALMER Department of Economics, Uppsala University and the National Social Insurance Board

SHELLEY PHIPPS Department of Economics, Dalhousie University

VELI-MATTI RITAKALLIO Åbo University, Finland

PETER SAUNDERS Social Policy Research Centre, University of New South Wales

TOSHIAKI TACHIBANAKI Kyoto Institute of Economic Research

PANOS TSAKLOGLOU Department of International and European
Economic Studies, Athens University of Economics and Business
JIŘÍ VEČERNÍK Institute of Sociology, Academy of Sciences of the Czech
Republic
TADASHI YAGI Faculty of Economics, Nagoya University

1 What's behind the increase in inequality? An introduction

PETER GOTTSCHALK, BJÖRN GUSTAFSSON
AND EDWARD PALMER

1 The issues

The essays in this book examine the income distributional experiences of 15 developed economies during the last two decades.[1] The period covered was characterised by dramatic changes. Growth slowed, from an average 3 per cent to 4 per cent in the 1950s and 1960s, to around 2 per cent in the 1970s and 1980s. The period began with high inflation and low unemployment and ended with low inflation and, in many countries, chronically high unemployment.

Deregulation and the unleashing of market forces became the norm. Restrictions were lifted on the movement of capital. National financial bubbles emerged, grew and burst. The iron curtain fell, while market economies appeared to gain a strong foothold. Politics shifted to the right, and proponents of the 'Welfare State' found themselves increasingly on the defence.

This book focuses on the equally dramatic changes in the distribution of household income that accompanied these political and economic events. While countries such as Sweden, with centralised labour markets, for a long time have had more equal distributions than countries with more decentralised labour markets, such as the United States, inequality barely changed in the developed economies during the 1950s and 1960s. As Henry Aaron stated, watching the distribution of income change was somewhat like watching the grass grow.

This all changed in most industrialised countries during the 1980s. Earnings became markedly less equal as demand for skilled workers outpaced the growth in their supply. Some countries managed to stem the tide, but most did not or could not. As a result, inequality of market incomes increased across a wide variety of countries.

Government reaction to these shifts in market forces differed. Some countries with centralised labour markets, such as Germany, managed to limit the increase in earnings inequality. Other countries, such as Canada,

1

offset the increase in earnings inequality through redistributive taxes and transfers. As a result, increases in inequality of family income were smaller than increases in inequality of labour market income in most countries.

One of the aims of this volume is to bring together a set of comparative studies that examine changes in inequality of both earnings and family incomes.[2] Most essays provide rich detail on a single country. Two essays offer direct comparative material. Gottschalk's contribution compares the experience of the US with six other countries, while Gardiner's essay places the United Kingdom in an international context.

The studies of Australia and Ireland present extensive overviews of research in their countries and provide comprehensive pictures of what has driven the distribution of income in these countries in recent years. The studies of France, Germany, Japan, the Netherlands and Sweden build on previous studies by covering more recent data and by providing new insights into the processes influencing the distribution of income in the 1980s. The contributions from Finland, the Czech Republic, Greece, Hungary and Israel present data on countries that have not been widely accessible to an international readership.

Inequality of household income increased in all but two of these countries, Finland and Ireland. In Finland, there was no significant change in inequality of household income in the 1980s, and in Ireland, where inequality was high to begin with, inequality declined. At the other extreme, increases in inequality of family income in Hungary and in earnings inequality in the Czech Republic were very large.

Table 1.1 summarises the findings of the essays in this volume by categorising countries according to the levels of and trends in earnings and income inequality.[3] These classifications are necessarily crude, because they are based on country-specific data that use somewhat different definitions and are not always for the same years. However, several patterns clearly emerge. First, eastern European countries had the lowest level of earnings and income inequality but the largest increases. The movement from centralised towards market economies had a major impact on the distribution of family income. Second, western European countries with traditionally more centralised labour markets, such as Finland, Germany, the Netherlands and Sweden, had the lowest levels and trends in earnings inequality. Likewise, countries with more extensive income protection systems, such as France, Canada, and the above countries, had lower levels and trends in income inequality. Third, in three of the major market economies with weaker built-in social protection mechanisms – Japan, the UK and the US – income inequality increased noticeably.

The common change in the direction of the development of inequality in the early 1980s makes it tempting to look for a common cause for these

Table 1.1 *Trends in earnings and income inequality*

Country	Earnings inequality		Income inequality	
	Level	Trend 1983–90	Level[a]	Trend 1983–90
Australia	high	(+) moderate	high	(+) moderate
Canada	moderate	(+) moderate	moderate	(+) low
Czech Rep.	very low	(+) very high	na	na
Finland	low	(+) moderate	low	no change
France	moderate	(+) slight	moderate	(+) slight
W.Germany (FRG)	moderate	(+) slight	moderate	(+) slight
E.Germany (GDR)	na	na	low	(+) very high
Greece	na	na	na	(+) moderate
Hungary	very low	(+) very high	low	(+) very high
Ireland	high	no change	high	(−) slight
Israel[b]	high	(+) very high	high	(+) slight
Japan	na	na	high	(+) moderate
The Netherlands	low	(+) slight	moderate	moderate
Sweden	low	(+) low	low	(+) moderate
UK	high	(+) high	moderate	(+) high
US	high	(+) high	high	(+) high

Notes:
[a] Table 1 in Gardiner's contribution in this volume provides Gini coefficients for 9 of the countries included in this study in the mid 1980s. By a 'low level', we mean a Gini of 0.20–0.25, moderate would be 0.26–0.30 and high over 0.30.
[b] Based on Gini for factor income from Achdut's study.

changes. The general picture may be deceiving, however, as a number of factors have been at work. The essays in this volume identify several different factors operating in different directions that, when taken together, have moved the balance in the same direction. In the following section we attempt to place these changes in a broader context by examining the changing economic and social environments facing many of these countries.

2   The changing economic and social environment

The chapters in this volume largely focus on changes in inequality of family income. Table 1.1 shows that all countries (other than Finland and Ireland) experienced increases in inequality, though some countries experienced substantially larger increases than others. Since family income comes from many sources (earnings, private non-labour income, public transfers), the increased inequality could reflect changes in any one, or any combination, of the sources. However, since earnings make up roughly 70 per cent of family income it seems likely that the change in labour markets was a dominant force affecting the distribution of family income.

The importance of changes in the economic environment is seen starkly in the increase in inequality of centralised economies that moved to more market-oriented systems. Sharp increases in earnings inequality in former eastern bloc countries are vividly documented in this volume by Večernick in the chapter on the Czech Republic and Éltetö in the chapter on Hungary.

Although less dramatic, changes in market forces in western industrialised countries led to large changes in inequality. Several chapters in this volume and essays in Freeman and Katz (1994) document that labour market income became considerably less equally distributed, especially in countries with decentralised labour markets. Earnings inequality grew dramatically in the US and the UK, two countries with market-oriented economies. Smaller but appreciable increases in earnings inequality were observed in countries as diverse as Canada, Australia, the Netherlands and Sweden.

These increases in earnings inequality reflect more than occupational or industrial shifts. Tsakloglou finds that increasing inequality within occupational groups was a significant determinant of increasing inequality in Greece in the 1980s. Likewise, Hauser and Becker find for West Germany increasing inequality of income within groups defined by occupation.

The US and the UK were the leaders in the trend towards greater inequality of labour market earnings, but many other countries followed similar patterns. Those countries that managed to initially limit the increases in earnings inequality, such as Germany and Sweden, tended to have more centralised labour market institutions that buffeted workers from market forces. However, as the chapter on Sweden by Gustafsson and Palmer shows, market forces are gaining on the political forces behind wage solidarity.

Changes in labour market conditions were moderated in some countries by explicit changes in macroeconomic and social policies. While the US largely stood by, letting labour market conditions dominate changes in the distribution of after-tax and transfer income, other countries, such as Canada, took an active role in softening the blow from changes in labour market conditions.

During the 1950s and 1960s, the prevailing view in western economies was that full employment could be maintained by fine-tuning the economy. Holding down unemployment seemed to be more important than fighting inflation in a time when inflation was – by later standards – low. The first

OPEC agreement, however, resulted in large oil price rises and a new threat in the form of higher permanent inflationary pressure, with resulting pressure on wage demands, inflationary expectations and, as a consequence, pressure on fixed exchange-rate regimes.

During the 1950s and 1960s, there was also a tendency to emphasise the role of public institutions in protecting individual agents from the dark side of the market. In many western European and Scandinavian countries, wage setting became centralised either through centralised negotiations between large employers and unions or through direct government intervention. As a result, wages were somewhat insulated from market forces. Furthermore, national and local public services expanded to protect those who did not benefit from the rapid economic growth of that era.

Many of the social mechanisms influencing the labour market became less prominent during the 1980s. Less reliance was placed on fine-tuning to maintain full employment, as macroeconomists fled the Keynesian camp. The public sector's involvement in the economy became politically less popular. As a result, wage-setting became less centralised, and firms faced fewer regulations, including measures designed to limit wage increases. The UK and the US led the way. Although there had been other Conservative governments in the UK and Republican Presidents in the US, the governments of Thatcher and Reagan symbolised a change in political thinking about economic policy in the west.

The shift to less economic and social protection came to continental Europe later in the 1980s. Social Democratic governments were pushed out by coalitions from the right in France, Germany and Sweden, although in Sweden only intermittently. This shift to the right did not, however, always lead to distributional changes. In Sweden, inequality continued to decrease during the first non-social-democratic regime (1977–82) and began to increase with the return of the Social Democrats in 1983. In Germany, the increase in inequality was at most modest, but in the Netherlands inequality increased with coalitions including the right-wing. Hence, it is difficult to attribute the common trend in inequality experienced in western European countries during the 1980s to the emergence of conservative governments. Whatever was happening was a more general phenomenon.

Political changes, however, were crucial in eastern Europe. As state socialism came crashing down in 1989, centralised economic decision making began to be replaced by decentralised market decision making. As Éltetö (Hungary), Vecernik (Czech Republic) and Hauser and Becker (eastern Germany) show, one of the main reasons behind the large increase in inequality in the former state socialist economies was the move away from central involvement and the move towards greater reliance on the market, particularly in the determination of earnings.

If changes in the ruling parties in the western economies are not sufficient to explain changes in inequality, was the shift in emphasis from holding down unemployment to controlling inflation a driving force? As the job of regulating inflation was turned over to the central banks, inflation dropped, but the rate of unemployment rose. To what extent can the increase in inequality be attributed to this switch in goals?

In previous studies of the US (Blinder and Esaki 1978; Blank and Blinder 1986; Jäntti, 1994), of the UK (Weil 1984; Nolan 1986) and, of Canada (Buse 1982), increased unemployment has been found to be correlated with increased inequality. Adding to this body of evidence, Callan and Nolan report in this volume that the rise in unemployment in Ireland played a major role in the falling income shares of the second and third quintiles.

The impact of increased unemployment, however, depends on the safety net. Concialdi attributes part of the increase in inequality of household income in France during the second half of the 1980s to an increase in uncovered long-term unemployment. Likewise, Saunders's study concludes that in Australia, where unemployment benefits are flat-rate and means-tested, inequality varied in response to changing cyclical conditions in the economy. In contrast, the study of Canada by Osberg, Erksoy and Phipps concludes that insurance payments were an important source of stability in the distribution of income among Canadian men, offsetting the increase in the inequality caused by business cycle fluctuations during the 1980s. Likewise, Gustafsson and Palmer find the effect of unemployment on the income distribution to be very weak because of significant replacement rates in Swedish unemployment insurance and because of labour market policies that employ or train the cyclically unemployed.

The effect of inflation likewise depends on institutional factors. For example, Achdut finds that inflation in Israel had a substantial distributional impact despite indexation of taxes and transfers, because levels were not immediately adjusted. In contrast, the Swedish study finds that inflation had only minimal impact because pension and other social security benefits are indexed.

Perhaps the moral of this story is that the effects of unemployment and inflation can be mitigated where benefit schemes and indexation are designed to offset such effects. Among the countries in this volume, the US offers the least protection. In contrast, Canada cushioned the incomes of the unemployed by generous benefits, and in Sweden a combination of benefits, training programmes and public works more or less neutralised the effects of rising unemployment.

Countries also differed in their protection of those outside the labour market. Table 1.2 offers a rough ranking of the degree of social involvement by the countries in this volume. The highest protection was offered by the

Table 1.2 *Degree of social involvement*

High	Moderate	Low
Czech Rep.	Finland	Australia
Hungary	France	Canada
E. Germany	W. Germany	Greece
	Japan	Ireland
	The Netherlands	Israel
	Sweden	UK
		US

eastern European countries, followed by the Scandinavian and continental European countries.[4] In the 1960s and 1970s, many European and Scandinavian countries developed social security systems for the sick, disabled, unemployed, elderly and children. This led to vast public commitments to large groups in society.

In many of the countries in this volume, taxes were increased to fund this greater social protection. Governments found themselves spending between 40 per cent and 60 per cent of GNP on public expenditures, with Sweden leading the way. As economic growth subsided, so did the potential to continue to expand – or in some cases maintain – the welfare state.

In the course of the 1980s, more restrictive policies emerged in the more prominent welfare states. Cutting back the welfare state took on different tones in different countries. Muffels and Nelissen attribute some of the increases in inequality observed after 1983 in the Netherlands to a stepwise downgrading of benefits and the tightening of qualifications for unemployment and disability. This pushed previous recipients and new applicants into the local social assistance net, where help is generally means-tested and benefits are low. Concialdi shows that in France, benefit increases were halted in 1983, benefit entitlement criteria were made more restrictive and the rise in the minimum wage was stabilised, depressing the relative income of younger workers most severely.

In Germany, there was a tendency to extend coverage and introduce new benefits during the 1970s. In the 1980s, the tide shifted, and efforts were made to reduce benefits, tighten the rules for entitlements and change indexation of pensions. Sweden and Finland also tightened benefit levels and entitlement conditions. Sweden, however, did not abandon its commitment to universal social insurance and subsistence help for those who land in the safety net. In Australia, the targeting of payments took the form of tightening eligibility and entitlement rules, but was combined with considerable increases in the real benefit levels for some categories (e.g., families with children).

The trend in tax reforms in the 1980s was towards less progression in tax scales. Greater reliance was put on proportionate taxation (flat-rate contributions for social security, value-added taxes on commodities and services, proportionate income taxes with more limited deduction possibilities than previously). Since old-age social security pension schemes are almost exclusively financed on a pay-as-you-go basis, the increase in both benefits and the number of recipients meant that contributions had to be raised. For example, according to Concialdi's study, the contribution rate in France increased by 10 percentage points between 1973 and 1984. In Germany, contributions to social security increased continuously during the 1970s and 1980s. In Sweden, almost half of the growth in GDP was transferred from wage earners to pensioners as the earnings-related pay-as-you-go pension scheme matured in the 1970s and 1980s.

Highly progressive income taxes were introduced originally for redistributive reasons, based on arguments of equity and ability to pay. As more taxpayers moved into higher marginal rates and as some econometric studies indicated that high marginal tax rates had a negative effect on labour supply, it became popular to argue for less progressivity.[5] Reforms reducing the progressivity of income taxes were introduced gradually in the UK beginning in the late 1970s. The top marginal tax rate was reduced from 60 per cent to 40 per cent. Similar patterns were followed in the US, where the top rate was lowered to 33 per cent. The 1990 Oort tax reform in the Netherlands broadened the tax base and lowered marginal tax rates, apparently hurting single-earner low-income earners and benefiting high-income households. A comprehensive reform in Sweden in 1991 decreased the highest marginal tax rate to 50 per cent, from earlier heights exceeding 70 per cent.

How important were these tax changes? Gardiner concludes that changes in tax law in the UK in the 1980s made the system less progressive. However, this inequality-increasing effect was offset by the increased taxes collected as income gains moved more households into higher brackets. Likewise, Gottschalk shows that the net effect of changes in taxes was small in most countries, certainly much smaller than the impact of changes in labour markets. Muffels and Nelissen conclude that the redistributive effects of the Oort reform seem to be moderate. Gustafsson and Palmer offer the one exception. They conclude that the decreased progressivity of taxes in Sweden was as important a driving force in increasing income inequality as the increase in wage dispersion during the 1980s.

Increases in inequality that arise from deterioration at the bottom of the distribution might be of greater policy concern than those that arise from gains at the top. For this reason, several of the studies in this volume (Australia, Finland, Ireland, Israel and the Netherlands) devote separate sections to changes in the number of persons under poverty levels. In three of these countries (Australia, Israel and the Netherlands), income inequality increased in the 1980s. In Finland, income inequality remained practically unchanged, while in Ireland it decreased. What happened to poverty in the 1980s in these countries?

Poverty was almost eradicated in Finland during the 1980s. Ironically, Finland entered into a deep recession in 1991, as the effects of the world recession were compounded by the loss of longstanding markets and bilateral trade with the USSR. It will be interesting to look back at the 1990s to see how Finland's social policy will have weathered this storm.

In Australia, the poverty rate increased, from 9.4 per cent to 15 per cent during the 1980s, with the strongest increases for single parents. In Israel, poverty before transfers and taxes rose substantially. However, taxes and transfers offset these adverse trends, allowing poverty to rise only slightly. In Ireland, Callan and Nolan conclude that the relatively rapid rise in the number of persons receiving occupational pensions and social welfare support for the elderly, widows and single parents led to a decline in the proportion of these groups under the poverty line. However, the rise in unemployment led to a sharp increase in poverty. In the Netherlands the incidence of poverty remained rather stable, although for the (long-term) unemployed and disabled the incidence of poverty rose substantially, as also for the widowed elderly (single) persons and single-parent families.

3   Summary

One of the clear conclusions of this volume is that inequality of earnings has been on the rise. While countries with more centralised labour markets have limited the increase, few have been totally successful. The trend to greater inequality has little to do with increasing interoccupational differences. Instead, earnings dispersion is a phenomenon within specific occupations and appears to be steered by forces that have little to do with occupations per se. The resulting increase in earnings inequality is clearly a dominant force behind the increase in income inequality observed in many of the countries covered in this volume.

Rising unemployment has been a problem. As a result, inequality rose where benefit schemes and other forms of public support were not sufficient to counteract these forces. In the traditional welfare states, there has been a clear trend towards tightening entitlement requirements and/or benefit levels. Still, inequality of family income did not increase dramatically in the welfare states, suggesting that the changes in social security thus far have been marginal. In some countries (the UK, the US, and Sweden), tax reform has led to less progressive taxation and increasing inequality.

In countries with less extensive welfare systems, poverty became an increasing problem for single-parent households and, although less so, generally for households with children. High unemployment in these countries has exacerbated the problem. The aged, however, appear to have bucked the trend. They improved their relative lot, owing to the increasing numbers that have accumulated good benefits from occupational and income-related pension schemes.

Notes

The contributions in this volume were prepared for and, with a couple of exceptions, presented at a conference held in Fiskebäckskil, 21–23 June 1993, sponsored by the Swedish Council of Social Research (SFR) and Jan Wallanders Stiftelse.

1 We focus on changes in inequality. For an international comparison of levels of inequality, see Atkinson, Rainwater and Smeeding 1995.
2 Freeman and Katz 1994 also provide comparative studies. Their focus is on earnings, however, and not household income.
3 For a discussion of the Gini coefficient and alternative measures of inequality, see Lambert 1993 and Jenkins 1991.
4 The UK is placed in the moderate group, in spite of its far-reaching social safety net, because social security only provides a subsistence standard, whereas social security arrangements are generally geared towards income replacement in Finland, France, Germany, the Netherlands and Sweden.
5 One of the most influential studies was Hausman (1981), although as surveys of econometric studies suggest the empirical evidence of the negative effect is mixed.

References

Atkinson, A., Rainwater, L. and Smeeding, T. 1995. *Income Distribution in OECD Countries: The Evidence from the Luxembourg Income Study (LIS)* Social Policy Studies No. 18. Paris: OECD.

Blank, R. and Blinder, A. 1986. 'Macroeconomics, Income Distribution and Poverty', in Danziger, S. and Weinberger, D. (eds.), *Fighting Poverty, What Works and What Doesn't*. Cambridge, Mass.: Harvard University Press.

Blinder, A. and Esaki, H. 1978. 'Macroeconomic Activity and Income Distribution in Postwar United States'. *Review of Economics and Statistics*, 60: 604–8.

Buse, A. 1982. 'The Cyclical Behaviour of the Size Distribution in Income in Canada'. *Canadian Journal of Economics*, 40: 189–204.

Freeman, Richard and Katz, Lawrence. 1994. *Differences and Changes in Wage Structures*. Chicago: University of Chicago Press and NBER.

Hausman, J. A. 1981. 'Labour Supply', in Aaron, H. J. and Peckman, J. A. (eds.), *How Taxes Affect Economic Behaviour*. Washington DC: Brookings Institution.

Jäntti, M. (1994). 'A More Efficient Estimate of the Effects of Macroeconomic Activity on the Distribution of Income'. *Review of Economics and Statistics*, 76: 372–8.

Jenkins, S. 1991. 'The Measurement of Income Inequality', in Osberg, Lars (ed.), *Economic Inequality and Poverty: International Perspectives*. Armonk, NY, London: M. E. Sharp.

Lambert, P. 1993. *The Distribution and Redistribution of Income: A Mathematical Analysis*. Second Edition. Manchester and New York: Manchester University Press.

Nolan, B. 1986. 'Unemployment and the Size Distribution of Income'. *Economica*, 53:, 421–45.

Weil, G. 1984. 'Cyclical and Secular Influence on the Size Distribution of Personal Income in the UK: Some Econometric Tests'. *Applied Economics*, 16: 749–55.

2 Policy changes and growing earnings inequality in the US and six other OECD countries

PETER GOTTSCHALK

1 Introduction

It is now widely recognised that earnings inequality grew rapidly in the United States during the 1970s and 1980s.[1] The average earnings of educated workers pulled further apart from those of the less educated, and young workers lost relatively to prime-aged workers.[2] Not only did inequality increase between groups, but inequality also increased substantially within education and experience groups.[3] This increase in 'within-group' inequality accounted for the majority of the increase in inequality. Furthermore, the trend to greater within-group inequality was nearly universal across all groups, including groups such as professional prime-aged white males, who are often insulated from adverse changes in labour markets.

The increase in earnings inequality was accompanied by a substantial increase in the dispersion of family income in the US (Danziger and Gottschalk 1993; Blackburn and Bloom 1993). Changes in the distribution of other family members' earnings and other private income sources did not change sufficiently to offset the increase in inequality of earnings of heads of households. While the earnings of spouses were mildly equalising, their impact did not offset the trends in male earnings inequality (Cancian, Danziger and Gottschalk 1993). Furthermore, government tax and transfer policies did little to offset the increase in earnings inequality (Gramlich, Kasten and Sammartino 1993). As a result, inequality of income after taxes and transfers largely reflected the increase in earnings inequality. With moderate increases in mean income and substantial growth in inequality, poverty rates were substantially higher in 1995 than in 1973.

How did other countries fare during this period of growing inequality in the US? Previous research supports three conclusions.[4] First, the increase in inequality of earnings was not limited to the US. Measured either by overall summary statistics, such as the coefficient of variation, or percentile points, inequality grew in Australia, Canada, Sweden and the UK.

Furthermore, the pattern of growing inequality both within and across groups was widespread. Most countries experienced an increase in the education premium and an increase in inequality within groups. This strongly suggests that the economic forces affecting the US were ubiquitous. Second, while the US is not unique, it is the country with the largest increase in earnings at the top of the distribution and the country with the largest increase in the premium for going to college. The third conclusion is that countries with more decentralised wage-setting institutions experienced the smallest increases in inequality. For example, Germany and Italy, two countries with centralised labour markets, showed no increase in inequality.

While earnings inequality rose in most countries, this change in market-generated earnings need not translate into increases in inequality of family income, since other forms of income, such as government transfers can offset some or all of the increase in earnings inequality. In fact, Hanratty and Blank (1992) show that in spite of similar increases in inequality of market income, Canada managed to supplement the incomes of low-income families enough to keep poverty rates from rising.

In this chapter, I examine the relationship between increases in earnings inequality and family income inequality in several industrialised countries. I examine whether changes in the earnings of other family members or changes in taxes and transfers mediated the effects of rising inequality of wage rates. The focus is again cross-national. Comparing the US experience with that of other countries gives a context for evaluating the ability of the US to offset these adverse changes in the distribution of labour market earnings.

The remainder of the chapter is divided into three parts. Section 2 reviews the literature on inequality of earnings and family income in the US and the emerging literature on international comparisons of inequality. Section 3 presents the results. The final section draws conclusions from the data presented.

2   Review of literature

I start by reviewing the evidence on changes in the distribution of family income and individual earnings in the US. The focus then changes from the US experience to trends in other industrialised countries.

The recent increase in inequality of family income in the US is a departure from the post-war trend. In the most comprehensive review of long-run changes in income inequality, Williamson and Lindert (1980) place the post-World War II stability of inequality in the US into historical perspective. After documenting the dramatic levelling of income differences between the Great Depression and the end of World War II (1929 to 1948) they conclude that 'the leveling ceased by 1950. By almost any yardstick, inequality has changed little since the late 1940s. If there has been any trend, it has been toward slightly more inequality in pre-fisc income and slightly less inequality in post-fisc income. This stability has been extraordinary even by 20th century standards' (p. 92).

However, just as Williamson and Lindert were going to press, the 'extraordinary' stability in family income inequality was breaking down. While the Gini coefficient for family income had declined 0.013 points over three decades, it jumped 0.036 points in the next decade.[5]

Growth in mean family income in the US was rapid and widely shared between 1949 and 1969. The inflation-adjusted income of a family at the 20th percentile grew by 92 per cent, while the income of a family at the 80th percentile grew by 82 per cent. This period of rapid and equally distributed growth came to an end in the early 1970s. During the next two decades, mean income grew only slowly, and the growth accrued mostly to persons at the top of the distribution. Growth was substantial for families at the top of the distribution, while those at the bottom actually lost ground. In 1989, the real income of a family at the 20th percentile was 5 per cent below the 1969 level, while that of a family at the 80th percentile was 19 per cent higher.

This rise in inequality of family income reflects a secular trend, not a cyclical aberration. While the sharp increase in inequality between 1979 and 1983 can be attributed to the recessions of the early 1980s, the continued increase during the ensuing recovery was counter to previous expectations. The old conventional wisdom that 'a rising tide lifts all boats' was rejected. The cyclical recovery simply did not help all families equally. The income of families at the bottom of the distribution stagnated while the income of families at the top rose rapidly.

Why did the family income distribution become increasingly unequal? Since labour market income accounts for about 70 per cent of family income, changes in the distribution of earnings is likely to be a key factor in explaining changes in the distribution of family income. Recent studies of earnings inequality in the US find that wage growth varied dramatically between the upper, middle and lower tails of the distribution.[6] Since 1975, the real wages of males at the 90th and 75th percentiles increased 10 per cent faster than the median. In contrast, the real wages for the 25th and 10th percentiles declined sharply relative to the median (Karoly 1993). The increase in inequality in both weekly and hourly wage series indicates that the increase in annual wage dispersion in the US reflects primarily changes in the rate of pay, not changes in the distribution of annual hours worked.

Changes in the dispersion in the overall earnings distribution can be usefully decomposed into changes in between-group inequality and within-group inequality. The former traditionally focuses on increases in wage differentials between high school and college graduates and between new entrants into the labour market and older workers. Within-group inequality focuses on increased dispersion in the earnings distribution within education and experience groups.

Part of the observed change in the overall distribution of earnings reflects the large increase in the returns to education. During the 1980s, the returns to experience and education increased dramatically in the US, especially for younger workers. According to Katz and Murphy (1992), young college educated workers earned a little over 40 per cent more than high school graduates in the late 1970s. By 1985, the college premium had risen to almost 90 per cent. This is in sharp contrast to the decline in the returns to education during the 1970s. Meanwhile, returns to experience increased nearly as much. The earnings of young workers continued to fall behind those of older workers with more experience.

The increase in returns to education and experience resulted in a dramatic decline in the relative position of young high school graduates. Juhn, Murphy and Pierce (1993) illustrate this decline by noting that real wages of young high school graduates of the 10th percentile were roughly 18 per cent lower in 1987 than wages for the same group 15 years earlier. The wages of the least-skilled workers were rapidly falling away from the rest of the distribution.

In addition to the increased inequality between education and experience groups, studies find a striking increase in wage dispersion within groups defined in terms of education, age, industry and other demographic characteristics. Persons at the top of the earnings distribution experienced significant growth in real wages while those in the lower part of the distribution experienced slight growth or, in most cases, declines in real wages. In fact, Murphy and Welch (1992) find that the majority of the change in dispersion occurred within groups. They conclude that 'deindustrialisation', as captured by industrial shifts out of manufacturing and into services, explains only a fraction of the change in inequality. Most of the change occurred within industries for persons of similar age and education. Gottschalk and Joyce (1995) find similar patterns in other industrialised countries.

The recent availability of cross-country data has made it possible to make cross-national comparisons of changes in earnings and income inequality across a variety of countries. Studies in this volume complement previous studies, which include Australia and New Zealand (Saunders, Stott and Hobbes 1991), Germany (Abraham and Houseman 1995), Italy (Erickson and Ichino 1995), Korea (Kim and Topel 1995) and Sweden (Hibbs 1990;

Edin and Holmlund 1995). Several cross-national studies provide bilateral comparisons with the United States. Freeman and Needles (1991) compare the rise in inequality in the US and Canada; Borland (1992) compares Australia with the US; Katz and Loveman (1990) compare the US with the United Kingdom and France; while Katz and Revenga (1989) compare the US and Japan; Katz, Loveman and Blanchflower (1995) compare the US with France, the UK and Japan. Gottschalk and Joyce (1995) use data assembled in the Luxembourg Income Study (LIS) to study changes in the US, UK, Canada, Australia, France, the Netherlands and Sweden.[7]

The broad picture that emerges from these studies is that the US and UK led the increase in earnings inequality. Canada, Japan and, to a lesser extent, Australia, France, the Netherlands and Sweden also experienced increases in inequality. The only European countries to escape the trend in inequality were Italy and Germany.[8] While there was a general trend towards inequality, the changes were largest in those countries with the most decentralised and least unionised labour markets. Countries with centralised wage-setting institutions, such as Germany and Sweden, experienced substantially smaller increases in earnings inequality (Freeman 1994).

3   Data and methods

The LIS data are a collection of microdata sets obtained from annual income surveys in various countries.[9] The different surveys are similar in form to the Current Population Survey for the United States and the Survey of Consumer Finances for Canada.[10] The advantage of these data is that extensive effort has been made by country specialists to make the information on income and household characteristics as comparable as possible across data sets. Comparability is, however, seldom perfect since these data sets are administered by different governments for varying purposes. LIS does as good a job as possible to overcome the comparability problems common to all cross-national studies.

Since I am interested in changes in inequality, the study is restricted to the countries with two years of data (Australia, Canada, France, the Netherlands, Sweden, the United Kingdom and the United States). Although the years used were dictated by the years covered for each country in LIS, they represent a roughly similar time period: the first wave of data for each country is from the early 1980s, the second wave from the mid or late 1980s. For all countries other than Sweden and the Netherlands, unemployment rates were higher in the second year than in the first.

My general approach is to start with the best available measure in LIS of changes in the distribution of wages of individual workers as measured by the distribution of earnings of male heads of household working full time.[11] I then move incrementally to the distribution of family income after taxes and transfers, adjusted for needs. In essence, I show how adding other male and female heads, adjusting for family size and adding additional sources of income and taxes alter the income distribution. The primary focus of this chapter is in contrasting the distribution of labour market incomes of individuals with the final distribution of after-tax and transfer family income.

The measure of earnings used in this chapter is real annual gross wages and salaries.[12] Because this measure includes the effects of hours as well as wages, I start by focusing on male heads who report working full time, a group for which changes in earnings reflect primarily changes in the distribution of wage rates and not hours. Therefore, the sample is initially limited to male heads of households between the ages of 25 and 55.[13] Where possible I also screen on the full-time variable in LIS.[14] Since no full-time variable is available for France or Canada, I contrast the experiences of these countries with data from the US that also include part-time workers. Finally, to focus solely on labour market income, I exclude male heads of households who report any self-employment income.

This initial sample of male heads with a strong attachment to the labour market is chosen to capture changes in the distribution of wage rates. However, it excludes other non-aged male heads and all female heads whose earnings may have changed due to changes in the distribution of hours as well as wages.[15] The next step is thus to include these other non-aged male heads and all non-aged female heads. This introduces the effects of changes in hours and changes in the gender composition of heads.

Since changes in the distribution of heads' earnings may have been accompanied by changes in family size, I take account of differences in family needs by dividing the earnings of heads by the OECD needs standard.[16] This yields the distribution of earnings of heads per equivalent unit. I then add the earnings of other family members to see the net effect of changes in other earners' labour market income on the distribution of family earnings in equivalent units. The next step is to add private non-labour income (self-employment income, property income, alimony and private pensions) to the family's earnings to obtain the distribution of pre-transfer income adjusted for needs. Government transfers (social insurance and means-tested payments) are then added to obtain the post-transfer distribution of family income adjusted for needs. Finally, income is adjusted for taxes paid.

The results presented in this chapter contrast the distribution of different income measures. This purely descriptive exercise answers questions such as 'Did the distribution of after-tax and transfer income change as much as the distribution of earnings?' The answer to this question, of course, does not isolate the cause of the change in final income since changes in taxes and transfers may themselves have caused the increase in inequality of pre-tax and transfer income.

4   Changes in inequality in seven industrialised countries

4.1   The United States

Changes in earnings inequality in the seven industrialised countries covered in this study are shown in table 2.1, which shows the earnings of male heads of households at the 10th, 20th, 80th and 90th percentile, all measured as log deviations from the earnings of the median. For example, among full-time workers in the US in 1979, the person at the 50th percentile earned 80.7 per cent more than the person at the 10th percentile. By 1986, this had increased to 82.8 per cent. At the upper end of the distribution, the earnings of a person at the 90th percentile increased from 53.9 per cent of the median to 69.3 per cent.

While table 2.1 shows differences in the size of the changes in different countries, it also reveals a decline in relative earnings at the bottom of the distribution and an increase at the top in all countries. The relative earnings of those at the 90th percentile rose not only relative to the 10th percentile but also relative to the median. This indicates that the changes in inequality of earnings reflect more than a decline in earnings at the lower end of the earnings distribution. Not only was there a pulling apart of the distribution, the change in earnings was positively related to decile rank – with few exceptions the lower the decile, the larger the decline in earnings (or the smaller the growth).

Where the US stands out is in the magnitude of the increase in earnings of those at the top of the distribution. The 90th percentile (relative to the median) grew by 2.2 per cent annually in the US. In contrast, the next largest increase (in the UK) is only 1.07 per cent per year, and the smallest increase (in Australia) is only 0.75 per cent.

Thus, we see that all countries faced at least some increase in inequality in labour market income. Did these increases in earnings inequality translate into increases in inequality of family income after taxes and transfers adjusted for family size? To answer this question, I proceed to add income sources and adjust for family size. Detailed information is presented for the US, which is then compared with summary information on the other six countries.[17]

Table 2.2 presents the basic data on the distribution of earnings and earnings/needs for non-aged heads in the US.[18] The first two columns show the distribution of the earnings of male heads. The first column shows data for

Table 2.1 *Log percentile differentials, real annual wages and salaries, males 25–54*

	10–50	20–50	80–50	90–50
Full-time workers				
Australia				
1981	−0.476	−0.288	0.283	0.446
1985	−0.503	−0.289	0.302	0.476
yearly D	−0.0068	−0.0003	0.0048	0.0075
Netherlands				
1983	−0.326	−0.236	0.320	0.517
1987	−0.351	−0.233	0.314	0.549
yearly D	−0.0063	0.0008	−0.0015	0.0080
Sweden				
1981	−0.311	−0.189	0.240	0.433
1987	−0.324	−0.196	0.286	0.459
yearly D	−0.0022	−0.0012	0.0077	0.0043
United Kingdom				
1979	−0.422	−0.267	0.302	0.506
1986	−0.521	−0.337	0.372	0.581
yearly D	−0.0141	−0.0100	0.0100	0.0107
United States				
1979	−0.807	−0.498	0.357	0.539
1986	−0.828	−0.511	0.470	0.693
yearly D	−0.0030	−0.0019	0.0161	0.0220
All workers				
Canada				
1981	−0.863	−0.445	0.325	0.498
1987	−1.04	−0.511	0.365	0.531
yearly D	−0.0295	−0.0110	0.0067	0.0055
France				
1979	−0.485	−0.307	0.376	0.636
1984	−0.567	−0.361	0.382	0.670
yearly D	−0.0164	−0.0108	0.0012	0.0068
United States				
1979	−0.887	−0.531	0.356	0.568
1986	−1.038	−0.612	0.459	0.724
yearly D	−0.0216	−0.0116	0.0147	0.0223

Table 2.2 Distribution of head's earnings by gender of head

	Earnings				Earnings/needs			
	1 Male heads 25–54, working full time, not self-employed	2 All male heads	3 All female heads	4 All heads	5 Male heads 25–54, working full time, not self-employed	6 All male heads	7 All female heads	8 All heads
US 1979								
10/50th per cent	0.446	0.372	0.207	0.286	0.427	0.384	0.170	0.312
20/50th per cent	0.608	0.563	0.441	0.500	0.599	0.567	0.356	0.528
80/50th per cent	1.429	1.492	1.621	1.571	1.627	1.652	1.892	1.681
90/50th per cent	1.714	1.813	2.082	1.929	2.154	2.174	2.550	2.223
Coefficient of var.								
Full dist.	0.277	0.338	0.493	0.413	0.465	0.499	0.691	0.537
Truncated dist.	0.194	0.243	0.360	0.300	0.275	0.304	0.503	0.342
US 1986								
10/50th per cent	0.437	0.334	0.183	0.296	0.386	0.326	0.182	0.287
20/50th per cent	0.600	0.522	0.423	0.495	0.574	0.523	0.386	0.488
80/50th per cent	1.600	1.601	1.769	1.721	1.763	1.788	2.072	1.832
90/50th per cent	2.000	2.022	2.183	2.140	2.400	2.447	2.726	2.475
Coefficient of var.								
Full dist.	0.385	0.459	0.520	0.517	0.539	0.601	0.731	0.627
Truncated dist.	0.249	0.302	0.391	0.342	0.345	0.388	0.531	0.415

Annual abs. change in							
90/10	0.105	0.169	0.263	0.069	0.167	0.262	0.000	0.215
80/20	0.045	0.059	0.073	0.048	0.051	0.072	0.006	0.081
Coefficient of var.							
Full dist.	0.015	0.017	0.004	0.015	0.010	0.015	0.006	0.013
Truncated dist.	0.008	0.008	0.004	0.006	0.010	0.012	0.004	0.011

Note:
Coefficients of variation are for the distributions of positive income.

the sample of male heads with strong labour force attachment. The data in column 2 add all other non-aged male heads. These include persons who were not full-time workers, were younger than 25 or received self-employment income. Column 3 presents data for female heads. Columns 2 and 3 are summarised in column 4, which shows the summary statistics for all non-elderly heads. Columns 5 to 8 replicate the samples in columns 1 to 4 but adjust earnings by family needs, as measured by the OECD equivalence scale. The rows in table 2.2 show the incomes of heads at the 10th, 20th, 80th and 90th percentiles, all measured as proportions of median incomes, and two summary measures of inequality based on the coefficient of variation. The first includes all observations. The second adjusts for changes in top coding and other misreporting at the top of the distribution by calculating the coefficient of variation for the bottom 95 per cent of the distribution.

Table 2.3 shows the impact of adding other sources of income and subtracting taxes. The sample in all these columns is the same (families with positive family earnings), so changes across columns do not reflect changes in sample composition. Column 1 replicates column 8 of table 2.2 and shows the distribution of the earnings of heads of households, adjusted for family size. Column 2 of table 2.3 adds the earnings of persons other than the head. These include the spouse and other persons in the family. Comparison of columns 1 and 2, therefore, shows the impact of changes in the distribution of earnings of other workers in the household.

Column 3 further adds all other private sources of income, including dividends, rents, private non-labour market incomes and private transfers, such as alimony and private pensions. Social insurance and means-tested public transfers are added in column 4 which shows the resulting distribution of total family income. Differences between columns 3 and 4, therefore, show the impact of changes in the distribution of public transfers. Finally, column 5 subtracts taxes.

Column 1 of table 2.2 shows that the earnings of our selected sample of male heads at the 10th percentile fell (relative to the median), from 0.446 to 0.437 between 1979 and 1986, while the earnings of those at the 90th percentile rose from 1.714 to 2.000. As a result, the 90/10 ratio rose by 0.105 points per year, as shown in the bottom panel of table 2.2. Somewhat smaller declines are found in the 20/50 ratio, resulting in a 0.045 point increase in the 80/20 ratio. The coefficient of variation increased by 0.015 points per year for the full distribution and by 0.008 points for the truncated distribution. These increases in inequality are consistent with other studies that have found large increases in inequality of wage rates, especially at the upper tail, in the US during this period.

Column 1 focuses only on fully employed male heads in order to gauge

Table 2.3 *Distribution of alternative income/needs measure*

	1 Earnings of head	2 Total earnings	3 Total earnings, other income, private transfers	4 Post-transfer income	5 Post-tax and transfer income
US 1979					
10/50th per cent	0.312	0.341	0.364	0.393	0.440
20/50th per cent	0.528	0.537	0.551	0.568	0.609
80/50th per cent	1.681	1.610	1.620	1.614	1.508
90/50th per cent	2.223	2.049	2.062	2.044	1.854
Coefficient of var.					
Full dist.	0.537	0.435	0.451	0.431	0.300
Truncated dist.	0.342	0.299	0.290	0.273	0.215
US 1986					
10/50th per cent	0.287	0.321	0.335	0.358	0.392
20/50th per cent	0.488	0.522	0.532	0.546	0.579
80/50th per cent	1.832	1.738	1.703	1.691	1.595
90/50th per cent	2.475	2.219	2.221	2.184	1.999
Coefficient of var.					
Full dist.	0.627	0.509	0.546	0.520	0.385
Truncated dist.	0.415	0.346	0.336	0.316	0.261
Annual Abs. *change in*					
90/10	0.215	0.132	0.137	0.129	0.126
80/20	0.081	0.047	0.037	0.037	0.040
Coefficient of var.					
Full dist.	0.013	0.011	0.014	0.013	0.012
Truncated dist.	0.011	0.007	0.007	0.006	0.007

Note:
Coefficients of variation are for the distributions of positive income.

the changes in the distribution of wage rates. Many families, however, are not headed by fully employed male heads. Column 2 therefore adds all other male heads, and column 3 shows similar data for female heads. These data also show increases in inequality, either measured by the 90/10 ratio or by the coefficient of variation for both groups.

As a result of these changes and changes in the gender composition of heads, inequality of earnings of all non-aged heads, shown in column 4, increased somewhat less than for the selected sample of male heads when measured by the 90/10 ratio but by roughly the same amount when measured by the 80/20 ratio. Thus, the general conclusion that inequality of earnings grew in the US during the 1980s is generally applicable to all heads in the US.

Since we are ultimately interested in changes in the distribution of family income adjusted for family needs, it is necessary to take into account changes in family size. Columns 5 through 8, therefore, replicate columns 1 to 4 by dividing family earnings by the family's needs standard. These columns show the changes in the distribution of heads' earnings adjusted for family size.

Adjusting for family needs has substantial impact on the distribution of equivalent income for both male- and female-headed households. The resulting change in the distribution of equivalent earnings for all heads is shown in column 8 of table 2.2 (and column 1 of table 2.3). As a result of substantial increases in the earnings/needs ratio at the 90th percentile and a shift towards female-headed households, column 8 shows roughly twice as large an increase in inequality of earnings adjusted for needs than for unadjusted earnings of heads. This implies that the reduction in family size was larger at the top than at the bottom of the distribution.

I now turn to the impact of adding other income sources to move from heads' earnings to family income after taxes and transfers. Comparing columns 1 and 2 of table 2.3 shows that the impact of adding the earnings of wives and other family members is somewhat equalising. This is consistent with the findings in Cancian, Danziger and Gottschalk (1993). What is particularly important for our focus on changes in the distribution of income is the fact that inequality rose less when these other sources of income were included. The 90/10 differential went up by 0.132 instead of 0.215, and the 80/20 differential went up by 0.047 instead of 0.081 when the earnings measure expanded to include the earnings of non-heads. Therefore, changes in the earnings of other family members tended to counteract the increase in inequality of heads' earnings. Changes in other sources of private income, however, partially offset the equalising impact of earnings of other family members.[19] Comparing columns 2 and 3 of table 2.3 shows that the change in the 90/10 differential increased from 0.132 to 0.137 when all sources of private income are added.

As expected, public transfers reduce inequality by raising incomes at the bottom of the distribution more than at the top. For example, in 1979 transfers raised the 10/50 ratio by 0.029 (0.393 minus 0.364). As a result of increases at the median, the 90/50 of post-transfer income was lower than the 90/50 of pre-transfer income (2.044 versus 2.062).

While transfers equalised incomes in each year, there was relatively little change in the relationship between pre- and post-transfer inequality. In spite of some cutbacks in programmes for the poor and expansion in social security, the increase in post-transfer inequality was roughly as large as the increase in pre-transfer inequality. In fact, the 90/10 differential fell slightly from 0.137 in column 3 to 0.129 in column 4.[20]

Likewise, changes in taxes did little to either increase or decrease the rise in inequality. The pre-tax 90/10 rose by 0.129 while the after-tax ratio rose by 0.126. Clearly, government taxes and transfers were doing little to moderate the rise in inequality of pre-fisc income. Thus, for the US, changes in the labour market ended up being largely reflected in changes in the distribution of total family income.

Particularly important for this study is the small difference between the last three columns in table 2.3. Changes in government transfers and taxes did little to counter the effects of changes in private markets. The result was that the increase in after-tax and transfer income was about the same as the growth in pre-transfer inequality.

4.2   Other industrialised countries

Table 2.1 showed that the seven industrialised countries used in this study also experienced at least some increases in inequality of wages and salaries (as measured by the earnings of the selected sample of male heads). In this section, I present data which show that these increases in wage inequality were accompanied by very different changes in family income inequality in these countries.

The countries studied can be broken down into three broad groups. The first group, which includes the United Kingdom and Canada, experienced only slightly smaller increases in inequality of wage rates than that experienced in the United States. The second group, consisting of the Netherlands, France and Australia, had increases in wage inequality roughly one-third as large as in the United States. The final country, Sweden, experienced by far the smallest increase in inequality of earnings. We turn to each group in turn.

Table 2.4 *Annual change in the distribution of alternative income/needs measures*

	Earnings of selected male heads (1)	Earnings of all heads/ fam. needs (2)	Total earnings/ fam. needs (3)	Pre-transfer income/ fam. needs (4)	Post-transfer income/ fam. needs (5)	Post-tax and transfer income/ fam. needs (6)
Full-time workers[a]						
Australia						
90/10	0.035	0.085	0.012	0.040	0.023	0.074
80/20	0.009	0.022	0.014	0.008	0.002	0.030
The Netherlands						
90/10	0.033	0.089	0.038	0.038	0.069	0.048
80/20	0.004	0.055	0.004	0.004	0.023	0.017
Sweden						
90/10	0.014	0.301	0.282	0.084	0.005	0.011
80/20	0.014	0.026	0.045	0.034	0.008	0.005
United Kingdom						
90/10	0.069	0.066	0.081	0.087	0.061	0.044
80/20	0.038	0.018	0.030	0.025	0.020	0.013
United States						
90/10	0.105	0.215	0.132	0.137	0.129	0.126
80/20	0.045	0.081	0.047	0.037	0.037	0.040
All workers[b]						
Canada						
90/10	0.151	0.310	0.202	0.125	0.062	0.031
80/20	0.040	0.061	0.030	0.023	0.008	0.007
France						
90/10	0.076	0.091	0.038	0.064	0.019	0.012
80/20	0.024	0.038	0.026	0.024	0.001	0.001
United States						
90/10	0.220	0.215	0.132	0.137	0.129	0.126
80/20	0.060	0.081	0.047	0.037	0.037	0.040

Notes:

[a] Column 1 includes only male heads working full time. Other columns not affected.

[b] Column 1 includes male heads working full time and part time. Other columns not affected.

4.2.1   The United Kingdom and Canada

Table 2.4 replicates part of the bottom panel of table 2.3 and provides the corresponding changes in the 90/10 and 80/20 ratios for the other countries in this study. Inequality of earnings of male heads (as shown in table 2.1 and column 1 of table 2.4) increased substantially more in the US, UK and Canada than in the other countries. In spite of these similarities, these three countries experienced very different changes in inequality of adjusted family income. The interesting contrast between the US, UK and Canada is that only the US had a larger increase in inequality of after-tax family income than in earnings inequality. Changes in other income sources and changes in family structure had the net effect of offsetting inequality of wages in the UK and in Canada. In the US these other forces reinforced the trend towards inequality.

In order to get a better picture of the differences among these three countries, it is instructive to isolate the point along the chain where the divergence occurs from wage inequality to family income inequality. The major difference between the US and Canada is in the transition from pre-transfer inequality to post-transfer inequality. In fact, Canada had larger increases in the 90/10 ratio of family earnings than the US. It was only changes in the distribution of private non-market income that led to pre-transfer income growing by about the same rates in Canada and the US (0.125 versus 0.137 per year). While both countries experienced roughly equal increases in the distribution of pre-transfer income/needs, the rise in inequality of post-transfer income/needs was half as large in Canada as in the US (0.062 versus 0.129). This indicates that differences in growth of public transfers were more responsible for the lower growth in post-transfer inequality in Canada than in the US. Furthermore, changes in taxes continued to limit the increase in inequality in Canada, but had almost no effect in the US.

The importance of transfers in Canada is consistent with Hanratty and Blank's (1992) documentation that changes in social spending in the 1980s differed considerably in the US and in Canada. For example, they show that as a result of real reductions in payments of Aid to Families with Dependent Children (AFDC), the maximum monthly transfers for low income people fell 6.4 per cent between 1979 and 1986 in the US, while low-income transfers rose 9.6 per cent in Canada (Hanratty and Blank 1992, table IV, p. 248).

These differences in social spending are reflected in table 2.5, which shows social expenditures (social insurance including health insurance and public employee insurance, family allowances, public assistance and aid to war victims) as a proportion of GDP and public assistance as a proportion of social expenditures in the seven countries in this study. In the US, social expenditures were roughly constant, but public assistance declined. In con-

Table 2.5 *Social expenditures as a percentage of GDP and public assistance as a percentage of social expenditures by year and country*

	Social exp./ GDP	Pub. assist./ soc. exp.
Australia		
1981	0.112	0.046
1985	0.099	N.A.
Canada		
1981	0.136	0.176
1985[a]	0.156	0.179
France		
1980[a]	0.254	0.158
1984	0.275	0.131
Netherlands		
1983	0.308	0.091
1986[a]	0.277	0.033
Sweden		
1981	0.320	0.165
1983[a]	0.301	0.168
United Kingdom		
1979	0.165	0.157
1986	0.194	0.244
United States		
1979	0.121	0.247
1986	0.120	0.193

Note:
[a] Year closest to LIS year.
Source: The Cost of Social Security.Geneva: International Labour Organisation, 1988.

trast, Canada experienced both an increase in social expenditures as a proportion of GDP and an increase in public assistance as a proportion of social expenditures.

The role of changes in transfers and taxes in mitigating the impact of rising inequality of earnings was also somewhat larger in the UK than in the US (as indicated by the difference in the change of inequality in income before and after taxes and transfers for the UK). While the 90/10 ratio for the UK rose by 0.087 per year for pre-tax and transfer income, the rise was limited to 0.061 after transfers were added in column 5 and further reduced to 0.044 after adjustment for taxes.

The importance of changes in transfers is again reflected in the data on social expenditures in table 2.4. Social expenditures as a proportion of GDP increased, and the government's greater reliance on income testing resulted in public assistance growing as a proportion of social expenditures in the UK. While benefits to the unemployed were restricted in the 1980s, this contraction was not universal across means-tested programmes. As Atkinson, Hills and Le Grand (1986) conclude, 'The Thatcher Government is widely thought to represent a distinct break in welfare state policy, but its nature should not be exaggerated' (p. 12). They show that while substantial cutbacks occurred in housing and other forms of in-kind transfers, which do not enter our data but could affect well-being, both our study and their more detailed work indicate that the distribution of post-transfer income exhibited considerably less increase in inequality than the distribution of pre-transfer income (Atkinson, Hills and Le Grand 1986, table 2.6). This undoubtedly partially reflects cyclical increases in spending; however, the shift to greater income testing (which may later weaken the support for low-income programmes) and the real increases in benefits in many cash programmes did serve to counter the effects of market forces.

4.2.2 Australia, France and the Netherlands

Australia, France and the Netherlands all have wage-setting institutions that are more centralised than those in the US or UK. The 'Accord' between the Australian government and trade unions, instituted in 1983, moderated changes in the structure of wages during the period covered by LIS data.[21] Likewise, France and the Netherlands have had strong union pressures to moderate inequality over the survey period (Hartog, Oosterbeek and Tuelings 1993, Katz and Loveman 1990). Partly as a result of these institutions, France, the Netherlands and Australia experienced increases in inequality of labour market earnings (column 1) roughly one-third as large as in the US.

Column 4 indicates that increases in pre-transfer inequality, which were one-quarter to one-half as large in these three countries as in the US, largely mirrored the moderate changes in earnings inequality. However, these countries differ in the extent to which changes in taxes and transfers affected the distribution of post-transfer income. While France and Australia managed to further reduce the rise in inequality in post-transfer income, the Netherlands had a substantially larger increase in post-transfer inequality than in pre-transfer inequality (0.069 versus 0.038). Likewise, these three countries differ in the extent to which changes in taxes mitigated or reinforced the change in inequality of pre-tax income. Subtracting taxes reduces the increase in inequality in the Netherlands (0.069 to 0.048) and France (0.019 to 0.012) but exacerbates the increase in Australia (0.023

versus 0.074).[22] Nevertheless, even for Australia the increase in inequality of after-tax income is smaller than for the US.

The potential importance of cutbacks in transfers in the Netherlands is indicated in table 2.5, which shows that social expenditures were reduced from 30.8 per cent to 27.7 per cent of GDP and public assistance fell substantially as a proportion of social expenditures. This reflects the substantial retrenchment which started under the liberal Social Democratic Party in the early 1980s. Replacement rates for social security programmes (including disability and unemployment insurance) declined from 80 per cent to 70 per cent of prior year earnings. Increases in family allowances and social security were capped, the qualifying period for unemployment benefits was extended and the duration of unemployment benefits for young workers was reduced.

In contrast, many social welfare benefits were increased and coverage in programmes broadened in France and Australia. A new system of unemployment benefits was introduced in France in 1979 and a minimum family income was introduced in 1981. While other countries were cutting family allowances, the Mitterrand government expanded benefits when it came to power. When the budgetary consequences of these acts raised fiscal problems, the government raised additional revenues through higher taxes to partially fund the increased expenditures. However, the distributional impact of the changes in transfers far outweighed the impact of any changes in the distribution of taxes, as shown in table 2.5.

Similar events in Australia mitigated the effects of increases in inequality of market incomes. The Hawke government, elected in 1983, liberalised benefits while continuing to focus limited resources through income testing. The resulting expansion of transfers, especially for the poor, limited the growth in post-transfer inequality to roughly half the rise in pre-transfer inequality.

4.2.3 Sweden

As shown earlier, Sweden experienced the smallest increase in inequality of earnings among prime-aged, full-time male workers for the seven countries examined. Hibbs (1990) and others have argued that Sweden's solidaristic wage bargaining stemmed the tide of growing inequality found in other countries. This conclusion is reinforced by the simultaneous growth in wage dispersion and the weakening of centralised bargaining that occurred after 1982.

Table 2.4 also indicates that Sweden experienced the smallest rise in inequality of income after taxes and transfers. The small increases in inequality in wages and after-tax and transfer income, however, does not necessarily mean that other sources of income were unimportant. Rather, the stability of the distribution of post-transfer income reflects large but offsetting changes. The large rise in inequality of family earnings adjusted for family size (shown in column (3)) indicates that changes in family composition and changes in labour supply increased inequality in Sweden. This is largely driven by the change in the earnings distribution of male heads working part-time. This group comprises a sufficiently large proportion of all male heads in Sweden to have a significant effect on inequality of earnings. The inequality increasing effects of these factors were fully offset by changes in the distribution of non-labour income and changes in government transfers. While the 90/10 ratio of family earnings increased by 0.282 per year, pre-tax and transfer income increased by only 0.084 per year and after-tax and transfer income increased an even more modest 0.011.

5   Conclusions

In summary, the increase in inequality of earnings was not limited to the United States. While the US had the largest increase in inequality of earnings, all other countries in this study experienced at least some increase in inequality of labour market rewards. The fact that countries differed in the extent to which earnings became less equal indicates that other labour market factors mitigated but did not completely counter the underlying forces causing wage rates to become less equal.

Countries also differed substantially in the ways in which increases in inequality of labour market income were translated into changes in inequality of family income. The distribution of family income is not solely determined by the distribution of the earnings of heads. Earnings of other family members and other sources of unearned income often accompany changes in the distribution of wage rates as other family members adjust their earnings to these new circumstances. Furthermore, changes in government taxes and transfers can either reinforce or mitigate the increase in inequality of market income.[23]

The data in this paper have shown that while inequality of total family income rose more than inequality of earnings in the US, this was not the case in other countries in this study. A country like Canada, which experienced a similar increase in inequality of market income, managed to have only a moderate increase in inequality of family income. On the other hand, a country like the Netherlands, which experienced very modest increases in inequality of labour market income, ended up with a rise in inequality of income after taxes and transfers that was very similar to Canada's.

Notes

I would like to thank Tim Smeeding for the years of work it has taken to put the Luxembourg Income Study (LIS) data set together and Janet Gornick for the institutional information provided through LIS. Carol Kallman and Alpay Filiztekin provided outstanding computer assistance and Jean Feinschreiber excellent administrative assistance.

1 See Levy and Murnane 1992 for a review of this literature.
2 Murphy and Welch 1992 document that the college premium for new entrants was 1.8 times greater in 1989 than in 1978.
3 Moffitt 1990 finds that the standard error in a log earnings equation for white males increased from 0.843 in 1970 to 1.031 in 1987.
4 Gottschalk and Joyce 1995 and the essays in Richard Freeman and Lawrence Katz 1995 examine changes in earnings inequality in several industrialised countries.
5 The summary statistics on family income in the US are from Danziger and Gottschalk 1993.
6 Almost all studies reviewed by Levy and Murnane 1992 use the Current Population Survey (CPS) to examine the distribution of weekly or annual wages for males. To concentrate on changes in wages and not changes in hours worked, most of these studies select only persons working full time and a full year. Since the large changes in labour force participation of women confound labour supply and wage effects, most studies focus on the distribution of earnings of males.
7 Fritzell 1992 also uses the LIS data to compare five countries.
8 In contrast, the limited information on less-developed countries indicates that many experienced a decline in inequality (Davis 1992).
9 The data are stored in Luxembourg under the sponsorship of the Luxembourg government. See Smeeding 1986 for a detailed description of the data source and methods for accessing the data.
10 For details see Gottschalk and Joyce 1995.
11 For many countries, LIS does not offer data on earnings of non-heads. The sample is limited to full-time workers in order to try to focus on the distribution of wages rather than hours.
12 Current dollar values have been inflated to 1988 prices (each in their own currency) using the implicit price deflators from the OECD National Product Accounts.
13 Studies using the CPS data have found similar patterns of earnings inequality using heads or individuals.
14 The Australian and Dutch data are for full time last week rather than for the reference year.
15 'Non-aged' is defined as younger than 56.
16 The OECD needs standard adds 0.5 for each child and 0.7 for each adult beyond the head.
17 Detailed tables for all countries are available from the author.
18 Similar data for the other countries are available on request from the author.

19 Other private income includes: interest, dividends, rents, alimony, child support and private pensions.
20 The coefficient of variation also declined marginally, but the 80/20 ratio remained constant at 0.037.
21 See Saunders in this volume for details.
22 Changes in the after-tax distribution may partially reflect differences in the measurement of taxes in the two waves of the LIS data for Australia.
23 Changes in market income may, of course, themselves reflect behavioural responses to changes in government transfers.

References

Abraham, Katherine G. and Houseman, Susan N. 1995. 'Earnings Inequality in Germany', in Freeman, Richard and Katz, Lawrence (eds.), *Differences and Changes in Wage Structures*. Chicago: University of Chicago Press.

Atkinson, Anthony, Hills, J. and Le Grand, Julian. 1986. 'The Welfare State in Britain 1970–1985: Extent and Effectiveness'. Welfare State Programme Discussion Paper 9. London School of Economics.

Blackburn, McKinley and Bloom, David. 1993. 'The Distribution of Family Income: Measuring and Explaining Changes in the 1980's for Canada and the United States', in Freeman and Cards (eds.), *Small Differences that Matter: Labor Markets and Income Maintenance in Canada and the United States.* Chicago: University of Chicago Press.

Blanchflower, David G., Katz, Lawrence F. and Loveman, Gary. 1992. 'A Comparison of Changes in the Structure of Wages in Four OECD Countries'. Paper presented at the NBER Conference, July.

Borland, Jeff. 1992. 'Wage Inequality in Australia'. Paper presented at NBER Conference, April.

Cancian, Maria, Danziger, Sheldon and Gottschalk, Peter. 1993. 'Working Wives and Family Income Inequality among Married Couples', in Danziger, Sheldon and Gottschalk, Peter (eds.), *Uneven Tides*. Cambridge, Mass.: Harvard University Press, pp. 195–221.

Danziger, Sheldon and Gottschalk, Peter. 1993. 'Editors' Introduction', in Danziger, Sheldon and Gottschalk, Peter (eds.), *Uneven Tides*. Cambridge, Mass.: Harvard University Press.

Davis, Steven. 1992. 'Cross Country Patterns of Changes in Relative Wages'. NBER, April.

Edin, Per-Anders and Holmlund, Bertil. 1995. 'The Swedish Wage Structure: The Rise and Fall of Solidaristic Wage Policy', in Freeman, Richard and Katz, Lawrence (eds.), *Differences and Changes in Wage Structures*. Chicago: University of Chicago Press.

Erickson, Christopher L. and Ichino, Andrea C. 1995. 'Wage Differentials in Italy: Market Forces, Institutions, and Inflation', in Freeman, Richard and Katz, Lawrence (eds.), *Differences and Changes in Wage Structures*. Chicago: University of Chicago Press.

Freeman, Richard. 1994. *Working Under Different Rules.* New York: Russell Sage Foundation.

Freeman, Richard and Needles, Karen. 1991. 'Skill Differentials in Canada in an Era of Rising Market Inequality', in Card and Freeman (eds.), *Small Differences that Matter: Labor Markets and Income Maintenance in Canada and the United States.* Chicago: University of Chicago Press.

Fritzell, Johan. 1992. 'Income Inequality Trends in the 1980s: A Five Country Comparison'. The Luxembourg Income Study Working Paper No. 73 (April).

Gottschalk, Peter and Joyce, Mary. 1995. 'Is Earnings Inequality Also Rising in Other Industrialized Countries?' Mimeo, Department of Economics, Boston College.

Gramlich, Edward J., Kasten, Richard and Sammartino, Frank. 1993. 'Growing Inequality in the 1980s: The Role of Federal Taxes and Cash Transfers', in Danziger, Sheldon and Gottschalk, Peter, (eds.), *Uneven Tides.* Cambridge, Mass.: Harvard University Press, pp. 225–49.

Hanratty, Maria and Blank, Rebecca. 1992. 'Down and Out in North America: Recent Trends in Poverty Rates in the United States and Canada'. *The Quarterly Journal of Economics*, 107 (February).

Hartog, Joop, Oosterbeek, Hessel and Tuelings, Coen. 1993. 'Age, Wages and Education in the Netherlands', in Johnson, P. and Zimmerman, K. (eds.), *Labour Market Implications of European Aging.* London: Centre for Economic Policy Research.

Hibbs, Douglas A., Jr. 1990. 'Wage Dispersion and Trade Union Action in Sweden.' In Persson, Inga (ed.), *Generating Equality in the Welfare State: The Swedish Experience.* Oslo: Norwegian University Press.

International Labour Organisation. 1988. The Cost of Social Security. Geneva.

Juhn, Chinhui, Murphy, Kevin and Pierce, B. 1993. 'Wage Inequality and the Rise in Returns to Skill'. *Journal of Political Economy*, 101 (June): 410–42.

Karoly, Lynn A. 1993. 'The Trend in Inequality among Families, Individuals, and Workers in the United States: A Twenty-Five Year Perspective', in Danziger, Sheldon and Gottschalk, Peter (eds.), *Uneven Tides.* Cambridge, Mass.: Harvard University Press, pp. 19–97.

Katz, Lawrence F. and Loveman, Gary W. 1990. 'An International Comparison of Changes in the Structure of Wages: France, the United Kingdom and the United States'. Draft, Department of Economics, Harvard University.

Katz, Lawrence F., Loveman, Gary W. and Blanchflower, David G. 1995. 'A Comparison of Changes in the Structure of Wages in Four OECD Countries', in Freeman, Richard and Katz, Lawrence (eds.), *Differences and Changes in Wage Structures.* Chicago: University of Chicago Press.

Katz, Lawrence F. and Murphy, Kevin M. 1992. 'Changes in Relative Wages, 1963–1987: Supply and Demand Factors'. *Quarterly Journal of Economics*, 107 (February): 35–78.

Katz, Lawrence F. and Revenga, Ana L. 1989. 'Changes in Structure of Wages: The US. vs. Japan'. *Journal of Japanese and International Economics* (December).

Kim, Dae-Il and Topel, Robert H. 1995. 'Labor Markets and Economic Growth: Lessons from Korea's Industrialization, 1970–1990', in Freeman, Richard and Katz, Lawrence (eds.), *Differences and Changes in Wage Structures*. Chicago: University of Chicago Press.

Levy, Frank and Murnane, Richard J. 1992. 'U.S. Earnings Levels and Earnings Inequality: A Review of Recent Trends and Proposed Explanations'. *Journal of Economic Literature*, 30 (September): 1333–81.

Moffitt, Robert. 1990. 'The Distribution of Earnings and the Welfare State', in Burtles, Gary (ed.), *A Future of Losing Jobs*. Washington, DC: Brookings Institute, pp. 201–30.

Murphy, Kevin and Welch, Finis. 1992. 'The Structure of Wages'. *The Quarterly Journal of Economics*, 107 (February).

Saunders, Peter, Stott, Helen and Hobbes, Gary. 1991. 'Income Inequality in Australia and New Zealand: International Comparisons and Recent Trends'. *Review of Income and Wealth*, 37 (March): 63–79.

Smeeding, Timothy. 1986. 'Luxembourg Income Study'. *The Journal of Human Resources*, 21, 4 (Fall).

Williamson, Jeffrey and Lindert, Peter. 1980. *American Inequality: A Macroeconomic History*. Academic Press.

3 A survey of income inequality over the last twenty years – how does the UK compare?

KAREN GARDINER

1 Introduction

Reich (1991) gives a vivid description of the distribution of income in the United States in the 1950s and 1960s which could have similarly fit many developed nations in the post-war period, including the United Kingdom: 'Picture a symmetrical wave that's highest in the middle and then gradually slopes down and out on both ends until merging with the horizon.'

From the 1970s onwards this apparent stylised fact of a stable (or even slightly equalising) distribution of income, with most households grouped around the middle, has ceased to hold true. One by one, countries have seen the gap between the richest and poorest households begin to grow.

In the past 20 years in the UK there has been a reversal of the post-war trend of a slow but steady decline in income inequality. Using existing published results and analysis, this chapter first seeks to describe the UK experience in the context of what has been happening in other western countries over the same period. Second, an attempt is made to give insight into the forces behind the trends across countries. A simple analytical framework is set up which identifies the main income sources and structural influences that determine the overall distribution of household equivalised household income. Finally, a summary is given of the inequality trends and some of the factors which have shaped the distribution of income in the western industrialised countries during the past two decades.

2 The picture

By their nature, the results presented in this survey are not completely consistent or comparable. They come from a wide variety of data sources, cover different periods and countries and use several alternative income definitions and inequality measures. This apparent problem will be tackled in two ways: in some cases by giving 'broad brush' results which are reasonably robust across methodological choices; or where more detailed statistics are cited, the particular definitions used are highlighted so that it is clear to the reader where results are not entirely consistent.[1]

Where possible, an 'ideal' measure of income is used, with real household equivalised disposable income taken to be the best approximation to 'standard of living'. Total income from earnings, investment income, other market income and state benefits are added over the household. Direct taxes and social security contributions are deducted to calculate total disposable income for the household. It is assumed that each member within the household enjoys the same standard of living, but this will vary between different households with the same total income because of differences in size and composition. Consequently, an adjustment is made using an equivalence scale. These scales take a variety of forms but it is usual to give smaller weights for children, on the basis that they have fewer 'needs', and assume some economies of scale so that second and subsequent adults also have lower weights. Where references are made to 'overall inequality' or the income definition is not specified, then it should be assumed that this 'ideal' definition is used.[2]

2.1   The distribution of household incomes in the UK

Figure 3.1 illustrates the pattern of inequality in the UK for the 1970s and 1980s. Results from four different studies present a broadly consistent picture of the trend in this period despite using a range of inequality measures and income definitions.[3] The picture that emerges is one of a U-shape: falling inequality during the first half of the 1970s, followed by an upturn sometime after 1976. At first, the increase is slow but seems to increase rapidly in the second half of the 1980s. Between 1979 and 1988/9, 39 per cent of the rise in average equivalised disposable household income went to the richest 10 per cent of the population. If capital gains were included in the income definition, this would probably be even higher.[4]

Despite rapid increases in income inequality in the UK in the late 1980s, indicated by the above results, it has been suggested that these are likely to underestimate the upward trend due to the exclusion of capital gains and fringe benefits which have become increasingly important over time for richer income groups (Jenkins 1992).

2.2   Levels and trends of countries by income inequality

When trying to make cross-country comparisons, one is faced with the almost overwhelming problem of comparability – of income definitions, unit of analysis, data, year of survey and so on.[5] This problem is partially overcome by the Luxembourg Income Study (LIS), which includes surveys

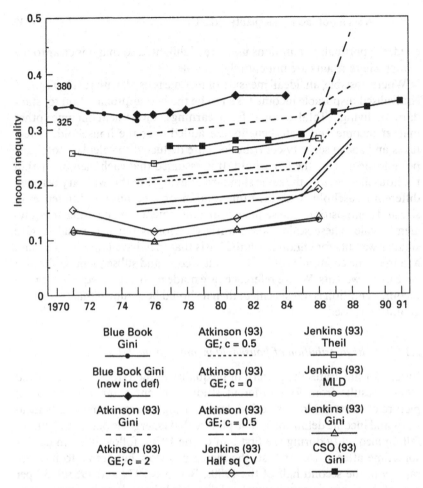

Figure 3.1 Trends in income inequality in the UK, 1970–1991
Notes: Blue Book: unequivalised annual tax unit disposable income from the
Survey of Personal Incomes; Gini coefficient are actually for financial years, e.g.,
Gini for 1970/1 shown as 1970 on the graph; note: break in series in 1975/6 due to
change in income definition – mortgage interest and other tax deductible items no
longer deducted; figures from table 1 of Atkinson 1993.

   Atkinson 1993: equivalised current family disposable income after housing
costs from the Family Expenditure Survey; 'GE' refers to generalised entropy
class measures and 'c' to the weight parameter; figures given in table 3.2.

   Jenkins 1993: equivalised current household disposable income from the Family
Expenditure Survey; 'Half sq CV' – half of the squared coefficient of variation;
'Theil' – Theil coefficient; 'MLD' – mean logarithmic deviation; figures given in
table 3.1.

   Jenkins 1993: equivalised household disposable income from Family
Expenditure Survey for 1971, 1976, 1981 and 1986

   CSO 1993: equivalised household disposable income from Family Expenditure
Survey supplemented by the Survey of Personal Incomes for those on high
incomes; note: this series is not completely consistent over time; figures given in
table 2, appendix 4.

Table 3.1 *Ranking of 12 countries by income inequality in the mid 1980s*

Ranking/country	Gini coefficient	Year
1st Finland[a]	0.20	1985
2nd Sweden	0.21	1987
3rd Luxembourg	0.23	1985
4th West Germany	0.25	1984
5th Netherlands	0.26	1987
6th Canada	0.28	1987
7th United Kingdom	0.29	1986
8th France	0.30	1984
8th New Zealand[b]	0.30	1985/6
10th Italy	0.31	1986
10th Australia	0.31	1985/6
12th USA	0.34	1986

Note:
Non-LIS studies in italics.
Sources: Whiteford and Kennedy 1993, table 2.5; McClements's equivalence scale.
[a] Uusitalo 1989, table 6.5; OECD equivalence scale.
[b] Saunders *et al.* 1989, table 10; LIS equivalence scale.

for around 20 countries with income and other variables which are roughly consistent across countries and over time. Many studies quoted in this chapter have used LIS data from two 'waves'. The precise year varies from country to country, but the most recent wave is from around the mid 1980s, and the previous wave is from the late 1970s/early 1980s.

Table 3.1 attempts to pull together several different studies that make cross-country comparisons of income inequality in the mid 1980s as measured by the Gini coefficient. Unless otherwise stated, the income measure is equivalised household disposable income, weighted by persons.[6] The first thing to notice about the rankings is that the countries are grouped very closely together, half of them having a Gini of between 0.28 and 0.31. This shows that any conclusions must be tentative; with a confidence interval around the calculated measure, an unambiguous ranking of many of the countries would not be possible. Nevertheless, the results presented here are consistent with other cross-country comparisons of smaller samples of countries (Fritzell 1992; Smeeding and Coder 1993; Jäntti 1993).

Perhaps the clearest way to analyse the table is to divide the countries into three groups: North European (Finland, Luxembourg, the

Table 3.2 *Trends in inequality of equivalised household disposable income*

Country	Turning-point	Source
U-shaped trend		
Australia	early 1980s	Atkinson 1993
Japan	1973	Bauer and Mason 1992
Netherlands	1983	Muffels and Nelissen 1993
New Zealand	early 1980s	Atkinson 1993
Sweden	1980/1	Atkinson 1993
United Kingdom	late 1970s	Atkinson 1993
USA	1973	Danziger and Gottschalk 1993
West Germany	mid 1980s	Guger 1989
Stable distribution during the 1980s		
Canada		Atkinson 1993
France		Atkinson 1993
Italy		Atkinson 1993
Falling income inequality during the 1980s		
Finland		Atkinson 1993
Norway		Atkinson 1993

Netherlands, Sweden and West Germany), Anglo-Saxon (Australia, Canada, New Zealand, the UK and the US) and Mediterranean (France and Italy). It seems that the North European countries had the most equal distributions of household incomes in the mid 1980s. Below these come the Anglo-Saxon countries, with Canada and the UK more equal than New Zealand and Australia. The Mediterranean countries fall in the middle of the Anglo-Saxon countries. Inequality in France and Italy in the mid 1980s appears to have been higher than for the UK or Canada but lower than for the US.

Fortunately, it is considerably simpler to find studies of the trends in income inequality within individual countries than for cross-country comparisons. Whilst the data sources and definitions used might not be completely comparable, results for trends tend to be much less sensitive to these factors than comparisons across countries at a particular point in time (Jenkins 1992; Cutler and Katz 1992).

The trends shown in Table 3.2 fall into three categories. The most common experience is inequality of disposable household income falling in the early 1970s but then reversing that trend. This group of countries can be most simply described as having a 'U-shaped' pattern of inequality. The UK and seven other nations share this familiar trend, but there are some considerable differences in the timing of the 'turning-point' when inequality stopped going down and began to climb. The countries where this occurred in the 1970s are Japan and the US,[7] with a turning-point in 1973, and the UK, where it has already been shown that the bottom of the 'U' was reached in the late 1970s.[8] Most countries in this group, however, did not see the gap between rich and poor begin to increase until the 1980s (turning-points in parentheses): Sweden (1980/1), Australia and New Zealand (early 1980s), the Netherlands (1983) and West Germany (mid 1980s).[9]

Whilst the most common experience, not all countries fall into the U-shape category. Canada, France and Italy appear to have had a constant level of inequality of equivalised disposable household income throughout the 1980s. In addition, there are two countries which have had a quite different experience: Finland and Norway are the only two out of the 13 countries included in this review where inequality fell in the 1980s. In Norway, this was preceded by a rise in the 1970s, but for Finland income inequality consistently declined throughout the 1970s and the 1980s (Ringen 1991).

3   Underlying factors

This section seeks to review the main contributory factors which have been put forward to explain the various trends. The focus is on explanations of the UK experience, but these are presented in light of existing evidence that the same influences are relevant across countries.

Figure 3.2 is a simple graphical representation of the factors which influence the distribution of household equivalised disposable income (box labelled Y11), the measure of standard of living used here. The 14 boxes which flow into this show the separate components and can be divided into two categories: income sources (Y1–Y10) and structural or compositional factors (C1–C4). Total earnings (including those from self-employment) depend on the effective hourly wage and the number of hours worked. In the diagram, therefore, the process begins with the distribution of individual hourly earnings (box Y1). It is box C1, the composition of the distribution of hours which shows how the variation in the number of hours worked feeds directly with box Y1 into the distribution of total individual earnings (box Y2).

The individual distribution of earnings is one of the three income sources which then flow into the distribution of individual market income (box Y5); the other two are the distributions of individual investment income (box

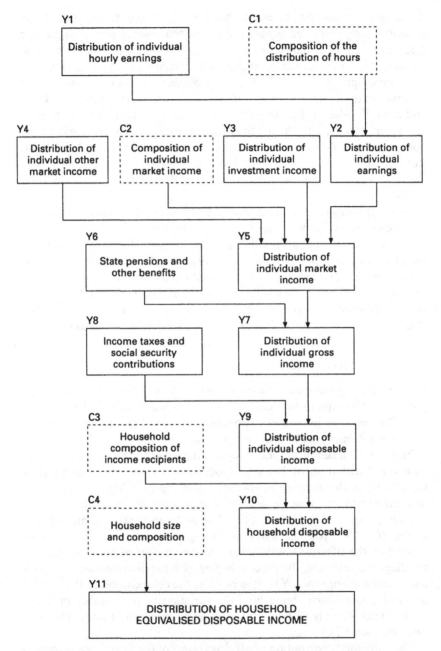

Figure 3.2 Composition of household equivalised disposable income

Y3) and other market income (box Y4). Other market income includes occupational pensions and private transfers, such as maintenance payments. However, income sources alone do not determine the distribution of market income. The importance of the link between these three income components is represented by box C2, the composition of the individual's market income. For example, it would be possible for the distributions of earnings, investment income and other market income to remain unchanged whilst the overall distribution of market income became more unequal. This could be the result of an increase in the 'correlation' between earnings and investment income, in other words if it became more likely that individuals with high earnings would also have high investment income. Such factors are shown separately in the diagram to emphasise how changes in the distribution of income cannot be explained by examining the income components in isolation.

The distribution of individual gross income (box Y7) is determined by adding state pensions and other benefits (box Y6) to market income. Income taxes and social security contributions (box Y8) are subtracted from gross income to get the distribution of individual disposable income (box Y9).[10]

The next stage of the process is to move from the level of the individual to the household. The distribution of household disposable income (box Y10), whilst clearly dependent on individual disposable income, is also influenced by the links between people in the household. It has already been seen that the individual's market income depends on the correlation between income sources, i.e., how likely it is that an individual with high earnings also has high investment and other income. In the same way, the household's disposable income depends on the correlation between people, i.e., how likely it is that an individual with high disposable income lives in a household with other people who are also relatively rich. This appears in the diagram in box C3, the household composition of income recipients. We see below, for example, that increased labour force participation of married women tends to make the distribution of individual disposable income more unequal. This is because they represent a group who previously were not counted, since they had no earnings, but enter the distribution with significantly lower earnings than the average. However, the effect on the distribution of household disposable income may be to make it more equal. If these women live in a household with other low-income earners, the overall effect is to shift low-income households closer to the mean. Once again, this shows how compositional factors have an important influence on the distribution of household income which may not at first be apparent.

The next and final stage involves adjusting the household's disposable income for the number of people in the household to obtain a measure of their standard of living: household equivalised disposable income. It is the distribution of household equivalised disposable income (box Y11) which this chapter seeks to explain. This adjustment is done using an equivalence scale. The household is assigned a weight, based on the total needs of the household, related to the number of members, the number of children and their age, for example. It is these factors household size and composition, which are represented by box C4, that translate the distribution of household disposable income (box Y10) into the actual standard of living enjoyed by the household (box Y11).

The following survey of five major explanations for changing income inequality across countries can be related to figure 3.2. The first three – earnings, investment income and direct taxes and transfers – are mutually exclusive income sources, appearing in the diagram in boxes Y2, Y3, and Y6 and Y8, respectively. However, as stressed above, different sources of income can also influence the distribution of household equivalised disposable income indirectly through the link between them (box C2). The other two factors considered here are unemployment and demographic and socioeconomic factors. These are more structural and may influence the final distribution of household equivalised disposable income in a variety of ways. For example, unemployment will clearly mean, *ceteris paribus*, that benefits (Y6) are a larger share of household disposable income and that market income (Y5) will become less important. But there may also be indirect influences on the labour market (Y1 and C1) and through the household composition of income recipients (C3).

3.1   *Earnings*

Results for full-time male employees for the period 1974–88 show a slight fall in earnings inequality in Great Britain over the 1970s, followed by a rapid increase in the 1980s (Schmitt 1992; Gregg and Machin 1993). After 1980, the real earnings of the 10th percentile hardly changed while those of the 90th percentile rose rapidly. Given what has happened in other countries, it is worth noting here that all parts of the income distribution experienced gains in real earnings over the 1970s and 1980s, even the 10th percentile. It appears that there has been a similar pattern for females with earnings inequality declining over the 1970s (but less consistently) and sharp increases in the 1980s.

There is clearly a similarity with the trend in earnings inequality and overall household income inequality: both have had a U-shaped pattern. This is not unexpected, because wages, salaries and self-employment income are the most important sources of household income in the UK. In 1986, the earnings of heads and spouses alone accounted for 78 per cent of total household disposable income on average, and 72 per cent of households had one or more earners. But the question to consider here is how much of what has happened to the structure of overall incomes – including all sources of income and all types of households – can be explained by these changes in labour market income alone.

Decompositions of total household disposable income in the UK for the 1970s and first half of the 1980s show that the shifts in earnings of the head of household were the most significant force driving overall inequality. In the first half of the 1970s, both overall inequality and the dispersion of heads' wages and salaries were falling. Then, in the late 1970s, the structure of household incomes shifted when inequality began to rise followed by the same trend in wages and salaries but with a slight lag in the date of the upturn. In the first half of the 1980s, however, it was labour market income in the form of heads' self-employment income which played a crucial role in explaining the increase in overall income inequality. This is an interesting distinction since, whilst self-employment income still constitutes earnings, it seems reasonable to assume that the factors underlying these shifts may be quite separate from those influencing the wage distribution.[11]

Results presented here for Australia, Canada and Sweden indicate that there was some evidence of increasing earnings inequality in all three countries for prime-aged males during the early 1980s.[12] The dispersion of wages also became more unequal throughout the 1980s for men and women in Japan, West Germany and the US. In fact, of the countries studied, France is the only country where earnings inequality was falling for men and women during the 1980s. It declined consistently from the early 1970s until around 1984, when differentials for both males and females widened.

The experience of France of falling wage inequality during the 1970s was more widespread. A similar pattern can be noted for men and women in Great Britain and West Germany and for women in the US. Earnings were becoming more unequal even during the 1970s for men and women in Japan and for male workers in the US.[13]

It seems that trends in income and earnings inequality more or less coincide in Australia, Japan, Sweden and the US, where it may be, therefore, that earnings are one of the most important factors driving the distribution of household income. However, in the case of Britain, France, Canada and West Germany there is clearly some other force at work. In the first two countries wage inequality was still falling when overall the dispersion of incomes was either stable (France in the early 1980s) or widening (Britain at the end of the 1970s). In West Germany and Canada in the early 1980s, earnings inequality was rising whilst the distributions of household disposable income remained fairly constant. Possible explanations of this apparent inconsistency between the trends in disposable household income and wage and salary income in Britain, Canada and West Germany are explored below under other determinants of income inequality trends.

The single most important factor driving the distribution of wages seems to be trends in relative supply and demand for skilled workers through the 1970s and 1980s. In Britain, France, Japan and the US, the result was a narrowing of skill differentials in the 1970s and then large increases in the 1980s (in France after 1984). There was a significant rise in the demand for highly educated workers in all four of these countries in the 1970s and then even more so in the 1980s. However, the entry of well-educated baby boomers into the labour market in the 1970s represented a sufficiently large offsetting increase in supply to result in falling skill differentials in the 1970s in these countries.

By the 1980s, the effect of the continuing rise in relative demand was to push up the premium on education, although there is some debate about what was actually driving this demand change. One view put forward, particularly for Britain but also for France and the US, is that the increased relative demand for skilled workers is a result of the decline in the goods-producing industries in the 1980s. Workers have shifted from manual occupations in manufacturing to non-manual employment in the service industry, where inequality tends to be higher.

Several studies have tried to test this 'deindustrialisation' hypothesis for Britain. The evidence is mixed. Stark (1989) finds that change in the relative sizes of the manual and non-manual sectors accounts for 30 per cent of the increase in overall earnings inequality between 1979 and 1988 for full-time male adults. On the other hand, Schmitt (1992), looking at the 1980s, finds that the increased inequality within industries is much more significant. For other countries, most of the evidence is that increases in within-industry earnings inequality have far outweighed the influence of the shifts between industries.

The introduction of technology was also an important factor in the shift in demand towards workers with higher skills in Great Britain. It has been argued that technological or work-organisation changes are likely influences behind the growth in within-industry inequality in Great Britain. Such an explanation has also been forwarded for the US and Japan. In the case of the US the appreciation of the dollar may have been responsible for technological change, explaining the increasing premium on education.

The supply and demand for a skilled labour force does not provide a complete story for the changes in earnings inequality for all these countries. Skill differentials fell in the 1970s and then rose in the 1980s, which fits with the overall picture of earnings inequality in Britain and France. However, in Japan and the US in particular, wages were becoming more unequal even in the 1970s, when the premium on education was declining.

High levels of unemployment in the 1980s are cited as responsible for increased earnings inequality in Great Britain and France. Where an increase in unemployment means excess supply of labour for particular jobs (often associated with young or unskilled workers), there will be relatively greater downward pressure on the wages offered for these jobs. For Britain, this was manifested in increases in within-group inequality, whilst for France youth unemployment was particularly high, which may be linked to the widening differentials by age during the second half of the 1980s. Similarly, the recession and high and rising unemployment were important factors in the 1980s in West Germany. It has been argued that in Japan the slowdown in growth in the 1970s led to a 'loosening' of the labour market which increased pay differentials. Within-group inequality was also increasing in the US in the 1970s and 1980s, which may be explained by the effect of lower inflation and higher unemployment in the US.[14]

In the case of Britain, the influence of trade unions, wages councils and incomes policies have been cited as reasons for the upturn in earnings inequality lagging behind the US. The same institutional differences between the two countries have been linked to the rising real wages combined with high unemployment outcome for British low-skilled workers as opposed to falling real wages but low unemployment in the US in the 1980s (Schmitt 1992). Others, however, acknowledge the influence of trade unions in Great Britain during the 1970s but argue that in the 1980s Britain's experience was much closer to that of the US. Indeed, analysis of data on semi-skilled workers in unionised and non-unionised plants in Britain has shown that the decline in unionisation over the 1980s accounts for 20 per cent of the increase in earnings inequality (Gosling and Machin 1993).

3.2   Investment income and the distribution of assets

While the major source of households' market income is earnings, investment income has also played a part in determining trends in the distribution of household equivalised disposable income. In terms of figure 3.2, the influence of investment income seems to be as important through its link with other forms of market income (box C2) as the trend in the inequality of investment income per se (box Y3).[15]

For the UK, investment income was the second most important factor in determining the overall rise in inequality, after the household head's self-employment income between 1981 and 1986. The disequalising influence was due to the distribution of investment income becoming less equal and increasingly correlated with other sources of income.

Evidence for the US shows that a growing share of total income came from capital in the 1980s and that this has become increasingly concentrated in the upper-income groups. The story in the US is, however, different from that in the UK. In the US, the distribution of investment income per se has in fact become more equal (only looking at those with any investment income), but this has been outweighed by the disequalising effect of this increase in the likelihood that a household with high investment income is also rich in other sources of income.

Increased income from interest, dividends and capital gains were important factors driving inequality in Japan in the 1980s. Two specific components of this have been what has been happening in the property and stock markets – the decline in homeownership and the rapid appreciation of stock prices. In Australia and New Zealand, it has been suggested that the growth in the proportion of gross income made up by property income for the top quintiles of the distribution was an important factor underlying the increase in income inequality in the early 1980s.[16]

Investment income has been instrumental in increasing overall inequality in the distribution of household equivalised disposable income in all the countries for which evidence has been presented. In the case of the UK and the US, investment income has become increasingly correlated with other sources of income which, for the US, has outweighed the effect of a fall in inequality of investment income. Finally, it is worth noting that in several of these countries, in the late 1980s there was a sharp slowdown or even decline in stock market values. This may have offset some of the increase in gains accruing in earlier years to better-off households.

3.3   Taxes and transfers

The state has had a powerful influence on the distribution of household disposable income through changes in the welfare state and direct taxation. Sandford (1992) states: 'The worldwide tax reform movement which has characterised the 1980s is remarkable in fiscal history. Every continent has been affected. . . . Perhaps even more remarkable than the widespread nature of tax reform in the 1980s is the similarity in the form it took across countries. The universal feature of the tax reforms of the 1980s (often with beginnings in the late 1970s) has been the reduction in rates of personal income tax.'

Whilst the redistributive impact of government taxes and benefits will generally be expected to make the distribution of income more equal, the extent to which this is true can alter over time. The equalising effect of policy has two determinants: the policies themselves and the population to which they are applied. Hence, there are two possible explanations of a change in redistributive effect: (a) the 'automatic stabilisation' effect, as a given system responds to changes in the distribution of market income and the demographic structure of the population and (b) explicit policy shifts.

Where policy has remained constant over time, any change in the redistributive impact of taxes and transfers will be purely the result of shifts in the underlying population and their market incomes. In general, the most important factor will be the trend in market income to which direct taxes and income-related benefits respond. However, the redistributive effect of a given set of policies will also be influenced by demographic changes, where benefits are contingent on numbers of children or disability for example. If the distribution of market income and the structure of the population were stable, the redistributive effect of policy would only change if policy was made more or less progressive (type b).

Table 3.3 shows the results of five studies covering eight countries, including the UK. For each country the table shows what is happening to the distribution of equivalised household disposable income, the trend in inequality of market income and the direction of change of the redistributive effect of tax and transfer policy. Three of the studies use Luxembourg Income Study data (Fritzell 1992; Smeeding and Coder 1993; Gottschalk 1993). All of these plus the results by Stark cover the period from the late 1970s to the mid 1980s. Jenkins's findings for the UK cover 1971–86, but for consistency only those for 1981–6 are presented in table 3.3.

In every country except the Netherlands, the results unambiguously show that inequality of market income was increasing. This would lead us to expect that, with policy unchanged, the redistributive effect of taxes and transfers would automatically increase (type (a) effect). In fact, in most but not all countries this seems to be the case. This suggests that tax and transfer reforms (type (b) effect) offset this automatic effect in several countries.

Looking at the UK, there is some evidence that changes in taxes and transfers have contributed to the increase in inequality of household income. In this case, whilst market income became more unequal in the early 1980s, the automatic increase in the redistributive impact of taxes and transfers that one would expect was more than offset by reforms which have made the system less progressive. What we know about the reforms made in the UK between 1979 and 1986 seems to suggest that they disproportionately benefited the well-off. Examples include the abolition of the unearned income surcharge, the breaking of the link between the basic state retirement pension and average earnings growth, the freezing of income tax allowances and increases in social security contributions with the ceiling only uprated in line with prices.

Fritzell estimates that with a constant redistributive effect between 1979 and 1986, inequality of household equivalised disposable income in the UK would have been 20 per cent lower. Probably due to the automatic response of the tax and transfer system to the growing inequality of market income,

Table 3.3 *Five studies of the change in the redistributive effect of tax and transfer policy for eight countries*

Country		Results from five studies				
		1	2	3	4	5
Australia	Redistributive effect of tax and transfer policy			↑		↑
	Overall income inequality ↑					
	Inequality of market income			↑		↑
Canada	Redistributive effect of tax and transfer policy	↑		↑		↑
	Overall income inequality stable					
	Inequality of market income	↑		↑		↑
France	Redistributive effect of tax and transfer policy					↑
	Overall income inequality stable					
	Inequality of market income					↑
Netherlands	Redistributive effect of tax and transfer policy			↓		↓
	Overall income inequality ↑					
	Inequality of market income			↓		↑
Sweden	Redistributive effect of tax and transfer policy	↓				↑
	Overall income inequality ↑					
	Inequality of market income	↑		↑		↑
United Kingdom	Redistributive effect of tax and transfer policy	↓	↑	↑	↑	↑
	Overall income inequality ↑					
	Inequality of market income	↑	↑	↑	↑	↑
USA	Redistributive effect of tax and transfer policy	↓		↓		↑
	Overall income inequality ↑					
	Inequality of market income	↑		↑		↑

Table 3.3 (*cont.*)

Country		Results from five studies				
		1	2	3	4	5
West Germany	Redistributive effect of tax and transfer policy	↑				
	Overall income inequality ↑					
	Inequality of market income	↑				

Sources: 1 Fritzell 1992. Market income inequality measure: growth in real equivalised household earnings where heads aged 20–64. Data: LIS data from early and mid 1980s.
2 Jenkins 1993. Market income inequality measure: market income – half the squared coefficient of variation.
Data: FES data from 1976, 1981 and 1986.
3 Smeeding and Coder 1993. Market income inequality measure: unequivalised market income – 80/20, 80/50, 50/20 percentile ratios. Data: LIS data from early and mid 1980s.
4 Stark 1989. Market income inequality measure: unequivalised market income – Gini coefficient. Data: FES for 1979 and 1986.
5 Gottschalk 1993. Market income inequality measure: household equivalised market income – 90/10 percentile ratio. Data: LIS data from early and mid1980s.

however, all other results find that its effect was to have a greater impact on reducing inequality over the same period.

Subsequently, major reforms were introduced in the Budget of 1988, when top marginal income tax rates were cut from 60 per cent to 40 per cent. Furthermore, given the nature of tax reform under the Conservative Government, it is important to remember that we are only looking at policy changes which influence disposable income. There has been a very significant shift towards indirect taxation. The rate of value-added tax increased, from 8 per cent in 1979 to 17.5 per cent presently, and in March 1993 in the Budget it was announced that the coverage of VAT is to be extended. The Poll Tax has also come and gone, a form of local taxation paid by all adults. None of these reforms is included in the findings presented here, although it has certainly been argued that they hit the living standards of low-income households significantly harder.

In the Netherlands, the expected automatic effect of a more equal distribution of market income combined with a constant tax and welfare system would be for taxes and transfers to become less redistributive. Smeeding and Coder find that taxes and transfers indeed became less redistributive during the early 1980s in the Netherlands. Gottschalk estimates a small increase in market income inequality and provides a summary of policy reforms in the Netherlands which may well have made the system more regressive. During this period, there was a limit imposed on increases in family allowances and social security, as well as changes to the unemployment benefit making it less easy to claim. It appears that taxes and benefits have become less redistributive over time in the Netherlands, possibly as a result of policy reform, and that this contributed to the overall increase in income inequality in the early 1980s (Muffels and Nelissen 1997).

The next group of countries to be considered are those where the distribution of market income became less equal and the effect of taxes and transfers was to offset this increase but not sufficiently to prevent a rise in inequality of disposable income. West Germany and Australia falls into this category. In some cases, however, the increase in the equalising impact of direct taxes and transfers offset the increase in inequality of market income, possibly in combination with other factors, with the result that the distribution of household disposable income remained stable. This was the case in Canada and France during the first half of the 1980s.

There is some evidence that reforms to taxes and transfers in the UK, Sweden and the US have made those systems less progressive, completely offsetting the automatic increase in the redistributive effect of policy resulting from greater inequality of taxable income. This suggests that from the late 1970s to the mid 1980s, the effect of changes in tax and transfer policy was to contribute to the rising inequality of household equivalised disposable income in each of these three countries.

This is most clear in the case of the US. Both studies of taxes and transfers in the US show that the trend from 1979 to 1986 was for policy to have a declining impact on reducing inequality. Indeed, Fritzell estimates that with the assumption of a constant redistributive effect, inequality would have been 35 per cent lower in the US. Gottschalk shows small net effects of taxes and transfers.

For Sweden, all three studies find that between 1981 and 1987 market income inequality rose but the results for the trend in the redistributive impact of taxes and transfers are mixed. Fritzell estimates that direct taxes and benefits contributed 41 per cent to the overall increase in income inequality, whilst the calculations by Smeeding and Coder show no clear shift in their equalising effect.[17]

3.4   Demographic and socioeconomic change

Demographic and socioeconomic trends are structural influences on the distribution of disposable income that are likely to have an effect through the 'compositional boxes' in figure 3.2. Shifts in the relative proportions of different household types, for example, will influence the household composition of income recipients (C3) as well as household size and composition generally (C4).

Despite the interest in the effect of ageing on inequality of household income, there is no evidence to suggest that it has had any influence in the UK (Jenkins 1993; Stark 1989). Studies of other countries produce similar results except in the case of West Germany and Japan. In both countries, the aging of the population has had a disequalising effect in the 1980s. In Japan, this is linked to the importance of inherited wealth.[18]

As with the impact of the ageing of the population, changes in household composition appear not to have influenced the level of inequality in other countries except West Germany and Japan (Fritzell 1992; Guger 1989; Bauer and Mason 1992). Findings for the UK are mixed. There is evidence both that household composition has not been a significant factor in explaining the trend in income inequality in the UK and that it has had a slightly disequalising effect on the distribution of income (Jenkins 1993; Fritzell 1992; Stark 1989).

The increase in participation of women in the labour force is a good example of where there can be a systematic breakdown in trying to explain the distribution of household equivalised disposable income by examining the dispersion of individual wages and salaries. Whilst it seems likely that women entering the labour force will probably make the distribution of earnings more unequal *ceteris paribus* because they tend to earn significantly below the average, it is less obvious what the effect will be on the distribution of household disposable income. This depends largely on whether these women are coming from rich or poor households. If it is the former, then the effect of them working is to make the household even more well-off, which is likely to increase inequality. On the other hand, if women from low-income households boost total income by going out to work, this will tend to make incomes more equal. Referring back to figure 3.2, these effects would feed into household composition of income recipients, box C3.

Decompositions of income inequality in the UK by income source suggest that throughout the period 1971–86 the impact of a spouse's earnings was to increase overall inequality. This influence was particularly strong in 1971–6, when the proportion of spouses with earnings increased from 29 per cent to 33 per cent. During this period, although inequality of women's earnings was actually falling, the share increased, as did the correlation with husband's earnings. In other words, the growth in participation of married women was disequalising because these women tended to belong to households which already had relatively high income (Jenkins 1993).

In West Germany, it appears that by far the most important influence reducing inequality in the 1970s and 1980s was the increase in labour force participation of women specifically and of multiple-earner households generally. Whilst this has the effect of pushing up the dispersion of individual wages (because women receive substantially lower wages) it has an equalising impact on the distribution of household income by increasing the incomes of poorer households relatively more. In 1985, equivalent household disposable income was 15 per cent higher on average in households with multiple earners, and incomes of multiple-earner households tended to have a narrower dispersion.

4   Summary and conclusions

The countries with the most equal distributions of income in the mid 1980s are those of northern Europe (not including the UK), which are also the only nations to have experienced falling inequality in the early 1980s. In most other countries, including the UK, the common pattern has been one of a consistently widening distribution of income since the early 1970s or mid 1980s. The steady rise in inequality seems to have been accompanied by contained periods of declining real income growth, particularly for the poorest households.

Much of the literature concentrates on the trends in earnings to explain what has been happening to the overall distribution of income. The evidence suggests that in about half of the countries studied there seems to be a similar pattern in trends in household disposable income and wages and salaries. The rise in relative demand for skilled workers seems to be a major factor driving changes in earnings. This shift in demand reflects a combination of shifts in final demand away from manufactures and the introduction of new technology. The macroeconomy appears to have been a very important influence on the labour market during the 1980s, as have the changes in labour market institutions, particularly for Great Britain and France.

The tax and benefit system in a country interacts with the distribution of market income to determine the distribution of disposable income. In most western countries during the early 1980s, there have been two competing forces at work: the increase in inequality of market income forcing up the extent of redistribution, and tax and benefit reforms, which have been largely regressive, reducing the redistributive effect of government policy. Consequently, there have been a variety of outcomes. It appears that there was a sufficient rise in the equalising effect of direct taxes and transfers in Canada and France (possibly in combination with other factors) to completely offset the increase in market income inequality and keep the overall distribution of disposable income constant during the first half of the 1980s.

In the US, Sweden and the UK, however, there is evidence that regressive policy reforms counteracted the automatic increase in redistribution and therefore contributed to the upward trend in income inequality in each of these countries during the 1980s. This is most clearcut for the case of the US, whereas the results are less conclusive for Sweden and the UK.

The increase in labour force participation of women has influenced trends in income inequality in the UK and West Germany. However, increases in female labour force participation had the opposite effect in these two countries. The females in West Germany who were going out to work tended to come from poorer households, so the net effect there was to reduce inequality of household disposable income. In the UK, however, such females were more likely to be married to rich husbands, so the consequence of adding the woman's earnings pushed an already high income even higher, and inequality rose as a result.

Finally, I offer some comments about the appropriate methodology for explaining inequality trends across countries. As has been stressed throughout, straightforward comparisons of trends in the individual distributions of various income sources with the overall distribution of household disposable income will fail to capture some of the important factors which influence the changing pattern of income inequality. Furthermore, trying to assess the extent to which inequality has the same 'ingredients' in different countries would be facilitated by using comparable measures, definitions and data sources, such as those provided by the Luxembourg Income Study. Ideally, we would produce inequality decompositions based on consistent and systematic analyses of the role of all income sources and linkages – between types of income and between individuals and households – across countries. Provided with such results, we will be one step closer to being able to identify precisely the economic and social phenomena which lie at the root of the trends in the distribution of living standards.

Notes

Karen Gardiner was a Research Officer with the Welfare State Programme at STICERD in the London School of Economics at the time of writing. She is now working in the Ministry of Finance and Economic Planning in Uganda. This paper was funded under the Joseph Rowntree Foundation's Programme on Income and Wealth. The author would like to thank all those who gave such helpful comments on earlier drafts, particularly John Hills, Stephen Jenkins and Holly Sutherland.

1 For a detailed analysis of the effect on income distribution statistics of different methodological choices, see Atkinson *et al.* 1993 and Coulter, Cowell and Jenkins 1992.

2 A variety of different inequality measures are used and no attempt is made here

to explain their relative properties, as this has been done very thoroughly else-where (Atkinson 1975; Cowell 1977).

3 The studies which use the 'ideal' income definition (equivalised household dis-posable income, weighted by persons) are Jenkins 1993 and CSO 1993.

4 This figure for the UK is calculated by Jenkins and Cowell 1993 on the same basis Krugman 1992 uses for the US. The comparable figure for the US is that 44 per cent of the growth in average family equivalised income between 1977 and 1989 went to the top 1 per cent of families (including capital gains).

5 For a discussion of some of these issues and their effect on cross-country comparisons, see Atkinson *et al.* 1993.

6 The results in Whiteford and Kennedy 1993 use LIS data and Saunders *et al.* 1989 use an LIS-type approach in calculating the Gini coefficient for New Zealand.

7 Official inequality statistics produced by the Census Bureau have published Gini coefficients in 1967/8 which make it appear that the upturn in inequality hap-pened much earlier than 1973. Seeking to explain the difference, Karoly (in Danziger and Gottschalk 1993) highlights two aspects of the official methodol-ogy which may have distorted the results: i) all families with only one person or where unrelated individuals live together are excluded; ii) income is not equival-ised to adjust for household size and composition.

8 Estimates of the trend in inequality in the US which use income data have been disputed on the grounds that misreporting of income and rapid growth in the provision of in-kind benefits to those on low incomes during the 1970s distorted the results. To address this, Cutler and Katz (1992) use expenditure data from the Consumer Expenditure Survey to examine the trends in inequality for several years between 1960 and 1988. They find similar patterns.

9 The income definition for the Netherlands is unequivalised.

10 In some countries, taxation may be on the basis of family earnings, but one or more individuals in the household will actually pay the taxes out of their gross income.

11 These results are from Jenkins 1993. Stark 1989 performs a similar analysis using the same data (the Family Expenditure Survey) but a different income definition: gross weekly household income. On the basis of concentration indices, he shows that 60 per cent of the overall increase in inequality between 1980 and 1986 was due to wages and salaries. Johnson and Webb 1992 find that one-sixth of the increase in inequality of equivalised household disposable income between 1979 and 1988 can be accounted for by changes in the distrib-ution of earnings. This seems to be much lower than other estimates but may have to do with the relatively high importance they give the impact of taxes and transfers due to their use of an alternative methodology (see section (iii)).

12 The conclusions for Australia are less clear because there were gains at the bottom and top offset by losses in the middle.

13 For more detail about what has happened to earnings in these countries, see Green, Coder and Ryscavage 1992 and Katz *et al.* 1992 for comparative analy-sis; Bauer and Mason 1992 for a study of Japan; Guger 1989 for evidence from

West Germany; and Levy and Murnane 1992 for a survey of results for the US.
14 For more detail, see Katz *et al*. 1992 on Great Britain, France, Japan and the US; Bauer and Mason 1992 on Japan; Guger 1989 on West Germany; and Levy and Murnane 1992 on the US.
15 There are two inadequacies with the findings described below. Firstly, this study would ideally include an examination of the distribution of interest payments and debt. Given the growth in homeownership in the West, the effect on the trends in income inequality could be substantial. A further caveat to the results presented here is that, unless stated, they do not include capital gains.
16 For more detail on the UK see Jenkins 1993; Cowell and Jenkins 1993 and Duncan *et al*. 1991 on the US; Bauer and Mason 1992 on Japan; and Saunders *et al*. 1989 on Australia and New Zealand.
17 Smeeding and Coder supplement their detailed analysis with a description of some subsequent policy reforms. In the case of the US, they note reductions in top marginal tax rates and social policy benefits. As far as the other nations are concerned, cuts in top marginal tax rates for most and in social security benefits for some seem to be the message.
18 For studies of other countries, see Fritzell 1992; Guger 1989; and Bauer and Mason 1992.

References

Atkinson, A. B. 1975. *The Economics of Inequality*. Oxford: Clarendon Press.
   1993. 'What is Happening to the Distribution of Income in the UK?'. Welfare State Programme Discussion Paper No. 87. London: London School of Economics.
Atkinson, A. B., Gardiner, K., Lechene, V. and Sutherland, H. 1993. 'Comparing Poverty in France and the United Kingdom'. Welfare State Programme Discussion Paper No. 84. London: London School of Economics.
   1994. 'Comparing Low Incomes in France and the United Kingdom: Evidence from Household Expenditure Surveys'. Microsimulation Modelling Unit Discussion Paper No. 4. Cambridge: Cambridge University.
Bauer, J. and Mason, A. 1992. 'The Distribution of Income and Wealth in Japan'. *Review of Income and Wealth*, 38, 4 (December).
Björklund, A. 1991. 'Unemployment and Income Distribution: Time-Series Evidence from Sweden'. *Scandinavian Journal of Economics*, 93, 3.
Blank, R. M. and Blinder, A. S. 1986. 'Macroeconomics, Income Distribution, and Poverty', in Danziger, S.H. and Weinberg, D.H. (eds.), *Fighting Poverty*. Cambridge, Mass.: Harvard University Press.
Buse, A. 1982. 'The Cyclical Behaviour of the Size Distribution of Income in Canada: 1947–78'. *Canadian Journal of Economics*, 15, 2 (May).
Central Statistical Office. 1993. 'The Effects of Taxes and Benefits on Household Incomes, 1990'. *Economic Trends*, 471: 147–87. London: CSO.
   1992. 'International Comparisons of Taxes and Social Security Benefits in 20 OECD Countries 1980–1990'. *Economic Trends* (December). London: CSO.

Coulter, F .A. E., Cowell, F. A. and Jenkins, S. P. 1992. 'Equivalence Scale Relativities and the Extent of Inequality and Poverty'. *Economic Journal*, 102: 1067–82.

Cowell, F .A. 1977. *Measuring Inequality*. Phillip Allen.

Cowell, F. A. and Jenkins, S.P. 1993. 'Changes in American Income Inequality in the 1980s'. London School of Economics. (mimeograph).

Cutler, David M. and Katz, Lawrence F. 1992. 'Rising Inequality? Changes in the Distribution of Income and Consumption in the 1980s'. *AEA Papers and Proceedings*, 82, 2 (May).

Danziger, S. and Gottschalk, P. (eds.). 1993. *Uneven Tides, Rising Inequality in America*. New York: Russell Sage Foundation.

Department of Social Security. 1993. 'Households Below Average Income: A Statistical Analysis 1979–1990/91'. London: HMSO.

Duncan, G. J .M., Smeeding, T .M. and Rodgers, W. 1991. 'W(h)ither the Middle Class? A Dynamic View'. Paper presented at Levy Institute Conference on Income Inequality, June.

Fritzell, J. 1992. 'Income Inequality Trends in the 1980s: A Five Country Comparison'. LIS-CEPS Working Paper No. 73. Walferdange, Luxembourg: Luxembourg Income Study.

Gosling, A. and Machin, S. 1993. 'Trade Unions and the Dispersion of Earnings in UK Establishments, 1980–90'. Centre for Economic Performance Discussion Paper No. 140. London: London School of Economics.

Gottschalk, P. 1993. 'Changes in Inequality of Family Income in Seven Industrialised Countries'. *AER* (May).

Green, G., Coder, J. and Ryscavage, P. 1992. 'International Comparisons of Earnings Inequality for Men in the 1980s'. *Review of Income and Wealth*, 38, 1 (March).

Gregg, P. and Machin, S. 1993. 'Is the UK Rise in Inequality Different?', in Glyn, A. (ed.), *Is the British Labour Market Different?* Cambridge: Cambridge University Press.

Guger, Alois. 1989. 'The Distribution of Household Income in Germany'. WIFO Working Papers No. 35. Austrian Institute of Economic Research. Vienna.

Jäntti, M. 1993. 'Changing Inequality in Five Countries: The Role of Markets, Transfers and Taxes'. LIS-CEPS Working Paper. Walferdange, Luxembourg: Luxembourg Income Study.

Jenkins, S. P. 1992. 'Recent Trends in UK Income Inequality', in Slottje, D. (ed.), *Research on Economic Inequality*, vol. II, JAI Press.

    1993. 'Accounting for Inequality Trends: Decomposition Analyses for the UK, 1971–86'. *Economica*.

Jenkins, S. P. and Cowell, F. A. 1993. 'Dwarfs and Giants in the 1980s: The UK Income Distribution and How It Changed'. Department of Economics Discussion Paper Series No. 93–03. University College of Swansea.

Johnson, P. and Webb, S. 1992. 'Explaining the Growth in UK Income Inequality, 1979–88'. Paper presented at the 1992 Royal Economic Society Conference, London.

Katz, L. F., Loveman, G. W. and Blanchflower, D. G. 1992. 'A Comparison of Changes in the Structure of Wages in Four OECD Countries'. NBER Conference, July.

Krugman, P.R. 1992. 'The Right, the Rich and the Facts: Deconstructing the Income Distribution Debate'. *American Prospect*, 11 (Fall).

Levy, F. and Murnane, R. J. 1992. 'US Earnings Levels and Earnings Inequality: A Review of Recent Trends and Proposed Explanations'. *Journal of Economic Literature*, 30 (September): 1333–81.

McWatters, C. J. and Beach, C. M. 1990. 'Factors Behind the Changes in Canada's Family Income Distribution and the Share of the Middle Class'. *Relations Industrielles*, 45, 1.

Muffels, R. and Nelissen, J. 1997. 'The Distribution of Economic Well-Being in the Netherlands, its Evolution in the 1980s and the Role of Demographic Change'. Chapter 12 in this volume.

Nolan, B. 1987. *Income Distribution and the Macroeconomy.* Cambridge: Cambridge University Press.

1988. 'Macroeconomic Conditions and the Size Distribution of Income: Evidence from the United Kingdom'. *Journal of Post Keynesian Economics*, 11.

Reich, R. B. 1991. *The Work of Nations.* London: Simon and Schuster.

Ringen, S. 1991. 'Households, Standard of Living, and Inequality'. *Review of Income and Wealth*, 37, 1 (March).

Sandford, C. 1992. 'Worldwide Tax Reform "How Does Australia Compare?"'. *The Australian Economic Review*, Q1 1992, Institute of Applied Economic and Social Research.

Saunders, P. 1992. 'Poverty, Inequality and Recession'. *Economic Papers*, 11: 1–22.

Saunders, P., Hobbes, G. and Stott, H. 1989. 'Income Inequality in Australia and New Zealand: International Comparisons and Recent Trends'. *Review of Income and Wealth*, 37: 63–79.

Schmitt, J. 1992. 'The Changing Structure of Male Earnings in Britain, 1974–88'. Centre for Economic Performance Working Paper No. 223, July. London: London School of Economics.

Smeeding, T. M. and Coder, J. 1993. 'Income Inequality in Rich Countries During the 1980s'. 1993 Conference, Eastern Economics Association.

Stark, T. 1989. 'The Changing Distribution of Income Under Mrs. Thatcher', in Green, F. (ed.), *The Restructuring of the UK Economy.* London: Harvester Wheatsheaf.

United Kingdom. *Hansard Parliamentary Debates*, July 1993, col. 1010.

Uusitalo, H. 1989. 'Income Distribution in Finland'. Central Statistical Office of Finland, Studies No. 148.

Whiteford, P. and Kennedy, S. 1993. 'Households Below Average Income: A Comparative Analysis'. Social Policy Research Unit Discussion Paper. York: University of York.

4 Economic adjustment and distributional change: income inequality and poverty in Australia in the 1980s

PETER SAUNDERS

1 Introduction

The 1970s saw the demise of Keynesian demand management policies and the end of full employment. In the 1980s, emphasis was given instead to the need to reduce inflation, cut public expenditure and lower taxes in the belief that this would create incentives and allow a less regulated private sector to prosper. The evidence shows that almost all OECD countries reduced the level of government expenditure relative to GDP in the latter half of the 1980s (Saunders 1993a), although tax receipts continued to rise relative to GDP in the majority of cases (Oxley and Martin 1991). The reduction of trade barriers and deregulation of capital and foreign exchange markets encouraged the search for new technologies designed to increase productivity and improve international competitiveness. These changes were embraced by some countries and imposed on others. They saw Australia deprived of much of its traditional market for agricultural exports which, in combination with fluctuating commodity prices, forced it to seek new trading relationships and diversify its range of tradable goods.

The consequences of these changes for income distribution received relatively little attention during the extended world recovery of 1983–90, when most economies experienced rates of growth well above post-oil crisis expectations. This changed with the onset of world recession in 1990 which forced the issues of unemployment, inequality and poverty back on to the policy agenda. Yet the delays involved in collecting and analysing reliable data on the distributional dimensions of performance mean that, even now, the effects of the recession on inequality remain for the most part unknown. Advances in data quality and analytical technique have made it easier to identify and monitor trends in inequality, but these tend to lag far behind what is currently happening. The advances have, however, facilitated the development of more accurate accounts of how the structure of inequality has been changing in the past and the role of various factors in the process of change.

The research available reveals a widespread, though not universal, trend towards increasing income inequality in the 1980s. In a recent review of this work, Atkinson (1993) concludes, 'The results cited cover only a selection of countries, but they are sufficient to demonstrate the risks in making any generalisation about the world-wide pattern of change in income inequality. A number of countries have experienced a rise in income inequality over the 1980s, but in others there has been no increase, or a fall. This in turn suggests that, while common economic forces have undoubtedly been at work, we have also to look at national factors, and particularly national policies, in seeking an explanation of changes in inequality' (p. 23).

One of the countries which Atkinson identified as having little change in inequality was Australia, at least for the period up to the mid 1980s. The availability of more recent data allows us to ascertain whether this has continued beyond then, and this chapter summarises a range of recent research on trends in inequality in Australia during the 1980s. The analysis adopts a similar framework to that used by researchers in other countries, thereby allowing common trends and differences to be more easily identified.

Research on inequality needs to be placed in a context if it is to be most valuable. With this in mind, section 2 of the chapter briefly describes several key features of and changes in the Australian tax-transfer system during the 1980s and outlines the major labour market changes of the period. This is followed in section 3 with a presentation of a range of evidence on changes in income distribution between 1981/2 and 1989/90. The use of this time period is determined by the availability of unit record data on household incomes, collected and released by the Australian Bureau of Statistics (ABS). The developments over the period are reviewed against a background of both shorter-run cyclical movements in inequality and the longer-run distributional trend. Section 4 discusses Australian evidence on the incidence of poverty, focusing on the role of housing costs and on the sensitivity of estimates of poverty to the methods used to derive them. The main conclusions of the analysis are summarised in section 5.

2   The policy and labour market context

The policy context

The processes generating and redistributing incomes in Australia have several singular features as compared with those of most other OECD countries. Amongst the most important of these are its centralised system of wage determination, a non-contributory social security system financed from general revenue and paying flat-rate means-tested benefits and a tax system which relies heavily on personal income taxation but raises total revenue which, in relation to GDP, is at a relatively low level by international standards. These features, it has been argued, have ensured that the distribution of wage income in Australia is relatively equal and that the tax-transfer system redistributes income effectively given the low level of taxes and transfers. However, while the comparative research evidence indicates that there is truth in both propositions (Bradbury 1993; Green, Coder and Ryscavage 1992; Mitchell 1991), other evidence from the Luxembourg Income Study (LIS) database indicates that the distribution of income in Australia is still not particularly equal when compared with other countries (Saunders and Hobbes 1988; Saunders, Stott and Hobbes 1991).

During the 1980s, wage, tax and transfer policies further strengthened those features which have traditionally been regarded as uniquely Australian. A cornerstone of economic policy since the election of the Australian Labor Party (ALP) to government in 1983 has been the 'Accord', a corporatist-style incomes policy agreed between the government and the trade union movement. The Accord is a social compact, being designed to achieve wage restraint in exchange for increased social wage provisions in health and social security and, increasingly, occupational pension coverage, as well as the introduction of reforms to the tax system designed to improve horizontal and vertical equity. While the Accord has provided a stable policy framework within which specific policy formulation has been fluid, its particular aims have been renegotiated several times in light of changes in economic and budgetary circumstances.

Linked to the wage determination aspects of the Accord has been the move to greatly increase the targeting of social security payments, mainly by tightening eligibility conditions and benefit administration (Saunders 1991) but also by the introduction of such measures as a benefit assets test in addition to the traditional income test. The only wide-ranging universal payment in the system – family allowance – became subject to both income and assets tests, and the introduction and extension of income-tested family benefits for low-income families saw the system of family income support become increasingly selective.

These moves to tighten benefit eligibility and reduce entitlements have resulted in considerable savings to the social security budget, by 1990/1 amounting to about A$1.4 billion, or 6 per cent of total outlays, according to one recent estimate (Whiteford 1992, p. 34). Changes to old-age pension eligibility alone have seen the proportion of the aged population receiving an old-age pension decline, from around 75 per cent at the beginning of the decade to 58 per cent by 1990 (ABS 1992, table 6.3.5).[1] At the same time, these and other restrictions have been accompanied by increased scope and generosity of payments to certain groups, mainly benefit and low-wage families with children and social security recipients in the private rental sector.

Changes to income taxation have seen the nominal rate schedule becoming flatter, as the top marginal rate has been reduced in stages from 60 per cent to 48 per cent, the first rate coming down from 30 per cent to 21 per cent and rates in between falling commensurately. These reduced rates have been slightly offset by the introduction of a levy (currently 1.4 per cent of taxable income) to finance the national health scheme (Medicare) introduced in 1984. A system of dividend imputation has also been introduced. At the same time, there have been significant moves to broaden the personal tax base, specifically through the introduction of a capital gains tax and a fringe benefits tax. Together, these changes have not resulted in a reduction in the overall reliance on income taxation. The ratio of personal income tax revenue to both total Commonwealth government tax revenue and to GDP were virtually the same in 1990/1 as they were a decade before.

Economic performance

The concern of this chapter is not the *overall* success of the Accord in achieving its basic objectives of non-inflationary growth and improvements in equity and social justice. Rather, this chapter's purpose is to analyse more specifically changes in inequality against the background of economic circumstances which prevailed under the Accord.[2] In relative terms, Australia's economic performance was generally good during the 1980s. During the decade, economic growth in Australia averaged 3.2 per cent a year, compared with an average OECD growth rate of 2.7 per cent. Between 1984 and 1989, growth in Australia was even higher: 4.5 per cent a year, compared with the OECD figure of 3.6 per cent.

That economic growth translated into a growth in employment which was also impressive by international standards. Over the decade, the level of employment in Australia grew by 2.3 per cent a year, more than twice the OECD average of 1.1 per cent, despite the greater severity of both Australian recessions. Between 1983 and 1989, Australia's employment record was even more impressive, employment increasing by 3.4 per cent a year compared with 1.2 per cent in the OECD as a whole. It is difficult to avoid the conclusion that the Accord played a major role in this context, a view for which there is support from labour market research. One study, for example, provides a conservative estimate that the Accord generated an extra 310,000 jobs between 1983 and 1989 as a result of its effects on structural wage relationships, although the authors note that the effect could be as large as half a million (Chapman, Dowrick and Junankar 1991, p. 41).

Employment trends over the decade saw the continuation of two longer-term labour market trends which other countries have also been experiencing: the increasing importance of part-time work and growth in the labour force participation of married women. The proportion of part-time jobs increased, from 16 per cent of all jobs in 1980 to more than 21 per cent in 1990. Female employment increased by 985,000, representing 60 per cent of total employment growth, while employment amongst married women rose by 646,000 and accounted for almost 40 per cent of overall employment growth.

The increased employment of married women saw the number of married couple families in which both partners were employed increase, from 39 per cent of all couple families in 1980 to almost 49 per cent by 1990. The percentage of couples with only one partner in employment declined by even more than this, while the percentage with neither partner in employment rose slightly, from 18 per cent to almost 22 per cent.

The labour market changes described above have important consequences for, and may in part result from, changes in income distribution, where the family (or some variant thereof) is the normal unit of analysis. Another important labour market development relates to the changing structure of employment opportunities. In a recent study, Gregory (1993) investigates this issue using data on the earnings distribution of full-time adult male non-managerial employees in May 1976 to construct earnings quintiles and quintile cut-offs expressed relative to median earnings in that year. These relative quintile cut-offs were then applied to median earnings in each survey between 1976 and 1990, and the growth in employment falling into each category was estimated.

The results, summarised in table 4.1, reveal that, for male employees, practically all of the net job growth occurred in the top and bottom quintiles, particularly in the bottom quintile.[3] A similar, though less marked, pattern is also apparent for females, and the substantial decline in middle-paying jobs is also apparent in both the public and private sectors. The growth of jobs in the highest quintile in the public sector is well below that in the private sector, an effect which Gregory attributes to the Accord. Overall, however, Gregory concludes that the Accord had little effect on retarding the growing dispersion of earnings in either the public or private sectors. A consequence of the relative decline in middle-paying jobs has been that displaced workers have taken low-paying jobs previously occupied by the least-skilled workers. This, Gregory argues, has made it even harder for displaced unskilled workers to regain employment, thus adding to the problems of the long-term unemployed.

In summary, the labour market trends discussed above indicate significant developments on both the supply and demand sides of the labour market which could, in principle, have led to an increase in inequality in Australia over the 1980s despite the policy context described earlier. Two aspects are worthy of special emphasis. The first is the increase in married women's labour force participation and the growing importance of two-

Table 4.1 *Employment growth by earnings quintile, 1976–1990 (thousands)[a]*

Quintile[b]	Male employees	Female employees	Public sector	Private sector	All employees
Lowest	176	114	111	178	983
Second	−51	24	29	−60	4
Third	−82	54	−4	−25	10
Fourth	15	104	89	30	139
Highest	94	50	35	117	243
Total	152	347	260	240	1,379

Notes:
[a] Full-time, non-managerial employees only.
[b] The quintile cut-offs are held at a constant percentage of median earnings in each year. Each quintile will thus not necessarily contain 20 per cent of earners in years other than in the base year (1976).
Source: Gregory 1993, table 1.1.

earner couples. The second is the relative decline in middle-paying jobs and the concentration of job growth in the lowest- and highest-paid positions.

Between the March quarter of 1983 (when the Accord came into operation) and the June quarter of 1990, average male earnings fell roughly 2.0 per cent in real terms, while real average female earnings fell 3.4 per cent. This partly reflects the change in the composition of employment towards more part-time work, although the average earnings of full-time male employees also fell slightly (by less than 0.5 per cent) while those for full-time female employees increased very modestly (by 1.5 per cent).

That real earnings could have been so constrained during a period of rapid employment growth is evidence of the impact of the Accord process on wage outcomes, this being made possible by Australia's centralised wage determination system.

Of more interest in the context of income distribution and living standards is figure 4.1, which shows movements in real household disposable income per capita (HDYC) over the decade. This is a more comprehensive income measure (derived from the National Accounts) whose scope extends beyond earnings to also include such items as imputed rent, personal benefit payments, grants to non-profit institutions, income taxes and other direct taxes, fees and fines.[4] Movements in HDYC are of particular interest, as this measure has been used to adjust the poverty line in most Australian poverty research (see section 4 below). While real HDYC follows

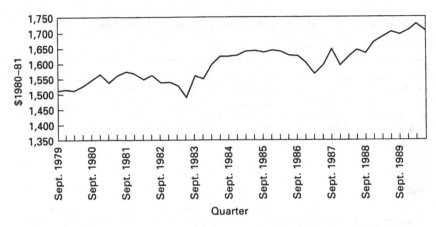

Figure 4.1 Trends in real household disposable income per capita

a marked cyclical pattern over the 1980s, the overall trend is clearly upward. During the period as a whole, real HDYC rose 13.3 per cent, while the increase after March 1983 was 11.7 per cent. On this measure, therefore, growth in the economy translated into higher average living standards, even though real earnings remained fairly static.

3   Trends in income inequality

Data issues

The data used here to describe trends in inequality and relative poverty in Australia in the 1980s are contained on the unit record files released by the ABS and based on the household income surveys undertaken in 1982 and 1990.[5] The income data refer to the financial years (commencing 1 July) 1981/2 and 1989/90. One advantage of these particular years is that they both represent approximately the same point in the business cycle: just before the onset of recession which led to a rapid rise in unemployment. It needs to be emphasised, however, that comparisons based on two points in time can be misleading if considerable variation took place in the intervening period.

Considerable effort has been made to ensure consistency in the data by, for example, recoding negative incomes to zero, and checks have been made to ensure that, wherever possible, the results conform with those published by the ABS itself. Despite these efforts, it needs to be acknowledged that perfect consistency of concept and definition is an ideal which will never be achieved in practice. Not only do statistical agencies themselves change their definitions, but even if definitional consistency were to be achieved, problems would still arise as a consequence of other changes which will impact on data of this kind to an unknowable degree.[6] Another issue relates to the calculation of personal tax payments. The unit record file based on the 1981/2 income survey contains no information on tax payments and these had to be estimated from the tax laws. In the later survey, tax information was estimated by the ABS itself prior to release of the unit record file. Finally, there are likely to be errors in the data themselves.

Income shares

Table 4.2 presents estimates of how the overall income distribution changed between 1981/2 and 1989/90 for the three income concepts now used most extensively in the distributional literature. The unit of analysis is the ABS income unit concept, which corresponds broadly to that used for the determination of social security entitlements. An income unit comprises single people, sole parents or married couples (*de jure* or *de facto*) with or without dependent children. Dependent children are unmarried persons living with their parents and either aged under 15 (under 16 in 1989/90) or full-time students aged 15–20 (16–20 in 1989/90). Young people who do not fit this definition of being dependent are treated as separate income units. In deriving the estimates shown in the third column of table 4.2, equivalent income has been distributed to all individuals in each income unit and the ranking and income shares have been based on individual weightings, making the individual the focus of analysis (O'Higgins, Schmaus and Stephenson 1990).[7]

In both years, the estimates in table 4.2 indicate that net income is more equally distributed among income units than gross income, and that the distribution of individual equivalent net income is more equal still. Using individual weights and adjusting for differences in need through the use of an equivalence scale has a far bigger impact on income inequality in both years than the progressivity of personal income taxes. For all three income measures, the Lorenz curve for 1989/90 lies wholly outside of that for 1981/2. All three distributions thus indicate more inequality in 1989/90 than in 1981/2, the most substantial change occurring in the highest decile, particularly in relation to its share of gross income. On the basis of the Gini coefficient, the degree of inequality increased by 10.7 per cent (gross income), 8.6 per cent (net income) and 7.4 per cent (equivalent net income). These increases were such that the estimated distribution of net income in 1989/90 was only slightly more equal than the distribution of gross income in 1981/2. The personal tax system (as well as the transfer system) thus continued to turn back the tide of inequality, but the tide itself was growing steadily stronger.

Table 4.2 *The distributions of gross income, net income and equivalent net income in Australia, 1981/2 and 1989/90 (decile shares)*

Decile	Gross income	Net income	Equivalent net income[a]
1981/2			
Lowest	1.8	2.2	3.2
Second	2.9	3.6	5.5
Third	4.3	5.1	6.6
Fourth	5.7	6.4	7.6
Fifth	7.5	7.9	8.6
Sixth	9.2	9.6	9.6
Seventh	11.2	11.4	10.8
Eighth	13.6	13.6	12.5
Ninth	17.2	16.6	14.8
Highest	26.7	23.7	20.9
Gini coefficient	0.40	0.35	0.27
Coefficient of variation	0.78	0.65	0.52
1989/90			
Lowest	1.6	2.0	3.0
Second	2.8	3.4	5.3
Third	3.9	4.7	6.4
Fourth	5.2	6.1	7.3
Fifth	6.8	7.6	8.3
Sixth	8.7	9.1	9.4
Seventh	10.8	11.0	10.8
Eighth	13.5	13.5	12.5
Ninth	17.4	16.9	14.8
Highest	29.5	25.7	22.4
Gini coefficient	0.43	0.38	0.29
Coefficient of variation	0.92	0.75	0.61

Note:
[a] Individual weighting is used in constructing this distribution.
Sources: 1981–2 Income and Housing Survey and *1990 Survey of Income and Housing Costs and Amenities;* unit record files.

Decomposition analysis

Table 4.3 focuses on how overall inequality changed between different income unit types. We turn now to a more formal decomposition of inequality within and between these income unit types. Given the significant changes in the employment status of family members, the analysis will

Table 4.3 *Within-group and between-group inequality: decomposition of* $CV^2/2$

Income concept and year	Within-group inequality	Between-group inequality	Aggregate inequality
Groups defined by income unit type			
Private income			
1981/2	0.301	0.138	0.439
1989/90	0.421	0.148	0.569
Gross income			
1981/2	0.221	0.093	0.313
1989/90	0.317	0.104	0.421
Net income			
1981/2	0.136	0.080	0.217
1989/90	0.192	0.089	0.281
Groups defined by the number of earners			
Private income			
1981/2	0.242	0.196	0.439
1989/90	0.346	0.222	0.569
Gross income			
1981/2	0.195	0.119	0.313
1989/90	0.278	0.144	0.421
Net income			
1981/2	0.119	0.098	0.217
1989/90	0.164	0.117	0.281

Sources: See table 4.2.

also be undertaken for groups defined according to the number of earners (i.e., individuals with positive earnings, including from self-employment) in the income unit. The groups defined for this purpose were: aged income units with no earners, non-aged income units with no earners, non-aged units with one earner and non-aged units with two or more earners. The inequality measure used, following Cowell (1984) and Jenkins (1992), is half the squared coefficient of variation ($CV^2/2$), which is a member of the generalised entropy family of inequality measures ($I(\alpha)$) discussed by Shorrocks (1984) for the case where $a=2$.[8]

The results from the application of this method to private (market) income, gross income and net income in each year are presented in table 4.3. These results indicate that inequality increased between 1981/2 and 1989/90 by about 30 per cent in the case of private income, 35 per cent for gross income and 30 per cent for net income.[9] Interestingly, the tax-transfer system performed the same overall redistributive task in both years, the degree of inequality of net income being just below half (49 per cent) of that of private income in both 1981/2 and 1989/90. The decomposition results also reveal a fairly consistent story, one similar to that provided by the recent analysis undertaken by Jenkins (1992) for the United Kingdom between 1976 and 1986.

For all three income concepts, both years and both groupings, the within-group inequality term is larger than the between-group term.[10] The between-group term is, however, a larger proportion of the within-group term when the groups are defined by the number of earners than when the groups are defined by income unit type. For the income unit type decomposition, the size of the within-group term relative to the between-group term is smaller for net income than for private income in both years. When the decomposition is based on the number of earners, the within-group term is approximately the same size relative to the between-group term for both private and net income in both years. For both decompositions, the within-group effect increased over time, to the extent that the relative importance of the within-group and between-group effects for net income in 1989/90 were much the same as they were for private income in 1981/2. That the between-group inequality term is larger (in relative terms) when the decomposition is based on the number of earners suggests that differences in the number of earners in families played more of a role in shaping the structure of income inequality in the 1980s than differences in the economic fortunes of different income unit types.[11]

With regard to changes in inequality, whichever decomposition is considered the change in within-group inequality dominates the change in between-group inequality. When the groups are defined by income unit type, the within-group change explains 92 per cent of the total change in private income inequality, 89 per cent of the change in gross income inequality and 87 per cent of the change in net income inequality. When the decomposition is based on the number of earners in the unit, the within-group change still dominates, although it declines somewhat in relative size. Whichever decomposition is used, the size of the change in the between-group term is larger for gross income than for private income and larger again for net income. Income inequality thus increased both within and between groups, however defined, and increased before transfers, after transfers and after transfers and taxes combined.

Increased earnings inequality was not, however, the only factor causing the greater disparity of private incomes. If, for example, the analysis is restricted to aged income units only – where earnings are of only minor significance – the changes in income inequality between 1981/2 and 1989/90 are of a similar magnitude to those for the whole population shown in table 4.2. This suggests that unearned income, particularly interest income resulting from high interest rates, played an important role in widening income disparities in the latter half of the decade. What does seem clear is that not all of the explanation of increasing inequality can be attributed to changes in the labour market, although they have been important. No comprehensive account of how inequality evolved in the 1980s in Australia can ignore the role of the tax-transfer system and how it has changed over time.

Inequality and unemployment

The above results establish that income inequality in Australia was more pronounced in 1989/90 than in 1981/2. This finding does not imply a unidirectional increase in inequality over the period, nor does it say anything about the impact of the government policies described earlier. In relation to the latter, the investigation of impact effects requires the specification of a counterfactual, and this has not been attempted. Even if such an exercise were undertaken, problems would arise because the observed changes in inequality in any particular period will partly reflect the impact of past policies, while current policies are likely to have an impact which extends beyond the period. Any conclusion that government policies have caused, or even contributed to, the observed increase in inequality would thus be premature and cannot be supported by the evidence presented here.[12]

To establish what may have happened to inequality and living standards in the period between 1981/2 and 1989/90, two possible approaches suggest themselves. The first involves simulating the distributional effects of labour market, demographic, social security, other income and income tax changes with the assistance of a microsimulation model designed specifically for this purpose. Such research indicates that a comparison of the simulated distributions of net income in 1983/4 and 1989/90 reveals an ambiguous trend in inequality, with the income shares of the first, second and fifth quintiles increasing at the expense of those of the third and fourth quintiles (Bradbury 1992, table 4.5). This result, when combined with the actual distributional changes described earlier, suggests that much of the observed increase in inequality between 1981/2 and 1989/90 may have occurred between 1981/2 and 1983/4, and if so was almost certainly associated with the recession and the rise in unemployment which accompanied it.

The second approach is more direct but also more aggregate and less complex. It involves using regression analysis to estimate the relationship between unemployment (and other macroeconomic variables) and income distribution, as has been done in a number of recent studies.[13] A recent application of this method to Australian data revealed a significant impact of unemployment on income inequality, at least among families containing more than one person (Saunders 1992). When the regression results were used to estimate the impact of the current recession in Australia, they indicated an increase in inequality between 1989/90 and 1991/2 of a similar order of magnitude to that which took place between 1981/2 and 1989/90. The regression results thus confirm the microsimulation results in suggesting that inequality will vary in the short run in response to changing cyclical conditions in the economy.[14]

Income distribution in the longer run

What of the longer-run distributional trend? Income distribution comparisons over long periods of time are hampered by the lack of reliable data and results for earlier years which can be replicated with any accuracy using more recent data. Such studies as have been undertaken in Australia have tended to suggest a considerable reduction in inequality amongst male income recipients between 1914/15 and 1968/9 (Jones 1975) and between 1932/3 and 1980/1 (McLean and Richardson 1986). Saunders (1993d) recently used the income survey data for 1989/90 to replicate a study of the distribution of individual incomes in 1942/3 undertaken by Brown (1957). Given the difficulties involved in such an exercise, combined with the fact that 1942/3 was a highly unusual year, the outcomes need to be interpreted very cautiously.

The results, summarised in table 4.4, are remarkable in that they indicate that the overall change in gross income inequality between 1942/3 and 1989/90 was very small. The only significant changes took place within the top three deciles, the share of the highest decile declining and those of the two deciles below it increasing commensurately. The decline in the Gini coefficient from 0.41 to 0.40 seems minuscule when placed alongside the enormous increase in the size and scope of social security programmes which occurred over the period.

One possible implication of this is that the expansion of these programmes (which are known to be vertically redistributive) has been accompanied by growing inequality of private income, this explaining the absence of any significant reduction in gross income inequality.[15] Perhaps of more significance, table 4.4 indicates that the increase in inequality between 1981/2 and 1989/90, when assessed on the same basis as the methods used to derive the 1942/3 estimates, is considerable when viewed in this longer-run perspective. In terms of both the change in the Gini coefficient and the upward redistribution in favour of those in the highest decile, the estimates

Table 4.4 *Estimates of the distribution of individual gross incomes (decile shares)*

Decile	1942/3	1981/2	1989/90
Lowest	2.3	2.4	2.4
Second	2.7	3.2	3.2
Third	4.3	4.1	4.0
Fourth	5.7	5.6	5.4
Fifth	7.6	7.6	7.3
Sixth	8.6	9.7	9.2
Seventh	11.1	11.5	11.0
Eighth	12.2	13.6	13.2
Ninth	14.3	16.5	16.3
Highest	31.2	25.7	28.1
Gini coefficient	0.41	0.38	0.40

Source: Saunders 1993d, tables 2 and 4.

in table 4.4 suggest that the increase in inequality between 1981/2 and 1989/90 may have reversed much of the redistributive change which occurred in Australia over the previous 40 years.

4   Relative poverty

Research on poverty in Australia dates back to the mid 1960s, most of it adopting the measurement framework developed by the Commission of Inquiry into Poverty which reported in 1975 (Commission of Inquiry into Poverty 1975). That framework focuses on income poverty using a poverty line proposed by the Commission and named after its chairman: the Henderson poverty line. The line was initially set (in 1966) equal to the level of the minimum wage plus family benefits for a one-earner couple with two children. Being an explicitly relative poverty standard, the line was subsequently adjusted by the Poverty Commission in line with movements in average weekly earnings. Since the early 1980s it has been adjusted by movements in household disposable income per capita (HDYC) to reflect a broader income concept and to link the poverty line to after-tax income, the same basis as that on which poverty status is itself determined.

In the absence of any reliable Australian equivalence scale, the scale used in the Henderson poverty line was derived from the 1954 Family Budget Standards produced by the Budget Standard Service of the Community Council of Greater New York. This scale is rather complex, varying not only with the number of adults and children in the income unit, but also

Table 4.5 *Poverty rates before and after housing costs (percentages)*

Income unit type	Before housing costs		After housing costs	
	1981/2	1989/90	1981/2	1989/90
Single, aged	10.1	27.4	6.0	8.1
Single, non-aged	12.0	17.0	12.1	19.0
Couple, aged	5.2	6.8	3.9	4.8
Couple, non-aged	3.4	6.3	2.8	5.8
Sole parent	43.8	57.5	38.3	54.4
Couples with children	7.1	10.4	7.4	14.4
Total	10.2	16.4	9.4	15.0

Sources: See table 4.2.

with their age and workforce status and the total number of people in the household within which each unit is living (Whiteford 1985).

Application of the Henderson poverty line framework produces the estimates shown in table 4.5.[16] Estimates are provided of poverty both before and after housing costs. The latter are derived by subtracting housing costs in the form of mortgage and loan repayments, rent and local government property rates from net income and comparing the resulting figure with a poverty line which excludes the housing cost element. The estimation of poverty after housing costs has traditionally been justified in Australia on the grounds that it provides a better measure of poverty amongst the elderly, many of whom have low incomes but because of their high rate of home ownership also have very low housing costs. It has to be acknowledged, however, that the approach ignores the imputed rental income associated with home ownership and takes no account of differences in housing quality.

The results in table 4.5 indicate an increase in poverty before and after housing costs, in aggregate and for each separate income unit type. In both 1981/2 and 1989/90, the overall poverty rate after housing costs is about one percentage point lower than poverty before housing costs. For non-aged income units, poverty rates after housing costs are higher than poverty before housing costs, and the increase in poverty between 1981/2 and 1989/90 is more pronounced. Sole parent families have the highest poverty rates, over four times as high as the overall rate in 1981/2 and three and a half times as high in 1989/90. Poverty is generally much higher in units with only one adult present than it is among couples. The large increase in poverty among the single aged reflects the fact that the level of the age pension on which most of this group rely is close to the Henderson poverty line, making head-count poverty estimates sensitive to relatively small

Table 4.6 *Net incomes after housing costs by housing tenure (1989/90 dollars)*

	Net income			Net income minus housing costs		
Housing tenure	1981/2 ($)	1989/90 ($)	Increase (per cent)	1981/2 ($)	1989/90 ($)	Increase (per cent)
Outright owner	22,570	24,740	9.6	21,800	23,720	8.8
Home purchaser	32,440	33,490	3.2	25,940	24,010	−7.4
Private renter	20,170	20,800	3.1	15,330	15,150	−1.2
Government renter	17,690	14,490	−18.1	14,400	11,490	−20.2
Other[a]	15,490	16,070	3.7	14,860	13,660	−8.1

Note:
[a] Other includes boarders and those living rent free.

changes in either the poverty line or in the level of the pension (an issue explored further below). The increase in poverty among aged couples is much lower, even though both the single aged and aged couples received virtually identical pension increases over the period.

Although the poverty estimates in table 4.5 before housing costs and after housing costs reveal the same general picture, housing costs them- selves have varied considerably over the period. There are a number of reasons for this, among the most significant being the impact of high inter- est rates on mortgage interest payments (which are not deductible for per- sonal taxpayers in Australia). Other notable factors include the considerable increases in social security payments to private renters in the latter half of the 1980s and the tendency for rents in government housing (which are determined by state governments) to be adjusted towards market rents and then, through a system of rebates, held at a fixed propor- tion of gross income. There have also been substantial changes in the composition of those in any specific tenure situation, particularly govern- ment renters, where increased priority of access has been given to sole parents and other social security recipients.

These factors are likely to have had different effects on the immediate living standards of those in different housing tenures. Table 4.6 reveals that, while mean net incomes rose in real terms in almost all cases, mean net incomes after housing costs fell in real terms between 1981/2 and 1989/90 for all groups except outright owners. The decline in real net income after housing costs was greatest for those in public housing, although this largely reflects the compositional change referred to earlier. Owner-occupiers were another group whose mean income after housing costs fell in real terms, although this group was acquiring an asset which attracts extremely favourable treatment in the tax-transfer system, owner-occupied housing being excluded from both the capital gains tax and from the assets test on social security benefits. Despite these longer-term advantages, higher interest rates cut into spending power and thus into living standards in the short run by raising mortgage repayments. Overall, table 4.6 shows that housing costs had a considerable immediate impact on changes in the living standards of most Australian families over the decade.

Table 4.7 explores the sensitivity of the estimates of poverty before housing costs to the level at which the poverty line is set.[17] These results indicate that varying the level of the poverty line does not markedly alter any of the major conclusions based on the Henderson poverty line shown in table 4.5. However, it is clear that a large proportion of the population in both years was on the margins of poverty, with incomes less than 20 per cent above the poverty line. The dominance result established by Atkinson (1987) indicates that for each poverty line shown in table 4.7 (i.e., from half the Henderson line to twice the Henderson line), poverty increased between 1981/2 and 1989/90 in aggregate and for each separate income unit type.

The degree of sensitivity is, however, more pronounced for some groups than for others. For example, precisely where the poverty line is set has an important impact on estimates of the poverty rate for the single elderly and also, to a lesser extent, for aged couples, and these in turn influence the structure of poverty. Poverty amongst income units with one adult is always well above poverty amongst couples, and sole parents always have the highest poverty rates. These results hold constant the equivalence scale which reflects differences in need, and further analysis of this issue is warranted along the lines pursued by Bradbury and Saunders (1990). Aside from this, it appears that conclusions about the level, composition and changes in poverty in Australia are robust with respect to where the poverty line is set within a fairly broad range.[18]

One final aspect of the results in table 4.7 is worth emphasising. As noted earlier, the poverty line on which these results are based has been adjusted over time in line with movements in estimates of HDYC based on National Accounts and demographic statistics. However, the National Accounts estimate of HDYC itself increased 10.1 per cent in real terms between 1981/2 and 1989/90, reflecting growth in the economy during the period. It is also significant that the data on the income survey unit record files considerably underestimate HDYC, by around 18 per cent in 1981/2 and 20 per cent in 1989/90. Because this downward bias increased during the period, the increase in real HDYC based on the income survey data (7.2 per cent) is somewhat less than the 10.1 per cent increase in the National Accounts measure.

Table 4.7 *Sensitivity analysis of the level and changes in poverty before housing costs, 1981/2 to 1989/90 (percentages in poverty)*

Income unit type	Poverty line as a proportion of the standard line (P):							
	0.5P	0.8P	0.9P	1.0P	1.1P	1.2P	1.5P	2.0P
1981/2								
Single, aged	1.5	2.8	3.9	10.1	26.8	40.4	61.0	82.8
Single, non-aged	3.4	6.9	9.1	12.0	14.4	16.7	24.1	37.1
Couple, aged	0.3	3.1	3.9	5.2	6.7	11.6	53.0	79.4
Couple, non-aged	0.8	2.2	2.6	3.4	4.5	7.7	14.8	29.4
Sole parent	4.8	20.6	32.1	43.8	53.4	60.2	72.8	89.2
Couples with children	0.6	2.5	4.6	7.1	9.7	13.2	28.9	63.3
Total	1.9	4.9	7.0	10.2	14.7	19.4	33.6	54.8
1989/90								
Single, aged	2.8	6.0	11.0	27.4	41.2	51.9	71.3	87.5
Single, non-aged	4.2	9.5	13.1	17.0	19.9	23.2	33.0	48.1
Couple, aged	1.5	3.8	4.9	6.8	11.4	24.8	59.6	83.1
Couple, non-aged	0.8	2.8	4.0	6.2	8.5	10.9	20.6	38.7
Sole parent	9.0	33.9	45.9	57.2	63.1	68.7	80.7	93.1
Couples with children	1.6	5.1	7.4	10.4	14.8	21.0	42.2	71.5
Total	2.9	7.7	11.1	16.4	21.3	27.2	43.3	62.9

Sources: See table 4.2.

If the poverty line had been held constant in real terms over the period, by 1989/90 it would have been only 90.8 per cent ($=1/1.101$) of the HDYC-adjusted line used to derive the results in tables 4.5 and 4.7. It is possible to gauge how poverty would have changed if the poverty line had been held fixed in real terms between 1981/2 and 1989/90 by comparing the 1981/2 poverty estimates based on the 1.0 P poverty line with the 1989/90 estimates based on the 0.9P poverty line. Such a comparison still shows a slight increase in the overall poverty rate, from 10.2 per cent to 11.1 per cent, and an increase in poverty for all groups except aged couples. Thus it is difficult to escape the conclusion that poverty in Australia increased over the period, unless one is prepared to abandon the Henderson framework entirely.

5   Summary and conclusions

The 1980s saw a combination of two factors in Australia which might have been expected to lead to reductions in both income inequality and poverty. The first was the existence for much of the decade of a federal government committed to equity and social justice. The second was the performance of the economy, at least between 1983 and 1989, which was moderately successful, particularly in terms of employment growth, though not extremely so in comparison with the 1950s and 1960s. The second factor provided the economic basis for the attainment of redistributive goals, whilst the first factor opened up the political avenues to achieve them. The Accord provided the broad policy framework which brought the two together in a manner absent in Australia since the late 1940s.

Against this background, the contextual description in section 2 of the chapter reveals that growth in employment after 1983 took place when the labour force participation of married women was also increasing rapidly. The result was a rapid increase in the relative importance of two-earner families. The Accord succeeded in restraining growth in real earnings, while increased employment and increases in unearned incomes saw a modest growth in household incomes even after adjusting for changes in prices and taxes and taking account of the increase in population. At the same time, structural changes in the economy were widening the distribution of job opportunities, as reflected in the relative decline in the number of middle-paying jobs.

The results in sections 3 and 4 consider the extent to which these forces tending to increase inequality were offset by countervailing tendencies, including changes in tax-transfer policies and changes in labour market behaviour within families. They reveal a considerable increase in income inequality between 1981/2 and 1989/90, most of it occurring within rather than between socioeconomic groups. They also indicate a rise in relative poverty as measured using the Henderson framework. Both findings seem quite robust within that framework, although there is evidence that changing the poverty measurement framework can cause estimates of the level and trend in poverty to vary. Although no formal analysis of the issue has been attempted, it appears that high interest rates exacerbated differences in living standards by increasing the incomes of those with financial assets while raising housing costs considerably for others.

No attempt has been made to assess the effectiveness of government tax-transfer policies on inequality and poverty, an exercise which is far more complex than that attempted here. The success of Australia's experiment with a more corporatist, social democratic approach to economic and social policy, encapsulated in the Accord, has not been addressed explicitly, although the Accord is central to understanding what happened over the period and why. Assessment of the overall impact of the Accord is, however, a task left for others. Such analysis might well reveal an optimistic assessment of the impact of government redistributive policies which could be set alongside the somewhat disappointing distributional outcomes actually experienced.

Notes

This chapter has benefited greatly from the comments of my discussant Göran Bergström, as well as from those provided by Bruce Bradbury, Anthony King, George Matheson, Ed Palmer and Phil Raskall. Research assistance was provided by George Matheson. None of these are in any way responsible for the views expressed in the chapter. Readers interested in a longer version of the chapter should consult Saunders (1993c).

1 These estimates exclude those individuals over pension age who are in receipt of service and other veterans' pensions paid through the Department of Veterans' Affairs.

2 These changes will reflect changes in tax, transfer and wage policies negotiated under the Accord framework, but the actual redistributive influence of the Accord is not analysed (even if it could be).

3 The quintiles shown in table 4.1 are not the same as those normally employed in distributional studies, because it is the quintile cut-offs (expressed relative to median earnings) which are held constant over time, not the percentage of the population in each quintile.

4 The difference between the growth in average earnings and household incomes cannot be attributed to changes in employer or employee social security contributions, because these do not exist in Australia.

5 Both surveys were based on a multi-stage area sample of dwellings representing approximately one-third of 1 per cent of the Australian population. The actual sample contains 31,700 individuals in 1982 and 30,400 individuals in 1990. Information is provided for individuals, for income units (defined below) and for households, although the income unit is the unit of analysis adopted here. The data from these surveys form the basis of virtually all quantitative research on poverty and income distribution undertaken in Australia and are summarised in a report recently released by the ABS (ABS 1992).

6 It has already been noted, for example, that both a capital gains tax and a fringe benefits tax, as well as a system of dividend imputation, were introduced in the mid 1980s. By closing existing tax loopholes, these tax measures are likely to have led to behavioural changes which may well have impacted upon the measurement and scope of income as recorded in income surveys.

7 The equivalence scale used to derive the distribution of equivalent income is explained in more detail in Whiteford (1985).

8 Members of the $I(\alpha)$ family have the property that overall inequality in a population can be additively decomposed into a weighted sum of inequality within each of a number of mutually exclusive and exhaustive sub-groups in the population and a between-group inequality term based on the mean incomes and sizes of the sub-groups. This and other properties of decomposable inequality indices, including $CV^2/2$, are discussed in Jenkins (1991).

9 The inequality measure being used here is sensitive to changes at the top of the distribution which, given the results in table 4.2, explains why these changes are so large.

10 This finding is supported by results from the decomposition analysis based on data from the Household Expenditure Surveys of 1984 and 1988/9 undertaken by Raskall and McHutchison (1992).

11 In a recent study, Saunders (1993b) shows that the earnings of wives in married couple families with husbands aged 25–54 reduced family income inequality in both 1981/2 and 1989/90 and that changes in the contribution of wives' earnings to family income had an equalising impact on the distribution of family incomes.

12 Harding and Mitchell (1992) consider more explicitly the role of government tax and transfer policies in the context of changes in poverty and inequality in the 1980s.

13 Blinder and Esaki (1978), Blank and Blinder (1986), Nolan (1988) and Bjorklund (1991).

14 The results also indicate that the size and composition of the effects of unemployment on inequality between 1989/90 and 1991/2 derived from the microsimulation and regression methods are broadly similar (Saunders 1992, pp. 18–19).

15 One of the factors likely to have contributed to this is associated with increased unemployment. Being in the midst of the war effort, 1942/3 was a year of full (if not over-full) employment, with an unemployment rate of 1 per cent. In contrast, the average unemployment rate during 1989/90 was 6.2 per cent.

16 Following the Poverty Commission, two groups have been omitted from the analysis, juveniles living in the parental home and self-employed income units, on the grounds that income as measured in income surveys provides an imperfect indicator of financial well-being in these cases. The self-employed are defined here as income units with either any income from self-employment during the survey period or who were self-employed at the time of the survey. Juveniles are single people aged under 20 (in 1981/2) or under 21 (in 1989/90) who are living with other family members.

17 A similar analysis based on poverty after housing costs produces the same broad conclusions.

18 This statement is only valid if the Henderson poverty line framework is used. In a recent study, Harding and Mitchell (1992) using a poverty line based on half median equivalent income, the OECD equivalence scales and a different income unit definition to that employed here, estimate that poverty declined from 11.0 per cent in 1981/2 to 9.5 per cent in 1989/90. Their results suggest that estimates of poverty in Australia are more sensitive to such issues as how families are defined and which equivalence scales are used than they are (within rather broad limits) to the level of the poverty line itself.

References

Atkinson, A. B. 1987. 'On the Measurement of Poverty'. *Econometrica* (December): 749–64.

1993. 'What is Happening to the Distribution of Income in the U.K?' Welfare State Programme Discussion Paper No. 87: STICERD, London School of Economics.

Australian Bureau of Statistics. 1992. *Social Indicators, Australia 1992*. Catalogue No. 4101.0. Canberra: Australian Government Publishing Service.

Binh, T. N. and Whiteford, P. 1990. 'Household Equivalence Scales: New Evidence from the 1984 Household Expenditure Survey'. *Economic Record*, 66 (September): 221–34.

Björklund, A. 1991. 'Unemployment and Income Distribution: Time-Series Evidence from Sweden'. *Scandinavian Journal of Economics*, 93: 457–65.

Blank, R. M. and Blinder, A. S. 1986. 'Macroeconomics, Income Distribution and Poverty', in Danziger, S. H. and Weinberg, D. H. (eds.), *Fighting Poverty – What Works and What Doesn't*. Cambridge, Mass.: Harvard University Press, 180–208.

Blinder, A. S. and Esaki, H. Y. 1978. 'Macroeconomic Activity and Income Distribution in the Postwar United States'. *Review of Economics and Statistics*, 60 (November): 604–9.

Bradbury, B. 1992. 'Unemployment, Participation and Family Incomes in the 1980s'. *Economic Record*, 68 (December): 328–42.

1993. 'Male Wage Inequality Before and After Tax: A Six Country Comparison'. SPRC Discussion Paper No. 42. Social Policy Research Centre, University of New South Wales, Sydney.

Bradbury, B. and Saunders, P. 1990. 'How Reliable are Estimates of Poverty in Australia? Some Sensitivity Tests for the Period 1981–2 to 1985–6'. *Australian Economic Papers*, 29 (December): 154–81.

Brown, H. P. 1957. 'Estimation of Income Distribution in Australia', in Gilbert, M. and Stone, R. (eds.), *Income and Wealth*, series VI. London: Bowes and Bowes, pp. 202–38.

Chapman, B. J., Dowrick, S. and Junankar, P. N. 1991. 'Perspectives on Australian Unemployment: The Impact of Wage Setting Institutions in the 1980s', in Gruen, F. H. (ed.), *Australian Economic Policy*. Conference Proceedings, Centre for Economic Policy Research, Australian National University, pp. 21–57.

Commission of Inquiry into Poverty. 1975. *First Main Report. Poverty in Australia*. Canberra: Australian Government Publishing Service.

Cowell, F. A. 1984. 'The Structure of American Income Inequality'. *Review of Income and Wealth*, 30: 351–75.

Green, G., Coder, J. and Ryscavage, P. 1992. 'International Comparisons of Earnings Inequality for Men in the 1980s'. *Review of Income and Wealth*, 38 (March): 1–15.

Gregory, R. G. 1993. 'Aspects of Australian and US Living Standards: The Disappointing Decades 1970–1990'. *Economic Record*, 69 (March): 61–76.

Harding, A. and Mitchell, D. 1992. 'The Efficiency and Effectiveness of the Tax-Transfer System in the 1980s'. *Australian Tax Forum*, 9: 277–304.

Jenkins, S. 1991. 'The Measurement of Income Inequality', in Osberg, L. (ed.),

Economic Inequality and Poverty. International Perspectives. New York: M.E. Sharpe Inc, pp. 3–38.

1992. 'Accounting for Inequality Trends: Decomposition Analyses for the UK, 1976–1986'. Study of Social and Economic Inequality, Working Paper No. 8. Centre for Applied Economic Research, University of New South Wales, Sydney.

Jones, F. L. 1975. 'The Changing Shape of the Australian Income Distribution, 1914–15 to 1968–69'. *Australian Economic History Review*, 15: 21–34.

Kakwani, N. 1980. *Income Inequality and Poverty. Methods of Estimation and Policy Applications*. Washington DC: Oxford University Press.

McLean, I. W. and Richardson, S. 1986. 'More or Less Equal? Australian Income Distribution in 1933 and 1980'. *Economic Record*, 62 (March): 67–81.

Mitchell, D. 1991. *Income Transfers in Ten Welfare States*. Aldershot: Avebury.

Nolan, B. 1988. 'Macroeconomic Conditions and the Size Distribution of Income. Evidence from the United Kingdom'. *Journal of Post-Keynesian Economics*, 11 (Winter): 196–221.

O'Higgins, M., Schmaus, G. and Stephenson, J. 1990. 'Income Distribution and Redistribution: A Microdata Analysis for Seven Countries', in Smeeding, T. M., O'Higgins, M. and Rainwater L. (eds.), *Poverty, Inequality and Income Distribution in Comparative Perspective: The Luxembourg Income Study*. Hemel Hempstead: Harvester Wheatsheaf, pp. 20–56.

Oxley, H., and Martin, J. P. 1991. 'Controlling Government Spending and Deficits: Trends in the 1980s and Prospects for the 1990s'. *OECD Economic Studies,* 17 (Autumn):145–189.

Raskall, P. and McHutchison, J. 1992. 'Changes in Income Inequality in Australia in the 1980s: A Lifecycle Approach'. Study of Social and Economic Inequality, Working Paper No. 6. Centre for Applied Economic Research, University of New South Wales, Sydney.

Saunders, P. 1991. 'Selectivity and Targeting in Income Support: The Australian Experience'. *Journal of Social Policy*, 20 (July): 299–326.

1992. 'Poverty, Inequality and Recession'. *Economic Papers*, 10 (September): 1–22.

1993a. 'Recent Trends in the Size and Growth of Government in OECD Countries', in Gemmell, N. (ed.), *The Growth of the Public Sector. Theories and International Evidence*. Aldershot: Edward Elgar, pp. 17–33.

1993b. 'Married Women's Earnings and Family Income Inequality in the Eighties'. *Australian Bulletin of Labour*, 19: 199–217.

1993c. 'Economic Adjustment and Distributional Change: Income Inequality in Australia in the Eighties'. Discussion Paper No. 47. Social Policy Research Centre, University of New South Wales, Sydney.

1993d. 'Longer Run Changes in the Distribution of Income in Australia'. *Economic Record*, 69 (December): 353–66.

Saunders, P. and Hobbes, G. 1988. 'Income Inequality in Australia in an International Comparative Perspective'. *Australian Economic Review*, 3: 25–34.

Saunders, P., Stott, H. and Hobbes, G. 1991. 'Income Inequality in Australia and New Zealand: International Comparisons and Recent Trends'. *Review of Income and Wealth*, 37 (March): 63–79.

Shorrocks, A. F. 1984. 'Inequality Decomposition by Population Subgroups'. *Econometrica*, 52: 1369–86.

Whiteford, P. 1985. 'A Family's Needs: Equivalence Scales, Poverty and Social Security'. Research Paper No. 27. Development Division, Department of Social Security, Canberra.

1992. 'Assessing the Impact of Anti-poverty Policies: The Australian Experience'. Paper presented to the Multidisciplinary Research Conference on Poverty and Distribution, 16–17 November, Oslo, Norway.

5 Unemployment, unemployment insurance and the distribution of income in Canada in the 1980s

LARS OSBERG, SADETTIN ERKSOY
AND SHELLEY PHIPPS

1 Introduction

This chapter examines changes in the distribution of income in Canada in the 1980s and focuses on (1) the accounting period used for analysis and (2) the consideration given to behavioural response for the perceived redistributional incidence of social transfers, especially unemployment insurance. We describe trends in the distribution of income in Canada, outline the reasons why unemployment has had a major impact on inequality and discuss why estimates of the impact of unemployment and unemployment insurance on the distribution of annual income may be misleading. We describe a microsimulation methodology for analysing redistributional impact over the course of a business cycle and present the results of such an analysis.

Section 2.1 argues that unemployment insurance played an important role in stabilising the level of income inequality in Canada in the 1980s despite increasing inequality in individual earnings. Section 2.2 outlines the methodology employed in this chapter to assess the distributional input of Canadian unemployment insurance. Section 3 describes our behavioural microsimulation model. Section 4 presents the main results and compares the distribution of income in a hypothetical steady state growth path and in the actual business cycle of the early 1980s. It compares the distribution of income with and without unemployment insurance and under alternative assumptions about the macroeconomic consequences of unemployment insurance. Section 5 presents conclusions.

2 Unemployment, unemployment insurance and the distribution of income

2.1 Unemployment, wages and the sources of change in inequality

The increase in concern of the 1990s with economic inequality has, in many countries, been a reflection of an actual increase in inequality in the 1980s.

As Levy and Murnane (1992) point out, when average real wages stagnate and there is a trend towards increased inequality in the distribution of earnings (as in the US since the early 1970s), low-income earners become absolutely worse off. As a result, there has been a surge of interest in the US in understanding the reasons for greater polarisation in the distribution of earnings.

As the chapters in this volume indicate, however, such trends are not unique to the US. As well as experiencing increases in inequality, many countries experienced historically high post-war unemployment during the 1980s. To what extent has the rising inequality of the 1980s reflected poor macroeconomic performance and misguided macroeconomic policy? Alternatively, does increasing inequality of earnings represent a structural, rather than a cyclical, change in labour markets?

We argue that much of the 1980s changes in Canadian earnings inequality can be explained by the macroeconomic business cycle and its labour market impact, but that these changes in earnings were offset by changes in unemployment insurance receipts, leaving the distribution of income less affected. Although much of the international debate on the polarisation of earnings in the 1980s has stressed the role played by structural change, Canada has been undergoing substantial structural change for at least the last 50 years. (See table 5.1 for trends in urbanisation and in labour force participation, especially for married women.)

However, over the last quarter century the Canadian labour market has been dominated by two major developments: the abrupt end of growth in average real wages in the mid 1970s, and a trend towards rising unemployment (averaging 9.5 per cent in the 1980s),[1] with increasingly severe cyclical fluctuations. Both represent a sharp switch from the earlier decades, when the Canadian economy produced low national unemployment and substantial increases in average real wages – a 35.9 per cent increase in average weekly wages in the 1950s and a 36.4 per cent increase in the 1960s in constant dollars (Rashid 1993).

Table 5.2 presents the quintile distribution of income among families and unattached individuals in the 1980s. During the period 1980–92, there is rather limited support for the 'polarisation' hypothesis, in that the income share of the middle quintile of Canadian families and unattached individuals fell from 17.8 per cent in 1980 to 16.7 per cent in 1992. However, cyclical factors may also have played a role. Most of the decline in the middle quintile's income share occurred during the recession of 1980–3 (a decline from 17.8 per cent to 17.1 per cent), followed by an essentially constant income share in the recovery years 1983–90, and a further decline with the renewed onset of recession in 1990/1. The share of the top 20 per cent rose from 42.1 per cent to 43.2 per cent during the 1980–3 recession, remained

Table 5.1 *Long-term trends in the income distribution and economic structure of Canada*

Family[a] income quintile	1951	1961	1971	1981	1986	1991
Per cent share of poorest 20 per cent 1	4.4	4.2	3.6	4.6	4.7	4.7
2	11.2	11.9	10.6	10.9	10.4	10.3
3	18.3	18.3	17.6	17.6	17.0	16.6
4	23.3	24.5	24.9	25.2	24.9	24.7
richest 20 per cent 5	42.8	41.1	43.3	41.7	43.0	43.8
Mean family[a] income, 1992 $	21,483	28,531	41,659	52,518	52,815	53,940
Mean unattached individual's income, 1992 $	8,289	11,391	17,462	23,058	22,498	22,857
Per cent urban labour force[b]	33.6	53.2	58.9	59.8	61.7	62.0
Per cent labour force in agriculture	15.7	9.9	5.8	4.3	3.9	3.5
Participation rate (aged 15–64)						
All men	84.4	81.1	77.3	78.4	76.6	74.8
All woman	24.1	29.5	39.4	51.7	55.1	58.2
Married women	11.2	22.0	37.0	50.5	56.1	61.4
Per cent of employment which is part-time	4.0	7.8	12.0	13.5	15.5	16.4
Per cent unemployment	2.4	7.2	6.3	7.5	9.5	10.3

Notes:
[a] Refers to economic families.
[b] 25 urban areas were defined as Census Metropolitan Areas in 1991. The total urban labour force is the sum of these Metropolitan labour forces in each census year.
Sources: Osberg, Lars and Phipps, Shelley (1992), 'A Social Charter for Canada' in McCullum, John (ed.), *A Social Charter for Canada? Perspectives on the Constitutional Entrenchment of Social Rights.* Toronto: C.D. Howe Institute, p. 5.
Statistics Canada (1992), *Historical Labour Force Statistics.* Cat. No. 71–201, annual.
Statistics Canada, *Income Distributions by Size*, 1990. Cat. No. 13–207, various issues.
Census of Canada, 1951, 1961, 1971, 1981, 1986, 1991.

Table 5.2 *Quintile shares of total income among all families and unattached individuals*

	Poorest 20 per cent				Richest 20 per cent	Total
1980	4.2	10.7	17.8	25.2	42.1	100.0
1981	4.6	10.9	17.6	25.2	41.7	100.0
1982	4.6	10.8	17.4	24.9	42.4	100.0
1983	4.3	10.3	17.1	25.0	43.2	100.0
1984	4.5	10.4	17.2	25.0	43.0	100.0
1985	4.6	10.4	17.0	24.9	43.0	100.0
1986	4.7	10.4	17.0	24.9	43.0	100.0
1987	4.7	10.4	16.9	24.8	43.2	100.0
1988	4.6	10.4	16.9	24.9	43.2	100.0
1989	4.8	10.5	16.9	24.6	43.2	100.0
1990	4.7	10.4	16.9	24.8	43.3	100.0
1991	4.7	10.3	16.6	24.7	43.8	100.0
1992	4.6	10.3	16.7	24.8	43.6	100.0

much the same in the 1983–90 recovery and rose again in the recession of 1991/2. The period as a whole saw essentially no change in the income share of the bottom 20 per cent after 1981.

The size distribution of family income is affected by the size and targeting of transfer payments, the distribution and rate of return of capital, and the demography of family composition and labour force participation. However, much of the recent debate on inequality has emphasised trends in the labour market. Table 5.3 therefore focuses on the labour forced and presents the quintile shares of individuals with positive incomes whose major source of income was wages and salaries. Overall, it is hard to find an aggregate trend in table 5.3. There are fluctuations from year to year, but for the period 1980–92 the middle quintile has much the same income share at the end (18.0 per cent) as at the beginning (17.9 per cent), and the same is true of the top quintile (42.7 per cent compared with 42.5 per cent). In relative terms, it is the bottom 20 per cent who advanced the most during these years.

Aggregate data on quintile income shares hide the trend towards greater inequality of earnings in Canada. Beach and Slotsve (1994) report that male workers with earnings beyond 75 per cent of the median rose from 26 per cent to 38 per cent between 1967 and 1984; and the decile mean ratio increased from 31 to 46.[2] (Polarisation of women's earnings was much less marked as the trend towards increased participation dominated change in

Table 5.3 *Quintile shares of income of individuals with income, whose major income source was wages and salaries*

	Poorest 20 per cent				Richest 20 per cent	Total
1980	2.8	10.6	17.9	26.0	42.7	100.0
1981	3.2	10.8	18.0	25.8	42.2	100.0
1982	3.1	10.8	18.0	25.8	42.3	100.0
1983	2.8	10.2	17.7	25.8	43.5	100.0
1984	2.9	10.5	17.8	25.9	42.9	100.0
1985	3.0	10.3	17.5	25.7	43.5	100.0
1986	3.1	10.5	17.7	25.8	42.8	100.0
1987	3.0	10.4	17.6	25.7	43.2	100.0
1988	3.1	10.3	17.4	25.8	43.4	100.0
1989	3.5	11.0	17.6	25.3	42.6	100.0
1990	3.5	10.9	17.7	25.1	42.9	100.0
1991	3.4	10.9	17.8	25.2	42.7	100.0
1992	3.2	10.9	18.0	25.4	42.5	100.0

Source: Statistics Canada, *Income Distributions by Size*, 1990, Cat. No. 13–207, p. 147.

rates of compensation.) However, if earnings losses are balanced by greater transfer payments, stability of the distribution of income is possible, as indicated in table 5.3.

In Canada, changes in the inequality of earnings during the 1980s were dominated by changes in the inequality of hours worked, not by changes in the inequality of hourly wages. Decomposing changes in the variance of the logarithm of annual earnings into changes in the variance of ln (annual hours) and ln (hourly wages), plus the co-variance of ln (hours) and ln (wages), MacPhail (1993) demonstrates that less than 10 per cent of the 1981–6 increase in the inequality of annual earnings of males can be ascribed directly to increased inequality in ln (hourly wages), while 50 per cent can be ascribed to increased inequality in ln (annual hours) and 41 per cent to the co-variance between ln (annual hours) and ln (hourly wages). The decline in earnings inequality between 1986 and 1989 appears to have been driven largely by the decline during that period in national unemployment rates, from 9.5 per cent to 7.5 per cent.

Morissette, Myles and Picot (1993) have in addition emphasised the role of increased dispersion in weekly hours of work in Canada – more people working very long hours and more people working part time. Unlike the US, Canada has not experienced an increase in the university/high school earnings differential. Although demand for highly educated labour surged in Canada in the 1980s, so did the supply (a 26.6 per cent increase between 1986 and 1991), and the result is a nearly constant return to education (see also Bar-Or *et al.* 1995 and Osberg 1994). Indeed, unlike in the US, there has been no aggregate increase in hourly wage inequality – a tendency to increased age/wage differentials being offset by the changing age composition of the population and decreased dispersion in hourly wages within age cohorts. In Canada, the trend towards increased earnings inequality has been driven by quantity, not price, changes, i.e., by growing polarisation in hours worked per week and hours worked per year.

Increased polarisation in earnings in Canada during the past 25 years can be directly related to increased unemployment. There are relatively few data points available in time series data, but a regression of the change in earnings polarisation on the change in unemployment indicates a clear relationship between changes in earnings polarisation and changes in the unemployment rate, particularly for Canadian men (Phipps 1994). Beyond any long-run structural trends affecting inequality in the distribution of individual earnings, the macroeconomic business cycle plays a major role in the determination of earnings inequality in Canada.[3]

From a welfare perspective, the broader issue is the distribution of total income among households. Trends in household formation, divorce and demographic structure have been broadly similar in Canada and in other affluent capitalist nations, but Canada appears to be one of the few advanced countries that did not exhibit a marked increase in inequality of income among households during the early 1980s. Fritzell (1992) used the Luxembourg Income Study (LIS) to examine trends in inequality in total household income during the early 1980s. Apparently Canada was an anomaly in that there was essentially no change in the inequality of household income, while there was a strong trend towards greater inequality in Sweden, the UK and the US and a weak trend towards greater inequality in Germany. Since there was an observed trend in Canada during this period towards greater inequality in the distribution of annual earnings, and since earnings inequality in Canada is strongly affected by changes in unemployment, it seems natural to ask whether the greater relative importance of unemployment insurance payments in Canada helped to stabilise the level of inequality in the distribution of income.

2.2   *Unemployment insurance and the distribution of income*

Table 5.4 uses the year when Canadian unemployment reached its post-war maximum (13.3 per cent, in March 1983) to make the point that, although total Canadian spending on social security transfers is on the low side by international standards, unemployment insurance in Canada has accounted for a relatively high percentage of that spending and a relatively high percent-

Table 5.4 *Unemployment insurance and social security expenditures, 1983*

	Social security expenditures as per cent of GDP	Unemployment insurance expenditures	
		as per cent of social security	as per cent of GDP
Canada	16.5	21.3	3.51
Germany	24.3	11.7	2.84
Sweden	33.3	3.5	1.17
UK	20.5	10.6	2.17
US	13.8	10.7	1.48

Source: Luxembourg Income Study Institutional Data Base.

age of total output. Given the automatic targeting of unemployment insurance on many of those adversely affected by rising unemployment, it is at least plausible that unemployment insurance in Canada functions to maintain the stability of the aggregate income distribution, offsetting the rise in the inequality of individual earnings that recessionary downturns produce.

Between 1981 and 1989, approximately 90.1 per cent of the Canadian labour force was covered by the unemployment insurance programme.[4] The redistributional impact of unemployment insurance in Canada has been studied by Kapsalis (1978), Cloutier and Smith (1980) and LeBlanc (1988). All these studies examine the unemployment insurance benefits (net of taxes and premiums) received by each quintile of the distribution of original income in particular years and conclude that unemployment insurance expenditures are not particularly pro-poor, because unemployment insurance is received by many households whose original income was relatively high.

However, unemployment insurance is a social transfer whose receipt depends on the occurrence of an event of uncertain duration. Spells of unemployment, like spells of dependence on social assistance or worker's compensation, occur in continuous time. Measurement of the redistributional impact of welfare state programmes is commonly done in discrete annual intervals, but the calendar year is an arbitrary accounting period within which to assess income distributional impact. Spells of unemployment can easily run over the beginning or end of the accounting period, and the apparent income distributional impact of unemployment insurance can depend heavily on the timing of the onset of an unemployment spell.

Figure 5.1 presents a schematic diagram illustrating this point. In 1990, the poorest quintile of families and unattached individuals in Canada was composed of those earning less than approximately $16,000, while the second quintile earned between $17,000 and $29,000, the third quintile

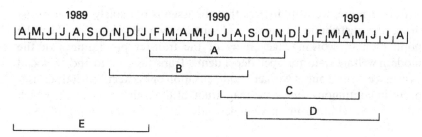

Figure 5.1 Unemployed spells

$30,000–$44,000, the fourth quintile $45,000–$64,000 and the fifth (richest) quintile more than $65,000 (Statistics Canada S.C. 13–207, p. 137).

To see how the choice of an annual time period for the measurement of income distribution can affect our understanding of the income-distributional effects of unemployment insurance, consider the following example. Suppose that five individuals had an identical monthly rate of pay of $6,000 but lost their jobs at different times. Assume they all have identical duration of unemployment of ten months before finding another job at the same rate of pay. Individual A in figure 5.1 had an unemployment spell lasting from 1 February to 30 November, implying that labour market earnings from her two months of employment in 1990 were $12,000, placing her in the bottom quintile of the 1990 income distribution. Individual B started his spell of unemployment on 1 November 1989 and found a job starting 1 September 1990 – $24,000 of earnings put him in the second quintile of 1990 income. Individual C lost her job on 1 July 1990, but earning $6,000 per month for the first six months of 1990 would place her in the third quintile. Individual D started unemployment on 1 September, meaning that earnings for the first eight months of the year totalled $48,000, placing him in the fourth quintile, while individual E started unemployment the previous April, and her earnings for 11 months of 1990 placed her in the top quintile of the income distribution.

Since spells of unemployment occur in continuous time, an annual accounting framework means that observed spells of unemployment in income distribution data are often interrupted spells.[5] Since it is arithmetic that longer unemployment within a given year means shorter employment and lower earnings, a calendar year accounting framework means that the timing of the onset of unemployment can significantly affect the perceived redistributional incidence of transfer payments. In the example given above, unemployment insurance payments could be counted as going to any of the quintiles of the Canadian income distribution, depending entirely on the timing of the onset of unemployment.

Furthermore, we would stress that the issue is not solely one of measuring the distributional impact of unemployment insurance. For the population of working age, many of the transfer programmes of the modern welfare state are 'spell dependent'. Transitions on to and off social assistance, in and out of worker's compensation or between marital statuses occur in continuous time – the magnitude of the transfer payments which they trigger within a given year depends heavily on the timing of these transitions within the given year.

A second issue is the extent to which these transitions are influenced by the incentives embedded in social transfer programmes. There is a large literature on the impact unemployment insurance might or might not have on the length of unemployment spells (for surveys, see Atkinson and Micklewright 1991 or, for the Canadian context, Osberg 1993b).[6] Analysis of the redistributional impact of unemployment insurance which proceeds by simply subtracting insurance payments from total income implicitly assumes that the influence of unemployment insurance on individual behaviour is zero – surely an extreme assumption.

If the real world were characterised by steady state growth and a constant unemployment rate, presumably there would be a constant degree of error introduced into distributional measurement by ignoring the interrupted nature of unemployment spells and the influence which unemployment insurance payments might have on the length of those spells. In a steady state world, one could ignore this error in making comparisons over time and across countries, because the annual accounting framework and the omission of behavioural response would not imply year to year changes in the measurement of inequality. However, the real world exhibits substantial swings in aggregate unemployment over the business cycle, and there is evidence that unemployed persons change their job search behaviour as aggregate unemployment changes (Osberg 1993a). Hence, the existence of the macroeconomic business cycle means a varying degree of error is introduced into inequality measurement if an annual accounting framework is used and if behavioural response is ignored.

This study takes the view that the business cycle is a more appropriate time period over which to measure the redistributional impact of unemployment insurance.[7] In the Canadian case, the national unemployment rate was 7.5 per cent in 1981, rising to 11.8 per cent in 1983 and declining gradually to 7.5 per cent again by 1989. Hence, we measure the distributional impact of unemployment insurance over this eight-year period for the population aged 16–64 in 1981. Measuring the impact of unemployment insurance over the business cycle does not eliminate the problem of truncation of unemployment spells, but it does minimise the impact, because only spells in progress in January 1981 and continuing past

December 1989 are truncated, and the measurement error is small as a percentage of total 1981–9 income. As well, one of the major rationales for the existence of unemployment insurance is protection of individual incomes from the fluctuations of the business cycle, which suggests that the business cycle is an appropriate time frame.

3 Microsimulation methodology

This chapter uses microsimulation methodology to address jointly the issues of behavioural response and accounting framework. The rationale underlying microsimulation is the idea that if we are to understand how the economy would have functioned under different external circumstances or different internal incentives, we have to take full account of the heterogeneity of individual characteristics, the interdependence of economic processes and the endogeneity of individual characteristics over time. The origins of microsimulation lie in the work of Orcutt and his colleagues (e.g., 1986). The basic idea is to take microdata on a representative panel sample of individual households and simulate the impact of alternative policy or environmental scenarios on each individual member of the panel.

This chapter builds on the model developed in Erksoy (1992) which embeds a behavioural microsimulation model in a time-varying macroeconomic environment. Since the time path of aggregate labour force totals, such as total employment, can be specified *a priori*, the microeconomic behaviour of individuals can be constrained to mimic in aggregate the actual historical evolution of the economy, and historical data can be used to calibrate model performance.

Using microsimulation, it is possible to explore the distributional implications of alternative assumptions about the macroeconomic consequences of social transfers. At the microlevel, it may be the case that more generous unemployment insurance incentives increase the reservation wage of individual unemployed persons. If so, one would expect that the abolition of unemployment insurance would have a bigger effect on the reservation wage of those with a high benefit/wage replacement rate than on those with a low benefit/wage replacement rate. But what are the macroeconomic implications of such changes in microbehaviour?

Would changes in incentives (such as the abolition of unemployment insurance) cause changes in the relative incidence of unemployment or changes in the absolute level of unemployment? If individual A (who had a relatively high benefit/wage ratio) drastically cuts her reservation wage, would this simply mean that the job she now accepts can no longer be offered to individual B? If the number of available jobs is set from the demand side of labour markets, then changes in unemployment insurance incentives can only affect the relative positions of individuals in the queue of the unemployed, not the aggregate rate of employment. We refer to this as the 'queue' scenario and distinguish it from the 'new classical' scenario in which unemployment comes entirely from the supply side of the labour market. If increases in the speed with which each individual finds a job have zero impact on the job finding chances of all other individuals, one can get the change in total unemployment by summing up the change in individual unemployment durations associated with a change in unemployment insurance incentives. We explore the distributional implications of unemployment insurance under both scenarios, using estimates of the impact of unemployment insurance on the aggregate unemployment rate available from the macro literature for the second (new classical) case.

Microsimulation enables us to model the likelihood that unemployment or labour force withdrawal will increase the future probability or duration of unemployment or the probability of future labour force withdrawal. This chapter uses the Labour Market Activity Survey of 1986/7 to estimate the structural determinants of labour force participation, unemployment incidence and unemployment duration.[8] However, since the public use sample of the 1986/7 LMAS does not link the behaviour of individuals within households, it is not possible to model accurately the interdependence of labour market behaviour within families. Because of this, and because an upward trend in the inequality of male earnings and male unemployment rates was especially marked during the early 1980s, the present chapter focuses on the impact of unemployment and unemployment insurance on the distribution of income of male Canadians aged 16–64 in 1981[9] who responded to the Asset and Debts Survey of 1983.

All nominal dollar amounts are deflated to 1981 dollars using the consumer price index. In the simulation scenarios involving the historical unemployment rate, the real weekly earnings of each individual are adjusted each year by the average change in real weekly earnings actually observed 1981–9. In the hypothetical scenario of steady state growth, real weekly earnings are adjusted by 0.56 per cent each year (the average rate of productivity growth 1977–81).

In the simulation model, as in real life, there is a positive probability that an individual will not participate in the labour force in any given year and a positive probability that an individual will not find any work even if a labour force participant for some or all of the year. Hence, although we start from a sample of men aged 16–64 with observed earnings (i.e., between $50 and $3,000 weekly), the model generates each year a fraction of the population with zero earnings. To reproduce 1981 aggregates, the model is 'run in' for the preceding two years (at assumed constant unemployment of 7.0 per cent) to generate 1981 estimates. Since individuals may move into or out of the labour force, and earnings may be zero in one year (perhaps with receipt of unemployment insurance from a previous year's entitlement) but positive in subsequent years, distributional statistics in this chapter are calculated for the sample as a whole, i.e., all males aged 16–64 (excluding wage outliers).

The simulation model works by first assigning each individual a particular number of weeks outside the labour force, based on demographic characteristics, labour market history, the regional unemployment rate and the weeks required to qualify for unemployment insurance in that local area. Notice that weeks outside the labour force are effectively aggregated into a single 'spell'. Equation 1 summarises an accelerated failure time model of labour force participation corrected for interval censoring,[10] which is used to predict expected weeks of labour force withdrawal for each individual. A random error term drawn from a distribution with variance consistent with the observed unexplained variance (G_i) in equation 1 is added to the conditional expectation of weeks of withdrawal to preserve the underlying stochastic element in labour force participation.

$$WKSNLF_{it} = F_1(X_{it}, WKSUN_{i,t-1}, LM_t, UI_t) + e_{1i} \tag{1}$$
$$(P_{it} WKSNLF_{it} < 52) = F_2(X_{it}, WKSUN_{i,t-1}, LM_t) + e_{2i} \tag{2}$$
$$(WKSUN_{it} P_{it} = 1) = F_3(X_{it}, WKSUN_{i,t-1}, LM_t, UI_t) + e_{3i} \tag{3}$$
$$WKSEMP_{it} = 52 - WKSNLF_{it} - WKSUN_{it} \tag{4}$$

F_1, F_2, F_3 –   estimated structural relationships (interval censored, Logit and Weibull)

e_{1i}, e_{2i}, e_{3i} –   random error term from corresponding structural equation

         i = individual

         $t, t\text{-}1$ = period

X_{it} –   personal characteristics

$WKSUN_{it}$ –   weeks unemployed

$WKSNLF_{it}$ –   weeks not in labour force

P_{it} –   probability of unemployment

UI_t –   parameters of UI system

LM_t –   local labour market condition

$WKSEMP_{it}$ –   weeks employed

Given participation in the paid labour force, a Logit model is used to predict the probability that an individual will experience unemployment in a given year, as summarised in equation 2. For those individuals who experience unemployment, an accelerated failure time model of annual unemployment experience is estimated,[11] correcting for the bias which would otherwise arise as a result of the right-censoring of unemployment.

Adding a stochastic term, as in equation 3, gives a predicted annual experience of unemployment, conditional on experiencing unemployment, for each individual in the sample. Weeks of employment are obtained as a residual, as in equation 4.

The microsimulation model is embedded within a changing macroeconomic environment by allowing the macroeconomic unemployment rate to change over time and calculating the associated aggregate weeks of unemployment. Individuals are ordered in descending order of the probability (P_{it}) of experiencing unemployment in a given year and the cumulative sum of unemployment weeks is calculated (by summing $WKSUN_{it}$ across individuals). Unemployment is assigned to those with the highest probability of experiencing unemployment, up to the point where the total number of unemployment weeks experienced equals the aggregate unemployment experience for the year. The maintenance of a stochastic element (l_{1i}, l_{2i}, l_{3i}) in each equation serves to ensure that the simulation model retains some of the dynamic change of real world labour markets, while the deterministic component of the structural equations and the inclusion of lagged labour market experience as a determinant of current labour market outcomes serves to introduce the period-to-period correlation of outcomes which is also characteristic of the real world.

4   Results

The debate on polarisation of incomes has often focused on the distribution of male earnings, usually measured before tax, so this chapter examines the impact of unemployment insurance on the distribution of pre-tax income among Canadian males, aged 16–64.[12] Tables 5.5 to 5.6 each use a different income concept, while the columns of each table compare the simulated distribution of income under alternative scenarios.

Table 5.5 looks at inequality in the distribution of the discounted value of total earnings (plus unemployment insurance payments where applicable) over the period 1981–9. Income flows are discounted to 1981 at 5.5 per cent per annum, the average real cost of home mortgage indebtedness faced by Canadians over this period (i.e., 5.5 per cent is a reasonable proxy for the trade-off between present and future consumption faced by many Canadians). Since a spell of unemployment in a particular year is, in table 5.5, averaged in with other years of full earnings, the distribution of the discounted value of the 1981–9 income is more equal than the distribution of income in any given year, and the impact of unemployment on inequality is also smaller. Table 5.6 presents measures of the inequality in annual income flows in the year of peak unemployment (1983).

It is desirable to disentangle the impact of unemployment insurance

Table 5.5 The distribution of the present value of earnings (including unemployment insurance): Canadian males 16–64, 1981/9

	A Base: unemployment constant	B Shock: historical unemployment	C Shock minus unemployment insurance (incidence)	D Queue model (historical unemp.)	E New classical (historic – 3.5 per cent)
Per cent share					
bottom 30 per cent	0.110	0.110	0.102	0.110	0.114
40 per cent	0.356	0.356	0.352	0.355	0.358
top 30 per cent	0.524	0.524	0.535	0.529	0.519
Average income (real 81)					
bottom 30 per cent	52,117	49,826	44,862	49,252	53,234
40 per cent	127,340	121,723	116,886	125,291	126,399
top 30 per cent	250,629	239,823	238,178	250,676	245,810
Gini	0.344	0.347	0.360	0.353	0.345
CV	0.669	0.689	0.699	0.688	0.670
Mean earnings and UI 1981–9	141,794	135,616	131,699	140,117	140,295

from the impact of the rise of unemployment which triggered unemployment insurance payments. Columns A and B of each table contrast the distribution of individual male income (annual earnings plus unemployment insurance benefits) under the alternative hypothesis of steady state growth (column A) which implies a constant unemployment rate and the actual historical experience of the business cycle of the 1980s (column B).[13] Column C presents the distribution of earnings alone under underlying 'incidence' analysis which assumes that unemployment insurance has no effect on behaviour whatsoever, i.e., it simply omits unemployment insurance benefits from the historical shock scenario of column B.

Columns D and E both presume that the microbehaviour of individuals is affected by the incentives of unemployment insurance. The distribution of income is calculated, in both cases, on the presumption that the influence of unemployment insurance on individual behaviour is captured by the unemployment insurance variables contained in equations 1, 2 and 3. To model the hypothetical abolition of unemployment insurance, unemployment insurance variables are simply set to zero in the calculation of individual probabilities of labour force withdrawal, unemployment experience and unemployment duration.[14]

Columns D and E differ, however, in their assumptions as to the implications of changed individual behaviour for aggregate unemployment. Column D (the queue model) presumes that the total amount of unemployment is set from the demand side of the economy, hence the elimination of unemployment insurance causes a change in the relative incidence of unemployment but no change in aggregate unemployment.

The impact of unemployment insurance on aggregate unemployment remains a hotly contested empirical issue in Canada (Myatt 1993). Column D is consistent with those macroeconomic studies which find no statistically significant impact of unemployment insurance variables on aggregate unemployment; its interest lies in its indication that changes in the relative incidence of unemployment do have distributional implications, even though the aggregate rate of unemployment is constrained to be identical in columns B and D.

Since the thought experiment of columns D and E is the abolition of unemployment insurance, unemployment insurance would not be part of anyone's income. Hence, both D and E report the distribution of earnings for the population of all Canadian males aged 16–64. However, column E reports the distribution of earnings under the assumption that the abolition of unemployment insurance coincides with a drastic decline in aggregate unemployment. The outside estimate cited by Myatt (1993) is that unemployment insurance could be responsible for as much as 3.5 percentage points of unemployment. Hence, the thought experiment of column E is that aggregate unemployment declines in 1982 and subsequent years by 3.5 percentage points from its historical levels. Column E therefore mingles two issues: the elimination of a substantial transfer programme and a simultaneous drastic decline in aggregate unemployment. Those who dislike the supply-side interpretation of economic events which links these two phenomena causally are invited to consider the possibility of Keynesian demand stimulation partially financed by the abolition of social programmes.

Our hypothesis is that the size of the Canadian unemployment insurance system and the automatic targeting of its payments to those adversely affected by unemployment constitute an important source of stability in the Canadian income distribution. This hypothesis receives strong support in table 5.5. Column A reports summary measures of aggregate inequality in the distribution of the present value of income (earnings plus unemployment insurance payments) under the alternative scenarios of steady growth (column A) and the actual historical pattern of unemployment (column B). As can be seen, the high unemployment of the 1981–9 period produces declines in average incomes, but the degree of inequality in the distribution of income is essentially constant.[15] Column C reports the distribution of the present value of earnings alone under the shock scenario of historical unemployment rates (but under the maintained hypothesis that individual behaviour continues to be as it was when influenced by the incentives of unemployment insurance), and it can be noted that the removal of unemployment insurance (with unchanged behaviour) produces a significant increase in the level of inequality.

Column D (the queue model) reports the distribution of earnings under the hypothesis that 1) individuals would change their labour market behaviour as equations 1, 2 and 3 predict if unemployment insurance did not exist and 2) aggregate unemployment remains unchanged.[16] Note that setting the unemployment insurance variables to zero will have both direct and indirect effects on simulated labour market behaviour. First, there will be the direct effects on weeks of participation and duration of unemployment (e.g,. reducing the maximum duration of unemployment insurance benefits will reduce the duration of unemployment in the first and each subsequent year). A shorter duration of unemployment in the first year will, in itself, reduce the probability of being unemployed and the duration of unemployment in the second year. This effect will cumulate throughout the simulation period – effectively a reversal of the 'scarring' effects of unemployment.

The main message of column D is that behavioural changes can affect the distribution of income, even if all they do is change the relative impact of unemployment experience. The distribution of earnings reported in column D is not as equal as the distribution of income with unemployment insurance payments (column B), but it is more equal than the distribution of earnings presented in column C. The implication is that the elimination of the unemployment insurance system in Canada would produce behavioural responses resulting in greater relative declines in the unemployment of lower-income groups than of higher-income groups, serving to partially offset the increase in inequality which would otherwise be produced by their loss of transfer payments.[17]

The results presented in column E can be read as indicating the importance of the aggregate unemployment rate for inequality in the distribution of human wealth. In columns D and E, the relative probability of individuals' not being in the labour force, their relative probability of experiencing unemployment and their duration of unemployment are the same. In both cases, behaviour is influenced by the incentives of unemployment insurance, the only difference being the aggregate level of unemployment. Lower unemployment levels have their biggest impact on lower-income groups. Column E represents an income distribution which is unambiguously more equal than column D, but it is interesting that the summary measures of income inequality (the Gini, Theil and coefficient of variation) indicate a level of inequality which is approximately similar to the base case of steady growth with unemployment insurance.

However, as a comparison of table 5.6 with table 5.5 indicates, the inequality of income in a given year (1983) is considerably greater than the inequality in the distribution of the present value of income 1981–9. As well, if one compares columns B and C, which measure inequality in the distribution of individual male incomes with and without unemployment insurance payments under the historical scenario of cyclical unemployment, one can note that the change in inequality measures is greater in table 5.6 (which measures inequality in annual income) than in table 5.5 (which looks at the present value of income 1981–9). The conclusion we draw is that measures of the distributional incidence of unemployment insurance in a single year will show a greater inequality reducing impact than is apparent over the course of the business cycle as a whole.

Comparing the columns of table 5.6, one observes that in any given year unemployment insurance only partly counterbalances the increase in inequality produced by the economic recession of the early 1980s and the subsequent slow recovery. But simply subtracting unemployment insurance payments from total income produces an income distribution which is considerably more unequal than that associated with steady growth. However, a defect of models of the annual incidence of programmes without behavioural response (such as reported in column C) is that they involve a thought experiment in which one takes away the income associated with the social programme but leaves in place the behaviour which was

Table 5.6 *The distribution of annual earnings (including unemployment insurance): all Canadian men aged 16-64, 1983*

	A Base: unemployment constant	B Shock: historical unemployment	C Shock minus unemployment insurance (incidence)	D Queue model (historical unemployment)	E New classical (historic −3.5 per cent)
Per cent share					
bottom 30 per cent	0.070	0.062	0.045	0.057	0.064
40 per cent	0.370	0.368	0.366	0.367	0.372
top 30 per cent	0.551	0.559	0.577	0.568	0.557
Average income (real 81)					
bottom 30 per cent	4,354	3,787	2,627	3,467	3,974
40 per cent	17,606	16,865	16,154	16,733	17,507
top 30 per cent	35,158	34,367	34,194	34,676	35,117
Gini	0.398	0.410	0.437	0.420	0.410
CV	0.757	0.774	0.823	0.799	0.771
Mean ($)	18,900	18,194	17,512	18,143	18,733

partially motivated by that income. Column D reports the results of a thought experiment in which both unemployment insurance payments and the behaviour which is induced by unemployment insurance are simultaneously removed. It appears that behavioural change does matter, even if its only impact is to change the relative incidence of unemployment experience rather than the aggregate rate of unemployment.

Of course, the thought experiment conducted is an extreme one – politically, economically and statistically. Politically, it is not really feasible simply to abolish unemployment insurance in Canada without a replacement programme. As argued earlier in the text, unemployment insurance is an extremely important Canadian transfer programme. From an economist's perspective, it is also not really valid to assume that the structure of behavioural responses would be unaffected by a non-marginal change in the institutional environment. Finally, from a statistical perspective, it is of course inappropriate to forecast 'out of sample', and there is no historical evidence to judge the impact of, for example, a change in the benefit/wage ratio from 0.66 to 0. Thus, it would be more reasonable to simulate the distributional implications of marginal changes in unemployment insurance programme parameters. We conduct the more extreme thought experiment of abolishing unemployment insurance only for the purpose of comparing with traditional incidence studies.

5   Conclusions

Discussions of trends in earnings inequality should not simply exclude those individuals who have had their earnings reduced to zero because they have withdrawn from the labour force or experienced an entire year's unemployment. Hence, this study calculates income distributional statistics for the population of all Canadian men aged 16–64. We think it is a desirable feature of our model that some people receive zero earnings in some years and that this proportion varies with the rate of unemployment and increases with age.

The issue is empirically important because it affects the number of men whom we estimate to have zero earnings, which has, in turn, a major impact on measures of inequality. Although men with zero earnings have disappeared entirely from the empirical analysis underlying the debate on the polarisation of earnings (see, for example, Levy and Murnane 1992), their numbers are significant. Older men withdrew from the paid labour force in substantial numbers in the late 1970s and early 1980s. Osberg (1993c) uses the 1986/7 LMAS to argue that constraints on available work are empirically significant for older workers and that a significant fraction of 'retirement' decisions are influenced by the belief that there are 'no jobs available'.

In discussions of the impact of unemployment and unemployment insurance, those with zero earnings should not just be dropped from consideration. Particularly in the modelling of labour force participation, there are important unresolved issues as to how best to model something as drastic as the abolition of unemployment insurance.[18] We would reiterate that this chapter is only considering the thought experiment of unemployment insurance abolition to make a clear comparison with the types of decomposition of income inequality or the standard incidence analysis of transfer programmes, both of which implicitly assume zero behavioural response.

Nevertheless, at this stage in our research programme we conclude the following.

1　In the 1980s, Canada achieved some stability in the distribution of income, despite rising inequality of earnings, because the source of greater earnings inequality was greater inequality of hours worked, and the impact of unemployment on earnings was mitigated by unemployment insurance transfers.

2　An annual accounting period will not reliably capture the distributional incidence of a social programme whose payments depend on the onset and duration of a spell which occurs in continuous time.

3　Even if unemployment insurance incentives affect only the relative incidence of unemployment experience, the incentives of unemployment insurance can affect the inequality of the income distribution. Incidence models which assume that behavioural response to the unemployment insurance system is zero may overstate the inequality reducing impact of social transfers such as unemployment insurance.

Notes

This chapter reports results as of March 1995 of an ongoing research project. We can be reached for the latest results at (tel.) +1 902 494–2026 or (fax) +1 902 494–6917. This phase of our research was funded by the Social Sciences and Humanities Research Council of Canada under Award No. 499–89–0022.

1　In the 1950s, unemployment averaged 4.2 per cent, in the 1960s 5.0 per cent and in the 1970s 6.7 per cent.

2　These results for men in Canada are qualitatively similar to those for the US but quantitatively much less dramatic (Beach and Slotsve 1994).

3　Osberg and Phipps (1993) ask the question 'How would inequality in labour market earnings be affected by the removal of underemployment constraints, holding wage rates constant?' Using Atkinson indices ($r = -0.5$), earnings inequality for men falls from 0.355 to 0.248 if underemployment constraints are relaxed. For women, earnings inequality falls from 0.517 to 0.353.

4　In the 1980s, unemployment insurance replaced 60 per cent of insurable earnings for up to 50 weeks, and maximum insurable earnings are set each year at the average weekly earnings of the previous year. Phipps (1990) discusses the changes implemented in 1990. More recently, a change was made to finance unemployment insurance entirely from premiums. Also, it might be noted that unemployment insurance benefits are taxable income in Canada and that high-income recipients must repay a sizeable portion of any benefits received.

5 The interruption of unemployment spells has been well examined in the literature on measuring the duration of unemployment. For Canadian examples, see Ham and Rea (1987) or Corak (1992).

6 Both surveys emphasise the ambiguity of the effects of unemployment insurance on unemployment duration and the complexity of the unemployment insurance incentive structure. For this reason, in the present study we are careful to model many of the institutional characteristics of the Canadian unemployment insurance system.

7 Ruggles and Williams (1989) find much more short-run variation in the experience of poverty within a year than is indicated by annual incomes. Their research explores the implications of choosing a time interval which is less than a year while ours extends the time horizon beyond the year.

8 For details, see our Dalhousie University Working Paper (No. 93–07).

9 We consider the experience of women in other work (Erksoy, Osberg and Phipps 1993).

10 That is, within a year no one can be outside the labour market for more than 52 or less than zero weeks. We use the SAS LIFEREG procedure.

11 Again, all weeks of unemployment are aggregated into a single 'spell' which we call 'annual unemployment experience'.

12 In Canada, people older than 65 are ineligible for unemployment insurance. We consider the experience of women in other work (Erksoy, Osberg and Phipps 1993).

13 The aggregate unemployment rate in 1981 was 7.5 per cent, increasing sharply to 11.8 per cent in 1983 before declining gradually to 7.5 per cent in 1989. We stick with the period 1981–9 as indicating the swing of the business cycle as a whole, but our simulation uses the historical unemployment rates experienced by males, aged 15 and over, between 1981 and 1989, i.e., 7.0 per cent, 11 per cent, 12 per cent, 11.2 per cent, 10.3 per cent, 9.3 per cent, 8.5 per cent, 7.4 per cent and 7.3 per cent.

14 Although this is not very 'realistic', it is implicitly the scenario assumed in incidence studies which subtract the payments of unemployment insurance from individuals' incomes in order to assess distributional consequences.

15 The percentage income shares reported in columns A and B of table 5.5 are not in fact exactly identical, but they do round to the same numbers.

16 At this stage there are no wage effects built into the model. The elimination of unemployment insurance in this simulation is assumed to affect the relative ordering of individuals in terms of the probability and duration of unemployment. Any weeks of employment assigned to an individual are assumed to be paid at that individual's wage rate. No process of 'underbidding' another worker by offering to take a job at a lower wage is, as yet, modelled.

17 This finding should be qualified as preliminary; it may diminish or even dis-
    appear when we take account of demand-side limitations on the ability of the
    unemployed to obtain weeks of employment and when we calibrate the model
    to regional rather than national unemployment rates.
18 Should we, for example, model the abolition of unemployment insurance by
    setting the influence of unemployment insurance variables to zero (as done in
    this chapter) or by setting unemployment insurance parameters such as the
    minimum weeks to qualify in equation 2.1 to impossibly high levels?

References

Atkinson, A. B. and Micklewright, S. 1991. 'Unemployment Compensation and
    Labor Market Transitions: A Critical Review'. *Journal of Economic Literature*,
    29, 4 (December): 1679–727.
Bar-Or, Yuval, Burbidge, John, Magee, Lonnie and Robb, A. Leslie. 1995. 'The
    Wage Premium to a University Education in Canada 1971–1991'. *Journal of
    Labor Economics*, 13, 3 (October): 752–94.
Beach, C. M. and Slotsve, G. A. 1994. 'Polarization of Earnings in the Canadian
    Labour Market'. *In Stabilization, Growth and Distribution: Linkages in the
    Knowledge Era*, T. J. Courchene (editor) John Deutsch Institute, Queen's
    University, Kingston, Ontario.
Bordt, M., Cameron, G., Gribbele, S., Murphy, B., Rowe, G. and Wolfson, N. 1990.
    'The Social Policy Simulation Data Base and Model: An Integrated Pool for
    Tax/Transfer Policy Analysis'. *Canadian Tax Journal*, 38, 1 (January–
    February): 48–65.
Borjas, C. 1993. 'Immigration Policy, National Origin and Immigrant Skills: A
    Comparison of Canada and the United States', in Card, D. and Freeman, R.
    (eds.), *Small Differences that Matter: Labour Markets and Income Maintenance
    in Canada and the United States*. Chicago: University of Chicago Press, pp.
    21–44.
Burtless, G. 1990. 'Earnings Inequality over the Business and Demographic Cycles'.
    A Future of Lousy Jobs? The Changing Structure of U.S. Wages. Washington,
    DC: Brookings Institute, pp. 77–117.
Card, D. and Freeman, R. 1993. *Small Differences that Matter: Labour Markets and
    Income Maintenance in Canada and the United States*. Chicago: University of
    Chicago Press.
Cloutier, J. and Smith, J. 1980. 'The Evolution of an Alternative UI Plan'.
    Discussion Paper No. 159. Ottawa: Economic Council of Canada.
Corak, M. 1992. 'The Duration of Unemployment Insurance Payments'. Economic
    Council of Canada, Research Paper No. 42.
Erksoy, S. 1992. 'Distributional Effects of Unemployment and Disinflation in
    Canada: 1981–1987'. Unpublished Ph.D. thesis, Dalhousie University.
Erksoy, S., Osberg, L. and Phipps, S. 1993. 'The Distributional Implications of
    Unemployment – a Microsimulation Analysis'. Dalhousie University.
    Mimeographed.

Freeman, R. and Needels, K. 1993. 'Skill Differentials in Canada in an Era of Rising Labour Market Inequality', in Card, D. and Freeman, R. (eds.), *The Labour Market in Comparative Perspective: Lessons from the United States and Canada.* NBER, University of Chicago Press.

Fritzell, J. 1992. 'Income Inequality Trends in the 1980s: A Five-Country Comparison' (April). Stockholm University, Swedish Institute for Social Research. Mimeographed.

Ham, J. C. and Rea, S. A., Jr. 1987. 'Unemployment Insurance and Male Unemployment Duration in Canada'. *Journal of Labour Economics*, 5, 3: 325–52.

Harding, A. 1992. 'Lifetime Versus Annual Income Distribution: Evidence from Australia'. Paper presented at the 22nd General Conference of the International Association for Research on Income and Wealth, 30 August– 5 September, Flims, Switzerland.

Jenkins, S. 1992. 'Accounting for Inequality Trends: Decomposition Analyses for the U.K., 1971–1986'. Discussion Paper No. 92–10 (October). Department of Economics, University College of Swansea.

Kapsalis, C. 1978. 'Equity Aspects of the UI Program in Canada'. Discussion Paper No. 116. Ottawa: Economic Council of Canada.

LeBlanc, G. 1988. 'The Redistributional Effects of Unemployment Insurance'. Unemployment Insurance Program Analysis, Strategic Policy and Planning, Employment and Immigration Canada (August). Mimeographed.

Lemieux, T. 1993. 'Unions and Wage Inequality in Canada and the United States', in Card, D. and Freeman, R. (eds.), *Small Differences that Matter: Labour Markets and Income Maintenance in Canada and the United States.* Chicago: University of Chicago Press, pp. 69–108.

Levy, F. and Murnane, R. 1992. 'U.S. Earnings Levels and Earnings Inequality: A Review of Recent Trade and Proposed Explanations'. *Journal of Economic Literature*, 30, 3 (September): 1333–81.

MacPhail, F. 1993. 'Has the Great U-Turn Gone Full Circle?: Recent Trends in Earnings Inequality in Canada 1981–1989'. Working Paper No. 93–01 (January). Department of Economics, Dalhousie University, Halifax, Nova Scotia.

Morissette, R., Myles, J. and Picot, G. 1993. 'What is Happening to Earnings Inequality in Canada'. Research Paper No. 60. Analytical Studies Branch, Statistics Canada, Ottawa.

Myatt, T. 1993. 'The 1971 UI Reforms – 22 Years Later: What Do We Really Know?'. Paper presented at the Conference, Unemployment: What is to be done?, 26–7 March, at Laurentian University, Sudbury. In MacLean, B. and Osberg, L. (eds.), *The Unemployment Crisis: All for Naught.* McGill Queens University Press. (Forthcoming).

Orcutt, G. H., Merz, J. and Quinke, H. (eds.). 1986. *Microanalytic Simulation Models to Support Social and Financial Policy.* Amsterdam: Elsevier Science Publishers (North Holland).

Osberg, L. 1986. 'Behavioural Response in the Context of Socio-Economic

Microanalytic Simulation'. Statistics Canada, Analytical Studies (April) Research Paper No. 1, Ottawa.

1993a. 'Fishing in Different Pools: Job Search Strategies and Job-Finding Success in Canada in the Early 1980s'. *Journal of Labor Economics*, 11, 2 (April): 348–86.

1993b. 'Unemployment Insurance and Unemployment – Revisited'. Working Paper 93–04 (March), Economics Department, Dalhousie University, Halifax, N.S. In MacLean, B. and Osberg, L. (eds.), *The Unemployment Crisis: All for Naught.* McGill Queens University Press. (Forthcoming).

1993c. 'Is it Retirement or Unemployment? Induced 'Retirement' and Constrained Labour Supply Among Older Workers'. *Applied Economics*, 25 (March): 505–19.

1994. 'The Economic Role of Education, with special reference to Atlantic Canada'. Working Paper No. 94–01, January, Department of Economics, Dalhousie University, Halifax Nova Scotia, Canada.

Osberg, L. and Phipps, S. 1993. 'Large-Sample Estimates of Labour Supply: Results with Quantity Constraints'. *Oxford Economic Papers*, 45 (April): 269–91.

Phipps, S. 1990. 'The Impact of the Unemployment Insurance Reform of 1990 on Single Earners'. *Canadian Public Policy*, 3, 16: 252–61.

1994. 'Polarization of Earnings in the Canadian Labour Market: Comment', in Courchene, Thomas J. (ed.), *Stabilization, Growth and Distribution: Linkages in the Knowledge Era, The Bell Canada Papers on Economic and Public Policy,* vol. *II.* Kingston: John Deutsch Institute, pp. 349–58.

Rashid, A. 1993. 'Seven Decades of Wage Changes'. In *Perspectives on Labour Income*, Statistics Canada, Catalogue 75–001E, Ottawa, Summer 1993: 9–21.

Ruggles, P. and Williams, R. 1989. 'Longitudinal Measures of Poverty: Accounting for Income and Assets over Time'. *Review of Income and Wealth*, 3, 35: 225–82.

6 Distribution of economic well-being in Japan: towards a more unequal society

TOSHIAKI TACHIBANAKI AND TADASHI YAGI

1   Introduction

Japan experienced a considerable increase of inequality in the distribution of income and wealth in the 1980s and early 1990s. One of the present authors, Tachibanaki (1989, 1992), has presented statistical evidence and discussed several causes of the increasing inequality. Bauer and Mason (1992) provide a useful review article in this field. The present study provides an overview of income distribution, reports new evidence not covered by past works and discusses several unsolved issues in income and wealth distribution in Japan.

Section 2 presents a detailed overview of the distribution of household income and shows several of its general features. Section 3 shows how both wage and property income distributions have tended towards increasing inequality. Section 4 examines the issue of wealth distribution and describes the most important cause of increasing inequality in wealth distribution, namely the price of land, which increased considerably in the late 1980s. Finally, the results are summarized and policy issues are discussed.

2   Household income distribution

2.1   Overview

As of 1992, national income in Japan totalled 355.8 trillion yen. This amount is around six times as large as in 1970. During the same period, the price level increased 2.87 times. Thus, real national income increased 2.1 times from 1970 to 1992, equalling on average an annual real growth rate of around 3.4 per cent.

The composition of household income on a macrolevel is summarised in table 6.1. Employees received around 69 per cent of national income in the period 1989–91. This portion has been increasing since 1970–4. On the other hand, the portion of income received by the self-employed has been decreasing since 1970–4. In 1991, this value was 5.9 per cent, reflecting a

Table 6.1 *Changes in the composition of national income, 1977–1991 (per cent)*

	1970–4	1975–9	1980–4	1985–8	1989–91
Household income					
(1)Employee income	59.2	67.1	68.8	69.4	68.9
Wage	(54.3)	(60.4)	(60.4)	(59.9)	(59.0)
Other benefits	(4.9)	(6.6)	(8.4)	(9.5)	(9.8)
(2)Self-empolyee	15.8	13.3	9.1	7.6	6.4
Agriculture, forestry and fishery	(4.3)	(3.5)	(1.8)	(1.3)	(1.1)
Other industry	(11.5)	(9.7)	(7.4)	(6.4)	(5.3)
(3)Property income	12.1	12.5	14.6	14.2	14.6
Dividend and interest income	(11.2)	(8.1)	(9.1)	(11.5)	(10.8)
Rent	(0.6)	(0.8)	(0.7)	(0.7)	(0.7)
Imputed rent	(3.5)	(2.6)	(2.4)	(2.7)	(2.7)
Private enterprise income	12.4	7.7	9.1	10.6	9.2
Public enterprise income	0.5	−0.7	−1.9	−1.9	0.9
Total	100.0	100.0	100.0	100.0	100.0

Notes:
1 These values are before tax income.
2 'Other benefits' in the employee income contain contribution to the public pension system paid by employers and retirement allowances.
3 Private enterprise income does not contain dividends paid to shareholders.
4 The ratios of disposable household income to household income in each period are 94.4, 96.7, 95.7 and 95.1.
5 The ratios of disposable private enterprise income to the enterprise income in each period are 51.0, 31.4, 36.8 and 32.1 per cent.
Sources: Data for 1970–88 are given by Ishikawa (1991). The authors extended the data until 1991 using information in Economic Planning Agency, Annual Report on National Accounts (1993).

decrease in the number of workers in the agricultural sector and a decrease in the self-employed.

The answer to the question, 'Who owns what portion of wealth?' is basic to understanding the distribution of wealth. Table 6.2 shows the distribution of wealth as of 1991. Sixty three per cent of land, forest and sea, 37 per cent of gross total assets and 58 per cent of net assets are owned by households. Non-financial corporations own 26 per cent of net assets. Half of the national debt is attributed to financial institutions.

The Economic Planning Agency (1993) reports recent shifts in the composition of national wealth. As shown in figure 6.1, changes in wealth

Table 6.2 Closing balance-sheet account, 1991 (unit = 1,000 mill. yen)

	Non-financial corporation	Financial institution	Central government	Priv. non-profit institution	Households	Total
Inventory	69,332.6	17,700.2		30,299.3	9,751.8	79,084.4
Portion	0.88	0.02		0.03	0.12	1
Net fixed assets	475,413.4		283,182.8		236,790.6	1,043,386
Portion	0.46		0.27		0.23	1
Land, forest, sea	611,621.3	65,877.5	131,897.7	22,894.7	1,412,614	2,244,905
Portion	0.27	0.03	0.06	0.01	0.63	1
Financial assets	803,906.6	1,681,211	281,534.1	33,909.9	1,003,714.7	3,804,276
Portion	0.21	0.44	0.07	0.01	0.26	1
Gross total assets	1,960,275.505	1,764,788.746	696,614.9302	87,103.93924	2,662,872.08	7,171,655
Portion	0.27	0.25	0.10	0.01	0.37	1
Debt	908,021.9	1,566,746.9	307,372.2	26,206.6	340,948.3	3,149,296
Portion	0.29	0.50	0.10	0.01	0.11	1
Net assets (incl. stock)	1,052,252	198,041.8	389,242.4	60,897.3	2,321,922.8	4,022,356
Portion	0.26	0.05	0.10	0.02	0.58	1

Source: Economic Planning Agency, Annual Report on National Accounts (1993).

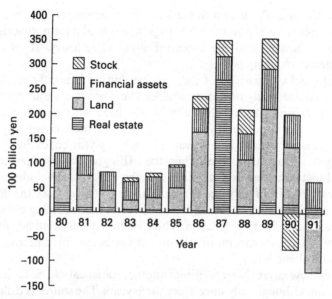

Figure 6.1 Changes in wealth components (household sector)
Source: Economic Planning Agency, Annual Report on National Accounts (1993)

components for the household sector and the non-financial corporate sector reflect the rise and fall of the so-called 'bubble economy'. For example, soaring land and stock prices in the late 1980s increased the value of land and stock holdings drastically, but drops in these prices in the early 1990s decreased national wealth.

2.2 *International comparison of the distribution of household income*

There has been common understanding that the distribution of household income in Japan is fairly equal in comparison with other industrialised countries. Sawyer (1976) showed two decades ago that Japan belonged to the group of OECD countries with the lowest degree of inequality in income distribution. Buss *et al.* (1989) confirmed this recently and proposed that income in Japan is equally distributed. Bauer and Mason (1992) conclude that the degree of income inequality in Japan is lower than in most OECD countries and attribute the lower inequality to a number of factors that have to do with the absence of poverty. Using data from the Family Income and Expenditure Survey (FIES) for the early 1980s, Bauer and Mason show that the poorest quintile's income share in Japan was around 10 per cent. In the US, the poorest quintile had only a 5 per cent share of total income. The income share of the richest quintile was around 35 per cent in Japan and 42 per cent in the US. Other important factors are the disappearance of rural poverty owing to post-war land reform, government subsidies to farmers and the decentralisation of industry, all of which contributed to reducing poverty.

International comparison of income distribution is a difficult subject because data are rarely fully comparable. There are two main difficulties peculiar to Japan. The first difficulty is associated with the treatment of farmers and owners of family-oriented firms. The most commonly used data source is the FIES, which is available for every year but excludes these two categories from its samples. Thus, the FIES gives a biased result. The second difficulty arises from the fact that the FIES also excludes households which consist of only one person. This again causes bias. In addition to these problems, it is often suggested that the underreporting of income is serious among the rich in Japan. Thus, we have to understand that the real story of Japanese income distribution is somewhat different from what is commonly believed.

The Japanese government publishes another statistical source for income distribution, although only once every three years. The source is called the Income Redistribution Survey (IRS) and is collected by the Ministry of Welfare. We examine this in detail here.

It is important to understand the differences between the IRS and the FIES with respect to their data gathering. The difference is related to the treatment of farmers and single families. First, the IRS includes all kinds of families and occupations. Thus, it more accurately represents the entire Japanese society. This suggests that the degree of inequality measured in the FIES is inclined to be lower than that measured in the IRS. Second, it is sometimes claimed that samples in the IRS are concentrated somewhat on lower-income classes, as the Ministry of Welfare is interested in knowing the socioeconomic conditions of lower-income families. We cannot judge whether or not the second claim is correct because we are not associated with the institutions involved in the design, composition and release of data.

Nevertheless, we understand that the IRS is fairly general and reliable in the sense that no particular groups, such as single families or farmers, are excluded from the sample. Also, it is conceivable that the inclusion of single families and farmers, who are in general lower-income earners, invites somewhat politically biased criticism favouring a more equal distribution. One problem here has been that the government has been somewhat reluctant to make this data source more accessible to the public. In sum, we find that the IRS must be examined more frequently, because it is basically more comprehensive and hence more reliable. This opinion has also been argued by Mizoguchi and Takayama (1984).

Table 6.3 *Estimated Gini coefficients for before-tax incomes (primary incomes) and for redistributed incomes for the income redistribution survey*

Income year	Before-tax income Gini coefficient (A)	Redistributed Gini coefficient (B)	Income degree of redistribution
1981	0.3491	0.3143	10.0 per cent
1984	0.3975	0.3426	13.8 per cent
1987	0.4049	0.3382	16.5 per cent
1990	0.4334	0.3643	15.9 per cent

Notes:
1 The degree of redistribution is measured by $(A-B)/A$.
2 Redistributed income is defined as before-tax income minus (tax and social security contributions) plus social security payments.
Source: Ministry of Health and Welfare, Income Redistribution Survey, 1981, pp. 84, 87, 90.

Table 6.3 presents the estimated Gini coefficients using the IRS for pre-tax incomes (i.e., primary incomes) and for redistributed incomes. The most important observation in table 6.3 is that the degree of income inequality for pre-tax incomes increased considerably from 1981 to 1990. The past ten years in Japan can be characterised by the constant and considerable increase in inequality in the distribution of primary income. Incidentally, the degree of the increase in inequality for after-tax income was somewhat lower than for primary income. Nevertheless, it is considerably high.

The estimated Gini coefficient for primary incomes increased about 0.1 during the past ten years. This is somewhat astonishing, and we would claim that no other major industrialised country had such a drastic increase in inequality of income distribution during such a short period. Atkinson (1993) reports an increase in the Gini coefficient of 0.08 from 1977 to 1988 for the UK, indicating an increase in measured income inequality. The worsening of the income distribution, according to recent information from the IRS, means that Japan can no longer be considered an industrialised country with a fairly equal income distribution.

Several caveats are necessary before completely accepting the above statement as correct. First, we have to keep in mind that the other statistical source, the FIES, does not produce a high degree of income inequality in terms of the Gini coefficient compared with income inequality measured in the IRS. The coefficient for the FIES was below 0.3 for all households. (Recall, though, our warnings about the differences between these two statistical sources.) Second, we used only the Gini coefficient to estimate the degree of income inequality. We must apply other indexes in addition to the

Gini coefficient to draw a more definite conclusion concerning income inequality.

Despite the above caveats, our conclusion is that income inequality in Japan has worsened, as supported by the IRS, and is based on the following reasoning. The estimated Gini coefficient for the IRS was calculated on the basis of individual household incomes, while the estimate for the FIES was based on average incomes for only five income classes. The latter method is likely to produce a downward biased estimator of the Gini coefficient. Therefore, the coefficient based on FIES data, namely that less than 0.3, must represent an underestimate, and the estimated Gini coefficient for the IRS, exceeding 0.4 in recent years, is more reliable. More importantly, we have to recognise the fact that the increase in the estimated Gini coefficient was observed for the common data source, i.e., the IRS which has a consistent policy of data collection and sampling method in past years. In sum, we believe that the estimated Gini coefficients for the IRS are reliable and robust and ought to be used to evaluate the development of the income distribution.

It is interesting to compare the estimated Gini coefficients for Japan with those for other industrialised countries. Our comparison is not comprehensive but includes several countries. O'Higgins, Schmaus and Stephenson (1989) present the results of a microdata analysis for seven countries. The estimated Gini coefficients for gross income (i.e., primary income) are as follows:

Canada	0.374
US	0.412
UK	0.365
Germany (West)	0.429
Sweden	0.329
Norway	0.356
Israel	0.395.

The comparable Japanese figures are 0.405 for 1987, 0.433 for 1990, 0.349 for 1981 and 0.398 for 1984. The earlier years are comparable with the results estimated by O'Higgins et al. (1989), because the observation years are nearly the same. Another study, by Atkinson (1993), shows Gini coefficients for the following countries and years:

UK	0.35	1988
US	0.40	1989
Australia	0.32	1985/6
Canada	0.404	1988
France	0.372	1984
Finland	0.20	1985

In sum, Japan can hardly claim to have one of the highest degrees of reported income equality among industrialised countries. In fact, inequality was higher in 1990 in Japan than in any of the above countries, as reproted in the above study.

2.3   Time-series analysis of income inequality in Japan

We have performed a simple regression analysis to examine the factors which affected changes in income inequality in Japan. The data source is the FIES. Figures for financial assets are based on the FSS. The dependent variable is the Gini coefficient calculated on the basis of the average household annual income of five income classes. The analysis covers annual data from 1963 to 1991, or 29 years of samples.

The simple regression analysis is summarised by the following equation

$$g_t = a_0 + a_1 y_t + a_2 y_t^2 + a_3 p_t + a_4 v_t + a_5 wi_t + a_6 fm_t + a_7 ne_t + u_t \qquad (1)$$

where the notations are as follows:

g_t: Gini coefficient for income distribution in year t
y_t: per-household GNP
p_t: the rate of increase in the consumer price index
v_t: the vacancy-to-job-seeker ratio
wi_t: per-household real net financial assets over income (including bank deposits, insurance, bonds and stock)
fm_t: the number of household members
ne_t: the number of income earners in a household
u_t: error term

Figure 6.2 shows how the different factors contribute to changes in the Gini coefficient for pre-tax incomes, i.e., primary incomes. The empirical findings are as follows.

First, the squared income term, y^2, explains a large part of the changes in Gini coefficients, especially in recent years. The R^2 of the equation which includes y^2 is 0.79, and that of the equation which excludes y^2 is 0.62. The t-value of y^2 is 4.33. Inclusion of the squared income term improves not only the figures for the Durbin–Watson statistics but also those of the t-values. The coefficient of y^2 is positive. It is possible to conclude that the U-shaped property of income inequality is supported statistically. The result suggests that income distribution tends to become more equal in the early stages of economic growth and then becomes less equal after the economy has reached some critical level of economic growth. This is inconsistent with the famous Kuznets inverted U-shape hypothesis (Kuznets 1955, 1963). We provide several reasons in subsequent sections as to why Japan reached a turning point and now shows a trend of increasing income inequality.

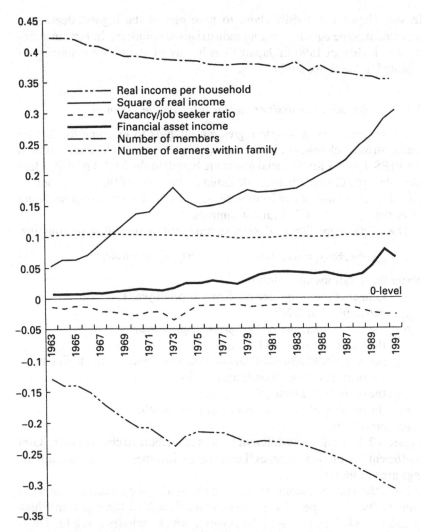

Figure 6.2 Factor analysis of changes in Gini (whole household)
Notes: The estimated regression equation is

$$g_t = -0.14 - 0.031y + 0.0029y^2 + 0.0058p - 0.02v + 0.001wi + 0.098fm + 0.061ne$$
$$\quad [0.48]\ [-2.29]\quad [4.33]\quad [0.26]\quad [1.83]\quad [0.56]\quad [2.04]\quad [1.08]$$

The figures in parentheses are *t*-values.
Source: Prime Minister Office, Statistics Bureau, Family Income and Expenditure Survey (1965–93).

Second, the rate of inflation does not have a significant effect on income inequality. Third, the number of household members, fm_t, has a positive influence on inequality. The positive coefficient implies that the decreasing trend in the number of household members, currently observed in Japan, lowers the degree of inequality. This is closely related to the issue of working wives (Tachibanaki and Yagi 1992).

Finally, per-household real financial assets over income does not give a statistically significant coefficient. Thus, we cannot support the previous finding, based on time-series data, that one of the most significant contributions to increasing income inequality in Japan was income from asset holdings. The distinction between cross-sectional data and time-series data seems to be crucial for deriving the role of asset income.

Some readers may not be convinced that the level of the Gini coefficient is a better dependent variable than the change of the Gini coefficient. We performed another regression analysis in which the change of the Gini coefficient is used as the dependent variable. The estimated results are worse statistically than that of the analysis which uses the level of the Gini coefficient, thus arguing for its application.

The analysis using the change of the Gini coefficient, however, produced some interesting results. The effect of the change in GNP after removing the effect of the level of squared form GNP is interpreted as the effect of the short-term business cycle. The negative value of the coefficient of change in GNP suggests that the short-term business cycle affects the change in income equality negatively. The t-value of y^2 is -1.89, i.e. the degree of income inequality decreases as growth increases while it worsens when growth decreases.

With respect to factors influencing changes in income inequality, Tachibanaki and Yagi (1994) shed light on the time-series change in a manner that differs from the above analysis.

Based on the time-series comparison and the cross-country comparison, we conclude that it is no longer true that Japan is one of the countries with the lowest degree of inequality in income distribution. The degree of inequality has increased very substantially in recent years. Why Japan has experienced such a trend will be explored in section 3.

2.4 Income redistribution

Concerning redistribution and the progressivity of income tax, using the Family Expenditure Survey, Itaba and Tachibanaki (1987) show that in 1980 tax legislation was more progressive in Japan than in the US. They used a modified version of the Kakwani measure of progressivity (Kakwani 1977, 1980). This measure is preferable because it is an overall index which

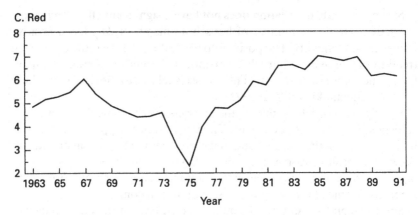

Figure 6.3 Coefficient of tax redistribution
Source: Family Income and Expenditure Survey (1964–92).

takes account of the shape of the income distribution. Itaba and Tachibanaki (1987) attribute the greater redistributive effect to the more equal income distribution in Japan and the higher tax elasticity with respect to income.

On the other hand, Ishizaki (1985) shows that changes in income distribution induced by Japan's tax system are considerably less than the average for OECD countries. In 1988, the tax system was changed and the marginal tax rate of the highest income bracket decreased, from 65 per cent to 50 per cent. For these reasons, the degree of progressivity should be reestimated using recent data to grasp the effects of the current Japanese tax system. In figure 6.3, we show the development of the coefficient of tax redistribution, using the coefficient as an index of progressivity and the FIES as a data source, i.e., only employed persons are examined. It is likely that the FIES excludes the richest and the poorest income classes, which generates a downward bias in measuring the degree of tax progressivity. Despite these defects, the FIES has some merits for time-series analysis because it is conducted every year. Figure 6.3 shows that the degree of progressivity defined by the coefficient of redistribution generally decreased until 1975, when it turned and generally increased until 1988. However, the coefficient started to decrease after the 1988 tax reform. The degree of progressivity in 1991 was still around the same level as in 1980. This declining contribution of the tax system to redistribution is a major feature of the 1988 tax reform.

Another important system with the potential to contribute to redistribution of income in Japan is the public pension system. Shimono and Tachibanaki (1985) examine the degree of income redistribution generated through the public pension system by using a two-period analysis. In their study, the public pension system in Japan is compared with that of the UK. The study showed that the low-income class is less well off in Japan. Tachibanaki and Shimono (1994) extend their previously published research empirically by using the Wage Structure Survey. They classify income classes by education completed. They also examine the degree of income redistribution through the public pension system as measured by differences in implicit rates of return. In the 1994 study, the implicit rates of return are calculated for employees with various school careers. Under the public pension system as of 1976, the implicit rate of return for university graduates was 11.94 per cent, that of senior high school graduates 12.17 per cent and that of junior high school graduates 12.21 per cent, all for employees who contributed to pension funds for 25 years. Under the current public pension system, these values dropped to 2.68 per cent, 2.86 per cent and 3.11 per cent for the corresponding educational levels and 25 years of contributions. For employees with 35 years of contributions, the values are 2.47 per cent, 2.61 per cent and 2.77 per cent, respectively. Based on these results, Tachibanaki and Shimono conclude that the public pension system in Japan results in intergenerational as well as intragenerational redistribution of income. That is, it is apparent that income is redistributed from the young to the old and from the rich to the poor through the public pension system in Japan.

Oguchi, Kimura and Hatta (1994) argue against redistribution of income through the public pension system. They estimate the size of intragenerational and intergenerational redistribution of income through the pension system and argue that the progressive income tax and social safety net are better schemes for redistributing income. Based on this argument, they propose a plan for reforming the public pension system in Japan. Contrary to Oguchi, Kimura and Hatta, Yagi (1991) argues that the public pension system has some advantages over the income tax system as a means of income redistribution to improve the living standards of the myopic poor. Yagi evaluates income redistribution through the public pension system and the linear income tax system by calculating the optimal redistributive levels and welfare levels for each system. The conclusions of Tachibanaki and Shimono (1994) are consistent with Yagi's conclusions, which demonstrate that a paternalistic government can redistribute income more effectively where people do not follow life-cycle saving behaviour.

Finally, we present the role of taxes and transfers in income redistribution using the IRS. Table 6.3 shows the results of income redistribution through tax and social security contributions. The degree of income redistribution is about 10.0 per cent–17.0 per cent for the 1980s. This implies that the degree of income redistribution through tax and social security contributions is neither particularly strong nor particularly weak. Japan is neither a welfare state in the European sense nor a highly developed capitalist country like the US, which is consistent with the modest degree of redistribution through taxes and social security contributions shown in the table.

More importantly, expenditure on social policies, such as pensions, medical care, unemployment compensation, child allowances, social payments to the poor and other social expenditures, are not as high as those in several European nations. Thus, the ratio of tax revenues and social security contributions to GNP is one of the lowest in the OECD. The role of the public sector in social support is limited in Japan, and individual families and enterprises are largely responsible for income support. Some specialists find that the minor role of the public sector (small-scale government) in income support and social policy has been effective for strong industrialisation and rapid economic growth, while other specialists have proposed that Japan should move towards the welfare state. We will not discuss this issue further here, because it is beyond the scope of this chapter. Nevertheless, it is important to recognise that Japan is not a welfare state. Recent changes in public policy, such as the introduction of value-added taxes and reduced progressivity in income tax, confirm this statement.

3   Wage and property income distributions

3.1   Wage differentials in Japan

To investigate the contribution of wages and property income to the distribution of primary income, it is useful to understand the component of each income source in total income. The IRS gives the following share of each income source to total income. (The figures are for 1990, and include all kinds of households.)

Wage income 82.5 per cent

Enterprise (self-employed) income 10.7 per cent

Farm income 1.6 per cent

Family-type wage income 0.4 per cent

Property income 4.3 per cent

Miscellaneous income 0.5 per cent

The share of wage income is by far the largest. Therefore, it is quite important to investigate how wages are distributed and how wages are determined to examine and understand the distribution in total income. Incidentally, the share of property income is only 4.3 per cent. This does not necessarily imply that property income is less important in investigating income distribution, though, because it accrues to relatively rich households. Finally, the share of enterprise (self-employed) income is about 10.0 per cent – considerably high.

Since wages represent the largest share of income, we will examine them first. Changes in wage distribution evidence the long-term tendency in the entire distribution. A tendency towards more unequal wage distribution is likely to persist, because the determination of wages involves firms' management policies, which evolve in reaction to changing economic conditions, and other institutional and social conditions. Thus, more inequality in the income distribution caused by an unequal distribution of wages will tend to reflect a long-term pattern.

Various studies have examined time-series changes in wage distribution, including the Economic Planning Agency's (EPA) comprehensive analysis of changes in wage differentials from 1975 to 1990. The findings of the EPA's report can be summarised as follows. First, the degree of wage dispersion has increased considerably since 1975. In other words, increased inequality in wage distribution is a fairly recent trend. Second, wage differentials between industries have also widened. Industries that have higher levels of wages than the average are electrical, gas and water and banking and insurance; those industries with lower wage levels are manufacturing, wholesale and retail trade and services. It is also important to note that the difference between wages in high-paying industries and low-paying industries has widened.

A third finding was that wage differentials according to firm size have also widened: Employees in larger firms receive much higher wages than employees in smaller firms, reflecting the dual structure of the Japanese industrial relations system. If non-wage payments such as fringe benefits and in-kind benefits are included, this dual structure is even more significant. Tachibanaki (1982) examines wage differentials in Japanese manufacturing industries by using the Wage Structure Survey. It provides the evidence that wage differentials by firm size widened during the period 1975–8. Tachibanaki (1993) also performs a comprehensive study on wage differentials by size of firm, from 1978 to 1988, using the Wage Structure Survey published by the Ministry of Labour.

Table 6.4 shows the advantages and disadvantages of wage payments by firm size estimated by Tachibanaki (1993) for a large number of variables, such as age, sex, job tenure, education, industry and occupation. Many other factors are used as controls. It is necessary to eliminate the contribution of various factors to wage differentials by size, because larger firms employ more males, more older workers, more longer tenured workers and more educated workers. Those workers normally receive higher wages and thus may be called 'advantaged workers'. These factors must be eliminated in order to estimate the advantages and disadvantages owing solely to size.

The pure size effect on wage differentials is obtained by estimating the wage equation as a function of the control variables described above and

Table 6.4 Advantages and disadvantages in wage payment by firm size (per cent)

Number of employees	1978			1988		
	Before		After	Before		After
5,000–	28.61 sample	(7,448)	23.11	32.10 sample	(8,647)	27.16
1,000–4,999	20.49 sample	(7,356)	17.03	21.86 sample	(7,091)	15.96
500–999	9.95 sample	(3,552)	5.61	9.24 sample	(3,667)	2.68
300–499	1.01 sample	(3,235)	−3.31	−1.55 sample	(3,038)	−5.60
100–299	−7.54 sample	(8,215)	−12.10	−11.93 sample	(7,271)	−15.37
30–99	−15.71 sample	(10,382)	−19.90	−20.29 sample	(9,330)	−23.36
10–29	−21.24 sample	(8,355)	−25.34	−25.34 sample	(7,329)	−28.78

Notes: Minus signs signify disadvantages. 'Before' means before controls and 'After' means after controls by a large number of quality variables.
Source: Tachibanaki (1993).

several size dummy variables. Some of the variables have not only a linear term but also a quadratic term. Also, some of the variables interact with other variables. The pure size effect is obtained as follows:

$$\ln(W_{ij}) = \text{const.} + (\text{size dummies with respect to } i\text{th firm size}) + (\text{many control variables})$$

in which W_{ij} stands for the hourly wage figure for the jth individual in the ith firm size. We consider seven classes of size of firms. The pure size effect (or premium) is given by

$$p_i = \frac{\hat{W} - \bar{W}}{\bar{W}}$$

in which p_i is the premium for the ith size class, $\hat{W}$ is the average estimated wage for the ith size class after the control and $\bar{W}$ is the overall average wage before the control.

Based on table 6.4, we find that the pure advantage and disadvantage associated with the size of firm increased substantially during the past ten years. This 'widening effect' associated with the size of the firm can be expected to have contributed very significantly to a greater wage distribution.

A fourth possible reason behind increasing wage differentials in general is the significant increase in the female labour force participation rate. Statistics give the following rates of female participation in non-agricultural sectors: 1970 26.7 per cent, 1980 29.3 per cent, 1985 31.6 per cent, 1988 32.8 per cent and 1991 36.4 per cent. We find also a steady increase in the number of female employees in industry. Unfortunately, females tend to work in lower-wage jobs, and a large number of females work as part-time employees. Therefore, the average observed wage of female workers is necessarily lower than that of male workers. Of course, it would be necessary to standardise male–female wage figures using control variables, as was done for the employer size effect, to draw more specific conclusions. We know of no studies of this kind for Japan. Thus, we cannot proclaim that pure male–female wage differentials have widened. Nevertheless, it is possible to propose that simple average observed wage differentials have increased because of the increase in female workers.

Katz and Revanga (1989) conclude that wage differentials by educational attainment and experience slightly widened from 1979 to 1987 in Japan and suggest a decreasing trend in wage differentials by age both for university and high school graduates. The result obtained in Katz and Revanga shows that the increasing inequality trend appears more sharply in various aspects in the US than in Japan. Katz and Revanga do not examine wage differentials by firm size. Genda (1994) examines changes in wage differentials in

Japan by education, age and firm size for the period 1978 to 1990 after removing the effects of tenure. According to his research, a change in tenure composition tended to decrease wage differentials by education and to increase wage differentials by age and firm size. A change in the rate of return to tenure tended to decrease all wage differentials and to decrease the variance in income distribution within a group of workers with identical attributes. Concerning wage differentials after removing the tenure effect, his results are consistent with Tachibanaki (1993) and Katz and Revanga (1989) in the sense that wage differentials by both education and firm size widened during the 1980s.

There are several other reasons for the trend towards wider wage differentials. First, competition among firms both within Japan and internationally has been so severe that differences between successful and less successful firms have become apparent and are likely to remain. Here, firm size is not a crucial determinant because successful firms, whether large or small, are able to pay higher wages, while unsuccessful firms, regardless of size, are unable to pay wages comparable to those paid by successful firms. The story is similar for industrial differentials. Hence, firms' 'ability to pay' is one of the most important factors behind the differential in wage payments.

Second, competition among employees has become more prevalent. In other words, the achievement and efforts of workers in a firm are evaluated, and there is a steady trend towards wage determination based on job evaluations and achievement rather than age and tenure; that is, incentive pay is becoming popular in Japan. This leads to a wider difference in wage payments among workers.

To predict the future of inequality in the wage distribution, we should consider the effects of the ageing trend in Japan. Recalling that older workers earn more than younger ones in the *nenko-joretsu* system, in which the wage rate increases proportionally with the worker's length of service, the current aging trend expands wage differentials. However, an increase in the proportion of older workers in a company increases labour costs and depresses profits. This implies that the ageing trend may eventually destroy the *nenko-joretsu* system. Thus, the overall effect of the ageing trend is uncertain.

In sum, all the available evidence makes clear that wage differentials and dispersion widened during the past decade. Inequality in the wage distribution is a recent trend and has contributed to inequality in income distribution.

3.2   *Income distribution and property income*

We mentioned that property income, such as interest, dividends and rent, is likely to contribute to a wider income distribution as the second most important source of total income inequality after wage distribution. Our time-series regression analysis showed that property income has not been important as a determinant of the change in inequality over time. Several cross-sectional studies, however, suggest an important role for property income in determining income inequality.

When considering the issue of property income, it is important to examine the effects of imputed rent on the income distribution. In the mid and late 1980s, land prices in Japan rose precipitously. Thus, the increase in land prices widened the gap between homeowners and renters. For homeowners, the increase in land prices increased their wealth. On the other hand, the increase in land prices became a severe burden for renters because it raised the actual rent. Thus, it would be interesting to compare primary incomes which include imputed rents for homeowners with those which do not include them for renters. In this chapter, we estimate the imputed rent in Japan from land value data and measure the inequality of income including income from financial assets and imputed rent.

We use microdata compiled by the Nikkei Shimbun called Nikkei Needs Radar. These microdata contain detailed information on household attributes, wage earnings, financial assets by type, land values, the state of homeownership and mortgage amounts. The sample size is 5,000, and the sample is randomly selected. The reliability of these microdata was examined by comparing the characteristics of these data with other official data.

The most important limitation of this data source is its narrow geographical coverage. The survey covers only the Tokyo metropolitan area. However, this does not make our analysis useless, because the problem of inequality between landowners and renters is most severe in the Tokyo metropolitan area. An analysis which focuses on this area will clearly reveal the importance of the problem.

There are mainly three methods for estimating imputed rent. The first is to estimate a rent function from other data concerning rented housing and apply the estimated rent function to the data. For this method, the data should contain detailed information on housing, such as the size of each building, number of rooms, equipment and structure. The second method is to estimate the opportunity cost of holding wealth in the form of land. With this method, an imputed rent is calculated by multiplying the interest rate of the financial asset with the land value, as shown by Smith (1990). This method is not as desirable if we are concerned with tenure choice behaviour. The third method is to estimate an imputed rent from the arbitrary conditions in tenure choice behaviour using land value data, as done by Skinner (1989) and King (1980).

The Nikkei Needs Radar does not contain any detailed information on the characteristics of buildings. The only parameter available to estimate

Table 6.5 *Inequality of earnings income and total income*

	Whole age	20–39	40–59	60–
Before-tax average earnings income	701.2	565.5	836.1	601.3
Gini coefficient of before-tax earnings income	0.304	0.259	0.283	0.380
Before-tax average total income	957.4	690.7	1,154.0	1,078.0
Gini coefficient of before-tax total income	0.371	0.308	0.348	0.437

Notes:
The unit of income is 10,000 yen. Total income includes income from financial assets and imputed rent.
Source: Japan Economic Newspaper, Nikkei Needs Radar (1990).

the imputed rent is land value. Thus, we used the third method to estimate imputed rent. Q_t and p_t denote the land value and the rent, respectively, at time t. Q_t and p_t then satisfy the following arbitrary condition.

$$Q_t = \sum_{j=t}^{\infty} p_j (1+r)^{t-j-1}$$

where r is the rate of interest. Assuming that rent p_t grows at the rate g_p, we have the growth equation of the rent:

$$p_{j+1} = (1+g_p)p_j$$

In this chapter, the annual growth rate of rent is set at 5 per cent according to the consumer expenditure survey.

Table 6.5 compares the degree of income inequality measured by primary income with that of total income, including wage income, imputed rent and income from financial assets. This table shows that the degree of inequality measured by total income is far larger than that measured by earnings income. Our decomposition analysis of inequality by income source (using the decomposition method in Fei, Ranis and Kuo 1978) shows that 32.8 per cent of total income inequality is attributed to imputed rents, while 54.2 per cent is attributed to earnings income for whole age classes, although imputed rent income is 1.77 million yen, and earnings income 7 million yen. The average income from financial assets is 0.78 million yen, and only 13 per cent of inequality is attributed to this.

Thus, we conclude that the degree of income inequality in Japan as estimated on the basis of earnings income alone is misleading. The large inequality between landowners and renters reflected in the high degree of total income inequality is an important characteristic of income distribution in Japan.

4   Wealth distribution

There is a common belief in Japan that the distribution of wealth considerably worsened in the 1980s. Two phenomena are behind this change. The first is the drastic increase in land prices in urban areas, such as Tokyo, Osaka and Nagoya. Between 1985 and 1989, the average price of commercial land increased 244 per cent, residential land 125 per cent and industrial land 124 per cent. These rates were calculated for six major cities. Households who had their own land and house benefited enormously. The second phenomenon is the increase in stock prices. Since only a small portion of households (around 11 per cent) own shares in Japan, the effect of the increase in stock prices has been enormous for shareholders.

The drastic increase in land prices and stock prices occurred in the late 1980s and gave the period its name: 'the bubble economy'. The bubble economy produced a considerably unequal wealth distribution, because the amount of wealth of households owning land and/or stocks increased considerably, while those without such assets were unaffected. Takayama *et al.* (1992) and Tachibanaki (1989, 1992) provide statistical evidence of increases in wealth inequality. Bauer and Mason (1992) summarise these figures on the inequality of wealth distribution. To avoid repetition, the present study does not provide statistical evidence on inequality but reviews the government's White Paper on the Japanese Economy (1993), which shows trends in inequality. Table 6.6 shows the historical change in wealth inequality, in particular inequality in land assets. The table clearly shows that wealth inequality has widened, especially in the late 1980s.

The bubble economy began deflating in the early 1990s. Prices of land in Tokyo, Osaka and Nagoya started declining in 1990 and 1991 after peaking in the late 1980s. The price of shares dropped considerably in the early 1990s, and stock market indices are roughly half as high as their historical peaks. These declining trends in land prices and stock prices are likely to have checked the rising trend of inequality in wealth distribution, and we predict that the degree of inequality in wealth distribution will have decreased marginally in recent years, although statistical evidence is not yet available.

However, we do not believe that the degree of inequality in wealth distribution, or more generally the degree of inequality in economic well-

Table 6.6 *Historical overview of inequality of land assets (Gini coefficients)*

	1983	1984	1985	1986	1987	1988	1989	1990
A)	0.4669	0.4334	0.4339	0.4410				
				0.4357	0.4821	05347	0.5202	0.5158
B)		0.4145					0.4175	
C)	0.6682	0.6677	0.6682	0.6723				
				0.6772	0.7038	0.7340	0.7258	0.7233
D)		0.6568					0.6668	

Notes:
1 These four groups of Gini coefficients were estimated for the following categories:
  A = value of land owned by landholders.
  B = area of land owned by landholders.
  C = value of land owned by landholders and renters (the value of renters' land is zero).
  D = area of land for both landholders and renters (the area of renters' land is zero).
2 The two figures shown for 1986 were estimated using different surveys. Through 1986, 1983 land samples and the land prices for each year were used. Beginning in 1986, 1988 land samples and the land prices for each year were used.
Source: Economic Planning Agency, White Paper on the Japanese Economy, 1993.

being, has declined substantially and thus returned to the state in which inequality is not so severe. Our reasons are as follows. First, the rate of decrease in land prices in urban areas is considerably slower than the rate of increase during the bubble economy. Moreover, there is no sign that land prices will return to the levels prior to the speculative bubble or prior to the rise in the price of land. Some specialists predict, for various reasons, that the prices of land in urban areas will begin to rise again in the near future without returning to previous levels. Second, as Barthold and Ito (1993), Tachibanaki and Shimono (1991) and Tachibanaki and Takata (1993) point out, intergenerational wealth transfers such as bequests and inheritance play a major role in determining inequality in wealth distribution in Japan, in particular distribution of physical wealth. Although in principle Japan's progressive inheritance taxes should help reduce the transfer of wealth inequality from one generation to the next, there are several exemptions and provisions which counteract this. Also, unlawful conduct is far from non-negligible, and tax evasion, illegal, is not uncommon. Third, although tax legislation prescribes not only inheritance tax but also income tax on interest and dividend income and various taxes on wealth, tax policy is not aimed at reducing the degree of inequality in wealth distribution. Thus, there is no reason to expect a decreasing trend in inequality in wealth distribution based on current government policies.

5 Summary and policy issues

We have presented an overview of distributional trends in Japan and new evidence on inequality in the income distribution. We found that it is incorrect to regard Japan as a country characterised by high equality in income. Various statistical evidence, based on both time-series data and cross-country data, suggests that Japan nowadays belongs to a group of industrialised countries in which inequality of income distribution is higher and that Japan's actual level of income inequality may be even higher. We concluded that this trend must be attributed to an increase in inequality of wage distribution, a long-term trend. Several causes of this worsening wage distribution were presented and discussed. Also, the effects of imputed rent and income from financial assets were examined.

We also examined the distribution of wealth. Increasing inequality in wealth distribution caused by the increase in land prices and stock prices was discussed extensively in Japan during the bubble economy. With the end of the bubble economy, the issue disappeared from the popular press. Nevertheless, we argue that the problem of worsening wealth inequality has not disappeared. Combining the persistent trend in inequality of wealth distribution with the long-term trend in inequality of income distribution, we can conclude that Japan is becoming a country of higher inequality. The picture of Japan as being an equality-oriented society is no longer true. Japan now belongs to that group of highly industrialised countries with the greatest inequality.

Is this development desirable for Japan? The answer in our view is 'No'. Tachibanaki (1989, 1992) discusses in detail the reasons for this trend, in particular the effects of public policies and general public opinion, which does not oppose this trend. Also, various policy issues were discussed. The main finding in these papers is that the majority of the Japanese do not care about the recent trend towards inequality induced by market forces and public policies, because their average living standard is currently fairly high. They are not concerned with the poor and the extreme rich, whose numbers are relatively small. What can we do? This is an open question for a society in which the majority of people are largely content with the status quo despite worsening inequality in economic well-being.

130   Toshiaki Tachibanaki and Tadashi Yagi

References

Atkinson, A. B. 1993. 'What is Happening to Distribution of Income in the UK?' Welfare State Programme Discussion Paper No. 87. London School of Economics.

Barthold, T. A. and Ito, T. 1993. 'Bequest Taxes and Accumulation of Household Wealth: US–Japan Comparison', in Ito, T. and Krueger, A. O. (eds.), *The Political Economy of Tax Reform*. NBER, The University of Chicago Press, pp. 235–92.

Bauer, J. and Mason, A. 1992. 'The Distribution of Income and Wealth in Japan'. *Review of Income and Wealth*, 38, 4: 403–28.

Buss, J. A., Peterson, G. P., Nantz, S. J. and Nantz, K. A. 1989. 'A Comparison of Distributive Justice in OECD Countries'. *Review of Social Economy*, 47: 1–14.

Economic Planning Agency. 1993. *White Paper on the Japanese Economy* (in Japanese).

Fei, J. C. H., Ranis, G. and Kuo, S. W. Y. 1978. 'Growth and the Family Distribution of Income by Factor Components'. *Quarterly Journal of Economics*, 92: 17–53.

Genda, Y. 1994. 'The Increasing Trend of Educational Attainments, the Increase in Middle Age Group, and Wage Structure' (in Japanese), in Ishikawa, T. (ed.), *Nihon no Shotoku to Tomi*. Tokyo University Press.

Ishikawa, T. 1991. *Shotoku to Tomi*. Tokyo: Iwanami Book Press.

Ishizaki, T. 1985. 'Is Japan's Income Distribution Equal? An International Comparison'. *Japanese Economic Studies*, 14, 2: 30–55.

Itaba, Y. and Tachibanaki, T. 1987. 'Measurement of Tax Progressivity when the Forms of both Income Distribution and Tax Function are Given'. *The Economic Studies Quarterly*, 38, 2: 97–106.

Kakwani, N. C. 1977. 'Measurement of Tax Progressivity: An International Comparison'. *Economic Journal*, 87, 1: 71–80.

1980. *Income Inequality and Poverty: Methods of Estimation and Policy Applications*. Oxford.

Katz, L. F. and Revanga, A. L. 1989. 'Changes in the Structure of Wages: The United States vs Japan'. *Journal of Japanese and International Economies*, 3: 522–53.

King, M. A. 1980. 'An Econometric Model of Tenure Choice and Demand for Housing as a Joint Decision'. *Journal of Public Economics*, 14: 137–59.

Kuznets, S. 1955. 'Economic Growth and Income Inequality'. *American Economic Review*, 45, 1: 1–28.

1963. 'Quantitative Aspects of Economic Growth of Nations: VIII. Distribution of Income by Size'. *Economic Development and Cultural Change*, 11, 2: 1–80.

Mizoguchi, T. and Takayama, N. 1984. *Equity and Poverty under Rapid Economic Growth*. Tokyo: Kinokuniya.

Oguchi, N., Kimura, Y. and Hatta, T. 1994. 'Redistributive Effect of Japanese Public Pension System' (in Japanese), in Ishikawa, T. (ed.), *Nihon no Shotoku to Tomi*. Tokyo University Press.

O'Higgins, M., Schmaus, G. and Stephenson, G. 1989. 'Income Distribution and

Redistribution: A Microdata Analysis for Seven Countries'. *The Review of Income and Wealth*, 35, 2: 107–32.

Sawyer, M. 1976. 'Income Distribution in the OECD Countries'. *OECD Economic Outlook*, July.

Shimono, K. and Tachibanaki, T. 1985. 'Lifetime Income and Public Pension: An Analysis of the Effect on Redistribution using a Two-Period Analysis'. *Journal of Public Economics*, 26: 75–8.

Skinner, J. 1989. 'Housing Wealth and Aggregate Saving'. NBER Working Paper No. 2842.

Smith, S. J. 1990. 'Income, Housing Wealth and Gender Inequality'. *Urban Studies*, 27, 1: 67–88.

Tachibanaki, T. 1982. 'Further Results on Japanese Wage Differentials: Nenko Wages, Hierarchical Position, Bonuses, and Working Hours'. *International Economic Review*, 23, 2: 447–61.

1989. 'Japan's New Policy Agenda: Coping with Unequal Asset Distribution'. *Journal of Japanese Studies*, 15: 345–69.

1992. 'Higher Land Prices as a Cause of Increasing Inequality: Changes in Wealth Distribution and Socio-Economic Effects', in Haley, J. O. and Yamamura, K. (eds.), *Land Issues in Japan: A Policy Failure?* Society for Japanese Studies.

1993. 'The Employer Size Effect on Wage Differentials in Japan, Revived'. Discussion Paper No. 377, Kyoto Institute of Economic Research.

Tachibanaki, T. and Shimono, K. 1991. 'Wealth Accumulation Process by Income Class'. *Journal of the Japanese and International Economies*, 5 (September): 239–60.

1994. *Savings and Life Cycle* (in Japanese). Nihon Keizai Shimbunsha.

Tachibanaki, T. and Takata, S. 1993. 'Bequest and Asset Distribution: Human Capital Investment and Intergenerational Wealth Transfer', in Tachibanaki, T. (ed.), *Savings and Bequests*. University of Michigan Press.

Tachibanaki, T. and Yagi, T. 1992. 'Welfare Improvement Caused by Changes in Income Distribution, Needs and Labour Supply: A Theoretical and Empirical Investigation'. Mimeographed.

1994. 'Recent Movement of Income Distribution in Japan' (in Japanese), in Ishikawa, T. (ed.), *Nihon no Shotoku to Tomi*. Tokyo University Press.

Takayama, N. *et al.* 1992. *Stock Economy* (in Japanese). Tokyo: Toyokeizai-shimposha.

Yagi, T. 1991. 'Why are Annuity Systems Used to Redistribute Income?' *The Economic Studies Quarterly*. 41, 2 (June): 134–54.

7 Income inequality and poverty under transition from rapid inflation to stabilisation: Israel, 1979–1990

LEA ACHDUT

1   Introduction

The implementation of a stabilisation policy in July 1985 was a turning point for the Israeli economy. During the period 1979–June 1985, Israel experienced extremely high inflation, which peaked at more than 450 per cent annually in the first half of 1985. In July 1985, the government introduced a sweeping package of measures which rolled the inflationary tide back to an annual level of 20 per cent and less during 1986–90. The price stabilisation policy, however, contributed to an expansion in unemployment, which had been emerging gradually since the end of 1979. In 1989–1990, unemployment intensified with massive immigration from the former Soviet Union.

High and unanticipated inflation, so the argument goes, has negative distributional effects and potentially devastating consequences for the poor. Failure to properly adjust the tax structure drives nominal incomes into higher tax brackets, thus raising the tax burden and further eroding real net incomes. Lags in the adjustment of social security benefits expose the more vulnerable sections of society to the risk of poverty and tend to expand income disparities between the poor and the rich. However, the distributional cost of inflation and its negative effects on the weak are somewhat moderated when, as is the case in Israel, the government takes steps to index various types of income. As early as 1973, the government of Israel introduced a widespread system of indexation that embraced wages, financial assets, the income tax structure and social security benefits. When inflation accelerated to higher levels, the government elaborated the updating mechanisms by raising the degree and frequency of indexation. However, these adjustments were not carried out immediately after the inflationary tides in 1980 and 1984, since it took time for policymakers and labour unions to fully recognise the adverse impact of inflation and to complete the necessary administrative and legal arrangements. When inflation declined in 1985, it had an immediate and favourable effect: The transition from a 20 per cent monthly rate of inflation to less than 2 per cent led to a one-time real increase in the income tax brackets and in social security benefits. With the stabilisation of prices, the income tax and the social security systems stabilised as well.

The purpose of this study is to examine trends in income inequality and poverty in Israel during the period 1979–90 against the background of macroeconomic developments and tax and welfare policies.[1] Data sources are the Annual Income Surveys, which the Central Bureau of Statistics has conducted since 1965.[2] The survey covers all households in urban localities whose head is either an employee or does not work, thus excluding the self-employed and the rural population.[3] Its data enable us to distinguish among three categories of income: (i) factor income (which includes earnings, interest payments, rents, dividends, occupational pensions, etc.); (ii) gross income (factor income plus cash transfer payments); and (iii) net income (gross income after the deduction of direct taxes – personal income tax and social insurance contributions). The study relates to each of these income categories to assess the impact of direct taxes and transfers on income inequality and poverty.

The structure of this chapter is as follows: section 2 describes concisely the main economic developments of the 1980s. Section 3 discusses trends in income inequality during the period of investigation, whereas section 4 inquires into trends in poverty. Changes in both income inequality and poverty are examined by alternative measures: the income inequality measures differ in their sensitivity to income changes at different ranges of the income distribution; the poverty measures differ in their sensitivity to different poverty dimensions. Section 5 concludes with a summary of the main results. The appendix to the chapter presents some results, based on Family Expenditure Survey data, on effects on income inequality and poverty and of including the self-employed in the investigated population.

2   Economic trends in the 1980s

Tables 7.1 and 7.2 provide a background to the analysis of trends in income inequality and poverty during the period 1979–90, with particular emphasis on the income tax and social security systems. During the first half of the 1980s, Israel experienced extremely high inflation. In July 1985, the government adopted an emergency programme (entitled 'Policy for Stabilisation of the Economy') aimed at combatting inflation and improving the balance of payments. The new programme combined fiscal and monetary measures to reduce public and private demand, such as cuts in government expenditure (mainly in subsidies to necessities and in child allowances), increased taxation on high-income individuals, a real wage

Table 7.1 *Indicators of main economic developments in Israel, 1979–1990*[a]

	1979	1980	1981	1982	1983	1984	1985	1986	1987	1988	1989	1990
Rate of inflation (per cent)	111.0	133.0	101.0	132.0	191.0	445.0	185.0	19.6	16.1	16.4	20.7	17.6
Rate of unemployment (per cent)	2.9	4.8	5.1	5.0	4.5	5.9	6.7	7.1	6.1	6.4	8.9	9.5
Index for change at constant prices: 1979=100												
GDP per capita	100.0	100.6	103.3	102.5	103.5	104.0	106.2	108.6	113.5	114.5	114.4	117.0
Private consumption per capita	100.0	94.0	104.5	110.7	122.5	107.7	106.6	120.5	129.2	132.5	130.3	133.0
Gross average wage per employee post	100.0	96.8	106.9	106.4	112.9	112.4	102.3	110.3	119.0	126.2	124.5	123.3
NII benefit payments	100.0	111.4	128.9	140.7	133.7	138.3	145.7	163.9	174.6	191.6	200.2	209.0
NII benefit payments per capita	100.0	108.8	123.6	132.3	124.2	125.9	130.3	144.4	151.3	163.3	167.8	169.8
Minimum wage as per cent of average wage	31.0	26.3	36.0	36.8	37.6	36.5	31.8	31.5	36.8	40.1	41.3	42.9
NII benefit payments as per cent of GNP	6.3	6.8	7.1	7.6	7.2	7.0	7.5	8.0	7.8	8.2	8.3	8.2
Disposable income	11.1	9.8	9.4	10.3	9.4	8.9	12.1	13.1	12.3	13.1	13.3	13.1

Note:
[a] Calculated for the calendar year, which is not identical to the period of the Income survey.

Table 7.2 Indicators of main developments in social security and income tax systems, 1979–1990[a]

	1979	1980	1981	1982	1983	1984	1985	1986	1987	1988	1989	1990
1 Real change in tax threshold (per cent)	0.2	-12.2	7.7	3.5	-3.3	-9.0	25.3	40.3	1.0	0.0	1.4	0.0
2 Tax threshold as percentage of average wage	40.7	36.0	36.6	36.5	33.6	31.2	39.8	55.0	50.3	47.3	47.6	53.7
3 Tax threshold as percentage of minimum wage	131.3	136.9	102.0	99.2	89.4	85.5	124.7	174.0	136.5	117.7	115.3	125.2
4 Real change in basic old-age pension (per cent)	-0.7	1.4	17.0	10.0	1.7	-1.1	2.0	-0.1	10.8	9.5	1.4	-0.1
5 Basic old-age and survivor's pensions as percentage of average wage[b]	12.1	12.4	13.7	14.5	14.0	14.0	15.1	14.7	14.8	15.3	15.4	15.9
6 Real change in minimum guaranteed income (per cent)	-0.6	10.8	9.5	10.4	1.0	-2.8	10.3	6.5	-6.1	9.0	0.6	-3.3
7 Minimum guaranteed income as per cent of average wage[b]	20.5	22.9	23.7	25.1	24.2	23.7	27.5	28.9	24.6	25.2	25.2	25.4
8 Real change in child allowance point[c] (per cent)	-8.3	-12.0	-6.7	-3.5	-2.7	-14.4	10.2	37.0	0.0	0.6	2.0	0.0
9 Child allowance point[c] as percentage of average wage	3.2	2.8	2.8	2.8	2.6	2.2	2.5	3.4	3.1	2.9	2.9	3.0
10 Real change in child allowances for families with four children (per cent)	-7.5	-10.6	2.1	3.3	3.7	-3.8	13.5	36.0	0.0	0.7	2.6	0.0
11 Child allowance as percentage of the average wage[d]	20.3	18.3	17.6	17.5	17.3	16.8	19.6	26.3	23.8	22.5	23.0	23.4

Notes:

[a] Calculated to fit the period of the Income Survey, which was not identical to the calendar year.

[b] For a single person.

[c] Child allowances are defined in terms of child allowance points, the number of which varies with family size.

[d] Also includes family allowance for veterans; only about 60 per cent of all large families receive family allowance for veterans.

erosion (by means of a temporary suspension of cost-of-living wage incre-
ments), a devaluation of the local currency followed by price regulation and
credit restrictions. This policy resulted in a drastic curb in inflation to a level
of less than 20 per cent during the years 1986–90. However, the emergency
policy also led to the expansion of unemployment. The unemployment rate
jumped, from 2.9 per cent in 1979 to 4.8 per cent in 1980, then to 6–7 per
cent in 1984–6, finally reaching 9–9.5 per cent in 1989–90. The initial jump
in unemployment in 1980 stemmed apparently from a restrictive budget
policy adopted by the government at that time. After the implementation
of the stabilisation policy, unemployment continued to expand, mainly
because freezing the foreign exchange rate (following a one-time devaluation of the currency) and sharp monetary restraint, which considerably
increased local interest rates, led to the financial breakdowns of firms. The
massive wave of immigration to Israel from the former Soviet Union
towards the end of the 1980s sharply increased the size of the labour force,
intensifying the unemployment problem.

Throughout the period of investigation, GDP per capita increased on
average 1.4 per cent annually (in real terms), and private consumption per
capita 2.6 per cent, the main increase occurring during the stabilisation
period. The real gross average wage (per employee-post) increased 1.9 per
cent annually on average. Real wages increased substantially in 1981–3 and
1986–8 but eroded in other years, especially in 1980 (when inflation accelerated), in 1985 (as part of government policy) and in 1989–90 (when
unemployment expanded). The years 1980 and 1984–5 also witnessed a
dramatic decrease in the minimum wage level, both in real terms and relative to the average wage.

National Insurance Institute (NII) benefit payments, which constitute
more than 80 per cent of total transfer payments in Israel, rose from an
amount equivalent to 6.3 per cent of GNP in 1979, to 8.2 per cent in 1990,
the main increases occurring in 1980–1 and 1985–6. As a percentage of disposable income, NII benefits fell, from 11.1 per cent in 1979 to 8.9 per cent
in 1984, but rose to 13 per cent in 1990. Over the whole period, NII benefit
payments per capita increased on average almost 5 per cent annually (in real
terms). This rate of increase was more or less the same for all NII benefits
with the exception of child allowances, unemployment benefits and income
support benefits. Child allowance payments per capita increased by less
than 1 per cent annually, whereas unemployment and income support benefits, the two major programmes guaranteeing income for the unemployed,
increased almost 20 per cent annually. The relatively large increase in total
NII benefit payments is attributed to a rise in the NII real benefit level and
to the number of NII benefit recipients increasing at a faster rate than
population growth. Since most NII benefits are related either to the average

wage in the economy or to the recipient's previous earnings and are adjusted over time according to the changes occurring in the average wage, the real increase in the NII benefit level is partially explained by the increase in real wages throughout the period. Moreover, government policy aimed at adjusting the benefit level more frequently and at temporarily taking account of changes in the price level and in wages through the adjustment mechanism. This policy, which was adopted whenever inflation surged or the real average wage was eroded, was more favourable towards the elderly and low-income families entitled to the minimum income guaranteed by the NII than towards other beneficiaries. In contrast, the updating mechanism of child allowances changed only once, in 1981, when the frequency of adjustment to the price level was raised from twice to four times a year. Therefore, child allowances suffered from continuous erosion during the inflationary period, reaching their lowest level in 1984. Only after the implementation of the stabilisation policy did the real value of the allowance point increase sharply, by almost 50 per cent.

To complete the picture, I will now describe the main changes in the direct tax system – income tax and NII contributions. The indexation mechanism for income tax brackets and tax credits (which is the same as for child allowances) remained almost unchanged during the inflationary period. Therefore, as inflation accelerated, nominal incomes were driven into higher tax brackets, the average tax rate rose and real net income eroded. The increase in the average tax rate was greater in the middle- and high-income ranges. Moreover, the failure to properly adjust income tax parameters led to a decline in the tax threshold, which is determined by the lowest marginal tax rate and personal tax credits. Consequently, more low-income individuals began to pay income taxes. Also, by the end of 1982, the maximum income liable to NII contributions was raised from twice to three times the average wage, a rise which further increased the average tax rate.

Contrary to that during the inflationary period, the government policy since 1985 resulted in a gradual reduction in the average tax rate. First, with the drastic curb on inflation, income tax brackets and tax credits increased in real terms, while wages were eroded as part of the stabilisation policy. Second, in mid 1984 the lowest marginal tax rate was reduced, from 25 per cent to 20 per cent, while in 1987 the 60 per cent and 50 per cent marginal tax rates were abolished, and the highest marginal tax rate was set at 48 per cent. Third, to reduce the regressiveness of steps taken in 1987, in 1990 the government introduced special tax credits, determined as a declining (with income) percentage of the tax liability up to a given income ceiling. Fourth, in 1990 the government abolished a special tax (10 per cent on tax liability) imposed in 1985 on taxpayers with very high incomes. Overall, these steps reduced the average income tax rate for middle- and high-income taxpayers but raised the tax threshold. For a married taxpayer whose spouse is not working, this rose to 65 per cent of the average wage, as compared with 31 per cent in 1984.

In sum, the 1980s were characterised by an intense inflationary tide followed by price stabilisation at low inflation rates, expanding unemployment, moderate real wage increases, decreased tax burden and restrained economic growth. NII benefit payments grew substantially, in real terms and relative to GDP, to disposable income and to wages. By the end of the decade, a larger part of NII benefits reached the elderly, the unemployed and low-income families.

3   Trends in income inequality

In analysing the trends in income distribution during the period under investigation, three measures of income inequality have been applied: the Gini coefficient, the extended Gini coefficient and the coefficient of variation. These different income inequality measures reflect different sensitivities to income changes at different ranges of the income distribution. The Gini coefficient is relatively more sensitive to income changes at the middle range, whereas the extended Gini coefficient attaches higher weights to variations at the lower tail of the income distribution (Kakwani 1980).[4] The coefficient of variation is more sensitive to income changes at the upper and the lower tails.

The major methodological issues in the analysis of income distribution relate to the choice of the unit of analysis, the type of income measured, the weighting of the units and the way by which they are ranked. In this study the unit under investigation is the household (hereafter 'family'). The incomes measured are the factor, gross and net incomes, all adjusted to family size using the equivalent scale adopted by the NII and the Israeli Central Bureau of Statistics.[5] In the calculation of the income inequality measures, each family is weighted by its number of persons and is ranked by the relevant adjusted income.

Table 7.3 presents the absolute values of the Gini coefficient, the extended Gini coefficient (for $k=3$) and the coefficient of variation for the three categories of income. To emphasise trends in inequality in the distribution of net income registered by different measures, their values in the various years have been normalised by their value in 1979. The normalised values of the inequality measures, which indicate percentage changes vis-à-vis the base year, are presented in figure 7.1. The figure reveals that all measures follow identical trends (excluding 1990) but of different magnitude. A careful analysis of the year-by-year changes shows relatively large differences in the extent of income inequality between the inflationary period

Table 7.3. *The effect of benefit and income tax systems on income distribution: selected indicators*

Indicator	1979	1980	1983	1984	1985	1987	1988	1989	1990
Gini coefficient									
1 Factor income	0.433	0.434	0.443	0.475	0.468	0.459	0.457	0.474	0.480
2 Gross income	0.366	0.369	0.362	0.400	0.373	0.370	0.370	0.377	0.376
3 Net income	0.318	0.324	0.302	0.328	0.312	0.319	0.322	0.324	0.326
4 (1)–(3) as per cent of (1)	26.6	25.4	31.8	31.0	33.3	30.5	29.6	31.7	32.0
5 (2)–(3) as per cent of (2)	13.1	12.2	16.7	17.9	16.5	13.9	12.9	14.0	13.0
Extended Gini coefficient (k=3)									
6 Factor income	0.693	0.695	0.708	0.741	0.736	0.727	0.729	0.743	0.755
7 Gross income	0.570	0.576	0.564	0.610	0.570	0.574	0.577	0.575	0.579
8 Net income	0.506	0.515	0.487	0.523	0.496	0.514	0.520	0.513	0.524
9 (6)–(8) as per cent of (6)	27.0	26.0	31.2	29.4	32.7	29.3	28.6	30.9	30.7
10 (7)–(8) as per cent of (7)	11.2	10.7	12.7	14.3	13.1	10.6	9.8	10.8	9.6
Coefficient of variation									
11 Factor income	0.840.	0.824	0.847	0.953	0.926	0.907	0.888	0.952	0.942
12 Gross income	0.731	0.720	0.708	0.822	0.766	0.752	0.754	0.790	0.758
13 Net income	0.640	0.653	0.566	0.638	0.611	0.617	0.653	0.649	0.626
14 (11)–(13) as per cent of (11)	23.8	20.8	33.2	33.0	34.0	32.0	26.5	31.8	33.5
15 (12)–(13) as per cent of (12)	12.5	9.3	20.0	22.4	20.0	18.0	13.5	17.8	17.4

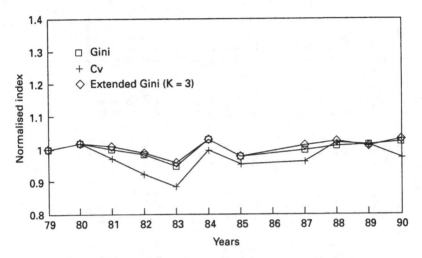

Figure 7.1 Measures of inequality (net income)

1979–84 and the price stabilisation period 1985–90 as well as within each period.

During the five-year inflationary period, there were differences between developments in 1980 and 1984, when inflation jumped to higher levels, and developments in 1981–3, when inflation was high but relatively steady. According to all measures, after a 2 per cent rise in net income inequality in 1980, the years 1981–3 witnessed a continuous decline: The Gini coefficient fell 6.8 per cent, and the extended Gini coefficient 5.5 per cent. The coefficient of variation declined even more – 13.3 per cent. In 1984, net income inequality rose again and to an even higher level than that of 1980 – 9 per cent and 7 per cent, respectively, according to the former two measures and 13 per cent according to the latter. These differences indicate that incomes at the upper tail of the distribution, to which the coefficient of variation is more sensitive, rose (or declined) at higher rates than did lower incomes.

The striking differences between developments in 1980 and 1984 and in 1981–3 are mainly due to the effects of inflation on government welfare programmes and on the income tax system, as well as to the rise in unemployment. When the different categories of income are compared (table 7.3), one finds that despite a 2–3 per cent increase in inequality in the distribution of factor income between 1980 and 1983, according to all measures inequality in the distribution of gross income declined 1.5–2 per cent. Furthermore, as mentioned above net income inequality declined even more. These findings indicate that the inequality-reducing effect of transfer payments and especially that of direct taxes strengthened between 1980 and

1983. For example, in 1983 transfer payments and income taxes reduced the Gini coefficient 32 per cent, compared with 25 per cent in 1980.

The increased contribution of transfer payments was a result of improvements in the level of benefits (mainly to low-income families) following the adjustment of indexation mechanisms to accelerating inflation. The inequality-reducing effect of direct taxes strengthened, first, due to the increased progressivity of the income tax system: erosion of the tax threshold and brackets (in real terms and relative to the average wage) drove nominal incomes into higher tax brackets, thus raising the tax rate – especially for middle- and high-income ranges. Second, raising the maximum income liable to NII contributions (from twice to three times the average wage) further increased the inequality-reducing effect of direct taxes. Comparing gross and net inequality measures, table 7.3 shows that the direct tax system reduced the Gini coefficient 12.2 per cent in 1980. This reduction increased to 16.7 per cent in 1983 and to 18 per cent in 1984 as a result of the failure to properly adjust income tax parameters to inflation.

The other inequality measures indicate the same development. This is especially accentuated by the coefficient of variation, which is more sensitive than the others to changes at the higher range of the distribution. As this measure indicates, direct taxes reduced gross income inequality 9.3 per cent in 1980. This percentage rose continuously, to more than 22 per cent in 1984. In spite of the growing contribution of direct taxes to reducing income inequality in 1984, the overall impact of transfer payments and direct taxes decreased. This was due mainly to renewed erosion in social security benefits caused by the inflationary tide that year. In 1984, the extent of inequality in the distribution of factor income, as measured by the Gini coefficient, rose 7 per cent, but that of gross income rose 10 per cent.

In 1985, the year the stabilisation policy was implemented, the trend reversed again, and net income inequality decreased 4–5 per cent according to most measures. This decrease emanated from a rise in benefit levels resulting not only from the introduction of temporary special indexation arrangements in 1984 to cope with the soaring inflation but also from the successful curb of inflation in the second half of 1985. While employees suffered a deliberate erosion in their real wages as part of government policy, NII low-income beneficiaries enjoyed real increases in their benefits. The inequality-reducing effect of transfer payments remained more or less stable until 1990. In contrast, income tax brackets increased in real terms after annual inflation slowed to 20 per cent and less which, combined with the abolition of the two highest marginal tax rates in 1987, led to a lower average tax rate, thereby reducing the progressivity of the income tax system and its favourable effect on income inequality. As shown in table 7.3, the rate of reduction in gross income inequality attributed to direct taxes

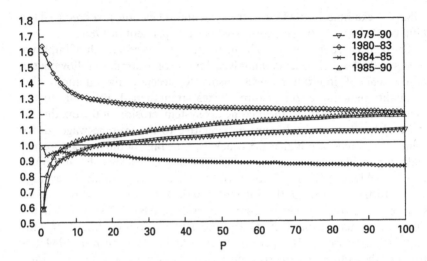

Figure 7.2 The ratio of real absolute income between two selected years, by percentile

declined, according to the Gini coefficient, from 18 per cent in 1984 to 13 per cent in 1990. Net income inequality in 1987–8 rose 3–5 per cent according to most measures despite a slight decrease in factor income inequality (in part a result of a significant rise in the minimum wage level) and in gross income inequality. In contrast, in 1989–90, with the expansion of unemployment, the factor income inequality rose about 4 per cent according to most measures and was accompanied by only a very small increase in net income inequality.

In sum, during the 12-year period 1979–90, inequality in the distribution of factor income increased 9–12 per cent,[6] depending on the inequality measure, but net income inequality rose only slightly, by 2–4 per cent. The coefficient of variation for net income even declined 2 per cent. The overall impact of transfers and direct taxes in reducing income inequality increased throughout this period: in 1990, transfer payments and direct taxes reduced the Gini coefficient 32 per cent, compared with 27 per cent in 1979. While the inequality-reducing effect of transfer payments increased, the contribution of direct taxes to reducing income inequality remained almost unchanged, according to the Gini coefficient.

Figure 7.2 shows, for each percentile of the income distribution, the increase in real absolute income adjusted for population growth (that is, the increase in real income per capita) between selected pairs of years. The continuous decrease in net income inequality from 1980 to 1983 was accompanied by an increase in real income per capita. As is clearly evident from figure 7.2, the rate of increase in real income declined continuously with the percentile of income distribution. The decrease in income inequality between 1984 and 1985 was, in contrast, accompanied by a decrease in real incomes. However, the decrease at the bottom of the distribution was smaller than that at the middle and the top of the distribution. Between 1979 and 1990, and mainly between 1985 and 1990, when income inequality rose, families in the low percentiles enjoyed less of an increase (and even suffered declines) in real income than did other families.

4   Trends in poverty

Basic trends and year-on-year changes in poverty are examined here using five poverty indices: the head count ratio H, the poverty gap ratio G, and the poverty indices proposed by Sen (1979) PS, Kakwani (1980) PK and Foster, Greer and Thorbecke (1984) PF. The first two indices, H and G, are the commonly used measures of poverty in empirical studies, although their weaknesses have been widely discussed in the literature. The head count ratio H does not reflect the 'depth' of poverty (i.e., how poor the poor are), and the poverty gap does not reflect the 'breadth' of poverty (i.e., the size of the poor population). Neither is sensitive to 'relative deprivation' among the poor (i.e., income inequality among the poor). The other three indices – PS, PK and PF – reflect all three dimensions of overall poverty. Each of these indices has the general form of the poverty index proposed by Sen, i.e., a normalised weighted sum of the poverty gaps of all poor individuals. The weights may be either the position of the poor individual in the poverty ladder, the poverty gap itself or both. Rank order weights have been applied in PS and PK, and poverty gap weights have been applied in PF.[7]

The poverty line applied to this study is based on the relative approach to poverty, by which income is considered 'low' and a population group 'poor' only with respect to the incomes or the well-being of the population as a whole. Aside from the well-known advantages of this over the absolute approach, this approach is also in line with the principle which guides the setting of most social security benefits in Israel (i.e., as a percentage of the average wage). More specifically, the poverty line in this study has been defined as 50 per cent of the median equivalent net income (using the Israeli equivalence scale). This poverty line is frequently used by social researchers in Israel; it is also officially adopted by the government in its poverty alleviation policy.

The head count ratio has been calculated in terms of families as well as of persons; the poverty gap ratio and the PS, PK and PF measures have been calculated on the basis of the family equivalent income, each family being weighted by its number of persons.[8]

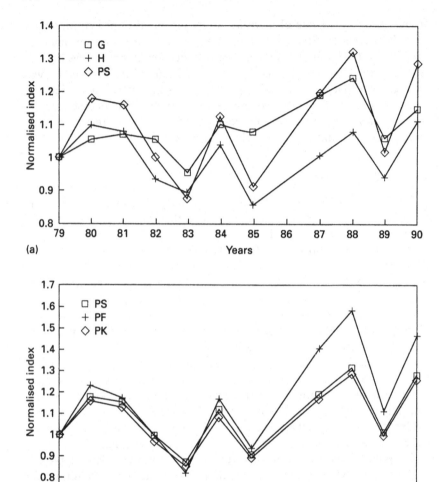

Figure 7.3 Poverty measures (net income)

Figures 7.3a and 7.3b illustrate the trends in poverty as indicated by the five poverty indices, calculated for net income and normalised by their values in 1979. As can be seen, all indices exhibit the same trends. In the inflationary period 1979–84, poverty declined gradually in 1981–3 but increased in 1980 and 1984. The head count ratio (in terms of persons), which rose from 15.2 per cent in 1979 to 16.7 per cent in 1980, declined to 13.6 per cent in 1983, and the poverty gap, which rose from 25.6 per cent of the poverty line in 1979 to 27 per cent in 1980, declined to 24 per cent of the poverty line in 1983. In 1984, the trend reversed again; the head count ratio increased to 15.8 per cent, and the poverty gap ratio rose to 28.2 per cent of the poverty line. In 1985, poverty decreased again, and the head count ratio reached its lowest level, 13 per cent. The poverty gap, however, remained almost unchanged. During 1987–90, when inflation was low and stable, poverty continued to fluctuate, increasing in 1987 and 1988, decreasing in 1989, then increasing again in 1990. In 1990, 16.9 per cent of the total population were poor, and their poverty gap was almost 30 per cent of the poverty line.

During the stabilisation period 1985–90, the head count ratio rose 30 per cent, and the poverty gap 6.5 per cent. Over the entire decade, the head count ratio rose more moderately, by 6 per cent, whereas the poverty gap increased at a higher rate, 15 per cent. The three poverty indices PS, PF and PK, that combine (and weight) all three dimensions of poverty, showed even greater changes in poverty. For example, according to the PS measure poverty increased 28 per cent.

To assess the combined effects of transfer payments and direct taxes on poverty, table 7.4 presents the values of three selected poverty measures for the three income categories (factor, gross and net). Factor income poverty increased gradually during the entire period mainly due to the expansion of unemployment, although the rise in the minimum wage level in 1981 and during the latter years of the 1980s probably helped moderate the adverse effects on poverty of growing unemployment.[9] In 1990, the head count ratio (in terms of persons) was 28 per cent higher than in 1979–80, the poverty gap ratio almost 14 per cent higher and the PS measure more than 40 per cent higher. However, net income poverty as indicated by all measures (with the exception of the poverty gap ratio) rose by much lower rates. This was due to the increased contribution of transfers to reduce poverty (from 1981) as well as to the gradual weakening of the adverse effect of direct taxes on poverty (from 1984).

As an illustration of the combined effects of taxes and transfers on poverty we will consider the head count ratio. Inspection of the factor, gross and net income poverty levels reveals that in 1990 transfers reduced poverty almost 50 per cent, compared with 44 per cent in 1979 and 1980, and direct taxes increased poverty only 10 per cent in 1990, compared with almost 24 per cent in 1980. The combined effect of transfers and direct taxes was to reduce poverty 44.4 per cent in 1990, compared with only 31 per cent in 1980. In 1980, the poverty reducing effect of transfers was the lowest, and the adverse effect of direct taxes was the greatest. The decline in poverty in 1981–3 is attributed only to the growing effect of transfers. In contrast, in 1984 transfers were less efficient in reducing poverty. The adverse effect of

Table 7.4 The effect of public transfers and income tax on poverty: selected indicators

Indicator	1979	1980	1983	1984	1985	1987	1988	1989	1990
Head count – families (per cent)									
1 Factor income	27.8	28.1	29.8	31.0	31.3	32.6	32.6	33.0	34.3
2 Gross income	16.4	13.9	11.2	13.1	10.3	12.7	13.3	11.4	13.4
3 Net income	17.7	15.7	12.6	14.8	11.4	13.8	14.2	12.8	14.3
4 (1)–(3) as per cent of (1)	36.3	44.0	57.7	52.3	63.6	57.8	56.4	61.2	58.3
Head count – persons (per cent)									
1 Factor income	23.8	24.2	24.3	25.9	26.3	27.3	28.0	28.0	30.4
2 Gross income	12.9	13.5	11.1	13.3	11.4	13.7	14.8	12.6	15.3
3 Net income	15.2	16.7	13.6	15.8	13.0	15.3	16.4	14.3	16.9
4 (1)–(3) as per cent of (1)	36.1	31.0	44.0	39.0	50.6	44.0	41.5	49.0	44.4
Poverty gap (per cent)									
1 Factor income	58.4	58.6	61.4	62.6	66.5	63.2	63.7	64.6	66.4
2 Gross income	27.8	29.2	25.9	30.2	28.8	32.2	33.2	29.0	30.9
3 Net income	25.6	27.0	24.4	28.2	27.6	30.4	31.8	27.1	29.4
4 (1)–(3) as per cent of (1)	56.2	53.9	60.6	55.0	54.3	51.9	50.2	58.0	55.7
PS[1]									
1 Factor income	0.188	0.191	0.198	0.213	0.227	0.228	0.235	0.238	0.262
2 Gross income	0.052	0.058	0.042	0.056	0.047	0.063	0.070	0.053	0.068
3 Net income	0.056	0.066	0.049	0.063	0.051	0.067	0.074	0.057	0.072
4 (1)–(3) as per cent of (1)	70.2	65.4	75.2	70.4	77.5	70.6	68.3	76.1	72.5
PF[2]									
1 Factor income	0.113	0.115	0.124	0.133	0.151	0.146	0.151	0.156	0.175
2 Gross income	0.016	0.020	0.013	0.018	0.015	0.023	0.026	0.018	0.024
3 Net income	0.017	0.021	0.014	0.024	0.016	0.024	0.027	0.019	0.025
4 (1)–(3) as per cent of (1)	85.0	81.7	88.7	82.0	89.0	83.6	82.2	88.0	86.0

Notes:
[1] PS is the poverty index proposed by Sen (1979).
[2] PF is the poverty index proposed by Foster, Greer and Thorbecke (1984).

direct taxes on poverty remained relatively strong during 1979–84, mainly because the income tax threshold eroded gradually, from 41 per cent of the average wage in 1979 to 31 per cent in 1984.

In 1985, the effect of transfers in reducing poverty strengthened significantly, and the adverse effect on poverty of direct taxes declined. In that year, the combined effect of transfers and direct taxes in reducing poverty was the highest, and a decline in net income poverty occurred despite a rise in factor income poverty. In 1987–90, the adverse effect of direct taxes continued to diminish, but the reducing effect of transfers on poverty weakened in 1987 and remained more or less stable thereafter.

Contrary to the rise in the percentage of poor persons in the total population between 1979 and 1990, the percentage of poor families declined, in terms of net income (table 7.4). This stemmed from the fact that poverty decreased sharply among elderly families but not among families with children. Tables 7.5 and 7.6 present selected indicators of changes in net income poverty among the elderly and large families, respectively. On average, during the decade 60–5 per cent of the elderly had a factor income lower than the poverty line. Since most of the elderly depend for their livelihoods on social security benefits (which constitute almost 90 per cent of their gross income), they are highly vulnerable to adverse changes in the level of benefits. Moreover, since the minimum income guaranteed to the elderly is set very close to the poverty line, even small changes in that income lead to relatively large changes in the head count ratio (but only to small changes in the poverty gap ratio). In 1979, the erosion of benefits was the deepest, and poverty among the elderly was the highest: 35 per cent had net income below the poverty line. Improvement in NII benefits in 1980–2 and again in 1985–6 led to a gradual decline in poverty. In 1982 and in 1985–90, transfers raised the income of 80 per cent of the poor elderly above the poverty line, and only 10–14 per cent of the elderly remained poor.

In contrast, families with children, the majority with members participating in the labour force, are more vulnerable to the adverse consequences of unemployment. The factor head count ratio of large families rose, from 43–45 per cent in 1979–87, to 50–51 per cent in the last three years. The increase in the level of NII benefits, particularly in the value of child allowances, and in the tax threshold during the second half of the 1980s did not suffice to offset the rise in factor income poverty. Poverty among large families remained high, and by the end of the decade 35 per cent of them were still poor.

5   Summary

We have examined trends in income inequality and poverty in Israel during the 12-year period 1979–90. The results show that the extent of inequality in

Table 7.5 Indicators of net income poverty among the elderly

Indicator	1979	1980	1981	1982	1983	1984	1985	1987	1988	1989	1990
1 Head count ratio	34.8	25.3	25.8	10.3	18.9	20.6	13.1	14.0	13.2	10.5	11.8
2 Poverty gap ratio	19.7	18.9	16.7	19.6	17.2	22.0	22.7	20.4	19.4	17.9	20.2
3 The elderly poor as a percentage of the poor population											
families	53.6	39.1	40.7	18.4	37.5	36.5	23.7	21.1	21.0	18.4	17.9
persons	29.0	18.3	19.5	9.2	17.6	16.8	11.9	10.9	9.7	8.8	8.4
4 Reduction in H after transfers and direct taxes	42.4	57.4	58.9	83.8	71.3	69.0	80.6	78.0	79.3	83.3	81.3

Table 7.6 *Indicators of net income poverty among large families*[a]

Indicator	1979	1980	1981	1982	1983	1984	1985	1987	1988	1989	1990
1 Head count ratio	26.4	36.2	36.4	35.4	31.0	34.4	31.2	26.6	36.4	28.0	35.3
2 Poverty gap ratio	24.7	29.8	30.4	26.9	24.0	30.6	29.1	26.1	27.6	26.1	25.3
3 Poor large families as a percentage of the poor population											
families	11.4	17.2	13.9	23.8	16.4	15.9	16.8	14.7	17.2	14.5	17.3
persons	30.5	37.8	32.1	41.5	37.0	36.3	34.5	29.6	34.4	29.2	34.3
4 Reduction in *H* after transfers and direct taxes	43.5	18.2	18.3	25.0	28.0	22.0	30.0	39.4	27.5	42.3	31.1

Note:
[a] Families with four or more children.

the distribution of factor income increased 9–12 per cent, depending on the inequality measure used. This increase is attributed to the expansion of unemployment, widening of wage disparities and increased inequality in the distribution of occupational pensions. It is likely that wage earners in strongly unionised industries succeeded more than others in protecting their real wages from high and unanticipated inflation. Moreover, when unemployment expanded, real wages declined, the greatest decline occurring in less-unionised, low-paying or non-professional labour-intensive industries. Evidently, these occurrences were moderated by the rise in the minimum wage level following a new minimum wage agreement in 1980 and minimum wage legislation in 1987. However, there have been relatively small changes in the extent of inequality in the distribution of gross and net income. Between 1979 and 1990, most measures rose slightly, by 2–4 per cent. The combined effect of transfers and direct taxes in reducing income inequality strengthened throughout this period. While the inequality–reducing effect of direct taxes grew stronger during the inflationary period 1979–84 and lessened thereafter, the inequality-reducing effect of transfers grew only moderately during the first period and strengthened during the second.

The trends in poverty were more or less similar. Poverty as measured by factor income increased substantially, among persons as well as among families, whereas net income poverty rose only slightly among persons and even declined among families. Government efforts to elaborate the indexation mechanisms of NII benefits, especially those paid to the elderly and to other low-income families, increased the contribution of transfers to reducing poverty. Moreover, the stabilisation policy was carried out with special attention to maintaining the purchasing power of NII benefits paid to weak populations, while wage earners suffered from substantial wage erosion. Also, the adverse effect on poverty of direct taxes strengthened in 1979–83 but weakened thereafter as a result of a sharp rise in the income tax threshold. Consequently, the percentage of persons in the total population with net income below the poverty line rose only from 15.2 per cent in 1979 to 16.9 per cent in 1990, and the percentage of families declined from 17.7 per cent to 14.3 per cent, respectively. While poverty rose among families with children, it declined significantly among the elderly. Thus, by the end of the decade the core of poverty in Israel shifted from the elderly to families with children, whom should be given high priority in the determination of anti-poverty policy.

Appendix   Income inequality and poverty in the total population, including the self-employed

As mentioned earlier, the analysis in this chapter is based on Income Survey data which relate only to households whose head is either an employee or

Table 7AI *Gini coefficients for the distribution of net income (Family Expenditure Surveys)*

	1979	1986	1992
Total	0.318	0.322	0.322
Employees and	0.314	0.319	0.324
non-workers[a]	(0.318)	(0.319)	(0.327)
Self-employed	0.338	0.345	0.305

Note:
[a] The coefficients in parentheses are those derived from the Income Surveys for each respective year.

Table 7AII *Net income head count ratio (percentage of persons. Family Expenditure Surveys)*

	1979	1986	1992
Total	17.4	16.5	15.0
Employees and	17.8	16.6	16.4
non-workers[a]	(15.9)	(15.3)	(17.2)
Self-employed	15.7	16.0	6.2

Note:
[a] The coefficients in parentheses are derived from the Income Surveys for each respective year.

does not work, hence excluding the self-employed. Another data source enabling us to follow trends in poverty and income inequality in Israel is the Family Expenditure Survey, which is however conducted less frequently (every 5–6 years). This survey covers all households, including the self-employed, in urban localities (defined more widely than in the Income Survey). Table 7AI presents the Gini coefficients derived from the last three Family Expenditure Surveys (1979, 1986 and 1992). The table shows, first, that the Gini coefficients for the employee and non-working population derived from the Family Expenditure Surveys are almost the same as those derived from the Income Surveys. Second, the extent of income inequality was higher among the self-employed (constituting 12–14 per cent of all household heads) than among employees and non-workers in 1979 and 1986, but lower in 1992. Third, the net income distribution of the self-employed was more equal in 1992 than in 1979 and 1986.

As regards poverty, table 7AII shows that the incidence of poverty among the self-employed was only slightly lower than among employees and non-workers in 1979 and 1986 but significantly lower in 1992.

Notes

I am indebted to the editors of this volume, to Gideon Yaniv and to an anonymous referee for many helpful comments and suggestions.

1 For earlier studies on poverty and inequality in Israel during the inflationary period, see Achdut and Bigman 1991, 1993.
2 With the exception of 1986.
3 The Annual Income Survey is conducted as an appendix to the current Labour Force Survey, by which a quarter of those surveyed in the latter are also questioned about their incomes. Although the Labour Force Survey includes the self-employed, income data in the Income Surveys are only provided for employees and non-workers living in urban localities (Jewish or mixed localities with 2,000 or more inhabitants and non-Jewish localities with 10,000 or more inhabitants). About 80 per cent of all households in Israel and 84 per cent of all persons are covered by the Income Survey sample. The sample size and the drop-out rate (refusals to respond, invalidated questionnaires, etc.) vary from year to year. In 1990, for example, the initial sample size (derived from the Labour Force Survey) was about 9,200 households, the drop-out rate being 28 per cent. Excluding the self-employed, the final sample consisted of about 5,900 households of employees and non-workers.
4 The extended Gini coefficient is given by

$$EG(k) = \frac{1}{\mu \phi_n(k)} \sum_{i=1}^{n} (\mu - y_i)(n+1-i)^k,$$

where n is the size of the population, μ is the mean income, y_i is the income of the ith unit $(i=1,...,n)$, k is a sensitivity parameter and $\phi_n(k) = \Sigma i^k$. The extended Gini coefficient is a general class of inequality measures of which the Gini index is a particular member for $k=1$.
5 The equivalence scale is given by:

Number of persons	1	2	3	4	5	6	7	8
Number of standard adults	1.25	2.00	2.65	3.20	3.75	4.25	4.75	5.20

where the weight of each additional person is 0.40.
6 The Income Surveys which serve as a database for this study also reveal that the Gini coefficient for earnings among family head earners grew, from 0.28 in 1979 to 0.32 in 1990, and that the Gini coefficient for the distribution of occupational pensions among pension recipients grew, from 0.58 to 0.60.
7 As shown by the respective authors, the poverty indices may be written in the following form, which emphasises the differences among them:

$$PS = H[G + (1-G)I_p]$$
$$PK = H[G + (1-G)EI_p]$$
$$PF = H[G^2 + (1-G)^2(CV_p)^2],$$

where I_p and EI_p are the Gini and the extended Gini coefficients of income inequality among the poor, respectively, and CV_p is the coefficient of variation of income of the poor. The above formulation of PF holds, however, only when the individual poverty gaps are weighted by the poverty gaps themselves (i.e., raised to the power of 1).

8 In computing PK, the extended Gini coefficient of income inequality among the poor (EI_p) was calculated for $K=3$ (see note 4).

9 While an increase in the minimum wage level could adversely affect employment, and thus poverty, there is no evidence that unemployment actually expanded because of the implied rise in employers' costs. Apparently, government efforts to reduce the costs of labour, for example by lowering employers' social security contribution rates, helped to more than counteract the effects of the former.

References

Achdut, L. and Bigman, D. 1991. 'The Anatomy of Changes in Poverty and Income Inequality Under Rapid Inflation: Israel 1979–1984'. *Structural Change and Economic Dynamics*, 2: 229–43.

1993. 'The Performance of National Insurance Old-Age Benefits'. *Bank of Israel Economic Review* (in English), 66: 53–68.

Foster, J. E., Greer, J. and Thorbecke, E. 1984. 'A Class of Decomposable Poverty Measures'. *Econometrica*, 52: 761–6.

Kakwani, N. C. 1980. 'On a Class of Poverty Measures'. *Econometrica*, 48: 437–46.

Sen, A. K. 1979. 'Issues in the Measurement of Poverty'. *Scandinavian Journal of Economics*, 81: 285–302.

8 Changes in inequality in Greece in the 1970s and the 1980s

PANOS TSAKLOGLOU

1 Introduction

During the first three post-war decades, the Greek economy was among the fastest-growing in the world. At that time, the economic debate in Greece primarily emphasised growth, and distributional issues appeared rarely at the top of the agenda. The picture changed dramatically in the late 1970s and, especially, in the early 1980s. Growth rates were low or negative, while acute claims for redistribution were raised by several population groups. Inequality became a central issue in public debate. Although there was no general agreement regarding the trend in aggregate inequality, there was broad consensus that a large part of inequality in Greece was due to differences between regions and/or differences between urban and rural areas and, to a lesser extent, between occupational groups (Tsakloglou 1988). As a result of the stagnation of the early 1980s and mounting budget deficits, in the late 1980s the emphasis of public debate shifted again towards growth, and distributional issues were relegated accordingly. Nevertheless, recently, partly as a result of several protracted stabilisation programmes which have affected the living standards of large segments of the population, inequality and, for the first time, poverty are on the forefront of public and academic debate in Greece.

This chapter builds on earlier work by the author (Tsakloglou 1988 and 1993) and examines changes in the levels of inequality and welfare in Greece in the 1970s and the 1980s as well as the structure of inequality in Greece using the microdata of three Household Expenditure Surveys (HESs) conducted by the National Statistical Service of Greece (NSSG) in 1974, 1981/2 and 1987/8.[1]

2 A short description of the main macroeconomic developments in the 1970s and 1980s

Greece entered the 1970s under a military dictatorship which lasted from 1967 until 1974. The economic policies pursued by the military junta did

154

not differ dramatically from those pursued during most of the period 1950–67. During that period, growth rates were spectacular (GDP per capita grew at an annual rate of 6.2 per cent from 1950 to 1973), and the economy was transformed rapidly, from an agrarian one to one based on industry and services. Unemployment was kept low by a combination of high international migration (more than one million persons emigrated permanently abroad during the quarter century following World War II) and a transfer of surplus labour from the rural to the urban areas. As a result of the latter and sometimes brutal repression of trade union activity, industrial wages remained low, returns to capital were high, and there were considerable foreign capital inflows, while investment (private and public) accounted for around one-quarter of GDP. At the same time, inflation was below the OECD average. Although no kind of planning – general or indicative – was applied during that period, the state did play an important role in economic life mainly through regulation and, particularly, through tight control of the financial system. Three other areas where the state played an important role were in fixing the exchange rate, in investment in infrastructure and in price support schemes for agricultural products. Most years the budget was balanced, and the welfare state was embryonic.

The situation changed dramatically after 1973. The first oil shock was accompanied by accommodative monetary policies, and at about the same time (1974) Turkey invaded and occupied the northern part of Cyprus in response to a coup staged by the Greek military regime on the island. These events brought Greece and Turkey to the brink of a war and resulted in the collapse of the dictatorship. As a consequence of these factors, prices increased rapidly, while output declined for the first time in the post-war period (between 1973 and 1974, output fell 4 per cent while inflation rose to almost 27 per cent). Furthermore, since that time relations between Greece and Turkey have been sour, and Greece devotes around 6 per cent of GDP to military expenditures, by far the highest proportion among NATO countries.

After the restoration of democracy in 1974, Greece had conservative governments between 1974 and 1981, while the socialists were in power between 1981 and 1989. Between 1974 and 1979, the economy continued to grow at rates that were respectable but lower than those of the preceding period: GDP per capita grew around 4 per cent per annum. At the same time, the activity of trade unions intensified, real wages and the share of salaries and wages in national income rose, profitability declined and the share of investment in GDP started to decline – a process which accelerated after 1979. Towards the late 1970s and particularly in the early 1980s, highly expansionary fiscal and monetary policies were pursued. These policies resulted in high inflation rates and rapid increases in the budget and balance of payments deficits, while output was hardly affected and unemployment rose substantially. Since 1974, inflation rates have been double digit, sometimes above 20 per cent, and since 1979 the average growth rate has been around 1 per cent. Within less than ten years, the accumulated public debt shot up from less than 40 per cent to more than 100 per cent of GDP. Two major macroeconomic stabilisation programmes have been undertaken since the mid 1980s to cope with this clearly unsustainable situation; one programme was judged partially successful but was abandoned after two years of implementation. In a typical case of clientelism, most of the increase in government spending was devoted to consumption (mainly hiring personnel in the public sector and other payroll increases), while for many years, along with private investment, public investment was declining both as a proportion of GDP and in absolute terms. On the revenue side, indirect taxation accounts for around 70 per cent of total tax revenues. Direct taxation plays a rather marginal role, and tax evasion is widespread. Among the top contributors to the budget deficit is the deficit of the social security system and, particularly, the part of it which is related to pensions. In the 1980s a combination of the ageing population, expansion of the social security system and early exit of large segments of the working population from the labour market led to an explosion in social security spending, while at the same time social security contributions rose very modestly. By the late 1980s, the deficit of the social security system was as high as 4 per cent of GDP.

However, the major event of the 1980s was the accession of Greece to the EC as a full member (1981). The main beneficiaries among the Greek population were farmers, who have enjoyed higher prices for their products through the Common Agricultural Policy, while the losers can be found in the industrial sector, which no longer enjoys protection from EC competition. Moreover, transfers from the EC cover a significant part of the chronic current account deficit. By the late 1980s, the net inflow of resources from the EC was as high as 6.5 per cent of GDP.[2]

In the final section, I attempt to link these developments with the results of the next sections concerning the level and trends in inequality in the 1970s and 1980s.

3   Data and methodology

The first choice one faces when dealing with economic inequality is 'inequality in the distribution of what?' Usually, when studying inequality we are ultimately interested in inequality in the distribution of welfare. Since welfare is not directly observable, a reasonably close approximation to it has to be used instead. Most empirical studies use either current consumption or current income as an indicator of welfare. Current consumption is usually considered a better approximation to life-cycle income than current income because individuals and households tend to save and dissave in different periods of their life-cycles in an attempt to smoothe out their consumption to maximise welfare (Sen 1976 and Deaton 1980), while current income is sometimes considered a better indicator of the ability of an individual or a household to achieve a particular welfare level. Nevertheless, the data used in empirical distributional studies can usually be considered, at best, approximations to the concepts of income and consumption a researcher would wish to use.

The existing studies on inequality in Greece use either grouped data from tax returns or HES data. The data from tax returns cover a long period (from 1959 to date) but have a number of disadvantages. Firstly, tax legislation does not require every household or working person to file a tax return. Large segments of the population (agricultural households, households with annual income below a certain threshold and so on) are effectively exempted from the payment of income taxes and, hence, do not file tax returns. In the early 1960s, only 10 per cent of the households were filing tax returns. Even though that proportion had risen to 75 per cent by the late 1980s, a large number of households are still excluded from the sample of the studies which use tax return data (these samples come, at best, from truncated distributions). Secondly, income in kind, consumption of own production, capital gains and some transfer payments are not included in the concept of income used by the tax authorities. Hence, this concept is not appropriate for welfare comparisons across households, especially in the case of Greece, where a considerable proportion of the total income of the poorest households is in the form of income in kind. Thirdly, it is widely accepted among Greek economists, politicians and the general public that tax evasion in Greece is widespread. Therefore, even the existing data may be of low quality and taxed income is just a small fraction of personal income reported in the National Accounts. Of the studies which utilise grouped tax returns data,[3] the most comprehensive are those of Livada (1988, 1991) who found that during the last three decades the income shares of the top and bottom population quintiles were declining while those of the middle-income classes were rising. As a result of intersecting Lorenz curves, some inequality indices record a declining and others a rising trend in inequality. Further, some of these studies assert that there is a high level of regional inequality in Greece. Unlike the tax returns data, which are available on an annual basis, there have been only three national HESs in Greece (1974, 1982 and 1988), and hence it is difficult to reach safe conclusions about the trend of inequality using these data sets. The HES data sets come from multistage stratified random samples covering the entire non-institutional population. Their samples are between

6,000 and 7,500 households. The main findings of the studies which utilise HES data sets[4] are that disparities between population groups do not play a very important role for the determination of aggregate inequality and that the level of inequality in Greece is higher than that of most EC or OECD countries. Moreover, some studies which use grouped HES data claim that there are substantial disparities between urban and rural areas and/or between sectors of economic activity.

The HESs contain both income and consumption expenditure information. In this chapter, consumption expenditure is used as a proxy for the concept of welfare.[5] This choice was dictated by both the theoretical reasons cited above and empirical considerations. The income information in the HESs is considered rather unreliable by the NSSG, and there are large discrepancies between the HES estimates and estimates of the relevant tables of the National Accounts. Furthermore, self-employment is widespread in Greece and, as several studies point out, the variability of the income of households headed by self-employed persons is considerably higher than that of the rest of the population, whereas the variabilities in consumption expenditure by the two groups do not differ substantially. The concept of consumption expenditure used here includes, apart from the value of purchased goods and services, consumption of own production, consumption of income in kind and imputed rent for owner-occupied accommodation evaluated at market prices. Expenditures on some lumpy items with normalisation periods unquestionably longer than the enumeration period of the HESs (one year), such as purchases of cars and home repairs and improvements, are excluded from the concept of consumption expenditure. A few households were removed from the samples on reliability grounds, and the data of each HES are expressed in constant mid-year prices in order to remove the impact of inflation. The distributions used are distributions of equivalent consumption expenditure per capita. Equivalence scales for the cost of children were estimated using three different models (Engel, Rothbarth and Barten, described in Tsakloglou 1991a and 1991b). Based on their results, weights of 1.00, 0.40 and 0.25 were assigned to each adult, child aged 6–16 and child aged less than 6, respectively. Then, the total consumption expenditure of each household was divided by the number of equivalent adults in it and the distribution of equivalent consumption expenditure per capita was derived by assigning the resulting figure to each household member.

4   Aggregate inequality and welfare

Our investigation begins by looking at the expenditure shares of the population deciles in table 8.1. The first three columns of the table report the percentage expenditure shares of deciles of the population ranked from the lowest to the highest expenditure person for 1974, 1982 and 1988, respectively. The last three columns report the absolute and in parentheses the relative changes in the expenditure shares of the deciles for the entire period 1974–88 and the two sub-periods. Between 1974 and 1982, a redistribution took place from the top two towards the bottom eight deciles.[6] In absolute terms, the main beneficiaries of this transfer were the five bottom deciles and the main loser the top decile. In relative terms, there was a substantial increase in the share of the two bottom deciles (14.2 per cent and 11.6 per cent respectively) and an important decline in the share of the top decile (−9.9 per cent).[7] Between 1982 and 1988, the changes were less dramatic. The shares of the middle deciles (third, fourth, fifth and sixth) remained unchanged, whereas the shares of the remaining deciles apart from the top declined marginally, and the share of the top decile rose 2.9 per cent in relative terms. For the entire period, we can observe an increase in the shares of the seven bottom deciles and a corresponding decline of the shares of the top two deciles.

Using the information in table 8.1, we can construct the Lorenz curves shown in figure 8.1. An interesting feature is that they do not intersect. The 1982 Lorenz curve dominates that of 1988 (although this is not clear in figure 8.1.), which in turn dominates the Lorenz curve for 1974. Therefore, all the indices which satisfy the axioms of symmetry, population independence, income-unit independence and the principle of transfers would rank the 1982 distribution as less unequal than the 1988 distribution and the 1988 distribution as less unequal than the 1974 distribution (Atkinson 1970 and Fields and Fei 1978). However, since each index of inequality corresponds to a different social welfare function, it is interesting to ask: 'By how much did aggregate inequality change between 1974 and 1988?'. An answer to this question is given in table 8.2, where estimates of the Gini index, the Atkinson index ($\varepsilon=2$), the two Theil indices and the variance of logarithms are reported for 1974, 1982 and 1988. Champernowne (1974) points out that the second Theil index, the variance of the logarithms and the Atkinson index for $\varepsilon=2$ are relatively more sensitive to changes at the bottom end, the first Theil index is more sensitive to changes at the top and the Gini index is more sensitive to changes in the middle of a distribution. The results of table 8.2 are in line with Champernowne's findings. Table 8.1 suggests that between 1974 and 1982 and, especially, between 1982 and 1988 most changes took place close to the tails of the distribution. As a result, the changes in the value of the Gini index reported in table 8.2 are far less dramatic than the changes in the values of the rest of the indices both for the entire period 1974–88 and for the two sub-periods. Even though all indices record a substantial decline in inequality during the

Table 8.1 *Decile shares of consumption expenditure*

Population decile	Year			Change		
	1974	1982	1988	1974–82	1982–8	1974–88
1 (bottom)	2.8	3.2	3.1	+0.4 (14.2)	−0.1 (−3.2)	+0.3 (10.7)
2	4.3	4.8	4.7	+0.5 (11.6)	−0.1 (−2.1)	+0.4 (8.5)
3	5.5	5.9	5.9	+0.4 (7.2)	0.0 (0.0)	+0.4 (7.2)
4	6.5	6.9	6.9	+0.4 (6.2)	0.0 (0.0)	+0.4 (6.2)
5	7.6	8.0	8.0	+0.4 (5.3)	0.0 (0.0)	+0.4 (5.3)
6	8.8	9.1	9.1	+0.3 (3.4)	0.0 (0.0)	+0.3 (3.4)
7	10.3	10.6	10.4	+0.3 (2.9)	−0.2 (−1.9)	+0.1 (1.0)
8	12.3	12.4	12.3	+0.1 (0.8)	−0.1 (−0.8)	0.0 (0.0)
9	15.6	15.4	15.2	−0.2 (−1.3)	−0.2 (−1.3)	−0.4 (−2.6)
10 (top)	26.3	23.7	24.4	−2.6 (−9.9)	+0.7 (2.9)	−1.9 (−7.2)

period 1974–82, the Gini index declined by 9.6 per cent, while the remaining indices declined between 15.5 per cent and 20.5 per cent. Similarly, between 1982 and 1988 the Gini index rose by just 1.9 per cent, whereas the rest of the indices rose between 4.1 per cent and 6.9 per cent. For the entire period, the Gini index declined by 7.9 per cent, the Atkinson index by 11.8 per cent and the remaining indices by 14–15 per cent.

The proxy for welfare used in this chapter is equivalent consumption expenditure per capita. Therefore, the next question one can ask is: 'What was the change in the equivalent consumption expenditure per capita in real terms during the period under examination?'. Using information from NSSG (1985, p. 417 and 1992, p. 484) on the level of the retail price index, it can be calculated that the mean equivalent consumption expenditure per capita rose in real terms by 51.7 per cent between 1974 and 1982 and by a further 6.8 per cent between 1982 and 1988. Until some years ago, many policymakers would consider this increase in average consumption expenditure an indication of an increase in the welfare of the population.

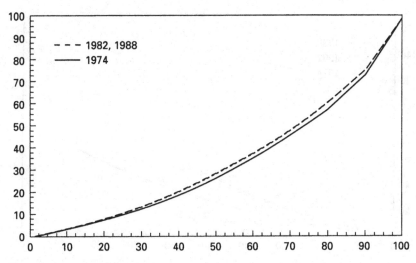

Figure 8.1 Lorenz curves
Note: 1982 and 1988 coincide in the figure

Table 8.2 *Changes in aggregate inequality measured by various indices*

		Year		Proportional change		
Index of				1974–82	1982–8	1974–88
inequality	1974	1982	1988	per cent	per cent	per cent
Gini	0.342	0.309	0.315	−9.6	1.9	−7.9
Atkinson ($\epsilon=2$)	0.323	0.273	0.285	−15.5	4.4	−11.8
First Theil	0.200	0.159	0.170	−20.5	6.9	−15.0
Second Theil	0.196	0.159	0.167	−18.9	5.0	−14.8
Variance of						
logarithms	0.387	0.318	0.331	−17.8	4.1	−14.5

However, nowadays it is recognised that social welfare is a function of both the mean expenditure (or income) and its distribution among the population.

Since the mean equivalent consumption expenditure rose considerably and inequality declined substantially between 1974 and 1982, there is no question that social welfare rose during that period. No such unambiguous answer can be given by just looking at the relevant data for the period 1982–8, when both mean expenditure and inequality rose. In this case, the technique of generalised Lorenz curves may help in providing an answer. A

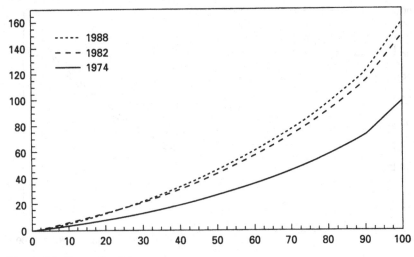

Figure 8.2 Generalised Lorenz curves

generalised Lorenz curve is a normal Lorenz curve scaled up by the mean of the distribution. Shorrocks (1983) demonstrates that if the generalised Lorenz curves of two distributions do not intersect, any social welfare function which is a non-decreasing function of all expenditures and follows the Lorenz criterion for ranking distributions with the same mean will give the distribution corresponding to the higher generalised Lorenz curve a higher welfare ranking. Figure 8.2 presents generalised Lorenz curves constructed using the information of table 8.1 and the estimates of the increase in mean equivalent consumption expenditure given above. Since the three curves do not intersect, it can be argued that social welfare in 1988 was higher than in 1982 and that the social welfare level of 1982 was higher than that of 1974.

Nevertheless, one can still ask: 'By how much did social welfare improve during the period under examination?'. In this case, different social welfare functions give different answers. As noted earlier, each index of inequality corresponds to a different social welfare function. Blackorby and Donaldson (1978) suggest a method of deriving these functions from the inequality indices. Their starting point is to take perfect equality as reference and scale the social welfare function so that social welfare is equal to the mean equivalent consumption expenditure, μ. Any departure from this point reduces the level of social welfare and social welfare is equal to zero in the case of complete inequality. Then, provided that the inequality index, i, takes values in the range zero to one, the proportional reduction in social welfare due to the existence of

Table 8.3 *Equally distributed equivalent consumption expenditure per capita*

| Year | Equally distributed equivalent consumption expenditure per capita according to | | | | |
	Gini	Atkinson ($\epsilon=2$)	First Theil	Second Theil	Variance of logarithms
1974	100.0	100.0	100.0	100.0	100.0
1982	159.3	162.9	159.5	158.7	168.8
1988	168.6	171.1	168.1	167.8	176.8

inequality is equal to the value of i and the actual value of social welfare, w, is simply given by

$$w = \mu(1-i) \tag{1}$$

In the present framework, w can be thought of as the 'equally distributed equivalent expenditure per capita according to i', that is, the average level of consumption expenditure which if equally distributed would produce a level of social welfare equal to the actual level of social welfare. Estimates of w corresponding to the inequality indices of table 8.2 are reported in table 8.3 taking as base year 1974 (1974: 100.0).[8] They indicate that between 1974 and 1982 social welfare in Greece rose 58.7–68.8 per cent, while between 1982 and 1988 it improved a further 4.7–5.7 per cent.

5 Structure of inequality

The present section is devoted to the measurement of inequality among the members of particular socioeconomic groups and the (one-way) decomposition of aggregate inequality, using the technique known as 'decomposition of inequality by population sub-groups'. This decomposition is achieved with reference to a set of factors. These factors are regional (region and locality of residence), occupational (sector of employment and occupational status of household head), demographic (age of household head) and educational (educational level of household head). For this section, extensive use is made of the second Theil index of inequality

$$L = (1/n)\Sigma_i \ln(\mu/y_i) \tag{2}$$

where y_i denotes the equivalent consumption expenditure of person i and n the size of the population. As Bourguignon (1979) and Shorrocks (1980) demonstrate, L is the only strictly additive decomposable index of

inequality which satisfies the axioms of symmetry, population independence, income-unit independence and the principle of transfers.
Additive decomposability means that if the population is grouped into
non-overlapping exhaustive groups, aggregate inequality can be expressed
as a weighted sum of the same index for the different groups ('within-
groups' component) plus the value of the index if the expenditure of every
person in each group is equal to the mean expenditure of that group
('between-groups' component). Thus, if the population is grouped into j
such groups, L can be written as follows (Anand 1983, appendix C)

$$L=\Sigma_j(n_j/n)L_j+\Sigma_j(n_j/n)\ln[(n_j/n)/(Y_j/Y)] \tag{3}$$

where Y is the total expenditure of the population, and Y_j, n_j and L_j are,
respectively, the total expenditure, the population and the value of L for
group j.[9] The first and the second terms in (3) are, respectively, the 'within-
groups' and the 'between-groups' components of aggregate inequality.[10]

The results of the measurement and decomposition of inequality are presented in table 8.4. Estimates of L are reported for all the socioeconomic
groups in the three survey years, along with their population shares and
arithmetic mean expenditures. The figures in parentheses are the percentage contributions of inequality 'within' the corresponding group to aggregate inequality. The contributions of 'within-groups' and 'between-groups'
inequalities to aggregate inequality are reported below the results for individual groups.

In the top panel of table 8.4, aggregate inequality is decomposed according to region of residence. No clear relationship between mean regional
expenditure and level of inequality is observed. Differences in mean
regional expenditures were relatively large only in 1974. In that year, the
ratio of the highest over the lowest regional mean equivalent expenditure
was 1.88. In the next two surveys, this ratio declined to 1.54 and 1.52. The
results of decomposition analysis suggest that in 1974 only 12.4 per cent of
the aggregate inequality was due to regional disparities. By 1982, this percentage had declined to 8.7 per cent and by 1988 it was almost half its 1974
level (6.6 per cent).

In the next panel, inequality is decomposed according to the size of the
locality of residence. Since, as noted earlier, it is widely accepted among
Greek policymakers that there are significant disparities between urban
and rural areas, the population is split accordingly into two groups only:
urban (living in municipalities with populations greater than 10,000) and
rural (living in municipalities or communes with populations less than
10,000). Despite the fact that the mean equivalent expenditure was considerably higher in the urban than in the rural areas, the results of decomposition analysis show that only 10.1 per cent, 9.3 per cent and 7.0 per cent of

the overall inequality could be attributed to disparities between urban and rural areas in 1974, 1982 and 1988, respectively.[11] These results, combined with the results of the top panel of the table, contrast sharply with the popular view that a large part of inequality in Greece emanates from disparities between regions or between urban and rural areas. For example, if in 1988 consumption expenditure disparities between regions or between urban and rural areas were eliminated but the level of inequality within each region or within urban and rural areas remained intact, aggregate inequality would not decline by more than 7.0 per cent.[12]

The next two panels of table 8.4 are devoted to the measurement and decomposition of inequality by occupational factors (sector of employment and occupational status of the household head). In both panels, two groups exhibit levels of inequality higher than or very close to the national average: 'Retired' and 'Other'. This is not surprising since both groups are extremely heterogeneous; in particular, 'Other' (members of households headed by housewives, students, the unemployed, unpaid family workers and so on) exhibits the highest level of inequality. Further, the mean equivalent expenditure of agricultural households and, to a lesser extent, households headed by retired persons are substantially lower than the national average, whereas the members of households headed by employers or persons employed in the financial sector ('Banks/insurance') enjoy, on average, consumption levels far above the national mean. Nevertheless, using either classification, the 'between-occupational-groups' component of aggregate inequality was only around 12 per cent in 1974, 10–11 per cent in 1982 and 8–9 per cent in 1988. Therefore, the view held by some Greek academics and policymakers that occupational differentials play an important role for the determination of aggregate inequality does not seem to be substantiated.

In the fifth panel of table 8.4, the population is grouped according to the age of the household head. A strong negative relationship can be observed between mean equivalent expenditure and age of the household head. Further, a positive relationship between age of household head and inequality 'within-age-groups' is also discernible. For two groups (members of households headed by persons in the age brackets '65–74' and particularly 'over 74') inequality is higher than or very close to the national average. This is consistent with the findings of the previous panels that inequality is high within the group of members of households headed by 'Retired' persons. Disparities 'between-age-groups' play a growing but not very important role in the determination of the national level of inequality. Only 2.9 per cent (1974), 4.6 per cent (1982) or 5.1 per cent (1988) of the aggregate inequality can be attributed to these disparities.[13]

The last panel of table 8.4 provides the results of measurement and

Table 8.4 Measurement and decomposition of inequality in Greece

Characteristic of household member or household head	Population share (per cent)			Group mean expenditure (overall mean: 100)			Index of inequality (second Theil index)		
	1974	1982	1988	1974	1982	1988	1974	1982	1988
Region									
Greater Athens	31.7	31.9	33.8	1.28	1.22	1.17	0.166 (26.9)	0.138 (27.7)	0.158 (32.0)
East Mainland and Islands	10.8	12.6	12.7	1.02	0.91	0.95	0.165 (9.1)	0.160 (12.7)	0.155 (11.8)
Greater Salonica	7.3	7.2	8.3	1.06	1.03	1.07	0.160 (6.0)	0.125 (5.7)	0.142 (7.1)
Central and West Macedonia	9.7	9.6	9.5	0.78	0.83	0.87	0.162 (8.0)	0.132 (8.0)	0.146 (8.3)
Peloponnese and West Mainland	13.1	13.6	11.9	0.89	0.90	0.88	0.165 (11.0)	0.151 (12.9)	0.146 (10.4)
Thessaly	9.8	8.1	6.7	0.82	0.82	0.78	0.207 (10.3)	0.148 (7.5)	0.182 (7.3)
Crete	5.1	5.0	4.9	0.79	0.95	1.00	0.179 (4.6)	0.135 (4.2)	0.158 (4.6)
Epirus	4.8	4.2	4.4	0.77	0.79	0.77	0.199 (4.9)	0.167 (4.4)	0.159 (4.2)
East Macedonia and Thrace	7.8	7.8	7.8	0.68	0.85	0.85	0.172 (6.8)	0.167 (8.2)	0.165 (7.7)
'Within-groups' component of inequality							0.172 (87.6)	0.145 (91.3)	0.156 (93.4)

'Between-groups' component of inequality							0.024 (12.4)	0.014 (8.7)	0.011 (6.6)
Locality									
Urban (more than 10,000)	56.8	59.1	62.9	1.16	1.13	1.11	0.174 (50.4)	0.145 (53.9)	0.155 (58.5)
Rural (less than 10,000)	43.2	40.9	37.1	0.77	0.80	0.80	0.179 (39.5)	0.143 (36.8)	0.155 (34.5)
'Within-groups' component of inequality							0.176 (89.9)	0.144 (90.7)	0.155 (93.0)
'Between-groups' component of inequality							0.020 (10.1)	0.015 (9.3)	0.012 (7.0)
Sector of employment of household head									
Agriculture	22.5	18.5	14.2	0.68	0.75	0.74	0.153 (17.5)	0.140 (16.3)	0.147 (12.5)
Manufacturing/ handicraft	14.9	15.1	15.7	1.04	1.03	1.01	0.157 (12.0)	0.122 (11.6)	0.131 (12.3)
Mining etc.[a]	10.0	10.6	8.2	1.00	0.95	0.94	0.146 (7.6)	0.151 (10.1)	0.139 (6.8)
Commerce/hotels/ restaurants	11.9	11.8	11.8	1.13	1.13	1.15	0.176 (10.7)	0.155 (11.5)	0.157 (11.1)
Transport/ communications	7.5	7.1	6.4	1.10	1.07	1.06	0.147 (5.6)	0.117 (5.2)	0.131 (5.0)
Banks/insurances	2.2	2.5	2.9	1.68	1.56	1.47	0.175 (2.0)	0.104 (1.7)	0.136 (2.4)
Services	10.9	11.1	13.6	1.29	1.27	1.22	0.161 (9.0)	0.132 (9.2)	0.138 (11.3)
Retired	13.0	15.6	21.7	0.88	0.83	0.84	0.215 (14.3)	0.156 (15.3)	0.172 (22.4)

Table 8.4 (cont.)

Characteristic of household member or household head	Population share (per cent)			Group mean expenditure (overall mean: 100)			Index of inequality (second Theil index)		
	1974	1982	1988	1974	1982	1988	1974	1982	1988
Other	7.0	7.7	5.5	1.08	1.04	1.06	0.250	0.173	0.203
							(9.0)	(8.3)	(6.7)
'Within-groups' component of inequality							0.172	0.142	0.151
							(87.7)	(89.2)	(90.7)
'Between-groups' component of inequality							0.024	0.017	0.016
							(12.3)	(10.8)	(9.3)
Occupational status of household head									
Employer	6.0	6.9	5.0	1.56	1.37	1.42	0.167	0.150	0.185
							(5.1)	(6.5)	(5.6)
Self-employed (agric. sector)	20.1	16.1	13.1	0.66	0.72	0.74	0.145	0.128	0.147
							(14.9)	(13.0)	(11.6)
Self-employed (non-agric. sector)	17.8	15.1	15.9	1.06	1.00	1.05	0.181	0.143	0.161
							(16.4)	(13.6)	(15.7)
Employee	35.9	38.2	38.6	1.08	1.09	1.08	0.153	0.136	0.131
							(28.1)	(32.7)	(30.3)
Retired	13.0	15.6	21.7	0.88	0.83	0.84	0.215	0.156	0.172
							(14.3)	(15.3)	(22.4)
Other	7.2	8.1	5.7	1.08	1.05	1.05	0.249	0.175	0.199
							(9.1)	(8.9)	(6.8)
'Within-groups'							0.172	0.143	0.154

component of inequality							(87.9)	(90.0)	(92.1)
'Between-groups' component of inequality							0.024 (12.1)	0.016 (10.0)	0.013 (7.9)
Age of household head									
Below 25	1.3	1.4	1.3	1.31	1.19	1.31	0.148 (1.0)	0.102 (0.9)	0.138 (1.1)
25–34	13.5	16.1	14.3	1.16	1.15	1.15	0.168 (11.6)	0.151 (15.3)	0.152 (13.0)
35–44	29.2	26.2	23.7	1.05	1.06	1.10	0.186 (27.7)	0.149 (24.6)	0.158 (22.5)
45–54	24.8	25.8	23.7	0.98	0.98	0.98	0.190 (24.1)	0.157 (25.5)	0.154 (21.9)
55–64	16.7	15.7	20.3	0.91	0.93	0.93	0.188 (16.0)	0.144 (14.2)	0.150 (18.3)
65–74	10.8	10.4	10.6	0.86	0.84	0.83	0.218 (12.1)	0.156 (10.2)	0.180 (11.6)
Over 74	3.7	4.4	6.0	0.72	0.69	0.72	0.246 (4.6)	0.170 (4.7)	0.191 (6.9)
'Within-groups' component of inequality							0.190 (97.1)	0.152 (95.4)	0.158 (94.9)
'Between-groups' component of inequality							0.006 (2.9)	0.007 (4.6)	0.009 (5.1)
Educational level of household head									
University graduate	6.4	9.1	14.8	1.93	1.58	1.46	0.139 (4.5)	0.118 (6.8)	0.128 (11.4)
Secondary educ. completed	12.8	16.5	26.3	1.46	1.29	1.16	0.146 (9.5)	0.131 (13.6)	0.138 (21.8)

Table 8.4 (*cont.*)

Characteristic of household member or household head	Population share (per cent)			Group mean expenditure (overall mean: 100)			Index of inequality (second Theil index)		
	1974	1982	1988	1974	1982	1988	1974	1982	1988
Primary educ. completed	54.7	55.6	44.1	0.92	0.90	0.85	0.149 (41.6)	0.129 (45.1)	0.134 (35.5)
Primary educ. not completed or no education	26.2	18.7	14.8	0.70	0.73	0.68	0.164 (21.9)	0.139 (16.4)	0.151 (13.4)
'Within-groups' component of inequality							0.152 (77.5)	0.130 (81.9)	0.137 (82.1)
'Between-groups' component of inequality							0.044 (22.5)	0.029 (18.1)	0.030 (17.9)
Total	100.0	100.0	100.0	1.00	1.00	1.00	0.196	0.159	0.167

Note:
[a] Mining/electricity/gas/water/construction/public utilities.

decomposition of inequality when the population is grouped according to the educational level of the household head. Human capital theory provides an explicit link between education and labour incomes. In broad terms, it implies that, other things being equal, in a perfectly competitive economy the incomes of persons with different educational characteristics may differ, but their consumption levels should not. Different levels of consumption can arise either because of imperfections in the markets for factors of production (capital, labour) or because education is related to other characteristics of the individual (for example, ability). Three interesting relationships are evident in this panel. First, there exists a strong positive relationship between educational level of household head and equivalent expenditure. Second, 'within-educational-groups' inequalities are considerably lower than the national average for all groups. Third, there are substantial differences in expenditure levels between groups. Further, a weak negative relationship between the educational level of household head and inequality among members of the relevant group can also be observed. Since inequalities 'within-educational-groups' are relatively low and there are substantial differences in the mean expenditures of the educational groups, the 'between-groups' component of inequality is relatively high. The proportion of aggregate inequality attributable to disparities 'between-educational-groups' was 22.5 per cent in 1974, 18.1 per cent in 1982 and 17.9 per cent in 1988.

The evidence of table 8.4 suggests that none of the factors used there has a contribution higher than 23 per cent in 1974 or 18 per cent in 1982 and 1988 in the determination of aggregate inequality. Hence, it may be interesting to ask whether the combined contribution of these factors is substantially higher. Although the present chapter does not deal with this question, the evidence of Tsakloglou (1992b) demonstrates that when the population is split into over 500 very fine locational–regional–occupational–demographic–educational groups and multivariate decomposition of the variance of logarithms is employed, 'between-groups' variations accounted for only about one-third of aggregate inequality in 1974 and for even less in 1982. These results, combined with the results of table 8.4, demonstrate very clearly that disparities 'within-groups' play a far more important role for the determination of aggregate inequality in Greece than inequalities 'between-groups'.

Careful examination of the estimates of table 8.4 reveals that between 1974 and 1982, inequality declined within the great majority of the socioeconomic groups, and in most cases this decline was substantial. As a rule of thumb, inequality declined proportionally more within those groups where it was relatively high in 1974. No clear pattern is observed regarding changes in the levels of inequality of the various groups between 1982 and

1988, even though when the population is grouped according to regional factors, inequality rose more where it was at its lowest in 1982. As a result of these factors and taking into account that, in absolute terms the overall change in inequality between 1974 and 1982 was far larger than the corresponding change between 1982 and 1988 (-0.039 against 0.008), the differences in the levels of inequality between most pairs of groups in 1988 were not as large as in 1974.

Table 8.5 is derived from table 8.4 and shows the absolute and relative changes in the 'between-groups' and 'within-groups' components of inequality when the population is grouped according to the above-mentioned factors, as well as their contributions to the change in aggregate inequality. Between 1974 and 1982, inequality declined both 'within-groups' and 'between-groups'. In most cases, the proportional reduction in the values of the 'between-groups' components was higher than the proportional reduction in the corresponding 'within-groups' components. Most 'between-groups' components continued to decline between 1982 and 1988, as well. However, all 'within-groups' components rose in the second subperiod. During the entire period 1974–88, all 'within-groups' components and all 'between-groups' components apart from one ('between-age-groups') declined substantially. In percentage terms, the decline in 'between-groups' components is impressive (from 30 per cent to 55 per cent). However, since the contribution of most 'between-groups' components to aggregate inequality is relatively low, in most cases between two-thirds and three-quarters of the decline in aggregate inequality is attributable to changes in the 'within-groups' components (when the population is grouped by size of locality, sector of employment and occupational status of the household head). However, when the population is grouped by region of residence or educational level of household head, almost half of the observed decline in inequality – 44.8 per cent and 48.3 per cent respectively – is attributed to the decreases in 'between-groups' components. The latter is in line with the arguments of Psacharopoulos (1982) that the expansion of the educational system in Greece had a strong equalising effect on the distribution of income.[14]

During the period under examination, there were several changes in the structure of the population in Greece. These changes are reflected in changes in the population shares of the various groups. It is interesting, therefore, to examine to what extent the observed changes in aggregate inequality can be attributed to these changes, rather than to changes in the level of inequality within specific groups and to changes in group mean expenditures. This can be done in the following way. Defining $v_j = n_j/n$ and $k_j = m_j/m$, taking into account that $Y_j = n_j m_j$ and $Y = nm$ and applying the difference operator on both sides of (3) gives the following

Table 8.5 *Changes in inequality 'within' and 'between' groups*

Characteristic of household member or household head	Absolute change multiplied by 10 in inequality index (L)			Relative change (percentage)		
	1974-82	1982-8	1974-88	1974-82	1982-8	1974-88
Region						
'Within-groups' component	-0.27	0.11	-0.16	-15.7	7.6	-9.3
Contribution to change in inequality	(-73.0)	(137.5)	(-55.2)			
'Between-groups' component	-0.10	-0.03	-0.13	-41.7	-21.4	-54.2
Contribution to change in inequality	(-27.0)	(-37.5)	(-44.8)			
Locality						
'Within-groups' component	-0.32	0.11	-0.21	-18.2	7.6	-11.9
Contribution to change in inequality	(-86.5)	(137.5)	(-72.4)			
'Between-groups' component	-0.05	-0.03	-0.08	-25.0	-20.0	-40.0
Contribution to change in inequality	(-13.5)	(-37.5)	(-27.6)			
Sector of employment of household head						
'Within-groups' component	-0.30	0.09	-0.21	-17.4	6.3	-12.2
Contribution to change in inequality	(-81.1)	(112.5)	(-72.4)			
'Between-groups' component	-0.07	-0.01	-0.08	-29.2	-5.9	-33.3
Contribution to change in inequality	(-18.9)	(-12.5)	(-27.6)			
Occupational status of household head						
'Within-groups' component	-0.29	0.11	-0.18	-16.9	7.7	-10.5
Contribution to change in inequality	(-78.4)	(137.5)	(-62.1)			
'Between-groups' component	-0.08	-0.03	-0.11	-33.3	-18.8	-45.8
Contribution to change in inequality	(-21.6)	(-37.5)	(-37.9)			

Table 8.5 (*cont.*)

Characteristic of household member or household head	Absolute change in inequality index (L)			Relative change (percentage)		
	1974–82	1982–8	1974–88	1974–82	1982–8	1974–88
Age of household head						
'Within-groups' component	−0.38	0.06	−0.32	−20.0	3.9	−16.8
Contribution to change in inequality	(−102.7)	(75.0)	(−110.3)			
'Between-groups' component	0.01	0.02	0.03	16.7	28.6	50.0
Contribution to change in inequality	(2.7)	(25.0)	(10.3)			
Educational level of household head						
'Within-groups' component	−0.22	0.07	−0.15	−14.5	5.4	−9.9
Contribution to change in inequality	(−59.5)	(87.5)	(−51.7)			
'Between-groups' component	−0.15	0.01	−0.14	−34.1	3.4	−31.8
Contribution to change in inequality	(−40.5)	(12.5)	(−48.3)			
GREECE	−0.037	0.008	−0.029	−18.9	5.0	−14.8

decomposition of the change in L (Mookherjee and Shorrocks 1982; Tsakloglou 1993)

$$\Delta L = \Sigma_j v_j \Delta L_j + \Sigma_j L_j \Delta v_j + \Sigma_j (k_j - \ln k_j) \Delta v_j + \Sigma_j v_j (k_j - 1) \Delta \ln \mu_j \qquad (4)$$

where Δ represents the change in the relevant variable from period t (1974 or 1982) to period $t+k$ (1982 or 1988). (4) decomposes the change in L into four terms that can be interpreted as: the effect of intertemporal changes in 'within-groups' inequality $(\Sigma_j v_j \Delta L_j)$, the effect of changes in population shares on the 'within-groups' component of inequality $(\Sigma_j L_j \Delta v_j)$, the effect of changes in population shares on the relative mean expenditures of the population groups $(\Sigma_j (k_j - \ln k_j) \Delta v_j)$ and the effect of relative changes in the group mean expenditures $(\Sigma_j v_j (k_j - 1) \Delta \ln \mu_j)$. The overall effect of demographic changes is given by the sum of the second and the third terms.

The results of the decomposition of the change in aggregate inequality according to (4) are presented in percentage terms in table 8.6. Unlike table 8.5, where base period weights are used, following Mookherjee and Shorrocks (1982), the aggregation weights in table 8.6 are the arithmetic mean values of base and final period weights. The impact of changes in the structure of the population on the change in the level of inequality between 1974 and 1982 was negligible with one possible exception. The exception is the change in the structure of the population when it is grouped according to the educational level of the household head. According to the results, if inequality 'within-groups' declined as it did and group mean expenditures changed in the way they did, the decline in aggregate inequality would have been about 8 per cent higher if the educational structure of the population in 1982 had remained the same as in 1974. In general, changes in the structure of the population had a negligible effect on the mild change in aggregate inequality between 1982 and 1988, too. There are two exceptions to this pattern. When the population is grouped by the occupational status of the household head, demographic changes tended to reduce inequality, whereas the changes in the educational structure of the population had a relatively strong inequality-enhancing effect. For the entire period, less than 6 per cent of the change in aggregate inequality, in absolute terms, can be attributed to demographic changes when the population is grouped by region, size of locality, sector of employment, occupational status or age of the household head. However, the same results show that, other things being equal, had the educational structure of the population in 1988 remained the same as in 1974, inequality would have declined by over 50 per cent more than what it actually did by 1988.

Table 8.6 *Decomposition of the change in aggregate inequality*

Characteristic of household member or household head	1974-82				1982-8				1974-88			
	(A)	(B)	(C)	(D)	(A)	(B)	(C)	(D)	(A)	(B)	(C)	(D)
Region	-70.9	-1.0	-1.0	-27.0	138.2	-4.3	-0.2	-33.7	-48.6	-3.8	-1.5	-46.1
Locality	-83.0	-0.1	-1.0	-15.9	130.0	0.5	-7.3	-23.2	-66.8	-0.5	-3.6	-29.1
Sector of employment of household head	-84.0	3.8	-3.1	-16.7	115.0	0.0	2.3	-17.2	-78.4	9.5	-6.1	-25.0
Occupational status of household head	-81.1	4.4	-2.8	-20.5	129.0	-0.2	-20.1	-8.7	-68.0	6.9	-13.0	-26.0
Age of household head	-102.5	0.1	1.6	0.8	95.9	0.3	-4.2	8.1	-103.2	2.1	0.4	0.8
Educational level of household head	-57.5	-3.5	11.5	-50.5	85.6	-8.6	60.4	-37.5	-58.4	-11.1	62.3	-92.8

Notes:
(A) Percentage of the total change due to changes in 'within-groups' inequality.
(B) Percentage of the total change due to the effect of changes in population shares on the 'within-groups' component of inequality.
(C) Percentage of the total change due to the effect of changes in population shares on the relative mean expenditures.
(D) Percentage of the total change due to changes in the relative mean expenditures.

6 Conclusions – possible developments

Several conclusions can be drawn from the results of the chapter. One-way inequality decomposition analysis shows that variations 'within-groups' were far more important in accounting for aggregate inequality than variations 'between-groups', according to any grouping of the population (regional, occupational, demographic or educational) in all survey years. This pattern became stronger in recent years. With the exception of the 'between-educational-groups' component of inequality, no other 'between-groups' component was found to contribute more than 12.5 per cent to aggregate inequality. Contrary to the widely accepted view, the results show that despite the observed differences in mean regional and urban/rural differences, if 'within-groups' disparities were kept constant, complete elimination of inter-regional or urban/rural disparities would reduce aggregate inequality by less than 12.5 per cent in 1974, by less than 9.5 per cent in 1982 and by less than 7.0 per cent in 1988. Aggregate inequality declined considerably between 1974 and 1982 and then rose mildly between 1982 and 1988. For the entire period, inequality declined both 'within' and 'between' population sub-groups. There were substantial proportional increases in the expenditure shares of the poorest population deciles and decreases in the share of the top decile. The impact of changes in the structure of the population on aggregate inequality was limited, with one exception. The results of the decomposition of the intertemporal trend of inequality show that, *ceteris paribus*, inequality would have declined even more if the educational structure of the population had remained unchanged during the period under examination. Finally, social welfare as measured by the equally distributed equivalent consumption expenditure per capita rose significantly between 1974 and 1982 and mildly between 1982 and 1988.

The overall picture painted by the results of our analysis is a rather rosy one. In fact, it is quite likely that the 'real' welfare level of the population improved at an even faster rate than that implied by the results, because between 1982 and 1988 some goods and especially services became either heavily subsidised or were provided gratis by the state. However, is this situation sustainable and what developments are likely after 1988? In order to answer these questions, it may be useful to put them in a historical context. Several changes in inequality between 1974 and 1988 were the outcome of market forces. For instance, as noted earlier, it is likely that the expansion of the educational system increased the supply of better educated workers which resulted in a decline in disparities 'between-educational-groups'. A number of other changes can be attributed to institutional changes. For example, Greece's participation in the EC resulted in higher prices for farmers' production through the Common Agricultural Policy, which in turn resulted in the relative improvement of the position of farmers and a corresponding decline in inequality 'between-occupational-groups'. Similarly, the fact that a significant proportion of the help that Greece received from the EC within the framework of the 'Structural Funds' was directed to the poorest areas of the country resulted in a decline in the disparities between regions and/or rural and urban areas. However, many of the observed changes were the result of the adoption of elements of welfare state policies. Greece never had a well-organised welfare state providing a 'safety net' for each citizen. Many functions of the welfare state are performed by the family, which plays a diminishing but still far more important role in Greek society than in the societies of most industrialised countries. The elements of welfare state policies that can be found came into existence mostly as a result of pressure from numerous special interest groups and were not taken within a general programme aimed explicitly to reduce inequality or eradicate poverty. As a consequence, several of these policies are costly and not targeted towards the least advantaged members of the society. Moreover, in almost no case was the introduction of these measures accompanied by a proper cost–benefit analysis.

As noted in section 2, a number of policies were introduced in the late 1970s and particularly in the early 1980s aiming to reduce inequality. While the economy was in the middle of a recession and productivity was declining, real average and minimum salaries, wages and pensions were increased administratively and very abruptly[15] and the social security system was extended to cover segments of the population which were not covered until then.[16] These policies had an immediate impact on inequality. As demonstrated in Tsakloglou (1988), about two-thirds of the very substantial decline in inequality between 1974 and 1982 took place between November 1981 and October 1982, that is during the period of the 1982 HES. This period coincided with the first year in government of the first socialist administration which embarked immediately on the above massive (but poorly designed) redistribution programme. The abrupt increase in labour costs dramatically reduced the profitability and competitiveness of many firms. Industrial production collapsed, resulting in loss of markets, serious deterioration of the balance of payments, redundancies of workers and stagnation of GDP.[17] In the 1980s, unemployment became a serious problem in the Greek economy for the first time in many decades.[18] The expansion of the social security system was not accompanied by corresponding increases in contributions and/or taxation to finance it, and the situation deteriorated further because the rise in unemployment and the early retirement of many workers resulted in fewer contributors and more claimants. Social security deficits were partly responsible for the huge expansion of budget deficits and the accumulated public debt which marred the Greek economy in the 1980s.[19] At the same time, there was a substantial decline in the savings ratio[20] and an expansion of the underground economy.[21]

If the above elements are added, the overall picture becomes far less rosy than that implied by the inequality statistics alone. Moreover, the above information implies, first, that several improvements may be unsustainable in the long run and, second, that a better targeting of resources is necessary. Indeed, two major macroeconomic stabilisation efforts were undertaken during the last ten years. The first was initiated in late 1985, lasted for two years and was followed by a period of political instability and loose macro-economic policies. The second was undertaken in 1990, was intensified after 1992 and is planned to continue in the immediate future. At least during their initial stages, both stabilisation programmes were accompanied by a stagnation or mild fall in GDP, increases in taxation, declines in real wages, salaries and pensions, rises in the rate of unemployment and cuts in welfare programmes. Therefore, it is likely that inequality has risen and, possibly, social welfare has declined since the last year covered by our analysis (1988). If this is correct, then an urgent priority for economic and social policymakers is better targeting of the limited resources devoted to welfare policies and, especially, policies aimed at poverty alleviation.

Notes

I am grateful to the editors E. Palmer, B. Gustafsson and P. Gottschalk, the discuss-ant M. Jäntti and seminar participants at Fiskebäckskil and the Catholic University of Portugal (Lisbon) for useful comments and suggestions.

1 The HESs of 1981/2 and 1987/8 were conducted mainly in 1982 and 1988, respectively, so we refer to them as 'the 1982 HES' and 'the 1988 HES'.
2 Detailed discussion of macroeconomic developments in the Greek economy during the post-war period can be found in Dimeli *et al.* 1992; for an in-depth analysis, see Alogoskoufis (1995).
3 Lianos and Prodromidis 1974; Prodromidis 1975; Tsoris 1975; Mourgos 1980; and Livada 1988, 1991.
4 Karayiorgas 1973, 1977; Carantinos 1981; Athanasiou 1984; Karayiorgas and Pakos 1985; Kanellopoulos 1986; and Tsakloglou 1988, 1992a, 1992b and 1993.
5 Unlike welfare, consumption is observable. However, the HES data refer to consumption expenditures – not consumption. Although the two concepts are closely related, they are not identical.
6 Perhaps the term 'redistribution' is not appropriate in this case because, as demonstrated below, between 1974 and 1982 and again between 1982 and 1988 the mean expenditure of all deciles rose.

7 Despite these changes, the expenditure share of the bottom deciles in Greece in 1982 was, on average, lower than those of the bottom deciles of other EC member states, whereas the share of the Greek top decile was substantially higher (Tsakloglou 1992a).

8 Expression (1) was used for the estimation of w in table 8.3, although the two Theil indices can take values greater than one. However, this is very unusual, and since the values of w are expressed as percentages of the relevant 1974 values, this inconsistency is not expected to affect the results seriously.

9 Since $Y=n\mu$ and $Y_j=n_j\mu_j$, the last term in (3) is equal to $\Sigma_j(n_j/n)\ln[(\mu/\mu_j)]$ which is the value of L if the expenditure of every person in group j is equal to the mean expenditure of the group.

10 In Tsakloglou 1993, aggregate inequality in 1974 and 1982 is measured and decomposed using the variance of logarithms and the first Theil index, as well. The results are very similar to those reported below.

11 It is possible that these 'between-groups' percentages understate the true 'between-groups' percentages because the classification of the NSSG includes a few prosperous suburban municipalities around Athens and Salonica in the 'rural areas', increasing the mean expenditure of the latter. Nevertheless, it is very unlikely that this understatement is serious enough to alter our conclusions.

12 These results could be different if different price indices were used for the various regions and/or for urban and rural areas. Such price indices are not available in Greece, but taking into account that Greece is a small country, regional price differentials are not expected to be substantial. Even though the contributions of regional disparities to aggregate inequality are relatively low, they are considerably higher than those reported in the case of several countries; see, for instance, the corresponding estimates of Gustafsson and Palmer for Sweden (1.7–3.8 per cent) in Chapter 13 of this volume.

13 Nevertheless, the results of this panel are likely to be sensitive to the equivalence scales used (especially if it is assumed that needs differ between age groups of adults).

14 According to these arguments, at the beginning of the period under consideration there was excess demand for skilled workers in the labour market resulting in significant premiums for the highly educated workers. The expansion of the educational system during the last 20 years (especially of tertiary and, to a lesser extent, upper secondary and vocational education) led to a considerable decline in the wage differentials across educational groups.

15 For instance, within a single year in which there was a mild decline in productivity (1981–2) real hourly wage earnings rose 10.1 per cent (IMF 1989, p. 379).

16 Social insurance expenditure as a proportion of national income rose, from 12.5 per cent in 1976 to 15.1 per cent in 1980, 22.8 per cent in 1985 and 25.5 per cent in 1988 (NSSG 1992, p. 142).

17 As noted in section 2, the average annual GDP per capita growth rate declined from 4.1 per cent for the period 1975–9 to 0.6 per cent for the period 1980–5 and then rose slightly to 1.4 per cent for the period 1986–90 (IMF 1989, p. 379; OECD 1992, p. 95).

18 Although strictly comparable unemployment statistics for the 1970s and the 1980s do not exist in Greece, it seems that the rate of unemployment gradually grew from a mere 2–3 per cent in the late 1970s to around 8 per cent in the late 1980s (OECD 1992, p. 35).

19 The budget deficit rose from 3.0 per cent of GDP in 1980 to 14.5 per cent in 1985 and 19.0 per cent in 1990. The accumulated debt increased accordingly from 39.4 per cent of GDP in 1980 to 85.1 per cent in 1985 and 111.6 per cent in 1990. About one-quarter of this debt is external (around US $19 billion in 1990), although this percentage exceeded 40 per cent in the mid 1980s (OECD 1992, p. 107).

20 Gross savings as a proportion of GDP declined, from 19.1 per cent in 1980 to 14.0 per cent in 1985 and 13.3 per cent in 1987 (IMF 1989, p. 379), and Greece's gross saving ratio was the lowest among OECD countries in the late 1980s (OECD 1992, p. 110).

21 No official estimates of the size of the underground economy exist in Greece. However, the work of several Greek economists suggests that the underground economy expanded rapidly in the 1980s and that by the end of the 1980s it was as large as 30–40 per cent of the 'official' economy.

References

Alogoskoufis, G. 1995. 'The Two Faces of Janus: Institutions, Regimes and Macroeconomic Policy in Greece'. *Economic Policy*, 20: 148–92.

Anand, S. 1983. *Inequality and Poverty in Malaysia: Measurement and Decomposition.* New York: Oxford University Press.

Athanasiou, L. 1984. *The Distribution of Income in Greece.* Scientific Studies No. 6 (in Greek). Athens: Center of Planning and Economic Research.

Atkinson, A. B. 1970. 'On the Measurement of Inequality'. *Journal of Economic Theory*, 2: 244–63.

Blackorby, C. and Donaldson, D. 1978. 'Measures of Relative Equality and Their Meaning in Terms of Social Welfare'. *Journal of Economic Theory*, 18: 59–80.

Bourguignon, F. 1979. 'Decomposable Income Inequality Measures'. *Econometrica*, 47: 901–20.

Carantinos, D. 1981. 'Aspects of Income and Wealth Distribution in Greece'. Unpublished Ph.D. thesis. University of Strathclyde.

Champernowne, D. 1974. 'A Comparison of Measures of Inequality of Income Distribution'. *Economic Journal*, 84: 787–816.

Deaton, A. S. 1980. 'Measurement of Welfare: Theory and Practical Guidelines'. World Bank Living Standards Measurement Study Working Paper No. 7.

Dimeli, S., Kollintzas, T., Prodromidis, K., Chalikias, Y. and Christodoulakis, N. 1992. *Main Characteristics of the Greek Macroeconomic Variables.* Athens: Athens University of Economics and Business.

Fields, G. S. and Fei, J. C. H. 1978. 'On Inequality Comparisons'. *Econometrica*, 46: 303–16.

Gustafsson, B. and Palmer, E. 1997. 'Changes in Swedish Inequality. A Study of Equivalent Income, 1975–1991'. In this volume.

International Monetary Fund. 1989. New York: International Financial Statistics Yearbook.

Kanellopoulos, C. N. 1986. *Incomes and Poverty in Greece: Determining Factors.* Scientific Studies No. 22 (in Greek). Athens: Center of Planning and Economic Research.

Karayiorgas, D. 1973. 'The Distribution of Tax Burden by Income Groups in Greece'. *Economic Journal*, vol. 83: 436–48.

1977. 'The Distribution of Tax Burden by Income Groups in Greece'. *Spoudai*, 27: 390–402.

Karayiorgas, D. and Pakos, T. 1985. 'Les inégalités économiques et sociales actuelles'. *Les Tempes Modernes*, 473: 960–74.

Lianos, T. and Prodromidis, K. 1974. 'Aspects of Income Distribution in Greece'. Center of Planning and Economic Research, Lecture Series No. 28. Athens.

Livada, A. 1988. 'Aspects of Income Inequality in Greece'. Unpublished Ph.D. thesis. University of Essex.

1991. 'Income Inequality in Greece: A Statistical and Econometric Analysis'. *Oxford Bulletin of Economics and Statistics*, 53: 69–82.

Mookherjee, D. and Shorrocks, A. F. 1982. 'A Decomposition of the Trend in UK Income Inequality'. *Economic Journal*, 92: 886–902.

Mourgos, S. 1980. 'Economic Development and Distributional Trends in Postwar Greece'. Unpublished Ph.D. thesis. New York University.

National Statistical Service of Greece. 1985. *Statistical Yearbook of Greece 1984* (in Greek). Athens.

1992. *Statistical Yearbook of Greece 1989* (in Greek). Athens.

Organization for Economic Co-operation and Development. 1992. *OECD Economic Surveys: Greece 1991/92*. Paris.

Prodromidis, K. 1975. 'Regional Distribution of Employment and Income in Greece: 1961–1971' (in Greek). *Spoudai*, 25: 529–50.

Psacharopoulos, G. 1982. 'Earnings and Education in Greece, 1960–1977'. *European Economic Review*, 17: 333–47.

Sen, A. K. 1976. 'Real National Income'. *Review of Economic Studies,* 43: 19–39.

Shorrocks, A. F. 1980. 'The Class of Additively Decomposable Inequality Measures'. *Econometrica*, 48: 613–25.

1983. 'Ranking Income Distributions'. *Economica,* 50: 3–17.

Tsakloglou, P. 1988. 'Aspects of Inequality and Poverty in Greece: 1974, 1982'. Unpublished Ph.D. thesis. University of Warwick.

1991a. 'Estimation and Comparison of Two Simple Models of Equivalence Scales for the Cost of Children'. *Economic Journal*, 101: 343–57.

1991b. 'Estimating the Barten Model of Equivalence Scales for the Cost of Children from Microdata'. University of Bristol Department of Economics Discussion Paper No. 90/273.

1992a. 'Inequality and Welfare in EEC Countries'. *Bulletin of Economic Research*, 44: 21–37.

1992b. 'Multivariate Decomposition of Inequality: Greece 1974, 1982'. *Greek Economic Review,* 14: 89–102.

1993. 'Aspects of Inequality in Greece'. *Journal of Development Economics,* 40: 53–74.

Tsoris, N. 1975. 'The Distribution of Income in Greece' (in Greek). *Spoudai,* 25: 646–50.

9 The development of income distribution in the Federal Republic of Germany during the 1970s and 1980s

RICHARD HAUSER AND IRENE BECKER

1 Introduction

During the two decades covered by this chapter Germany experienced vast economic and political change. In the beginning of the 1970s, the German economy was characterised by full employment, medium rates of growth of real national income per capita and a rate of inflation that was considered rather high by German standards. The 1974 oil shock definitively ended the period of high real growth and low unemployment, and since then several business cycles have ended with ever higher rates of unemployment. In 1989, the year the wall between East and West Germany fell, unemployment was high, but real growth and the rate of inflation were still at acceptable levels. Unification in 1990 was accompanied by a brief increase in real growth rates and a decrease in unemployment in the western part of Germany, but a near breakdown of the East German economy. In 1992 and 1993, the old and the new 'Länder' of Germany experienced very high unemployment, unknown since the early 1950s, with negative real growth rates in the West and low positive growth rates in the East accompanied by moderate inflation (Sachverständigenrat zur Begutachtung der gesamtwirtschaftlichen Entwicklung (SVR) 1994/5).

Fairly little is known about the changes in the distribution of personal income and wealth that accompanied this development. The independent German Council of Economic Advisers (Sachverständigenrat zur Begutachtung der gesamtwirtschaftlichen Entwicklung (SVR)), which was set up in 1963 and by law is obliged also to review the distribution of income, insists that the available data are not sufficient for a thorough analysis (most recently SVR 1992, no. 209–11). But a series of statistical tables on income distribution is published by the German Statistical Office (Statistisches Bundesamt) in four- or five-year intervals,[1] and recently estimates of average income of various socioeconomic groups based on the National Accounts for the years 1972 to 1993 were published.[2] In 1981 a Government Commission dealt intensively with the effects of the German transfer system but was also seriously hampered by the lack of statistical data.[3] Recently, the Deutsche Bundesbank reviewed the distribution of income since 1982 and the distribution of wealth.[4] Scientific studies based on official microdata,[5] on aggregate statistics,[6] on surveys done by universities or research institutes[7] or derived from simulations with income distribution models[8] are also available. These studies suggest only slight changes in personal income distribution during the various business cycles, with a general tendency towards increasing overall inequality since the end of the full-employment period in 1974. Furthermore, strongly growing numbers of social assistance recipients point to an increase in poverty.[9]

The political debate about the overall distribution of personal incomes was never very heated. It was mainly concentrated on distributional effects of single policy measures, during the past decade mostly seen as redistributing net income from bottom to top.[10] The assertion of the opposition parties that Germany is on its way to becoming a 'Two-Thirds Society' (with one third of the population being excluded from prosperity and threatened by poverty) was heavily rejected by the ruling coalition. But it cannot be denied that the word 'poverty', almost taboo during the 1970s, is now widely used in political discussions to characterise the problems of groups that were left behind or even marginalised by the economic, demographic and political changes of the past decade. This may be due partly to activities of the Commission of the European Communities, which in 1979 commissioned national poverty reports from independent experts covering all the member states for the first time.[11]

In this chapter we will use microdata from the official Income and Consumption Surveys (EVS) 1973, 1978 and 1983 as well as data from the German Socio-Economic Panel (GSOEP), referring to the years 1983, 1985, 1987 and 1990, to examine more closely trends in distribution of income in West Germany, also giving attention to the problem of poverty. In this attempt to bring together microdata from two very different sources to span a period of two decades, the main aim is primarily descriptive rather than explanatory in any causal sense, emphasis being given to the identification of the various factors that may play a role in determining changes in income distribution with arguments only based on a priori reasoning. Finally, we examine inequality in East Germany before and after unification, and compare the results to those for West Germany.

2   An overview of the German welfare state

The German welfare state can still be characterised as being of the Bismarck type.[12] Social protection for workers and employees against the risks of loss of income in case of unemployment, occupational accident, sickness, disablement, old age or the death of the breadwinner of a family is currently based on social insurance with contributions and benefits proportional to wage income but restricted by upper limits. Special arrangements for craftsmen, independent workers, civil servants (Beamte), professionals and farmers also exist, so only some groups of the self-employed are not covered by these compulsory social insurance schemes. The benefit rates range from 56 per cent of previous net income (means-tested unemployment assistance) to more than 80 per cent. Pensions depend on the relative earnings position achieved in each year of working life and on the length of the period for which contributions were paid. All these benefits are now indexed to increases in net wages with the consequence of similar changes in real terms.

The main social insurance schemes do not contain provisions for minimum benefits sufficient for a sociocultural subsistence minimum. If social security benefits and all other incomes of a family or of an independent person do not sum up to a government-defined sociocultural subsistence minimum, a general social assistance scheme financed by taxes provides additional means-tested benefits to reach this minimum. Since the right to social assistance for everybody residing in Germany was introduced in 1962, the nominal value of the guaranteed sociocultural minimum of subsistence has been adjusted regularly but at a slightly slower rate than the increase in average nominal net wages. These adjustments resulted in an increase of the real value of the sociocultural minimum of subsistence between 1963 and 1991 of at least 60 per cent.[13]

Child allowances, maternity leave, an educational allowance and a job guarantee for mothers temporarily interrupting work to care for their children, student benefits, tax allowances and family-related implicit transfers built into some social security schemes and into the income tax schedule contribute to reduce the cost of child raising and single-earner marriages. These benefits are also mainly financed by taxes but are not indexed. Discretionary adjustments have occurred at irregular intervals.

The costs of health care for workers, employees, pensioners and their family members up to certain earning limits are covered by a mandatory social health insurance. High earners, civil servants and most self-employed persons have to take out private health insurance. A social insurance scheme to cover the cost of permanent nursing has been discussed and was passed by parliament in 1994.

While there was a tendency to extend coverage, to increase benefits and to introduce new ones during the 1970s, the 1980s saw many efforts to reduce benefits, to tighten the rules for entitlement, to change the formula for indexing pensions and to increase the minimum age of retirement. Despite this reversal of social policy during the 1980s, the contribution rates increased continuously, from 26.3 per cent in 1970 to 32.4 per cent in 1980 and to about 38 per cent in 1994, half of which is paid by employers. In addition, employers pay the contribution rates for the occupational accident insurance in full. During the same period, social expenditure as a percentage of GNP rose from 26.2 per cent (1970) to 32.5 per cent (1980) and then fell to 30.4 per cent in 1989. After unification in 1990, social expenditure increased again to a new peak of 34 per cent in 1993 (for united Germany) due to large transfers in favour of East Germans, a considerable portion of which was financed via the social insurance system.

The German tax system relies on about equal proportions of direct and indirect taxation. In 1989, taxes on income, wages and corporate profits amounted to about 47 per cent of total tax revenue. Taxes on income and wages are moderately progressive, with the highest marginal tax rate reaching 53 per cent, but have many loopholes to avoid high taxes, especially on income from self-employment and from capital. A tax on long-term gains from capital investment by private households does not exist, and houses and land are for tax purposes grossly undervalued. During the 1980s, several tax reforms reduced the progressivity of the tax schedule.

The institutional setting of the German labour market can be characterised as a three-tier system. Basic rules to protect workers are set by law, but there is no legal minimum wage. Labour unions and employers' associations have the constitutionally protected right to negotiate wages and working conditions, but agreements on working conditions can only deviate from the minimum standards set by law in favour of workers. Finally, individual labour contracts can again only deviate from the agreements in favour of the respective worker or employee. Practically the entire labour market is covered by union–employer agreements, because the Ministry of Labour has the power to declare agreements binding even for parties not belonging to the employers' associations or unions.

As a reaction to large increases in unemployment, the labour unions increasingly changed their strategy to demanding reductions in weekly working hours, at first with full-wage compensation but gradually accepting smaller wage increases. The goal of a 35-hour work week is not yet attained but some hours have been cut from the working week in all industries.

In general, this system of wage determination works rather efficiently, as judged by the comparatively low numbers of working hours lost due to strikes. The main limit to excessive wage increases is the stringent monetary policy of the Deutsche Bundesbank that, since the end of the 1970s, has closely adhered to the monetarist creed in setting and enforcing targets for monetary expansion. The aim of price level stability has increasingly dominated stabilisation policy, and the aim of full employment – considered

equally significant during the 1960s and 1970s – considerably lost importance. Consequently, the labour market policy of the government since the
middle of the 1970s refrained from the use of Keynesian expansionist
instruments and relied on training and retraining measures, on early retirement and on financing temporary jobs in the fields of public and social
work that would not be done otherwise (Arbeitsbeschaffungsmaßnahmen).

After unification, the institutional setting of the former West Germany
was transferred to East Germany, but the benefit levels of the social security system were related to the much lower East German wage level – about
half of West Germany's – and were to increase only in line with East German
net wages. At the beginning of the unification process, East German wages
were expected to rise quickly to the West German level, but the view now is
much more pessimistic, assuming that wage levels will not equalise until the
beginning of the next century. Therefore, an analogous discrepancy will also
persist in benefit levels. On the other hand, the transformation of the East
German pension system led to increases in most pensions so that recipients
improved their positions relative to wage earners. This effect was reinforced
by temporarily granting supplements to low pensions and to low unemployment benefits that do not exist in West Germany.[14]

3   Macroeconomic development and changes in the relative positions
      of various socioeconomic groups

3.1   An overview based on macroeconomic indicators

The economic development of the Federal Republic of Germany since the
beginning of the 1970s – starting at quite a high level in an international
perspective – has resulted in a considerable increase of national income. In
real terms (using the price index for a family of four with mid-range
income) national income per capita in 1993 was at a level of 157 per cent of
its value in 1970.[15] However, the upward trend did not proceed continuously as Table 9.1 shows.

The percentage changes in real national income per capita (column 1)
indicate two distinct, though not very regular, business cycles (from 1975 to
1981 and from 1982 to 1993). But the periods of prosperity were longer
than those of recession. The cyclical changes of growth rates were accompanied by a delayed or an even anti-cyclical development of the rate of
inflation (column 2) and an upward trend in the unemployment rate
(column 6). The unemployment rate rose in times of little or negative
growth but did not decline by an equal extent during periods of recovery.
During the 1970s, the labour force participation rate remained quite stable
at a level of about 44 per cent and increased during the 1980s to 48 per cent.

Table 9.1 *Selected economic indicators of the Federal Republic of Germany (West), 1972–1993*

Year	Percentage change in real national income per capita (prices of 1985) 1	Rate of inflation[a] (in per cent) 2	Labour force participation (inclusive of self-employed)[b] (in per cent)			Unemployment rate[c] 6	Long-term unemployed[d] (as per cent of all unemployed persons) 7
			self-employed 3	wage earners 4	all 5		
1972	3.49	5.4	6.56	37.44	44.00	1.1	—
1973	4.40	6.7	6.39	37.91	44.30	1.2	—
1974	−0.07	6.8	6.14	38.06	44.20	2.5	—
1975	−1.57	6.0	5.93	38.07	44.00	4.6	—
1976	5.45	4.5	5.59	38.31	43.90	4.5	—
1977	3.08	3.4	5.37	38.63	44.00	4.3	14.3
1978	5.29	2.6	5.34	39.06	44.40	4.1	14.7
1979	3.61	3.8	5.22	39.68	44.90	3.6	15.6
1980	−0.42	5.2	5.14	40.26	45.40	3.6	12.9
1981	−2.88	6.4	5.08	40.82	45.90	5.1	13.0
1982	−2.12	5.2	4.97	41.33	46.30	7.2	17.9
1983	2.21	3.3	5.00	41.60	46.60	8.8	24.9
1984	3.45	2.3	4.93	41.87	46.80	8.8	28.8
1985	2.59	2.0	5.02	42.38	47.40	8.9	31.0
1986	6.59	−0.2	5.00	42.80	47.80	8.5	31.9
1987	3.38	0.1	4.92	43.18	48.10	8.5	31.8
1988	3.74	1.1	4.90	43.30	48.20	8.4	32.6
1989	2.28	2.9	4.84	43.16	48.00	7.6	31.4
1990	4.02	2.7	4.75	43.25	48.00	6.9	29.7

Table 9.1 (*cont.*)

Year	Percentage change in real national income per capita (prices of 1985)[a] 1	Rate of inflation[a] (in per cent) 2	Labour force participation (inclusive of self-employed)[b] (in per cent)			Unemployment rate[c] 6	Long-term unemployed[d] (as per cent of all unemployed persons) 7
			self-employed 3	wage earners 4	all 5		
1991	2.94	3.6	4.74	43.16	47.90	6.1	28.3
1992	−0.48	4.0	4.83	42.87	47.70	6.5	26.6
1993	−5.18	3.8	5.19	42.01	47.20	8.1	26.0

Notes:

[a] Consumer price index of a family of four with middle-range income.

[b] Workers and employees (inclusive of the unemployed) and self-employed as per cent of the whole population.

[c] Unemployed as per cent of all workers and employees (inclusive of the unemployed).

[d] Period of uninterrupted unemployment, 12 months or more.

Sources: Sachverständigenrat: Jahresgutachten 1994/5 zur Begutachtung der gesamtwirtschaftlichen Entwicklung, Bundestagsdrucksache 13/26, pp. 339, 355, 426. Bundesanstalt für Arbeit: *Amtliche Nachrichten (ANBA)*, vol. 40 (1992), p. 84 and vol. 41 (1993), p. 85; and own computations.

But a structural shift in the labour force towards wage earners continued during the whole period. In 1972, almost 15 per cent of the labour force consisted of self-employed persons (including farmers); in 1993 this fraction fell to around 11 per cent.

Table 9.2 shows changes in the composition of income for the household sector from 1972 to 1993.

Profits (including the earnings of the self-employed) displayed the usual cyclical behaviour, with lower shares during recessions, and a slight downward trend. The share of gross earnings of workers and employees developed countercyclically. If these tendencies are seen in conjunction with changes in the composition of the labour force (table 9.1, columns 3 and 4), we should expect a pronounced divergence in the per capita market incomes of workers and the self-employed.

On the other hand, the share of interest and dividends nearly doubled, from 3.7 per cent in 1972 to 7.1 per cent in 1993, thus presumably strengthening tendencies favouring the self-employed, who can be assumed to own on average much higher assets than workers.

Employers' social security contributions, which may be considered a part of wages in a wider sense, also grew faster than the gross market income of the household sector. In 1982, their share amounted to 14.5 per cent, in contrast with 11.2 per cent in 1972, and remained at about the same level from then on. This tendency of a wage-related income component is a consequence of the expansion of the social security system during the 1970s and the corresponding increase in social security contribution rates. Hence, transfers paid by the household sector (personal taxes and social security contributions of employees and employers) also rose considerably during the 1970s in relation to gross market income (column 6 of table 9.2). Monetary transfers received by the household sector (column 7 of table 9.2) increased a little more in relative terms,[16] but in the 1980s their share declined continuously, to 26.8 per cent in 1991, despite high rates of unemployment and an increase in the share of long-term unemployed (columns 6 and 7 of table 9.1). Obviously, the various measures taken by the Christian Democrat and Liberal Government, which came into power in 1982, to curb social expenditure had an effect. Only in 1993, when regressive development continued, did transfers received increase again to about 30 per cent of gross market income, the same level as at the start of the 1980s.

3.2   Changes in relative welfare positions of various socioeconomic groups

Changes in the relative positions of various socioeconomic groups can be gauged by looking at each group's average equivalent income – defined

Table 9.2 Gross market income of household sector and its components in the Federal Republic of Germany (West), 1972–1993

Year	Gross market income of household sector (million D-Mark)[a] 1	Income components as per cent of gross market income					
		Employers' social security contributions 2	Gross earnings of workers and employees 3	Profits (inclusive of retained earnings of unincorporated business)[b] 4	Interest and dividends 5	Transfers paid[c] (in per cent of col. 1) 6	Transfers received (in per cent of col. 1) 7
1972	607,637	11.19	61.57	23.51	3.73	39.18	23.13
1973	676,917	11.56	62.58	21.77	4.08	42.18	23.47
1974	727,865	12.18	64.10	19.55	4.17	43.91	24.68
1975	761,292	13.00	63.47	19.20	4.33	44.58	29.10
1976	836,986	13.31	62.04	20.40	4.25	45.61	28.61
1977	893,010	13.10	62.83	19.79	4.28	45.99	28.34
1978	953,092	13.38	62.63	19.95	4.04	45.45	28.03
1979	1,029,446	13.44	62.74	19.34	4.48	45.28	27.83
1980	1,085,914	13.80	64.71	16.29	5.20	46.83	28.28
1981	1,123,419	14.16	65.49	14.38	5.97	47.57	29.87
1982	1,163,502	14.47	65.01	14.04	6.48	47.95	30.45
1983	1,210,220	14.29	63.66	16.18	5.88	47.48	29.83
1984	1,273,211	14.31	62.50	16.94	6.25	47.38	29.03
1985	1,335,416	14.17	61.94	17.28	6.60	47.57	28.54
1986	1,426,393	14.13	60.92	18.72	6.24	46.61	27.89
1987	1,477,385	14.11	61.43	18.57	5.89	47.32	28.39

1988	1,562,943	14.04	60.27	19.69	5.99	46.75	28.08
1989	1,651,019	13.65	59.87	19.90	6.58	46.87	27.80
1990	1,802,285	13.71	59.01	20.49	6.78	44.99	27.12
1991	1,924,014	13.78	59.82	19.65	6.74	46.63	26.83
1992	2,013,990	13.96	60.54	18.38	7.12	47.72	27.35
1993	1,998,614	14.43	61.66	16.76	7.14	49.56	29.59

Notes:

[a] Inclusive of employers' social security contributions.

[b] According to the conventions of national accounting, profits are calculated by using depreciation based on replacement cost. Retained earnings are calculated as a difference of all other components of national income, thus comprising all errors and omissions. The housing sector regularly shows a large negative value of retained earnings that dominates the positive value of retained earnings of unincorporated companies. (Comp. Schüler, K./ Spies, V.: 'Einkommen aus Unternehmertätigkeit und Vermögen', in: *Wirtschaft und Statistik*, vol. 10/1991, pp. 653–66.)

[c] Income tax, social security contributions of employers and employees and other transfers.

Sources: Statistisches Bundesamt (III B) 1994: Verfügbares Einkommen, Zahl der Haushalte und Haushaltsmitglieder nach Haushaltsgruppen-Aktualisierte Ergebnisse der Volkswirtschaftlichen Gesamtrechnungen für die Jahre 1972 bis 1993 – Wiesbaden (Sonderdruck); and Statistisches Bundesamt (III B) 1994: Einkommensverteilung nach Haushaltsgruppen und Einkommensarten-Aktualisierte Ergebnisse der Volkswirtschaftlichen Gesamtrechnungen für die Jahre 1972 bis 1993 – Wiesbaden (Sonderdruck).

more precisely below – in relation to the overall average equivalent income. These averages are influenced by the population shares of the various groups and their changes. Conventionally, the socioeconomic groups are distinguished by the social status of the head of household – derived from the main income source – and family members are classified accordingly.

The share of farmers (including their family members) fell continuously, from 3.9 per cent in 1972 to 1.5 per cent in 1993, i.e., by far more than one half. The share of the self-employed (excluding farmers) also decreased, from 8.0 per cent to 7.0 per cent, with most of the reduction occurring during the first decade. The population share of blue-collar workers fell, from 37.6 per cent to 26.0 per cent. While the population share of civil servants increased during the 1970s and has decreased since the mid 1980s to 6.7 per cent, the share of white-collar workers increased considerably from 20.4 per cent to 24.8 per cent. This change is mostly due to a shift from blue- to white-collar workers and to an increase in the labour force participation rate of women who take on white-collar jobs to a larger extent.

The biggest increase in population share occurred for groups of persons who live mainly on public transfers. Taking all family members of heads of households not gainfully employed, we find an increase from 23.0 per cent to 33.9 per cent. Among them, the share of the group of recipients of social old-age and survivor's pensions increased by more than four percentage points (to 21.7 per cent), but in relative terms the share of the unemployed grew most: to more than seven times its original size (up to 3.6 per cent), followed by the recipients of social assistance, whose share more than tripled (to 2.4 per cent).

The development of the relative welfare positions of these groups are shown in table 9.3 and figure 9.1. We define the relative welfare position of a socioeconomic group as the ratio of the group-specific average equivalent income to the average equivalent income of the total population.[17] The equivalent income of a person is derived from the net income of that person's household. Net income of a household equals the sum of all kinds of gross market incomes and transfers less social security contributions of workers and personal taxes. The equivalent income of each member of a household is then derived by dividing the net income of the household by the sum of the weights of the household members as defined by an equivalence scale.

A striking pattern holds true during the whole period observed: In all years since 1972, the self-employed have been best off, and – not surprisingly – persons living mainly on social assistance have been worst off. Moreover, the ranking of the various groups, with the exception of farmers, has remained the same. Compared with their initial position in 1972,

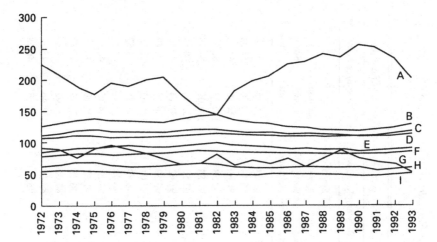

Figure 9.1 Relative welfare positions by status of head of household, FRG, 1972–1993
Notes: A: self-employed (without farmers). B: state pensions for civil servants. C: civil servants. D: white-collar workers. E: recipients of social old-age and survivor's pensions. F: blue-collar workers. G: farmers. H: recipients of unemployment benefits. I: social assistance recipients.
Source: See table 9.3.

farmer households dropped two ranks to 1981 and then another rank; in 1993 they were on average only slightly better off than the group living mainly on social assistance. But one must recall the problems of calculating comparable income figures for farmers. Since their relative welfare position has proved to be rather volatile, this decrease may be reversed quickly, although a downward tendency cannot be denied. Second in rank are retired civil servants with special state pensions (Beamte), and third are active civil servants (Beamte). The only other group that is above average is that of white-collar workers (Angestellte); they are only slightly below active civil servants. In descending order follow recipients of social security pensions for old age, survivors and disability (Rentner), blue-collar workers (Arbeiter), recipients of unemployment benefits, and, finally, recipients of social assistance, the basic means-tested benefit available to all persons with insufficient resources.

In 1993, the differences in the relative welfare positions between the various groups were considerable. While the self-employed reached a relative level of 199.0 per cent, social assistance recipients had to live on only 48.9 per cent of average equivalent income. In comparing the relative welfare positions realised by households with a gainfully employed head with those of households with a retired head, it is striking to find that

Table 9.3. *Relative welfare positions^a by status of head of household in the Federal Republic of Germany (West), 1972–1993*

| Year | Annual average equivalent income in D-Mark | Group-specific average equivalent income in per cent of overall average equivalent income by status of head of household | | | | | | Not gainfully employed with ... as main source of income | | |
		Farmers	Self-employed (without farmers)	Civil servants (Beamte)	White-collar workers	Blue-collar workers	Unemployment benefits	Social old-age and survivor's pensions	State pensions for civil servants	Social assistance
1972	11,000	90.00	224.54	110.91	106.36	77.27	60.91	83.64	125.45	53.64
1973	11,800	88.14	207.63	113.56	107.63	78.81	63.56	86.44	129.66	54.24
1974	12,500	75.20	188.80	118.40	110.40	80.80	67.20	89.60	134.40	54.40
1975	13,700	88.32	175.91	119.71	109.49	81.02	67.15	89.78	137.23	52.56
1976	14,700	94.56	193.88	116.33	106.80	78.91	62.59	91.84	134.01	51.70
1977	15,600	87.18	188.46	115.38	107.05	80.13	59.62	93.59	133.33	50.64
1978	16,700	81.44	198.20	114.97	107.19	80.24	59.88	91.62	131.14	48.50
1979	17,900	72.07	202.79	114.53	107.82	81.01	60.89	90.50	130.17	47.49
1980	18,600	62.90	174.19	117.20	109.14	83.33	62.90	93.01	136.02	47.85
1981	19,300	63.73	151.30	119.17	110.88	84.97	64.25	94.82	140.41	47.67
1982	19,900	78.89	141.71	118.09	112.06	83.92	62.81	96.98	141.71	47.24
1983	20,800	61.54	179.81	115.38	110.58	82.21	58.65	93.27	134.13	46.15
1984	21,600	68.98	195.37	113.43	109.72	81.48	57.41	91.67	130.09	46.30
1985	22,400	63.84	203.57	113.84	108.93	81.25	57.14	90.18	128.12	47.77
1986	24,000	72.08	222.92	111.25	107.50	80.42	57.50	87.08	122.92	46.67
1987	24,700	58.70	227.13	111.74	108.10	80.57	59.11	87.45	121.46	47.37
1988	26,200	72.14	238.55	110.31	106.49	79.77	58.40	85.50	117.56	46.18

1989	27,200	84.93	234.19	109.56	107.35	79.04	57.35	86.40	117.65	45.96
1990	29,500	72.20	253.22	107.46	107.12	79.32	57.97	83.39	115.93	44.07
1991	30,300	66.67	248.84	109.24	107.26	79.54	52.81	84.82	118.81	44.55
1992	31,200	63.14	231.41	112.18	108.65	80.45	55.77	85.90	121.79	46.80
1993	30,900	49.84	199.03	116.18	111.33	83.17	57.61	88.03	126.86	48.87

Note:

[a] The relative welfare position is defined as group-specific average equivalent income in per cent of overall average equivalent income. Equivalent income is based on an equivalence scale used by the Statistisches Bundesamt (Federal Statistical Office) : the head of household is weighted by a factor of 1.0, other household members of 15 years or more are weighted by a factor of 0.7, household members up to 15 years by a factor of 0.5.

Source: Statistisches Bundesamt (III B) 1994: Verfügbares Einkommen, Zahl der Haushalte und Haushaltsmitglieder nach Haushaltsgruppen – Aktualisierte Ergebnisse der Volkswirtschaftlichen Gesamtrechnungen für die Jahre 1972 bis 1993, Wiesbaden (Sonderdruck).

retired civil servants reach a higher relative level (126.9 per cent) than the active group (116.2 per cent), and that retirees on social security pensions are better off (88.0 per cent) than blue-collar workers (83.2 per cent). For all groups of retirees, it can be supposed that their smaller household size compared with the household size of the active groups is the chief reason for this advantageous position.

Let us now turn to changes in the relative welfare positions of the various groups during the two decades from 1972 to the beginning of the 1990s. At the beginning of the 1970s, the data indicate a shift in welfare positions from the households of the self-employed to the households of workers and civil servants and to households whose heads were not gainfully employed. The relative gains of persons living mainly on transfers were greater than those of blue- or white-collar households. During the following period (1975–8), changes in the opposite direction occurred. The relative position of persons living in households of the self-employed rose, from 175.9 per cent to about twice of overall average equivalent income, whereas the relative welfare position of farmers, blue- and white-collar workers, civil servants and civil service pensioners, the unemployed and social assistance recipients fell. The unemployed suffered the worst drop in relative welfare position. Only retirees living on social old-age and survivor's pensions were able to maintain their favourable position gained during the first period.

The development was reversed again for several groups towards the end of the 1970s (1978–82). These years can be characterised as a period of intensified distributional battles in an era of increasingly serious government budget problems. From 1982, after the change of coalition government, the data show more uniform trends than for the 1970s. The most remarkable development is the continuous and sizeable increase in the relative welfare position of persons living in the households of the self-employed, from 141.7 per cent to 253.2 per cent in 1990. The recession of the early 1990s reversed this development again but left the self-employed on a level double the average equivalent income (1993), comparable with the corresponding value of the boom year 1978. Farmers experienced ups and downs but remained on average in the same below-average position. The relative welfare position of all other groups decreased continuously until 1990. In this period, the drops in relative welfare positions were greatest for persons living mainly on money from the state (civil service pensioners, civil servants and retirees with social old-age and survivor's pensions). Although this tendency seems to have reversed itself since 1990, those living in households with a not gainfully employed head are in relative terms still worse off than they were in 1982.

Last but not least, we want to point out the negative development for persons living mainly on unemployment benefits and for those on social assistance. The relative welfare position of the recipients of unemployment benefits decreased particularly in the period from 1982 to 1985, from a level of 62.8 per cent to 57.1 per cent, and remained approximately at the lower level the following years. The relative welfare position of the recipients of social assistance was reduced continuously by about nine percentage points, from 53.6 per cent at the start of the 1970s to a level of only 44.1 per cent in 1990, then increasing again to 48.9 per cent. This result is quite contrary to the view held by the general public and in political circles that social assistance has grown faster than net wages and has become too generous.

4   Changes in the distribution of wage earnings

While the results of the previous section referred to changes in the relative positions of socioeconomic groups defined by the social status of the heads of household, we now turn to an analysis at the individual level looking only at wage earnings.

The microdata available to us are somewhat limited in scope and thus preclude a comprehensive analysis for the total resident population of West Germany. The Income and Consumption Surveys (EVS) 1973, 1978 and 1983 exclude households with a foreign head, households with a monthly net income of more than DM 15,000 (1973), DM 20,000 (1978) and DM 25,000 (1983), households with more than six persons and the institutionalised population.[18] Although the waves of the German Socio Economic Panel (GSOEP) referring to the years 1983, 1985, 1987 and 1990 include foreigners, for the sake of comparability they are excluded from the following calculations.[19] These limitations of the data used have to be kept in mind when interpreting the results.

Additionally, we have to mention that since it is our intention to analyse changes in the inequality of regular earnings, we performed bottom-coding by leaving out the sub-group of persons having received wage earnings of less than DM 1,200 during the whole year.[20] Since we use two different data sets that fortunately overlap in 1983, we show for this year results derived from both sources (EVS 1983, GSOEP 1983) to give an impression of the effects of the methodological differences between them.

All the benchmark years were years of sizeable positive real growth, so we need not consider a possible bias in our comparison. The level of inequality of wage earnings, presented in table 9.4, seems to be within the range known from other studies.[21] During the first decade (1973–83), inequality of earnings rose continuously but moderately. A causal relation to the rise in unemployment seems plausible. The smallest changes occurred in the Gini coefficient. In (EVS) 1983 it reached 0.345, a level about 6 per cent higher than ten years earlier. As the other inequality mea-

Table 9.4 *Indicators of inequality of earnings[a] in the Federal Republic of Germany (West) 1973–1990*

Inequality measures	1973	1978	1983 (EVS)	1983 (GSOEP)	1985	1987	1990
Gini coefficient	0.3256	0.3330	0.3452	0.3594	0.3743	0.3693	0.3693
Atkinson index							
$\epsilon=0.5$	0.0975	0.1046	0.1112	0.1179	0.1296	0.1243	0.1281
$\epsilon=2.0$	0.4654	0.5181	0.5435	0.5519	0.5914	0.5757	0.5992
Theil index[b]	0.2359	0.2598	0.2769	0.2210	0.2428	0.2334	0.2443
Quintile shares in per cent							
1st quintile	4.85	4.41	4.25	3.96	3.42	3.72	3.63
2nd quintile	13.08	13.04	12.76	12.20	11.61	11.72	11.98
3rd quintile	19.82	19.91	19.46	18.90	18.99	18.93	18.94
4th quintile	24.96	24.94	24.58	24.98	25.09	25.05	24.71
5th quintile	37.29	37.70	38.95	39.76	40.87	40.49	40.72

Note:
[a] Reference group: all German persons having reported wage earnings, bottom-coding at the level of DM 100 per month.
[b] Strictly decomposable version of the Theil index, which is bottom sensitive.
Sources: Col. 1–3: EVS 1973, 1978, 1983; col. 4–7: GSOEP, waves 1984, 1986, 1988, 1991; own computations.

sures increased more during that period, it appears that greater changes occurred at the bottom and at the top of the wage scale. The Atkinson index (with an inequality aversion of 2.0) rose 11 per cent during the first five years and during the second five years 5 per cent. Likewise, the Theil index rose by more during the first sub-period (10 per cent) than during the second (6.6 per cent). These changes are consistent with the development of the quintile shares. The shares of the bottom quintile of wage earners fell 9 per cent to 1978 and by another 4 per cent to (EVS) 1983, whereas those of the three middle groups diminished very little. On the other hand, wage earners belonging to the top quintile realised an increase in their share of aggregate gross wage earnings of 1 per cent (1978) and 3 per cent (EVS 1983), respectively.

Comparing the results for 1983 EVS and GSOEP, we find the GSOEP data show a slightly higher inequality of earnings than the EVS data. Therefore, we compare the results of the following years only with 1983 GSOEP. The development (GSOEP) from 1983 to 1990 does not seem to follow a trend as unequivocal as that of the first decade. All inequality indicators reported in table 9.4 continued to rise until the mid 1980s and then declined before increasing once more. Again, the Gini coefficient turned out to be quite stable, indicating only little change in the middle range of the earnings distribution with a high population density. During the period from 1983 to 1985 (GSOEP), the Atkinson indices and the Theil index showed the strongest increases. In line with this change, the lower quintile shares decreased considerably – the first by nearly 14 per cent and the second by 5 per cent – while the fifth quintile increased its share by about 3 per cent. During the latter half of the 1980s, however, the losses of the two lowest quintiles were partly reversed, although they were far from reattaining the shares customary at the beginning of the 1970s.[22]

As mentioned in section 3, many factors influenced the pattern of inequality during these two decades: changes in the share of earnings in gross market income of the household sector, an increase in the labour force participation rate, especially of women, changes in wage structure, a reduction in hours worked per month, an increase of the numbers of part-time jobs and 'minor jobs' and, finally, increased unemployment. Also, the fact that the risk of becoming unemployed is not evenly distributed across the various levels of education has its influence. We would require much more detailed information than can be gathered from our data sources to gauge the relative importance of each of these factors on the distribution of annual wage earnings. This question, therefore, has to be left to future studies.

5   **Changes in the distribution of equivalent income among persons in West Germany from 1973 to 1990**

We now turn back to the equivalent income perspective as it was shown in section 3, but instead of looking at the distribution problem at the meso-level of socioeconomic groups, we focus on the microlevel of individuals. As an indicator of well-being, equivalent income of persons is based on house-hold net income weighted accordingly and, therefore, includes all kinds of incomes and deductions as well as all members of a household, whether or not they are income recipients.

Table 9.5 depicts several inequality measures derived for the benchmark years.[23] These measures differ in the assumed basic social welfare function and, hence, in the normative implications and sensitivity with respect to income ranges.[24]

We can confirm the well-known fact that the distribution of equivalent income among all persons is much less unequal than the distribution of earnings among wage earners. But it is amazing to find that the distributional changes during the 1970s and the 1980s were quite moderate with a very slight tendency to growing inequality, while during the first decade the

Table 9.5 *Indicators of income inequality in the Federal Republic of Germany (West) based on equivalent income,[a] 1973–1990*

Inequality measures	1973	1978	1983 (EVS)	1983 (GSOEP)	1985	1987	1990
Gini coefficient	0.2537	0.2535	0.2548	0.2504	0.2595	0.2517	0.2601
Atkinson index							
$\epsilon=0.5$	0.0527	0.0539	0.0534	0.0505	0.0552	0.0518	0.0557
$\epsilon=2.0$	0.1765	0.1774	0.1877	0.1944	0.1943	0.1828	0.2008
Theil index[b]	0.1038	0.1051	0.1065	0.1057	0.1177	0.1100	0.1186
Quintile shares in per cent							
1st quintile	10.36	10.40	10.08	10.09	9.84	10.09	9.85
2nd quintile	14.12	14.15	14.18	14.23	13.99	14.31	14.09
3rd quintile	17.53	17.53	17.72	17.87	17.77	17.78	17.60
4th quintile	22.12	22.06	22.38	22.64	22.67	22.44	22.49
5th quintile	35.87	35.86	35.64	35.16	35.65	35.38	35.96

Notes:
[a] Equivalence scale derived from the scale specified in social assistance law: head of household: 1.0; other household members, aged 22 years or more: 0.80; aged 16 to 21 years: 0.90; aged 12 to 15 years: 0.75; aged 7 to 11 years: 0.65; aged up to 6 years: 0.45. The calculations for all years refer only to the sub-population with a head of household of German nationality. Data for households with a non-German head referring to the years 1973–83 are not available. Calculations with the GSOEP data for the years 1983–90 including households with a foreign head showed only very slight differences in the inequality measures (mostly less than 1 per cent, maximum 1.9 per cent).
[b] Strictly decomposable version of the Theil index, which is bottom-sensitive.
Sources: Col. 1–3: EVS 1973, 1978, 1983; col. 4–7: GSOEP, waves 1984, 1986, 1988, 1991; own computations.

relative welfare positions of the various socioeconomic groups narrowed the distance and then, during the second decade, diverged again (table 9.3).

During the first decade, the Gini coefficient remained nearly constant, at about 0.254. During the 1980s, however, the Gini coefficient first moved up nearly 4 per cent then fell back close to the level of 1983 GSOEP and rose again by more than 3 per cent to 0.2601 in 1990. As the Gini measure is most sensitive with respect to income ranges with high population density, the distribution within the middle range of equivalent income seems to be quite stable. The Atkinson index based on low inequality aversion shows a similar pattern with a slight indication of growing inequality. The Atkinson measure based on high inequality aversion and the Theil measure indicate more strongly an increase in inequality, the only exception being the year 1987, in which inequality was reduced although the macroeconomic conditions had improved but little. In particular, during the periods from 1978 to 1983 (EVS) and from 1987 to 1990 the Atkinson measure (with high inequality aversion) rose considerably, by 6 per cent and 10 per cent, respectively. During the first period, this increase in inequality coincides with a strong increase in unemployment, but during the second period the further increase is accompanied by a reduction of unemployment. An explanation for these opposite changes could be that the effect of less unemployment on the distribution of equivalent income was more than offset by the various measures taken to curb social benefits and to tighten the rules as they were sketched in section 2.

The very moderate trend towards increasing inequality is also evident in a study of the equivalent income shares of population quintiles – a more disaggregated presentation of the income distribution. From 1973 to 1983 (EVS), the quintile shares remained nearly constant with only very small losses of the lowest as well as of the top quintile to the advantage of the three middle quintiles (EVS between 1978 and 1983). However, during the 1980s the quintile shares went up and down. Comparing 1983 GSOEP with 1990, inequality has definitely increased with losses by the four lower quintiles in favour of the top quintile. This is also the message from the various summary inequality measures.[25] But on the whole, the changes have not been very grave.

Another informative way of looking at income inequality is shown in table 9.6. It presents distributions of persons by relative welfare positions, defined as brackets of equivalent income that are delimited by multiples of the overal average equivalent income.

Again, the changes during the whole period appear to be only minor. As expected with a skewed distribution, the fraction of persons below the mean was much greater than the fraction above. In all the years covered, about 60 per cent were found to be below the mean. The fraction of the population that belongs to the lowest group with less than half of mean equivalent income fluctuated but in general tended to increase – during the first decade more than 10 per cent and during the second period about 5 per cent. If one accepts the frequently used relative poverty line of 50 per cent of mean equivalent income, the increasing population share in the lowest bracket can be considered an indicator of growing poverty.[26]

6   Changes in inequality between and within socioeconomic groups

The amazing discrepancy between changes in the relative welfare positions of the socioeconomic groups – a convergence during the first decade and a

Table 9.6 *The distribution of persons by relative welfare positions^a in the Federal Republic of Germany (West), 1973–1990 (in per cent of all persons in private households with a German head)*

Year	Relative welfare position (in relation to average equivalent income)					
	<0.5	0.5–0.75	0.75–1.0	1.0–1.25	1.25–1.5	>1.5
1973	7.1	28.3	26.9	16.4	9.2	12.0
1978	6.9	28.5	27.1	16.8	9.1	11.6
1983 (EVS)	7.9	26.9	26.3	17.2	9.7	11.9
1983 (GSOEP)	8.3	25.6	25.5	17.9	9.9	12.7
1985	8.5	26.6	24.8	16.3	11.0	12.8
1987	7.7	25.6	26.7	18.0	10.2	11.4
1990	8.8	25.6	24.8	17.8	10.0	13.0

Note:
^{a} Equivalence scale derived from the scale specified in social assistance law.
Sources: Rows 1–3: EVS 1973, 1978, 1983; rows 4–7: GSOEP, waves 1984, 1986, 1988, 1991; own computations.

divergence during the second – and the continuous tendency to a slight increase of overall inequality poses questions.[27] One possible explanation would be that the socioeconomic groups traditionally distinguished in Germany are extremely heterogeneous so that changes of their relative average equivalent incomes are very misleading for the appraisal of changes of overall inequality. Changes of the relative size of the various groups may also play a role.

One approach to tackle this problem consists of a decomposition of the overall inequality into inequality within groups and between groups. Fortunately, the Theil index (in contrast to the Gini and Atkinson measures) is additively decomposable. This means, that 'for any non-overlapping exhaustive grouping of the population, the total inequality can be expressed as a weighted sum of the same index for the different groups (the "within-groups" component) plus the value of the index for the population as a whole, where each member is given the average income of its particular group (the "between-groups" component)'.[28] The Theil index used in this chapter is strictly decomposable and bottom-sensitive.

In row 1 of table 9.7, the overall Theil index is repeated from table 9.5. This overall index is decomposed according to population groups characterised by the occupational status of the head of household. All family members are assigned to the group of the head of household. For

Table 9.7 Decomposition of overall inequality by occupational status of head of household, based on equivalent income,[a] Federal Republic of Germany (West), 1973–1990 (resident foreigners excluded)

	1973	1978	1983 (EVS)	1983 (GSOEP)	1985	1987	1990
Overall Theil index	0.1038	0.1051	0.1065	0.1057	0.1177	0.1100	0.1186
Share of within-groups inequality (in per cent)	79.1	79.3	83.8	84.1	85.7	85.0	86.8
Share of between-groups inequality (in per cent)	20.9	20.7	16.2	15.9	14.3	15.0	13.2
Occupational status of head of household			Group-specific Theil index				
Self-employed	0.1430	0.1740	0.1531	0.1389	0.1677	0.1649	0.1582
Farmers	0.0647	0.0708	0.0728	0.1004	0.0777	0.1009	0.1117
Civil servants	0.0730	0.0696	0.0693	0.0789	0.0719	0.0763	0.0797
White-collar workers	0.0817	0.0777	0.0853	0.0864	0.0962	0.0805	0.1012
Blue-collar workers	0.0593	0.0567	0.0579	0.0759	0.0759	0.0647	0.0803
Not gainfully employed	0.1001	0.0979	0.1125	0.0950	0.1246	0.1223	0.1193

Note:
[a] Equivalence scale derived from the scale specified in social assistance law.
Sources: Col. 1–3: EVS 1973, 1978, 1983; col. 4–7: GSOEP, waves 1984, 1986, 1988, 1991; own computations.

weighting the 'within-groups' component, we have used the population shares of the respective groups as derived from our microdata.

The results of the decomposition of the Theil index are given in rows 2 and 3. They show, first, a clear prevalence of the total within-groups inequality in all benchmark years and, second, a pronounced tendency to an increase in the total within-groups inequality, amounting to 6 per cent during the first decade and 3 per cent during the second period. For Germany, this is a striking result. The occupational status, often associated with a specific income range, seems to contribute much less to overall inequality than is frequently assumed, and this contribution is even diminishing.

Looking at the group-specific Theil indices (the second group of rows in table 9.7), those of persons living in households of the self-employed are by far the highest but follow no clear pattern over time. At the other extreme, the Theil indices for the population living in households of blue-collar workers are the lowest ones in nearly all years. In the 1970s and early 1980s, the results for white-collar workers, fluctuating around 0.08, were less stable than for their blue-collar colleagues. The group-specific Theil index for civil servants was mostly at a level between those of blue- and white-collar workers but with less fluctuations. Inequality within the population group living in households of farmers, with one exception (1985), rose considerably – during the first decade about 12 per cent, during the following period 11 per cent. Farmers seem to become a more heterogeneous group.

Finally, persons living in households of not gainfully employed heads seem to be an even more heterogeneous group, especially when compared with the sub-groups of blue- and white-collar workers. In nearly all benchmark years, the Theil indices for that population sub-group came nearest to that of the self-employed. The values fluctuated in the range of 0.10 to 0.125 with increasing tendency. The large discrepancy between social assistance recipients and rich people living on income from their wealth explains only part of the heterogeneity. More important seems to be that due to the principle of maintaining the relative standard of living that is incorporated in the German social insurance system, inequality of earnings during the working period is maintained while receiving social transfers. Summarising the changes for the entire period under review, it seems that the increase in the share of within-groups inequality (row 2) is mainly caused by the white-collar workers and the not gainfully employed, because their population shares rose as well as their group-specific Theil index, while the effect of the increase of the group-specific Theil index of the self-employed and of farmers was compensated by a reduction in their population shares.

7   A first look at inequality in East Germany before and after unification in comparison to inequality in West Germany

The historically extraordinary event of the unification of a country divided for more than 40 years not only by political boundaries but also by two radically different economic and social systems happened in autumn 1990. Although Germany has been one country since then, it will continue to be a dual economy and a dual society for a long time to come. During the transition period characterised by different wage and social benefit levels, for example, it seems appropriate to maintain the distinction between the population of the former German Democratic Republic, now East Germany, and the former Federal Republic of Germany, now West Germany, and to compare only income distribution within each sub-population instead of comparing levels of well-being by using measures of real income.[29]

Fortunately, the GSOEP was extended to the former German Democratic Republic (GDR) just before unification with West Germany, and since then has been conducted regularly once a year using a slightly modified questionnaire.[30]

To provide a picture of the inequality of equivalent income in the two parts of Germany before and after unification, table 9.8 presents some inequality measures.[31] Though not completely comparable with table 9.5 because of some differences in the basic income concept (see footnote *a* to table 9.8), table 9.8 gives an impression of the distributional discrepancies, on the one hand between West Germany (1990) and the former GDR (1990), and on the other hand for East Germany under the old and the new regime.

The differences in the inequality of equivalent net income in West Germany and the German Democratic Republic in 1990 were actually very substantial, especially if measured by the Atkinson index. For both levels of inequality aversion used in table 9.8, the Atkinson measure for West Germany was about double its value for the German Democratic Republic, whereas the respective Gini coefficient amounted to a little less than 150 per cent. This indicates that great differences existed especially at the bottom and at the top of the equivalent income scale. This impression is supported by comparing the quintile shares. The share of equivalent income of the first quintile in West Germany is 20 per cent lower and the share of the fifth quintile is about 20 per cent higher than the respective shares for the German Democratic Republic. However, the differences with respect to the middle range are less the higher the quintile. Although there was considerable inequality in the German Democratic Republic, based on a socialist model, these inequalities were much less pronounced than in the Federal

Table 9.8 *Indicators of income inequality^a in the Federal Republic of Germany (FRG; 1990), the German Democratic Republic (GDR; 1990) and East and West Germany after reunification*

Inequality measures	East Germany				West Germany			
	1990	1991	1992	1993	1990	1991	1992	1993
Gini coefficient	0.185	0.198	0.200	0.216	0.267	0.263	0.264	0.274
Atkinson index								
$\epsilon=1$	0.055	0.067	0.066	0.078	0.114	0.109	0.111	0.119
$\epsilon=2$	0.109	0.136	0.133	0.157	0.216	0.208	0.209	0.225
Quintile shares in per cent								
1st quintile	11.8	11.3	11.1	10.6	9.4	9.5	9.5	9.2
2nd quintile	15.8	16.1	15.9	15.5	14.0	14.0	14.1	13.8
3rd quintile	19.2	18.9	19.1	18.8	17.7	17.8	17.7	17.7
4th quintile	22.9	22.3	22.5	22.7	22.5	22.8	22.8	22.8
5th quintile	30.2	31.2	31.3	32.4	36.4	35.9	35.9	36.5

Note:
^{a} The figures refer to the distribution of equivalent income. The basic equivalence scale is derived from the scale specified in social assistance law. In contrast to table 9.5, a different income concept has been used: to net household income reported for one month (FRG: March or April; GDR: May) one twelfth of single payments as well as the imputed rental value of owner-occupied houses and apartments has been added. Additionally, resident foreigners are included.
Source: Müller, Klaus, Frick Joachim, and Hauser Richard (1995), 'Die hohe Arbeitslosigkeit in den neuen Bundesländern und ihre Verteilungswirkungen', in: Andreß, Hans-Jürgen (ed.), *Zur Entwicklung von Sozialstruktur und Arbeitsmarkt in Ostdeutschland – Parallelen und Differenzen zu Westdeutschland*, Berlin–New York (forthcoming).

Republic of Germany. Other computations not shown here[32] also depict much less poverty as measured by the head-count ratio at the 50 per cent line in the GDR than in the FRG. Two main reasons for this more favourable situation are obvious: In the German Democratic Republic, practically nobody willing to work was unemployed, and the labour force participation rate of women was as high as for men. Moreover, minimum pensions existed at a level slightly above the poverty line, housing costs were almost negligible and basic goods were cheap because of subsidies. On the other hand, very high incomes practically did not exist, because persons could not receive high incomes from large holdings of private wealth.

After unification, the distribution of equivalent income in East Germany immediately turned to more inequality. The Gini coefficient rose by about 7 per cent, the two Atkinson indices increased by more than 20 per cent within one year.[33] But in 1991 the inequality of the income distribution in East Germany was still far away from the situation in West Germany.

Between 1991 and 1992, there was nearly no change of overall inequality in East Germany or in West Germany, perhaps because of the effects of several state programmes to subsidise employment. Thereafter, all indicators presented in table 9.8 rose again considerably – in East Germany more pronounced than in West Germany. For example, from 1992 to 1993 the Gini coefficient increased by about 8 per cent in East Germany but by less than 4 per cent in the western part. Hence, the inequality of equivalent income in East Germany again moved towards the respective level in West Germany. The difference between the Gini coefficients has been reduced to 27 per cent of the East German value (1993) compared to 44 per cent in 1990.[34]

In this transformation process, the results shown in table 9.8 are only a snapshot of a quickly changing situation. Although the West German system of social protection was transferred to the East with some additional minimum regulations that do not exist in West Germany, this did not hamper an increase in inequality. One factor is rising unemployment (a rate of 11.2 per cent in East Germany in 1991 and 15.8 per cent in 1993, compared to West Germany's 6.1 per cent and 8.1 per cent). Another factor is the new opportunities to earn income as a self-employed person or from capital that can be mobilised by selling private land, which has greatly increased in market value. Analyses of the following waves of the GSOEP will give more insight into the further development and speed of social change.

8   Summary

This chapter sketches the changes in the distribution of well-being during the period from 1972 to 1993 against the background of West Germany's economic and demographic development and compares the distribution of well-being in East Germany before and after unification. We rely on equivalent income of persons as the main measure of well-being but also look at the distribution of gross wage income of workers and employees. Estimates made by the Federal Statistical Office referring to the meso-level of average equivalent income of socioeconomic groups as well as various distributional measures we have computed on a microlevel (Gini coefficient, Atkinson measure, Theil measure and quintile shares) are used to gauge changes in the distribution. The computations are based on two sets of microdata available to us, namely the official Income and Consumption

Surveys (Einkommens- und Verbrauchsstichproben), referring to the benchmark years 1973, 1978 and 1983, and the German Socio-Economic Panel (GSOEP), referring to the years 1983, 1985, 1987 and 1990 for West Germany and to the years 1990–3 for West and East Germany.

At the meso-level, we find substantial changes in the relative welfare positions of the ten socioeconomic groups. While the ranking of the groups remained nearly constant during the whole period under review, we find a considerable decrease for the self-employed and an increase for all groups of wage earners during the first decade; among the not gainfully employed, pensioners and recipients of unemployment benefits improved their positions slightly, but social assistance recipients experienced a decrease. During the second decade, these tendencies were reversed with a strong increase for the self-employed and slight declines for other groups. During the recession starting in 1992, some of these tendencies were reversed.

Due to limitations of our data at the microlevel, only persons living in households with a German head are included. We find slight increases in the inequality of gross earnings during both periods. The distribution of well-being as measured by equivalent income of persons seems also to have become slightly more unequal during the whole period, but the changes are very small and partly reversed during sub-periods. Poverty as measured by the head-count ratio at the 50 per cent line also increased slightly, to a level of almost 9 per cent in 1990. A decomposition of overall inequality by occupational status of the heads of household using the Theil measure gives two interesting results: more than 80 per cent of overall inequality is due to within-groups inequality compared with less than 20 per cent due to between-groups differences, and the share of within-groups inequality was rising continuously. The two groups that contribute more than their population shares to overall inequality are the self-employed and the not gainfully employed. Finally, we found that before unification the distribution of well-being in East Germany was much less unequal than in West Germany. That inequality is rising, although it has by far not reached West German levels.

Notes

Revised version of a paper presented at the conference 'The Distribution of Economic Well-Being in the 1980s – An International Perspective', 21–3 June, 1993 in Fiskebäckskil, Sweden. We thank the editors, Björn Gustafsson, Peter Gottschalk and Edward Palmer, and the discussant of our paper, Leif Nordberg, for very helpful comments on the first version. All the remaining errors are ours.

This study was partly funded by the National Institute on Aging, Program Project #1–PO1–AG09743–01, 'The Well-Being of the Elderly in a Comparative

Context'. The study is co-financed by the Hans-Böckler-Foundation, Düsseldorf, Project #93–537–4.

1 Statistisches Bundesamt (various years), Euler 1983b.
2 Statistisches Bundesamt 1994a.
3 Transfer-Enquête-Kommission 1981.
4 Deutsche Bundesbank 1991, Deutsche Bundesbank 1993.
5 Hauser and Semrau 1990, pp. 27–36; Schlomann 1992.
6 Huster 1993; Schäfer 1991, 1992 and 1993; Krause and Schäuble 1986; Lindner 1986.
7 Hauser and Engel 1985; Klein 1987; Krupp and Hanefeld 1987; Krupp and Schupp 1987; Rendtel and Wagner 1991; Berntsen 1992.
8 Annual publications of results, e.g., Bedau 1990; see also Deutsches Institut für Wirtschaftsforschung 1993a and 1993b.
9 Hauser and Hübinger 1993. Compare also the broader overview in Döring, Hanesch and Huster 1990.
10 Teichmann and Zwiener 1991.
11 Compare the report on Germany by Hauser, Cremer-Schäfer and Nouvertné 1981. The report of the Community is published as Commission of the European Communities, 'Final Report from the Commission to the Council on the First Programme of Pilot Schemes and Studies to Combat Poverty' (Brussels, 1981) COM (81) 769 final.
12 For an overview, compare Lampert 1991 and the official publication of Bundesminister für Arbeit und Sozialordnung 1991.
13 Compare Hauser and Hübinger 1993, p. 51.
14 See Bundesminister für Arbeit und Sozialordnung 1991, Texterganzung (Kapitel 26 Übergangsregelungen für die neuen Bundesländer).
15 Calculated from Bundesminister für Arbeit und Sozialordnung 1994, tables 1.8, 2.1, 6.11.
16 The relative difference between transfers received and transfers paid decreased from 41 per cent (1972) to about 37 per cent (1982) of transfers paid. Nevertheless, the amount of transfers paid always is far above the aggregated transfers received because non-monetary goods and services provided by the state are not included in the term 'transfers received'.
17 The following results are derived from estimates of group-specific average equivalent income recently published by the Federal Statistical Office. These estimates are based on data from the National Accounts and structural information from several statistics and inquiries. The equivalence scale used to derive equivalent income assigns a weight of 1 to the head of household, weights of 0.7 to additional family members over 15 years and weights of 0.5 to children under 15 years. Compare Statistisches Bundesamt 1994a and Spies 1992, pp. 418–30.
18 The EVS are official surveys with voluntary participation comprising about 45,000 to 50,000 households each. The original quota sample is reweighted using data from the respective microcensus, in which participation is compulsory. The EVS data result from two interviews and diaries covering the whole

year of investigation. Retained earnings of unincorporated business are included. The data were edited by the Federal Statistical Office. The anonymous microdata available to us consist of a reweighted 98.5 per cent random sample of the original data. Compare Euler 1972, pp. 375–7; Euler 1977, pp. 576–9; Euler 1982, pp. 433–7; Euler 1983a, pp. 813–18.

19 On the other side, households with more than six persons – not covered by our EVS sample – have not been excluded from the GSOEP data. This inconsistency seems to be negligible because of the minor size of that population group.

The first random sample of the GSOEP comprised about 6,000 households including households with a foreign head but excluding most of the institutionalised population. The decline in sample size of later waves due to panel attrition is corrected by a reweighting procedure. The GSOEP data are based on a single interview per year. During this interview, each household member over 15 years is questioned about his or her monthly net income at the time of the interview as well as about all kinds of gross market incomes and transfers received and contributions and taxes paid during the previous year. The income components are checked by various methods. Our analyses are based on annual income of the previous year, i.e., the information contained in the first wave surveyed in 1984 refers to calendar year 1983, and so on. Because of these slight conceptual differences we show in parallel results based on the EVS 1983 and on the GSOEP 1983 marked as 1983 (EVS) and 1983 (GSOEP), respectively. We use these data only in a cross-sectional perspective. The GSOEP is described in Hanefeld 1987; Projektgruppe Panel 1990, pp. 141–51; and in Burkhauser and Wagner 1994.

20 A second way of bottom-coding would have consisted in cutting out all earnings from so-called 'geringfügige Beschäftigungen' (minor jobs) that are exempt from social security contributions and do not earn any social insurance benefit entitlements. The maximum amount to be earned on such a minor job was about DM 500 in 1991; the maximum amount is indexed. They are considered minor jobs for housewives, students and so on. If persons accumulate (illegally) several of these minor jobs to make a living, they would be implicitly included.

A third method – to concentrate only on earnings of full-time workers – was rejected, because, given the increase in the numbers of part-time jobs, the connection to the distribution of equivalent income would have become too loose.

21 Burkhauser and Holtz-Eakin 1993.

22 A recent paper by Katherine G. Abraham and Susan N. Houseman (1992) emphasises the general stability of the West German wage structure but finds a narrowing of differentials at the bottom half of the distribution. This finding need not be in contradiction to our results of a slight increase in the inequality of earnings, because Abraham and Houseman concentrate on full-time workers only, while we include all wage earnings above DM 1,200 per year. Moreover, Abraham and Houseman include foreign workers resident in West Germany, whom we excluded, in their calculations. Abraham and Houseman refer mainly

to indicators of inequality different from those in table 9.4 (relative median earnings of percentiles). Compare Abraham and Houseman 1992.

23 The following computations are based on an equivalence scale derived from the German social assistance law. It differs slightly from the less differentiated scale used by the Federal Statistical Office in calculating the results reported in table 9.3. In our computations, the head of household gets a weight of 1.0, and additional adults older than 21 get weights of 0.8; children 0–6 years are assigned 0.45; 7–11 years 0.65; 12–15 years 0.75; and 16–21 years 0.90. This scale has been in effect for nearly the whole period covered. Only recently, this scale was slightly changed. A sensitivity test has been performed on the results reported in table 9.5 using the equivalence scale of the Federal Statistical Office. The values of the inequality measures were very close to the ones reported above, and the trends remained the same. It has to be pointed out that the equivalence scale used assigns comparatively high weights to additional household members. A drastically different equivalence scale could lead to a reversal of some results. Compare Buhmann, Rainwater, Schmaus and Smeeding 1988, pp. 115–42.

24 As in section 4, the results refer only to persons living in households with a German head. This introduces a slight bias towards underestimating inequality. Based on the GSOEP data that include foreigners, we recalculated some inequality measures for the total resident population and found slight differences of not more than 1.9 per cent for the various benchmark years. The results differ in methodology from those of Guger 1989, who refers to DIW-data that present the distribution of income per household unadjusted for household size. Many studies show that such a distribution is much more unequal than the personal distribution of equivalent income as used here.

For a discussion of various measures of inequality and their normative implications, see Atkinson 1992.

25 The reversal of this tendency between 1985 and 1987 should be interpreted with caution because of possible distorting effects of panel mortality. The questionnaire of the fifth wave of the GSOEP included, for the first time, some detailed questions concerning wealth that have caused a higher panel attrition rate than usual. Since it can be assumed that especially wealthier participants refused to continue with the panel, this may have resulted in a seeming reduction of inequality.

26 A tendency towards growing poverty from 1973 to 1983(a) and 1983(b) to 1986 is also shown in Hauser and Semrau 1989, but the levels are higher. For these computations, imputed rent of owner-occupied housing was added to net household income. This correction has a double effect. On the one hand, it raised average equivalent income and, therefore, the poverty line and the head-count measures of poverty. On the other hand, some persons with sizeable imputed rent are lifted out of poverty, resulting in a reduction of the head-count measure. Additionally, it has to be remembered that in our study as well as in Hauser and Semrau's, foreigners are excluded from the data. This has a similar double effect on the results. Calculations by other authors based on the GSOEP

data from 1983(b) to 1990 including foreigners depict an almost stable tendency
of the poverty head-count measure. Compare Habich and Krause 1992, pp.
482–95.

27 It has to be kept in mind that the two analyses are not strictly comparable,
because our computations based on microdata exclude foreigners, while the
figures of the Federal Statistical Office refer to the whole resident population.

28 Compare Rodrigues 1993, p. 6.

29 Even comparisons of income distributions have to be done very cautiously
because in socialist economies, income is a much worse indicator of well-being
than in market economies. The main reasons, taking the former German
Democratic Republic as an example, are the following: distortion of the price
system with high subsidisation of basic goods and housing, rationing, special
privileges for the nomenklatura and other groups, fulfilment of many 'social
tasks' by state enterprises, differences in goods provided free by the state, a job
guarantee, the use of working time for many private purposes and a considerable share of private barter trade. For a more systematic analysis, see Hauser
1992, pp. 37–72.

30 The methodology is described in Schupp and Wagner 1990, pp. 152–9.

31 Many aspects of inequality are discussed in the conference volume Glatzer
and Noll 1992; see also Berger, Hinrichs, Priller and Schultz 1993; Hauser,
Müller, Wagner and Frick 1991; Frick, Hauser, Müller and Wagner 1993,
pp. 204–28.

32 Compare Hauser, Müller, Wagner and Frick 1991; table 9.2; Krause 1993.

33 These computations include all persons resident in the GDR in 1989 before unification, although they may have moved afterwards. Upon closer inspection one
finds that this first increase in inequality was mainly due to the several hundred
thousand persons who moved from the East to the West and took on jobs at
western pay levels and to a great number of commuters who resided in the East
but worked in the West.

34 See also Hauser, Frick, Müller and Wagner 1994.

References

Abraham, K. G. and Houseman, S. N. 1992. 'Earnings Inequality in Germany.'
Paper prepared for the NBER Conference on Differences and Changes in
Wage Structures, revised version, 23–24 July, Cambridge, Massachusetts.

Atkinson, A. B. 1983. *The Economics of Inequality.* 2nd edn Oxford.
1992. 'Measuring Inequality and Differing Social Judgements', in Smeeding,
T. M. (ed.), *International Comparisons of Economic Inequality*, Series Research
on Economic Inequality, vol. 3: 29–56. Ed. D.J. Slottje. Greenwich, Conn.,
London.

Bäcker, G. 1992. 'Sozialpolitik zwischen Überforderung und Strukturreformen'.
WSI-Mitteilungen, 11/92: 711–21.

Bedau, K.-D. 1990. 'Das Einkommen sozialer Haushaltsgruppen in der
Bundesrepublik Deutschland 1988'. *Wochenbericht*, 22/90: 304–13. Ed.
Deutsches Institut für Wirtschaftsforschung.

Bedau, K.-D., Freitag, B. and Göseke, G. 1987. 'Die Einkommenslage der Familien in der Bundesrepublik Deutschland in den Jahren 1973 und 1981', in *Beiträge zur Strukturforschung*, vol. 97. Berlin: Deutsches Institut für Wirtschaftsforschung.

Berger, H., Hinrichs, W., Priller, E. and Schultz, A. 1993. 'Veränderungen der Struktur und der sozialen Lage ostdeutscher Haushalte nach 1990'. Working Group Social Reporting, Discussion Paper P93–105. Berlin: Wissenschaftszentrum Berlin für Sozialforschung.

Berntsen, R. 1992. *Dynamik in der Einkommensverteilung privater Haushalte. Eine empirische Längsschnittanalyse für die Bundesrepublik Deutschland.* Frankfurt/Main–New York.

Buhmann, B., Rainwater, L., Schmaus, G. and Smeeding, T. M. 1988. 'Equivalence Scales, Well-Being, Inequality, and Poverty: Sensitivity Estimates Across Ten Countries Using the Luxembourg Income Study (LIS) Database'. *The Review of Income and Wealth*, 32: 115–42.

Buhmann, B., Rainwater, L., Schmaus, G. and Smeeding, T. M. (eds.). 1994. *Statistisches Taschenbuch 1994.* Bonn.

Bundesanstalt für Arbeit. 1992. *Amtliche Nachrichten (ANBA)*, vol. 40. Nürnberg.
   1993. *Amtliche Nachrichten (ANBA)*, vol. 41. Nürnberg.

Bundesminister für Arbeit und Sozialordnung (ed.). 1991. *Übersicht über die soziale Sicherheit*, 2nd edn Bonn.

Burkhauser, R. V. and Holtz-Eakin, D. 1993. 'Changes in the Distribution of Wage Earnings During the Growth Years of the 1980s: A Cross-National Comparison of the United States and Germany'. Paper prepared for the German Socio-Economic Panel Users Meeting, 7–8 June, Berlin.

Burkhauser, R. V. and Wagner, G. 1994. 'The Socio-Economic Panel after Ten Years', in Burkhauser, R. V. and Wagner, G. (eds.), *Proceedings of the 1993 International Conference of German Socio-Economic Panel Study Users.* Vierteljahresheft zur Wirtschaftsforschung, Heft 1/2, S. 7–9.

Commission of the European Communities. 1981. 'Final Report from the Commission to the Council on the First Programme of Pilot Schemes and Studies to Combat Poverty'. COM (81) 769 final. Brussels.

Danziger, S. H. and Taussig, M. K. 1979. 'The Income Unit and the Anatomy of Income Distribution'. *The Review of Income and Wealth*, 25: 365–75.

Deutsche Bundesbank. 1991. 'Die Entwicklung der Einkommen und ihre Verteilung in Westdeutschland seit 1982'. *Monatsberichte der Deutschen Bundesbank*, 43, 8.
   1993. 'Zur Vermögenssituation der privaten Haushalte in Deutschland'. *Monatsberichte der deutschen Bundesbank*, 45, 10.

Deutsches Institut für Wirtschaftsforschung. 1990. 'Das Einkommen sozialer Haushaltsgruppen in der Bundesrepublik Deutschland 1988'. *Wochenbericht*, 22/90: 304–13.
   1993a. 'Zur Entwicklung der Einkommensverteilung in der Bundesrepublik Deutschland, Gutachten im Auftrag der Hans-Böckler-Stiftung' (bearbeitet von K.-D. Bedau, V. Meinhardt, F. Stille, D. Teichmann, R. Zwiener). Berlin. Mimeographed.
   1993b. 'Verteilungsprobleme in Westdeutschland'. *Wochenbericht*, 37/93: 501–7.

Döring, D., Hanesch, W. and Huster, E.-U. (eds.). 1990. *Armut im Wohlstand.* Frankfurt/Main.

Euler, M. 1972. 'Die Einkommens- und Verbrauchsstichprobe 1973'. *Wirtschaft und Statistik*, 7/72: 375–7.

1977. 'Die Einkommens- und Verbrauchsstichprobe 1978'. *Wirtschaft und Statistik*, 9/77: 576–9.

1982. 'Die Einkommens- und Verbrauchsstichprobe 1983'. *Wirtschaft und Statistik*, 6/82: 433–7.

1983a. 'Genauigkeit von Einkommensangaben in Abhängigkeit von der Art der statistischen Erfassung. Dargestellt am Beispiel der Einkommens- und Verbrauchsstichprobe 1978'. *Wirtschaft und Statistik*, 10/83: 813–18.

1983b. 'Die Einkommensverteilung und -entwicklung in der Bundesrepublik Deutschland 1962–1978 nach Ergebnisssen der Einkommens- und Verbrauchsstichproben'. *Konjunkturpolitik, Zeitschrift für angewandte Wirtschaftsforschung*, 29: 199–228.

EVS. 1973, 1978, 1983, data files of the Einkommens- und Verbrauchsstichproben, 1973, 1978 and 1983 (Income and Consumption Surveys) with a limited catalogue of variables held by the author in a data bank system at the University of Frankfurt/Main.

Foster, J. E., Greer, E. J. and Thorbecke, E. 1984. 'A Class of Decomposable Poverty Measures'. *Econometrica*, 52: 761–6.

Frick, J., Hauser, R., Müller, K. and Wagner, G. 1993. 'Die Auswirkungen der hohen Unterbeschäftigung in Ostdeutschland auf die personelle Einkommensverteilung', in Neubäumer, R. (ed.), *Arbeitsmarktpolitik kontrovers, Analysen und Konzepte für Ostdeutschland.* Darmstadt, pp. 204–28.

Glatzer, W. and Noll, H.-H. (eds.). 1992. *Lebensverhältnisse in Deutschland: Ungleichheit und Angleichung, Soziale Indikatoren XVI.* Frankfurt/Main–New York.

Göseke, G. and Bedau, K.-D. 1974. 'Verteilung und Schichtung der Einkommen der privaten Haushalte in der Bundesrepublik Deutschland 1950–1975'. *Beiträge zur Strukturforschung*, no. 31. Ed. Deutsches Institut für Wirtschaftsforschung. Berlin.

GSOEP, 1983, 1985, 1987, 1990. Public use file of the Sozio-oekonomisches Panel (German Socio-Economic Panel) held by the author in a data bank system at the University of Frankfurt/Main.

Guger, A. 1989. 'The Distribution of Household Income in Germany'. WIFO Working Paper No. 35. Vienna.

Habich, R., Heady, B. and Krause, P. 1991. 'Armut im Reichtum-Ist die Bundesrepublik Deutschland eine Zwei-Drittel-Gesellschaft?', in Rendtel, U. and Wagner, G. (eds.), *Lebenslagen im Wandel: Zur Einkommensdynamik in Deutschland seit 1984.* Frankfurt/Main–New York, pp. 488–509.

Habich, R. and Krause, P. 1992. Niedrigeinkommen und Armut. In *Datenreport*, ed. Statistisches Bundesamt, in cooperation with Wissenschaftszentrum Berlin für Sozialforschung and Zentrum für Umfragen, Methoden und Analysen, Mannheim, Bonn, pp. 482–95.

Hanefeld, U. 1987. *Das Sozio-ökonomische Panel. Grundlagen und Konzeption.* Frankfurt/Main–New York.

Hauser, R. 1992. 'Die personelle Einkommensverteilung in den alten und neuen Bundesländern vor der Vereinigung. Probleme eines empirischen Vergleichs und der Abschätzung von Entwicklungstendenzen'. *Sozialpolitik im vereinten Deutschland II, Schriften des Vereins für Socialpolitik*, 208/II: 37–72, ed. G. Kleinhenz. Berlin.

Hauser, R., Cremer-Schäfer, H. and Nouvertné, U. 1981. *Armut, Niedrigeinkommen und Unterversorgung in der Bundesrepublik Deutschland-Bestandsaufnahme und sozialpolitische Perspektiven.* Frankfurt/Main–New York.

Hauser, R. and Engel, B. (eds.). 1985. *Soziale Sicherung und Einkommensverteilung. Empirische Analysen für die Bundesrepublik Deutschland.* Frankfurt/Main–New York.

Hauser, R., Frick, J., Müller, K. and Wagner, G. G. 1994. 'Inequality in Income: A Comparison of East and West Germans before Reunification and during Transition'. *Journal of European Social Policy*, 4: 277–95.

Hauser, R. and Hübinger, W. 1993. *Arme unter uns. Ergebnisse und Konsequenzen der Caritas-Armutsuntersuchung*, vol. I. Freiburg.

Hauser, R., Müller, K., Wagner, G. and Frick, J. 1991. 'Incomes in East and West Germany on the Eve of Union – Some Results Based on the German Socio-Economic Panel'. Discussion Paper No. 34. Berlin: Deutsches Institut für Wirtschaftsforschung.

1992. 'Einkommensverteilung und Einkommenszufriedenheit in den neuen und alten Bundesländern', in Glatzer, W. and Noll, H.-H. (eds.), *Lebensverhältnisse in Deutschland: Ungleichheit und Angleichung, Soziale Indikatoren XVI.* Frankfurt/Main–New York.

Hauser, R. and Semrau, P. 1989. *Trends in Poverty and Low Income in the Federal Republic of Germany.* Sfb 3-Arbeitspapier No. 306. Frankfurt/Main–Mannheim.

1990. 'Zur Entwicklung der Einkommensarmut von 1963–1986'. *Sozialer Fortschritt*, 2: 27–36.

Huster, E.-U. (ed.). 1993. *Reichtum in Deutschland. Der diskrete Charme der sozialen Distanz.* Frankfurt/Main–New York.

Kammann, H. W. 1980. *Umverteilungswirkungen und zeitliche Entwicklung des Sozialtransfer-Systems.* Frankfurt/Main.

Klein, T. 1987. *Sozialer Abstieg und Verarmung von Familien durch Arbeitslosigkeit. Eine mikroanalytische Untersuchung für die Bundesrepublik Deutschland.* Frankfurt/Main–New York.

Krause, D. and Schäuble, G. 1986. *Einkommensquellen und Lebenschancen. Eine Untersuchung zur Einkommenssituation der Haushalte in der Bundesrepublik Deutschland.* Berlin.

Krause, P. 1993. 'Einkommensarmut in Ostdeutschland nimmt nicht mehr zu'. *Wochenbericht*, ed. Deutsches Institut für Wirtschaftsforschung, 51–2/93: 750–2.

Krupp, H.-J. and Hanefeld, U. 1987. *Lebenslagen im Wandel: Analysen 1987.* Frankfurt/Main–New York.

Krupp, H.-J. and Schupp, J. (eds.). 1987. *Lebenslagen im Wandel: Daten 1987.* Frankfurt/Main–New York.

Lampert, H. 1991. *Lehrbuch der Sozialpolitik*. 2nd edn. Berlin–Heidelberg.

Lindner, H. (ed.). 1986. *Aussagefähigkeit von Einkommensverteilungsrechnungen für die Bundesrepublik Deutschland, Gutachten im Auftrag des Bundesministers für Wirtschaft*. Tübingen.

Müller, K., Frick, J. and Hauser, R. 1995. 'Die hohe Arbeitslosigkeit in den neuen Bundesländern und ihre Verteilungswirkungen', in Andreß, H.-J. (ed.), *Zur Entwicklung von Sozialstruktur und Arbeitsmarkt in Ostdeutschland-Parallelen und Differenzen zu Westdeutschland*. Berlin–New York (in press).

Projektgruppe Panel. 1990. 'Das Sozio-ökonomische Panel für die Bundesrepublik Deutschland nach fünf Wellen'. In *Vierteljahreshefte zur Wirtschaftsforschung*, ed. Deutsches Institut für Wirtschaftsforschung, 2–3/90: 141–51.

Rendtel, U. and Wagner, G. (eds.). 1991. *Zur Einkommensdynamik in Deutschland seit 1984*. Frankfurt/Main–New York.

Rodrigues, C. F. 1993. 'Measurement and Decomposition of Inequality in Portugal. 1980/81–1989/90'. CISEP Documentos de trabalho, no. 1. Lisbon.

Sachverständigenrat zur Begutachtung der gesamtwirtschaftlichen Entwicklung (SVR). 1992/3. Jahresgutachten 1992/3. Bundestagsdrucksache 12/3774.

1993/4. Jahresgutachten 1993/4. Bundestagsdrucksache 12/6170.

1994/5. Jahresgutachten 1994/5 Bundestagsdrucksache 13/26.

Schäfer, C. 1991. 'Zunehmende Schieflage in der Einkommensverteilung-Zur Entwicklung der Einkommensverteilung 1990'. *WSI-Mitteilungen*, 10/91: 593–613.

1992. 'Das "Teilen" will nicht gelingen-Zur Entwicklung der Einkommens-verteilung 1991-'. *WSI-Mitteilungen*, 10/92: 629–51.

1993. '"Armut" und "Reichtum" sind die verteilungspolitischen Aufgaben-Zur Entwicklung der Einkommensverteilung 1992 -'. *WSI-Mitteilungen*, 10/93: 617–34.

Schäfer, D. and Schmidt, L. 1993. 'Abschreibungen nach verschiedenen Bewer-tungs- und Berechnungsmethoden'. *Wirtschaft und Statistik*, 12/93: 919–31.

Schlomann, H. 1992. *Vermögensverteilung und Altersvorsorge*. Frankfurt/Main–New York.

Schüler, K. and Spies, V. 1991. 'Einkommen aus Unternehmertätigkeit und Vermögen in den Volkswirtschaftlichen Gesamtrechnungen. Erläuterungen zu den Berechnungen und revidierten Ergebnissen 1970 bis 1990'. *Wirtschaft und Statistik*, 10/91: 653–66.

Schupp, J. and Wagner, G. 1990. 'Die DDR-Stichprobe des Sozio-ökonomischen Panels-Konzept und Durchführung der "Basiserhebung 1990" in der DDR'. *Vierteljahreshefte zur Wirtschaftsforschung*, ed. Deutsches Institut für Wirtschaftsforschung, 2–3/90: 152–9.

Spies, V. 1992. 'Verfügbares Einkommen nach Haushaltsgruppen'. *Wirtschaft und Statistik*, 7/92: 418–30.

Statistisches Bundesamt. Wirtschaftsrechnungen, Fachserie 15, Einkommens- und Verbrauchsstichprobe 1983, no. 6, Einkommensverteilung und Einkommens-bezieher in privaten Haushalten. Stuttgart-Mainz.

Various years. Wirtschaftsrechnungen, Fachserie 15, Einkommens- und Verbrauchsstichprobe 1983.

Statistisches Bundesamt (III B). 1994a. Einkommensverteilung nach Haushaltsgruppen und Einkommensarten-Aktualisierte Ergebnisse der Volkswirtschaftlichen Gesamtrechnungen für die Jahre 1972–1993. Wiesbaden (Sonderdruck).

1994b. Verfügbares Einkommen, Zahl der Haushalte und Haushaltsmitglieder nach Haushaltsgruppen-Aktualisierte Ergebnisse der Volkswirtschaftlichen Gesamtrechnungen für die Jahre 1972 bis 1993. Wiesbaden (Sonderdruck).

Stolz, I. 1983. *Einkommensumverteilung in der Bundesrepublik Deutschland. Eine theoretische und empirische Untersuchung.* Frankfurt/Main–New York.

Teichmann, D. and Zwiener, R. 1991. 'Steuerentlastung 1986/90 und Steuerbelastung 1991: Umverteilung der Einkommen von unten nach oben'. *Wochenbericht*, 14/91: 178–84. Deutsches Institut für Wirtschaftsforschung.

Transfer-Enquête-Kommission. 1981. *Das Transfersystem in der Bundesrepublik Deutschland.* Stuttgart.

Wagner, G. 1991. 'Die Erhebung von Einkommensdaten im Sozio-ökonomischen Panel (SOEP)', in Rendtel, U. and Wagner, G. (eds.), *Lebenslagen im Wandel: Zur Einkommensdynamik in Deutschland seit 1984.* Frankfurt/Main–New York, pp. 26–33.

Wagner, G., Hauser, R., Müller, K. and Frick, J. 1992. 'Einkommensverteilung und Einkommenszufriedenheit in den neuen und alten Bundesländern Lebensverhältnisse in Deutschland: Ungleichheit und Angleichung', in Glatzer, W. and Noll, H.-H. (eds.), *Soziale Indikatoren XVI*, Frankfurt/Main–New York, pp. 91–137.

Welzmüller, R. 1989. 'Kräftige Gewinnsteigerung durch unerwarteten Wachstumsschub-Zur Entwicklung der Einkommensverteilung im Jahr 1988'. *WSI-Mitteilungen*, 7/89: 361–75.

10 Income inequality and poverty in Ireland in the 1970s and 1980s

TIM CALLAN AND BRIAN NOLAN

1 Introduction

In the early 1970s, Ireland's economic prospects appeared bright. Joining the European Community in 1973 (along with the United Kingdom and Denmark), Ireland became a member of the 'rich nation's club' and could expect to share in the prosperity of the expanded Community. Indeed, as the poorest member state, Ireland joined with promises of substantial resource transfers from its new partners to ease the transition. Together with economic growth, social expenditure could be expected to increase as the welfare state expanded. The promise was of 'a rising tide lifting all boats'. By the late 1980s, the reality looked rather different. Almost one in five of the labour force was unemployed. Reckless pump priming in the small and extremely open economy through the late 1970s in the face of international recession exacted a price, which was paid for in very low growth from 1980 to 1987 as public sector borrowing was brought under control. Servicing the public debt, now among the highest in relation to GDP in the EU, consumed a substantial proportion of tax revenue. No longer the poorest EU member after the expansion to include Spain, Portugal and Greece, Ireland was still receiving very substantial transfers from the Community to promote convergence. As economic growth stagnated and unemployment reached unprecedented levels, the role of social expenditure did indeed increase but primarily as a response to greater demands. From such an optimistic point of departure, what had happened to living standards and the distribution of economic well-being?

In this chapter we examine what happened to the distribution of income and to poverty in Ireland during this period. Recent research internationally has highlighted the increase in income inequality during the 1980s in a number of industrialised countries, notably the UK and the US, though this trend has not been universal. The contributions to this volume look in depth at the way inequality and poverty have evolved in various countries, enabling the identification of similarities and differences across countries in outcomes and causal factors. The aim of this chapter is to allow the Irish experience to be set alongside these others, adding to the international perspective. Section 2 looks at the distribution of income, focusing first on trends over time and then on the level of inequality compared with other western countries. Section 3 deals with poverty, again examining how it has changed over time and then how the Irish situation compares with other countries. Section 4 summarises the main points.

2 Income inequality

2.1 *Measuring income inequality in Ireland*

Studies of the distribution of income in Ireland rely on household surveys rather than administrative tax or social security records. The first survey on which income distribution estimates for the state could be based was the Household Budget Survey (HBS) carried out by the Central Statistics Office in 1973 (Nolan 1978; Murphy 1984). This was primarily an expenditure survey but contained detailed income data with questions, time period and recipient unit very similar to those used in the British Family Expenditure Survey (FES). Unfortunately, the HBS has been carried out only at seven-year intervals – in 1973, 1980 and 1987 – which is clearly a severe limitation for analysis of changes over time. The other major limitation is that the data tapes are not released to data archives or outside researchers. Some special analyses of the data have been carried out at arm's length, so we are not entirely reliant on the published reports, but the scope for in-depth investigation is constrained.

A separate household survey was carried out by the Economic and Social Research Institute (ESRI) in 1987 to provide data for research on income distribution, poverty and use of state services. (A full description is given in Callan *et al.* 1989.) The income information obtained is similar to that gathered in the HBS, and the major advantage of this source is that the microdata can be analysed directly. However, an important difference is that the farm income information obtained in the ESRI survey referred to 1986, which was a particularly bad year, whereas the HBS used farm accounts for 1987, when farm incomes were on average more than 25 per cent higher, which one would expect to produce differences in the income distribution between the two surveys. In the distribution analysis, the aggregate income measures employed here are gross income (market income plus social security payments received) and disposable income (gross income less income tax and employees' social security contributions paid). The time period is generally the preceding week, with the weekly average over a

Table 10.1 *Decile shares in gross income for Irish households, 1973, 1980 and 1987*

Decile	1973	1980	1987
bottom	1.5	1.6	1.9
2	3.0	3.0	3.1
3	4.8	4.5	4.2
4	6.4	6.1	5.4
5	7.7	7.6	7.0
6	9.2	9.2	8.8
7	10.9	10.9	10.9
8	13.2	13.3	13.6
9	16.6	16.8	17.6
top	26.7	27.0	27.5
all	100.0	100.0	100.0

Source: Rottman and Reidy (1988), table 7.4 (derived from 1973 and 1980 HBS tapes), 1987 from HBS Report (CSO).

longer period (usually a year) used for self-employment income. The recipient unit is the household.

2.2   Trends in income inequality

Table 10.1 shows the decile shares in gross household income from the HBS for 1973, 1980 and 1987. Between 1973 and 1980, the shares of the bottom quintile increased slightly, but those of the top three deciles also rose, with the losers being deciles 3, 4 and 5. The Lorenz curves for the two distributions thus cross, though the main change between the two years is the transfer from the bottom half of the distribution to the top quintile. This is reflected in the increase in the Gini and the Theil summary measures shown in table 10.2.[1] (Inequality rose even more for income before cash transfers, but transfers offset some of this increase (Murphy 1984; Rottman and Reidy 1988)). The pattern is similar for 1980–7 but more pronounced. The shares of the bottom two deciles increased substantially, but the shares of the top three deciles rose rather more, with the losers then being deciles 3, 4, 5 and 6. The summary inequality measures increased by more than they had between 1973 and 1980. Over the entire period from 1973 to 1987, then, the share of the bottom quintile rose by 0.5 per cent of total income, but that of the top quintile rose by almost 2 per cent of total income. The Gini coefficient for gross income rose by 5 per cent, and the Theil index by 8 per cent.

Table 10.2 *Gini and Theil coefficients for Irish households, gross income, 1973, 1980 and 1987*

Inequality measure	1973	1980	1987
Gini	0.379	0.385	0.398
Theil	0.236	0.243	0.255

Source: Calculated from decile shares in table 10.1.

Table 10.3 *Ireland: decile shares in disposable household income, 1973, 1980 and 1987*

Decile	1973	1980	1987
bottom	1.7	1.7	2.2
2	3.3	3.5	3.7
3	5.0	5.1	5.0
4	6.5	6.6	6.3
5	7.8	7.9	7.6
6	9.2	9.3	9.2
7	10.9	11.0	11.0
8	13.0	13.0	13.4
9	16.2	16.2	16.6
top	26.4	25.7	25.0
all	100.0	100.0	100.0

Source: Rottman and Reidy (1988), table 7.4 (derived from 1973 and 1980 HBS tapes), 1987 unpublished data supplied direct by CSO.

For disposable income the pattern was rather different, as shown in table 10.3. Between 1973 and 1980, the share of the bottom quintile rose slightly but those of deciles 3–7 also rose, while that of the top decile declined substantially. The Lorenz curves therefore do not intersect, 1980 Lorenz-dominates 1973 and the Gini and Theil coefficients fall, as seen in table 10.4. Between 1980 and 1987, the share of the bottom quintile rose substantially, and that of the top decile again fell. Deciles 3–6 then experienced a decline in share, however, with those of deciles 8 and 9 rising. Although the Lorenz curve for 1987 lies inside that for 1980 at most points, the curves do cross, and there is no unambiguous dominance. Nonetheless, the Gini and Theil coefficients show a decline in inequality between 1980 and 1987 which is slightly larger than between 1973 and 1980.

During the entire period 1973–87, inequality in the distribution of

Table 10.4 *Ireland: Gini and Theil coefficients, disposable income, 1973, 1980 and 1987*

Inequality measure	1973	1980	1987
Gini	0.367	0.360	0.352
Theil	0.221	0.211	0.200

Source: Calculated from decile shares in table 10.3.

disposable household income in the HBS fell, with 1987 Lorenz-dominating 1973 and the Gini coefficient falling from 0.37 to 0.35. This reflects the fact that the share of the top decile fell by 1.4 per cent of total income and that of the bottom quintile rose by 0.9 per cent. The other gainers were not in the bottom half of the distribution but rather deciles 8 and 9. However the pattern still contrasts with the increase in inequality observed for gross income, during both sub-periods and 1973–87 as a whole. The redistributive impact of income tax and employees' social insurance contributions on the gross income distribution therefore increased substantially over the period, as seen in the growing gap between the summary inequality measures for gross and disposable income. In 1973, the Gini coefficient for disposable income was 97 per cent of that for gross income, but by 1987 it was only 88 per cent, while the corresponding percentages for the Theil measure were 93 per cent and 77 per cent.

It is worth noting though that income distribution in the 1987 ESRI survey is more unequal than in the 1987 HBS, with a larger share going to the top decile, primarily because self-employment income is higher. This is only partly attributable to the difference in timing between the two surveys which, as already mentioned, leads to higher farm incomes in the HBS; it also reflects the fact that one household in the ESRI survey had very high income from self-employment. This illustrates the sensitivity of such estimates to sampling and the subsequent treatment of high-income 'outliers', an important and neglected issue in making income distribution comparisons. For our purposes, it means we rely on the HBS in assessing inequality trends over time while making use of the ESRI survey in looking at trends towards the bottom of the distribution later in this chapter.

It would be desirable to carry out the corresponding comparisons over time having adjusted household incomes for differences in size and composition, in other words to analyse the distribution of equivalent household incomes. Unfortunately, it is not possible to do this as comprehensively as one would wish given the current situation regarding access to the HBS (though recent legislation means that it may be possible in the future for the CSO to provide data tapes for the 1994 and subsequent surveys to researchers). Roche (1984) presents the equivalent gross and disposable income distributions for 1973 and 1980 using a set of equivalence scales based on the social security rates paid in 1973. On this basis, the distribution of gross equivalent income became unambiguously less equal between 1973 and 1980, while for disposable income the share of the bottom and top deciles fell and the remainder of the top half gained, with the Gini coefficient indicating a fall in inequality. Corresponding estimates from the 1987 HBS using a similar though not identical equivalence scale suggest that between 1980 and 1987 the distribution of disposable equivalent income once again became if anything more equal.

It is important to place these changes in income inequality in the context of the evolution of average real incomes, particularly in this case because average household income grew by about 25 per cent in real terms between 1973 and 1980 but fell by about 4 per cent between 1980 and 1987. Generalised Lorenz curves provide a convenient way of incorporating information about average living standards and inequality into the comparison of the level of social welfare yielded by different distributions: cumulative mean incomes instead of cumulative income shares are plotted against cumulative population shares (Shorrocks 1983; Jenkins 1991). Figure 10.1 shows the generalised Lorenz curves for the distribution of disposable (unadjusted) income among households in the 1973, 1980 and 1987 HBS. Both 1980 and 1987 lie above 1973 at all points because of the substantial increase in mean income between 1973 and 1980. With mean income slightly lower (in real terms) but the income share of the bottom deciles slightly higher in 1987 than 1980, however, the curves for those two years cross. While 1980 and 1987 are seen as preferable in social welfare terms to 1973, then, no unambiguous ranking of 1980 and 1987 is possible on this basis.

2.3   Explaining trends in inequality

Why did inequality in Irish income distribution evolve in this way during the years 1973–87? Without access to the HBS microdata it is not possible to address this question directly using for example the type of decomposition analysis performed by Atkinson (1993) and Jenkins (1992) with British FES data. However, the striking increases in both unemployment and direct personal taxation in the 1970s and 1980s appear to have been central. (Evidence is not available to assess whether increased inequality in the earnings distribution, examined by Gottschalk in this volume for a number of countries, also contributed.)

Rising unemployment is likely to have been a major influence on the

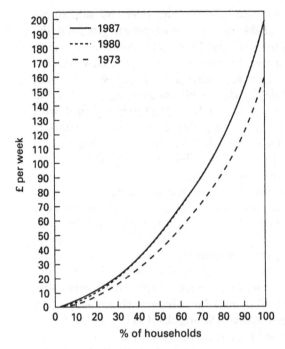

Figure 10.1 Generalised Lorenz curves for household disposable income: Ireland, 1973, 1980 and 1987

distribution of gross income. The rate of unemployment doubled to 7–8 per cent of the labour force between 1973 and 1980, and between 1980 and 1987 increased much more rapidly, exceeding 18 per cent of the labour force. This is likely to have played a major part in the falling gross income shares of the second and third quintiles of the unadjusted distribution, where the unemployed are most heavily concentrated.[2] In the Irish case, an unusually high proportion of the unemployed are married men living in families who would conventionally be termed 'household heads', rather than secondary earners.[3] Despite the fact that social security support rates increased in real terms, unemployment in general did result in a substantial decline in income for those affected.[4] Rates of social security support grew particularly rapidly for the elderly, who make up a significant proportion of the bottom quintile (in the unadjusted distribution) that saw an increase in share.

Total tax revenue including social security contributions rose, from 31 per cent of GDP in 1973, to 34 per cent in 1980 and 40 per cent in 1987, and taxes on personal income plus employees' social security contributions became more important within this increasing total, rising from 29 per cent

Table 10.5 *Suits progressivity index and average tax rate for income tax and PRSI contributions, 1973, 1980 and 1987*

	1973 per cent	1980 per cent	1987 per cent
Average tax rate			
income tax	7.8	12.9	15.4
PRSI contributions	2.0	2.2	3.5
total	9.8	15.1	18.9
Suits progressivity index			
income tax	0.194	0.207	0.275
PRSI contributions	−0.074	0.056	0.133
total	0.138	0.185	0.249

Source: 1973 from Nolan (1981), 1980 and 1987 calculated from HBS Reports.

of total taxation in 1973, to 37 per cent in 1980 and 40 per cent in 1987.[5] This reflected not only the growing burden of unemployment on the public purse but also the expansion in other areas of state expenditure associated with the ill-fated pump-priming fiscal policy adopted in 1977–9, with its legacy of extremely high public debt and associated debt service payments.[6] The impact on households in the HBS is shown in table 10.5. In 1973, income tax and employees' social security contributions (PRSI) came to just less than 10 per cent of gross household income; by 1980, it was 15 per cent, and by 1987, it had reached 19 per cent. The growing redistributive impact of income tax and social security contributions was also attributable to an increase in their progressivity. In table 10.5, the Suits progressivity index shows that in 1973, income tax was progressive, but social security contributions were mildly regressive (as indicated by the index's negative value). By 1980, social insurance contributions were also progressive. Between 1980 and 1987, income tax became a good deal more progressive, and so did social insurance contributions. The Suits index for tax and contributions combined increased 34 per cent in the earlier period and 35 per cent in the later one.

2.4   Income inequality in Ireland in an international perspective

Great care is needed in making cross-country comparisons of income inequality, as emphasised in the chapter by Gardiner in this volume, because of differences in income definitions, units of analysis and data. The income distribution database assembled by the Luxembourg Income Study

Table 10.6 *Decile shares of households in disposable annual income, Ireland and selected LIS countries, mid 1980s*

Decile	Ireland	Australia	Canada	Germany	Sweden	UK	US
1	2.0	1.7	2.0	2.8	1.8	2.0	1.4
2	3.5	2.8	3.7	4.4	4.4	4.0	3.2
3	4.8	4.1	5.2	5.7	5.5	5.1	4.6
4	6.0	5.6	6.6	6.9	6.8	6.3	6.1
5	7.4	7.5	8.1	8.2	8.0	7.8	7.8
6	9.0	9.3	9.6	9.6	9.3	9.3	9.4
7	10.8	11.2	11.3	11.1	11.4	11.1	11.3
8	13.1	13.5	13.4	12.8	14.2	13.2	13.6
9	16.3	16.8	16.2	15.3	16.6	16.2	16.9
10	27.0	27.5	24.0	23.2	22.0	25.0	25.7

Source: Ireland from 1987 ESRI survey; other countries from Bishop, Chow and Formby (1993), table A3, part B.

(LIS) is designed to overcome these obstacles to the greatest extent possible, and Gardiner pulls together from various studies based on LIS income inequality results for a number of countries, not including Ireland. It is therefore worth comparing Ireland with other countries in LIS, again on the basis of published results. The preferred income concept in the LIS is annual rather than weekly, so rather than the Irish results from the HBS discussed above, estimates of the distribution of annual income from the 1987 ESRI survey are used.

Callan and Nolan (1992b) show that the Gini coefficients for annual gross and disposable income in the 1987 ESRI survey are higher than the corresponding figures for most of the seven LIS countries studied in O'Higgins, Schmaus and Stephenson (1989). Ireland was not Lorenz-dominated by most of these countries, because the share going to the bottom quintile was relatively high. The data for the other countries in that comparison were from the LIS first wave for about 1980 and income inequality had risen in some of these by 1987, so a comparison with second-wave LIS data for the mid 1980s, now available, is more useful. Table 10.6 compares the Irish estimates from the ESRI survey with the decile shares in annual disposable income among households[7] for Australia, Canada, Germany, Sweden, the UK and the US around the mid 1980s derived from LIS by Bishop, Chow and Formby (1993).[8] Ireland Lorenz-dominates Australia, but otherwise what is striking is the relatively high share going to the top decile in Ireland – even compared with the US – and the relatively

Table 10.7 *Percentages below relative poverty lines, Ireland, 1973, 1980 and 1987*

	1973 HBS	1980 HBS	1987 HBS	1987 ESRI
40 per cent line				
per cent of households	8.0	8.5	7.3	10.0
per cent of persons	8.5	10.4	10.4	12.8
50 per cent line				
per cent of households	18.2	17.2	16.2	18.9
per cent of persons	17.8	19.2	20.9	22.9
60 per cent line				
per cent of households	27.8	27.9	26.6	29.0
per cent of persons	28.7	29.7	31.6	33.5

Source: 1973, 1980 and ESRI 1987 from Callan *et al.* (1989), HBS 1987 from special analysis.

low shares not of the bottom but of deciles 2–5 compared with Canada, Germany, Sweden and the UK. Some caveats about this comparison must be noted. The fact that annual income in the ESRI sample had to be estimated from limited information could serve to overstate inequality, though this would also be true of some of the other countries. Despite the best efforts of LIS, some differences in definition, etc. between countries remain. Finally, we have already seen that the distribution of income in the ESRI sample is more unequal than that in the HBS for the same year, and that this was most pronounced at the top of the distribution. While factors contributing to this difference have been identified, it means that a question mark has to be placed over the estimate of the share of the top decile in the Irish case.

It is therefore also of interest to compare the distribution of gross and disposable weekly income in the 1987 HBS with the corresponding figures from the British FES, since the Irish HBS and the FES are very similar in terms of the concepts and measures employed. Such a comparison for 1973 (Nolan 1981) shows the Irish distribution to be more unequal than the UK one, but by 1987 that was no longer the case. The quintile shares for gross income in the two countries were by then very similar, as were the Gini coefficients at 0.40. For disposable income, Ireland actually had a slightly lower Gini coefficient by 1987. This highlights the divergence of trends in disposable income inequality between the two countries during the 1970s and 1980s, with UK income becoming markedly less equal while Irish income became more equally distributed.

3   Poverty and living standards

3.1   Trends in relative poverty 1973–1987

A series of studies using the 1987 ESRI survey applies a number of different approaches to measuring poverty in Ireland, including relative income lines, subjective lines based on the Leyden approach and the combination of income and indicators of deprivation (Callan *et al.* 1989; Callan, Nolan and Whelan 1993; Callan and Nolan 1994a). Here our primary interest is in trends over time, and for this purpose it is again necessary to rely on the HBS for 1973 and 1980 as points of comparison. We therefore concentrate on results which can be replicated from those surveys, using relative income poverty lines constructed as a particular percentage of average equivalent income in the sample. This approach has in any case a number of advantages in making comparisons over time or across countries, in that the identical procedure can be readily applied in each case and the sensitivity of the results to the particular line or equivalence scale chosen can be examined. We look at the numbers falling below 40 per cent, 50 per cent and 60 per cent of mean equivalent household income. The equivalence scale employed is the one which has been used in a number of comparative studies for the EU, where the household head is given a value of 1, each additional adult is 0.7 and each child 0.5. These lines were applied to the HBS for 1973 and 1980 and to both the HBS and the ESRI samples for 1987. Table 10.7 shows the percentage of households and persons falling below each line.

Comparing 1980 with 1973, the percentage of households falling below the 40 per cent line rose, the percentage below half average income fell and the percentage below the 60 per cent line was virtually unchanged. There was a consistent increase in the percentage of persons living in households below these lines, because the average size of these households was rising over time. Now, comparing the 1980 and 1987 HBSs, the percentage of households falling below each of the three lines decreased, but once again the average size of these households rose. Thus, there was an increase in the percentage of persons below the 50 per cent and 60 per cent lines while the percentage in households below the 40 per cent line remained unchanged. A higher percentage of households and persons fell below each of the relative lines in the 1987 ESRI survey than in the HBS for that year, the much lower levels of income from farming in the ESRI survey apparently being the principal explanation. Comparing the 1980 HBS with the ESRI sample results for 1987 thus shows a consistent increase over time in the percentage of households and persons below each of the relative lines.

The sensitivity of these trends in relative poverty over time to the equivalence scale employed is tested in Callan *et al.* (1989), which shows that the general pattern held across the range of scales tested. As well as the head count of households and persons below the lines, per capita 'poverty gaps' and the distributionally sensitive summary poverty measure proposed by Foster, Greer and Thorbecke (1984) also consistently show an increase in measured poverty between 1973 and 1980, and between 1980 and the 1987 ESRI survey.[9] An alternative perspective for the 1980–7 period is provided by a cross-country study carried out for Eurostat which employed relative poverty lines based on equivalised household *expenditure* rather than income and applied these to the 1980 and 1987 HBS for Ireland (Eurostat 1990). The results show a fall in the percentage of households but an increase in the percentage of persons below the 40 per cent and 50 per cent poverty lines between 1980 and 1987. Application of relative poverty lines to the available Irish data therefore consistently shows that the percentage of persons below such lines rose between 1973 and 1980 and again between 1980 and 1987. The magnitude of the increase over the 1973–87 period varies depending on the proportion of mean income chosen, the equivalence scale used and whether the ESRI or HBS samples are the basis for the 1987 results. Nonetheless, the robustness of the overall conclusion as to the direction of change is to be emphasised. We look in the next section at some of the principal factors underlying this trend.

3.2   Explaining trends in poverty

Major changes in composition of households falling below the relative income poverty lines occurred over the period, and these provide insights into the processes at work. In 1973, almost half the households below the 50 per cent line had a head who was retired or 'in home duties', and only 10 per cent had an unemployed head. By 1980, the former had fallen to 36 per cent, and the latter had risen to 15 per cent. By 1987 (using the ESRI survey), only about 20 per cent of the households below half average income had a head who was retired or in home duties, while over one-third now had an unemployed head. Similar trends in composition are seen with the other relative lines. The increase in unemployment described earlier is therefore of central importance to understanding the evolution of poverty in Ireland in the 1970s and 1980s. The *risk* of poverty for households headed by an unemployed person did not in fact rise: the dramatic rise in the numbers unemployed in the population accounts for the growth in the numbers unemployed below the poverty line. At the same time, the relatively rapid rise in social security support levels for the elderly and improved provision for widows and other lone parents, as well as wider coverage of occupational pensions, contributed to the decline in the proportion of the poor from those groups.

This compositional change explains why the average size of the house-holds below the relative poverty lines rose so consistently and substantially over the period. Households with a retired head were effectively 'replaced' among the poor by those with an unemployed head, and far more of the latter households contained children, so the risk of poverty for children rose markedly. In 1973, 16 per cent of children were in households below half average income, but by 1987 this had risen to 26 per cent. While the precise percentage of children in that situation at a point in time varies with the equivalence scale adopted, the increase over time is not sensitive to the choice of scale (Nolan and Farrell 1990). These trends clearly have major implications for the design of policies to combat poverty. Improved social security for the elderly played an important role in reducing their risk of poverty over the 1970s and 1980s, but the current profile of the 'poverty population' makes reliance on transfers much more problematic. While income support for the unemployed is crucial to cushioning the impact of unemployment, the constraints in terms of both the burden on public expenditure and the impact on incentives have become all too obvious in Ireland as elsewhere. Tackling poverty is therefore even more closely linked to labour market policies than before.

3.3   Poverty in Ireland in an international perspective

To see the extent of relative poverty in Ireland compared with other EU member states in the mid 1980s, one can draw on several cross-country studies carried out for the EU Commission or Eurostat. O'Higgins and Jenkins's (1990) study, using relative income poverty lines, and Eurostat (1990), using expenditure-based lines, show Ireland having a level of rela-tive poverty higher than most member states, similar to Spain and Greece and lower than Portugal. More recent estimates prepared for Eurostat by Hagenaars, de Vos and Zaidi (1994) apply both income and expenditure lines to budget survey data for the late 1980s (in the Irish case the 1987 HBS). Their main results using a poverty line set at 50 per cent of average equivalent income or expenditure in the country in question are presented in table 10.8 and show a somewhat different picture.

On an income basis, Ireland is shown as having about the same percent-age of households in poverty as Spain, France, Germany and Italy, lower than Greece, Portugal and the UK, which now has the highest rate. On an expenditure basis, Ireland has a poverty rate (in terms of households or persons) similar to Spain, France or the UK, lower than Greece, Portugal or Italy. We will not dwell on the conceptual and empirical issues involved in choosing to measure poverty in terms of expenditure rather than income, though the gap between income- and expenditure-based poverty rates for

Table 10.8 *Percentage of households/persons below half national average equivalent income and expenditure, EC countries, late 1980s*

Country	Income poverty households per cent	Expenditure poverty	
		households per cent	persons per cent
Belgium	6.0	6.6	7.4
Netherlands	7.4	6.2	4.8
Denmark	11.9	4.2	3.9
Italy	12.8	22.0	21.1
Spain	12.9	17.5	16.9
Germany	13.6	12.0	10.9
France	14.0	14.9	14.7
Ireland	14.9	16.4	15.7
Greece	18.6	20.8	18.7
Portugal	20.2	26.5	24.5
UK	22.4	17.0	14.8

Source: Hagenaars, de Vos and Zaidi (1994), tables 1, 2 and 6.

some countries is striking. The main reason Hagenaars *et al.*'s income-based poverty rate for Ireland is considerably lower than the one derived from the 1987 HBS in the earlier Eurostat study and ours in table 10.7 above seems to be that the equivalence scale they employ is a good deal less 'generous' to larger households.[10] For non-EU countries, Buhman *et al.* (1988) apply a relative income poverty line based on the median to some countries in the (wave 1) LIS data set. Applying such a line to the ESRI sample suggests that Ireland around 1987 had a proportion of persons below half median income higher than Sweden, Norway or Switzerland, but lower than the US.

3.4 Real incomes

As noted earlier, the pattern of real income growth in Ireland was very different in the two sub-periods analysed here, with rapid growth between 1973 and 1980 followed by a slight fall between 1980 and 1987. This means that poverty lines held constant in real terms, rather than changing *pari passu* with average income, would show very different patterns in the two sub-periods. Between 1973 and 1980, a substantial fall in the numbers below such 'absolute' lines would be registered. In the 1980–7 period, on the other hand, there would be an increase in the number below 'absolute' lines which was slightly greater than that seen with relative lines.

An interesting perspective on the implications of taking differences in real incomes into account in cross-country poverty comparisons is provided by Hagenaars, de Vos and Zaidi (1994). As well as country-specific relative lines, they present results for the percentages in each member country below a Community-wide poverty line set at half average expenditure. The divergence in poverty rates across countries is then very much wider than with relative lines. The Irish poverty rate of 30 per cent is now very similar to those of Spain and Greece, well below that of Portugal. All of these are much higher than with country-specific relative lines, while those for the richer member states are much lower. Whether one would wish to base a poverty measure on a standard common across all countries rather than relative to the living standards and expectations in each depends, among other things, on the purpose of the exercise, but quantification of the difference made by adopting one rather than the other is clearly very valuable.

4   Conclusions

In this chapter we have used the limited data available for Ireland to examine changes over the 1970s and 1980s in income inequality, poverty and real living standards. Survey data on which estimates of the distribution of income and poverty can be based are available only for the years 1973, 1980 and 1987, when the official Household Budget Surveys were carried out by the Central Statistics Office and a specially designed survey was also carried out in 1987 by the ESRI. The analysis was also constrained by the fact that the microdata from the HBS cannot be analysed directly.

The degree of inequality in the distribution of gross income among Irish households widened from 1973 to 1987, but for disposable income inequality declined. The unprecedented rise in unemployment, to close to one-fifth of the labour force by 1987, is likely to have been a major contributor to the increased inequality in gross incomes. For disposable income, this was more than offset by the effects of the sharp rise in the proportion of income taken in income tax and social security contributions, and the fact that both became more progressive over the period. From this perspective, the main difference between Ireland and the UK, for example, is that similar macroeconomic factors produced a widening of inequality in market and gross incomes, but the policy adopted with respect to direct taxes was very different. The increase in the importance and the progressivity of direct tax was to a significant extent a response to the size of the public sector deficit and debt with which Ireland found itself as a result of reckless fiscal expansion in the 1970s, though social security support rates were also raised in real terms.

The percentage of persons falling below relative income poverty lines rose from 1973 to 1987 across different relative lines and equivalence scales. While unemployment was rising so substantially, private and public pensions for the elderly improved. This produced a marked change in the composition of those below the relative poverty lines, with the unemployed becoming much more important and the elderly much less so, and was accompanied by a significant rise in the risk of poverty for children. The percentage falling below country-specific relative poverty lines in Ireland was similar to that in a number of other EU member countries though lower than in Greece or Portugal.

During the 1970s, real incomes grew relatively rapidly in Ireland. During the period from 1980 to 1987, however, average household income fell slightly in real terms. Thus, although quite similar patterns of change in inequality and relative poverty were seen in 1973–80 and 1980–7, they occurred in quite different settings. Whereas the numbers below poverty lines held fixed in real terms would have fallen significantly in the 1970s, they would have risen in the 1980s. Applying a common standard to measure poverty across all EU countries would clearly rank Ireland with Spain, Greece and Portugal as the member states with the highest poverty rates.

Since 1987, the Irish economy has returned to growth and real incomes have been rising on average. However unemployment is still close to 14 per cent, having fallen in the late 1980s, and appears unlikely to fall very much below that level in the short to medium term. While the average rate of income tax remains high, top tax rates have been sharply reduced, with Ireland belatedly following the international trend and the top income tax rate now down to 48 per cent, from 58 per cent in 1987. In the absence of suitable household survey data, one can only attempt to infer the impact of such changes on income inequality and poverty,[11] although data for 1994 from both the Household Budget Survey and the first wave of the European Household Community Panel will soon be available.

Notes

1 These summary measures are calculated from the decile shares, since only these were available for 1987, although Murphy 1985 presents both measures calculated from discrete data and decile shares for 1973 and 1980. The Theil values here differ from Murphy's, because he uses $\log_{10}$ whereas we follow usual practice in using $\log_e$. Like the decile distributions, the summary measures use the household as the unit of analysis, without weighting for the number of persons in each household.

2 A detailed analysis of the 1973 and 1980 HBS by the CSO (Murphy 1984) shows that the increasing number of households with an unemployed head was an important factor in increasing inequality in market incomes.

3 OECD Employment Outlook 1990.
4 Callan and Nolan 1994b using the ESRI 1987 sample show that the average income replacement rate for the unemployed was less than 50 per cent.
5 OECD Revenue Statistics 1994, tables 3, 11 and 15.
6 The increase in direct tax revenue was achieved by a higher standard rate and by failure to index allowances and tax bands for inflation. The top income tax rate in fact fell from 80 per cent to 58 per cent.
7 The LIS database aims to harmonise as far as possible to an annual time period and the household as recipient unit but cannot always do so. For example, the Canadian data refer only to related individuals living together, the Swedish to the tax unit rather than to the household and the UK to current rather than annual income (Smeeding and Coder 1993, p. 3).
8 These provide a more direct basis for comparison than the summary inequality measures for some second-wave countries produced from LIS by Fritzell 1992 and Jäntti 1993 or the percentile ratios on which Smeeding and Coder 1993 rely.
9 Both income gaps and the Foster–Greer–Thorbecke measure are calculated on a household and a person basis, and the same pattern is shown in each case (Nolan and Callan 1989).
10 Hagenaars, de Vos and Zaidi use the 'modified OECD' scale, in which for each extra adult a household needs 0.5 of the resources for the first adult and 0.3 for each child (under 14), in their main results while also looking at alternative scales. The earlier Eurostat study uses a scale of 0.7 for each additional adult and 0.5 for each child as we do in table 10.7.
11 See Callan and Nolan 1992a for such an examination of the 1987–91 period.

References

Atkinson, A. B. 1993. 'What is Happening to the Distribution of Income in the UK?', Welfare State Programme Discussion Paper No. 87, London School of Economics.
Bishop, J. A., Chow, K. V. and Formby, J. P. 1993. 'The Redistributive Effect of Direct Taxes: An International Comparison of Six LIS Countries'. Luxembourg Income Study Working Paper 93. Luxembourg: CEPS/INSTEAD.
Buhman, B., Rainwater, L., Schmaus, G. and Smeeding,T. 1988. 'Equivalence Scales, Well-Being, Inequality and Poverty: Sensitivity Estimates Across Ten Countries Using the Luxembourg Income Study Database'. *Review of Income and Wealth*; Series 34: 115–42.
Callan, T. and Nolan, B. 1992a. 'Distributional Aspects of Ireland's Fiscal Adjustment'. *Economic and Social Review,* 23: 319–42.
    1992b. 'Income Distribution and Redistribution: Ireland in Comparative Perspective', in Goldthorpe, J. H. and Whelan, C. T. (eds.), *The Development of Industrial Society in Ireland.* Oxford: Oxford University Press.
    1994a. 'Income Poverty in Ireland', in Nolan, B. and Callan, T. (eds.), *Poverty and Policy in Ireland.* Dublin: Gill and Macmillan.

1994b. 'Unemployment and Poverty', in Nolan, B. and Callan, T. (eds.), *Poverty and Policy in Ireland*. Dublin: Gill and Macmillan.

Callan, T., Nolan, B. and Whelan, C. T. 1993. 'Resources, Deprivation and the Measurement of Poverty'. *Journal of Social Policy*, 22: 141–72.

Callan, T., Nolan, B., Whelan, B. J. and Hannan, D. F. with Creighton, S. 1989. *Poverty, Income and Welfare in Ireland*. General Research Series No. 146. Dublin: The Economic and Social Research Institute.

Eurostat. 1990. *Poverty in Figures: Europe in the Early 1980s*. Luxembourg: Eurostat.

Foster, J. E., Greer, J. and Thorbecke, E. 1984. 'A Class of Decomposable Poverty Measures'. *Econometrica*, 52: 761–6.

Fritzell, J. 1992. 'Income Inequality Trends in the 1980s: A Five-Country Comparison'. Luxembourg Income Study Working Paper 73. Luxembourg: CEPS/INSTEAD.

Hagenaars, A. J, de Vos, K. and Zaidi, M. A. 1994. 'Patterns of Poverty in Europe'. Paper for the Seminar on the Measurement and Analysis of Social Exclusion. Centre for Research in European Social and Employment Policy, University of Bath.

Jäntti, M. 1993. 'Changing Inequality in Five Countries: The Role of Markets, Transfers and Taxes'. Luxembourg Income Study Working Paper 91. Luxembourg: CEPS/INSTEAD.

Jenkins, S. 1991. 'The Measurement of Income Inequality', in Osberg, L. (ed.), *Economic Inequality and Poverty: An International Perspective*. New York: M. E. Sharpe, Inc.

1992. 'Accounting for Inequality Trends'. Department of Economics Discussion Paper 92–10. University College of Swansea.

Murphy, D. 1984. 'The Impact of State Taxes and Benefits on Irish Household Incomes'. *Journal of the Statistical and Social Inquiry Society of Ireland*, 25: 55–120.

1985. 'Calculation of Gini and Theil Inequality Coefficients for Irish Household Incomes in 1973 and 1980'. *Economic and Social Review*, 16: 225–49.

Nolan, B. 1978. 'The Personal Distribution of Income in the Republic of Ireland'. *Journal of the Statistical and Social Inquiry Society of Ireland*, 23: 91–139.

1981. 'Redistribution of Household Income in Ireland by Taxes and Benefits'. *Economic and Social Review*, 13: 59–88.

Nolan, B. and Callan, T. 1989. 'Measuring Trends in Poverty Over Time: Some Robust Results for Ireland 1980–1987'. *Economic and Social Review*, 20: 309–28.

Nolan, B. and Farrell, B. 1990. *Child Poverty in Ireland*. Dublin: Combat Poverty Agency.

O'Higgins, M. and Jenkins, S. P. 1990. 'Poverty in the EC: Estimates for 1975, 1980 and 1985', in Teekens, R. and Van Praag, B.M.S. (eds.), *Analysing Poverty in the European Community*. Luxembourg: Eurostat.

O'Higgins, M., Schmaus, G. and Stephenson, G. 1989. 'Income Distribution and Redistribution: A Microdata Analysis for Seven Countries'. *Review of Income and Wealth*, 35: 107–31.

238 Tim Callan and Brian Nolan

Organisation for Economic Co-Operation and Development. 1990. *Employment Outlook*. Paris: OECD.

1994. *Revenue Statistics*. Paris: OECD.

Roche, J. 1984. *Poverty and Income Maintenance Policies in Ireland*. Dublin: Institute for Public Administration.

Rottman, D. and Reidy, M. 1988. 'Redistribution Through State Social Expenditure in the Republic of Ireland 1973–1980'. Report No. 85. Dublin: National Economic and Social Council.

Shorrocks, A. F. 1983. 'Ranking Income Distributions'. *Economica*, 50: 3–17.

Smeeding, T. and Coder, J. 1993. 'Income Inequality in Rich Countries During the 1980s'. Luxembourg Income Study Working Paper 88, Luxembourg: CEPS/INSTEAD.

11 Income distribution in France: the mid 1980s turning point

PIERRE CONCIALDI

1 Introduction

Although inequality in France declined rather steadily in the 1970s, an official French report in 1989 noted that the range of incomes had probably begun to widen again in the second half of the 1980s (CERC 1989). Some of the characteristic features mentioned in that report were an increase in wage inequality, rapid growth of wealth income and revised taxation and social policies. Several studies have since elaborated on these findings or looked at the French experience in relation to that of other developed countries.[1]

In addition to a detailed discussion of this issue, this chapter provides an update using the most recently available data, in particular data covering the evolution of household disposable income. The second section reviews the main institutional changes of the past decade. This will enable a better understanding of the nature of the changes that occurred in the second half of the 1980s. The distribution of earned and unearned income is described and commented upon in section 3. In section 4, we examine the role of taxes and cash transfers and the way that redistribution might have corrected income inequality resulting from the distribution of market incomes. Section 5 summarises the empirical findings and their likely impact on the economic welfare of households. Some concluding remarks point out the major changes of the decade.

2 Policy changes

Politically and institutionally, the past decade seems far less uniform in France than in other countries, such as the United States or the United Kingdom. A brief chronology of institutional changes will help better identify their sometimes contradictory impact on employment rules, wage determination, taxation and, more broadly, redistribution policy.

The 1980s opened with Socialist Francois Mitterrand's election to the presidency in 1981. The accession to power of a left-wing government led by Pierre Mauroy as prime minister was a major political event for a country like France, where politics had been dominated by the conservatives for more than 20 years. During the first year in office, the new government implemented a Keynesian expansionary policy which heralded its determination to reduce inequality through large increases in the French minimum wage (*salaire minimum interprofessionnel de croissance* or SMIC), family allowances and the guaranteed minimum income for the elderly and the disabled and a reduction of the legal retirement age to 60. A wealth tax was created as a symbolic measure. The government also changed employment regulations by shortening the length of work time (reducing the working week from 40 to 39 hours and introducing a statutory fifth week of paid holidays) and by tightening the rules regarding jobs without security ('temping' and fixed-term contracts). Structural reforms were gradually introduced through the Auroux labour laws which established, among other things, annual statutory collective bargaining at the firm level.

The new government's determination to increase employment without creating inflationary pressure led to a wage and price freeze between June and October 1982. At the end of this period, the government urged employers and trade unions not to exceed the official forecasts for inflation during wage negotiations, thus setting up a process of indexing wages on prices *ex ante*. While inflation was contained by price controls, the government organised an annual dialogue between employers and trade unions. That dialogue focused on recent economic trends and their consequences on the income distribution as stated by the annual report produced by the Centre d'Etude des Revenus et des Coûts (CERC).

In 1983, a major shift in government policy took place. The government's Keynesian policy had quickly come up against international economic constraints. A debate over protectionism had been raging inside the administration, and in the end the anti-protectionist faction won. The decision to open France to outside forces was accompanied by wage restraint and reduced social expenditure on the domestic front. The formation of a new government in 1983 without Communist ministers was a concrete sign of the change of direction.

In 1984, Fabius succeeded Mauroy at the head of the government. The principle of combining an unemployment insurance system, managed by employers and trade unions, and a 'national solidarity' scheme, funded by the state, was firmly established with the reform of unemployment benefits. At the same time, the government implemented a 'social' strategy for dealing with unemployment with the creation of the community work scheme, *travaux d'utilité collective* (TUC). In the following years, various programmes of 'sandwich' courses, combining practical work experience and school, were introduced with the aim of helping young people secure careers.

In 1986, the conservatives gained a parliamentary majority and Chirac became prime minister, thus initiating the period of 'cohabitation'. The new administration instituted a series of deregulatory measures: lifting price controls, ending government authorisation for lay-offs, relaxing rules on temping and fixed-term contracts and simplifying rules for profit-sharing. The government abolished the wealth tax and cut income taxes for the highest and lowest income brackets.

Mitterrand was reelected president in 1988. Following the new parliamentary elections, Rocard became head of the Socialist government. The new government created a minimum income (*revenu minimum d'insertion* or RMI) together with a wealth tax (*impôt de solidarité sur la fortune* or ISF) that was supposed to finance the new benefit. In 1989, employers and trade unions agreed on rules regarding temping and short-term contracts. The same year, the government introduced lower taxes on unearned income.

Despite the heterogeneity of policy changes in the 1980s, some conclusions regarding the structural features of the French system stand out. First, there is no doubt that the Socialist government succeeded in curbing inflation. The structural inflation gap between France and Germany has disappeared during the past decade. Second, the *'lois Auroux'* have had some success in promoting decentralisation of the bargaining process. Because these laws were implemented at a time when the influence of trade unions was in decline, they may have stimulated a greater differentiation of wages among employees.

3   Market income

Here we consider three types of market income, namely wages and salaries, self-employment income and unearned income. Wages and salaries are the main source of primary income for over 85 per cent of the labour force today. We shall therefore devote a large part of this section to analysing wages.

Wage restraint has been one of the key features of the 1980s. Between 1980 and 1990, the average wage increased only 3.4 per cent (0.3 per cent a year) in real terms.[2] This situation greatly differs from the 1970s. From 1970 to 1978, the increase in the purchasing power of the average wage was 3.7 per cent annually. The rate of change was faster for total compensation from salaried work, including all employee and employer taxes and social welfare contributions, than for net wages. The increase in social welfare contributions has greatly influenced the evolution of net wages since the

242   Pierre Concialdi

Table 11.1 *Wage dispersion since 1984*
(Full-time employees in the private and semi-public sectors)

	1984	1988	1989	1991	1992	1993
C90/C10	2.91	2.97	3.03	3.03	3.04	3.07
C90/C50	1.92	1.94	1.96	1.97	1.98	1.99
C50/C10	1.52	1.53	1.54	1.54	1.54	1.55

Source: See appendix A; provisional estimates for 1992 and 1993.

early 1970s. The share of net wages in the total pay of employees steadily declined, from 70.5 per cent in 1970 to around 65 per cent in 1980, and then dropped to under 60 per cent in 1990. In the second half of the 1980s, increases in social welfare contributions mostly affected employee contributions, while the rate of employer contributions stayed the same. This levelling off of employer contributions is seen in other EU countries as well.

We find essentially the same pattern when looking at more detailed data on wages for full-time, full-year equivalent employees in the private and semi-public sectors (these statistics cover approximately 70 per cent of the overall population of employees). In real terms, the increase in the average net wage was around 0.7 per cent a year from 1980 to 1989. It should be noted that the increasing qualifications of the work force explain the biggest part of this rise (around 0.5 per cent a year alone). In other words, the price of labour virtually did not increase during this period. This phenomenon is even more noticeable in the public sector, where the price of labour fell in real terms 0.9 per cent a year during 1978–88.

Private-sector employees thus apparently gained a bit more than public-sector employees. However, public-sector employees have the advantage of job security, whereas a number of employees in the private sector lost their jobs and consequently experienced an erosion of purchasing power. When these differences are taken into account real wages in both sectors actually stagnated between 1974 and 1987 (Chassard and Concialdi 1989).

3.1   Greater inequality in wage distribution

Wage restraint in the 1980s had more impact on wages at the lower end of the distribution. As shown in table 11.1, wage dispersion has increased slightly since 1984. A closer look at the statistics reveals that this growing inequality has affected especially male employees and mainly managers and highly qualified jobs (table 11.2). Similar trends have been observed in other studies (Katz, Loveman and Blanchflower 1993; Gottschalk 1993).[3]

Table 11.2 *Wage dispersion by sex and qualification*

		C90/C10			C90/C50			C50/C10		
		1978	1982	1986	1978	1982	1986	1978	1982	1986
Senior management	Men	3.55	3.51	3.96	1.92	1.91	1.96	1.85	1.84	2.02
	Women	4.29	4.14	3.89	1.85	1.88	1.83	2.32	2.24	2.13
Middle or junior management	Men	2.38	2.40	2.68	1.56	1.56	1.67	1.52	1.54	1.60
	Women	2.33	2.37	2.37	1.52	1.48	1.46	1.53	1.60	1.62
Clerical and technical staff	Men	2.47	2.42	2.61	1.59	1.58	1.66	1.55	1.53	1.57
	Women	2.27	2.21	2.20	1.50	1.47	1.45	1.51	1.50	1.52
Manual labourers	Men	2.20	2.18	2.10	1.48	1.46	1.47	1.49	1.49	1.43
	Women	2.22	2.44	2.21	1.42	1.43	1.41	1.56	1.71	1.57

Source: CERC 1989.

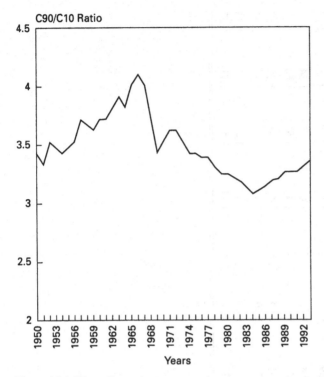

Figure 11.1 Wage dispersion among private sector employees (Both sexes)
Source: See appendix A.

This change broke a trend towards decreasing wage dispersion
which had started in the late 1960s and continued without interruption
into the 1970s (figure 11.1). However, due to a change in the wage
definition, data shown in table 11.1 cannot be compared directly with
those published earlier (see appendix A for details on methodology).
When correcting for the change in wage concept, one can say that today's
wage dispersion is at the same level as in the mid 1970s, slightly below
that of the late 1960s level and very similar to that observed in the early
1950s. We find quite the same pattern when we look at separate wage
data for men and women. Figure 11.2 exhibits a continuous trend
towards increasing dispersion since the mid 1980s. Accordingly, for both
men and women, today's wage inequality looks very similar to the mid
1970s levels.

The above figures only include full-time employees and therefore underestimate both the magnitude of and changes in wage differentials. The pro-

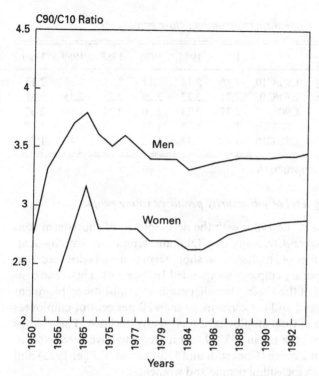

Figure 11.2 Wage dispersion among private sector employees by gender
Source: See appendix A.

portion of part-time employees rose steadily, from 5 per cent in 1974, to more than 11 per cent in 1989 (3 per cent for men and 22 per cent for women). These part-time employees have lower hourly wages than full-time employees. Incorporating them in the statistics would magnify the increase in inequality of the 1980s.[4] This limitation is particularly important when considering wage differentials between men and women.[5]

The above statistics exclude some categories of employees, such as those working for the state whether or not they are civil servants (more than 20 per cent of persons employed by the state do not have the employment status of civil servants). Data for this group indicate a similar but rather slight trend of increasing inequality. As can be seen in table 11.3, net wage statistics show an increase in inequality between 1986 and 1989, while data on basic salaries do not. That means that the increasing wage dispersion is attributable to the wage supplements (mostly premiums) that complement the basic salaries of state employees.

Table 11.3 *Wage dispersion among state employees*

		1982	1984	1986	1988	1989	1990
Basic salary	C90/C10	2.16	2.13	2.11	2.11	2.10	2.15
Gross wage	C90/C10	2.24	2.22	2.20	2.23	2.25	2.31
Net wage	C90/C10	2.27	2.23	2.20	2.24	2.26	2.32
Net wage	C90/C50	1.58	1.57	1.55	1.53	1.53	1.57
Net wage	C50/C10	1.43	1.42	1.42	1.46	1.47	1.50

Source: See appendix A.

3.2   Decreasing level of job security penalises young people

Job security eroded in the 1980s with the development of short-term contracts (*contrats à durée déterminée* or CDD) and temporary employment.
In 1984–8, the number of employees on short-term contracts doubled, and
the number of temporary employees expanded 160 per cent. This trend continued until the end of the 1980s. Overall, permanent full-time employment
remains the norm and still concerns more than 80 per cent of employees
today, but its share in total employment has greatly declined. This change
appeared throughout the EC in 1983–9, but it seems to have been particularly pronounced in France (Concialdi and Guillaumat-Tailliet 1993) and
was a major concern for young people and women.

It is often argued that the SMIC restrains employment prospects for
young people in France. There is no doubt that the unemployment rate of
French young people is higher than in other countries. But there is no strong
evidence of a direct link between the SMIC and these unemployment figures.
First, it should be emphasised that the unemployment rates must be related
to the labour force participation rate, especially for young people. For French
young people, the participation rate appears to be very low by international
standards, therefore inflating traditional unemployment rates. In fact, the
ratio of unemployed young people to all young people aged 15–24 years is
not higher in France than in other industrialised countries (table 11.4) and
is quite similar to that in the US. Second, studies by the OECD that have
tried to assess the effects of the SMIC on youth employment do not provide
strong evidence of such adverse effects, if any (Bazen and Martin 1991). Last
but not least, it should be noted that in the case of France, this debate
remains a somewhat theoretical one. During the 1980s, several types of jobs
with reduced labour costs combining traineeships and other kinds of training schemes were developed as part of a package for dealing with unemployment.[6] These 'semi-jobs' have been aimed particularly at young people and,
in effect, have made circumvention of the institutional constraint of the

Table 11.4 *Employment and activity status of young people (15 to 24 years old)*

	Unemployed	Employed	Inactive
Japan	1.9	42.2	55.9
Sweden	2.5	64.6	32.9
Germany	3.3	56.5	40.2
France	7.0	29.4	63.6
United States	7.2	60.4	32.4
United Kingdom	10.5	67.5	22.0
Italy	13.7	29.8	56.5
Spain	16.5	34.7	48.8

Source: Elbaum and Marchand 1993.

Table 11.5 *Net annual average wage by age: full-time private- and semi-public-sector employees*

	Average index = 100		Variation of real wage per cent
	1980	1987	1980–7
under 18	33.7	20.0	−37.0
18–20	51.9	49.0	−0.3
21–25	71.4	67.2	−0.7
26–30	88.3	83.6	0
31–40	110.2	103.6	−1.2
41–50	118.0	122.7	+9.8
51–60	121.3	122.0	+6.2
61–65	127.6	162.8	+34.7
over 65	140.7	169.3	+27.0
Total	52,720 francs	93,037 francs	+5.5

Source: Chassard and Concialdi 1990.

minimum wage (SMIC) possible without having any definite effect on employment (Cornilleau, Marioni and Roguet 1990). As a consequence of the growth of these 'semi-jobs', the labour cost for the employer is actually less than the SMIC for an estimated one out of five young employees.

However, it is true that the growing difficulties of the young entering the labour market have affected their hiring and pay conditions, even for those who have succeeded in getting full-time jobs. As a result, earnings disparities by age grew between 1980 and 1987 (table 11.5).

Table 11.6 *Growth of purchasing power, 1984–1991*

	1984–91	Rate of annual growth	1991 level (FF/month)
C 90	9.3	1.3	15,370
Average wage	7.1	1.0	9,530
Median wage	6.5	0.9	7,810
C 10	5.0	0.7	5,080
SMIC	4.5	0.6	4,500

Source: See appendix A.

The figures for the youngest and oldest age groups are coloured by some biases. The lengthening of education means that employees in the youngest age group are on average increasingly less qualified. This selection effect works in the opposite way for the oldest employees, because a growing proportion of those who continue to work after 60 are professionals. However, the comparison of the middle age groups is significant. In 1980, employees aged 41–50 earned 34 per cent more than employees aged 26–30 and 65 per cent more than those aged 21–25. The differences between these same age groups in 1987 was 47 per cent and 82 per cent, respectively. The deterioration of the relative position of young people in the distribution of wages also seems to have occurred in other countries, such as the US, at least for employees with the lowest qualifications (Levy and Murnane 1992).

3.3   Some factors that explain growing inequality

Imbalances between labour resources and the demand for labour at the highest education levels probably do explain some changes in the wage distribution in France (Concialdi and Madinier 1990). Other studies have also emphasised the connection between supply and demand and changes in the wage structure, especially to explain diminishing wage inequality that resulted from a large number of young graduates coming on to the labour market (OECD 1985; Katz and Murphy 1992). The widening of the wage range in the 1980s may thus reflect a shortage of skilled labour.[7]

The declining role of the SMIC may have been another factor in growing wage inequality since 1984. After the SMIC was substantially increased by the new Socialist administration upon Mitterrand's arrival in 1981, the impetus for change was short-lived. Since 1984, the minimum wage has increased much more slowly than the average wage (table 11.6). In real terms, the SMIC even dropped twice, in 1988 and 1989, due to rises in social welfare contributions.

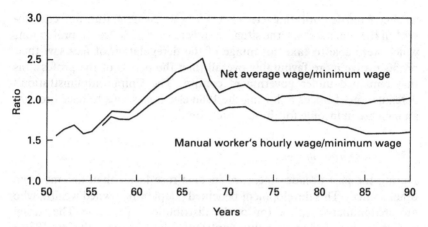

Figure 11.3
Source: Girard, J. P. and Lhéritier, J. L. 'Les salaires en 1990 – vol. I: Le secteur privé', INSEE.

While the level of the minimum wage was brought closer to the level of a manual worker's wage in the early 1980s, the differential hardly budged after 1985. A similar change had happened in the previous decade. The difference between the minimum wage and the wage of a manual worker had dropped following sharp rises in the SMIC in 1973 and 1974. The difference then stabilised from 1974. In relation to the average wage, the gap marginally widened in the second half of the 1980s and is today at a level comparable with what it was in the early 1960s (figure 11.3).

3.4   Self-employment income

Sluggish growth since 1974 has translated into slow income growth for the self-employed. Farmers have experienced a substantial drop in profits since 1973. At constant prices, their net average income fell more than 15 per cent in the second half of the 1970s and has stayed roughly constant since 1980. At the end of the 1980s, farmers' average profits were the same as 20 years earlier. In contrast, the average profit in the professions has risen about 15 per cent since 1973 (at constant prices), while for artisans and shopkeepers it stayed about the same.

Overall, these developments have contributed to the widening of the income range for self-employed professionals, but this change has been especially marked in the 1970s (CERC 1989; Concialdi 1990).

The evolution of relative prices seems to have played a predominant role in these income changes. For example, the drop in farm income mainly resulted from deteriorating terms of trade between agriculture and customers.[8] In the other sectors, the situation was less clear. However, professions which were able to take advantage of the deregulation of fees saw their profits evolve more favourably overall than the profits of the professions that remained under government control. The Chirac administration's deregulation of prices following the 1986 elections seems to have brought an increase in income for those professions.

3.5   Unearned income

During the past decade, unearned income rose faster than income from other sources. This development benefited people who owned wealth, who are predominantly at the top of the distribution of income. The strong growth of unearned income thus contributed (at least until the late 1980s) to the increasing inequality of income between households.

Unearned income includes rent, income from securities (interest, dividends, etc.) and income from land (farm rent and rent in kind). Rents fell in the 1970s but started to rise in 1985. During the 1980s, rents rose more than 5 per cent annually in real terms.

The recovery of company profits and the increase in the return on capital which resulted were accompanied by a sharp rise in dividends starting from 1986. In addition to these yields, there were substantial capital gains fuelled by speculation in the stock market and real estate, a feature of the 1980s. The real overall performance (yields plus capital gains) of financial investments rose sharply on average, from 0.5 per cent a year in the 1970s to 2.6 per cent in 1980–7, with particularly high returns on shares (12 per cent a year). The stock market crash of 1987 and the collapse of the commercial property market in the beginning of the 1990s may indicate a reversal of the trend since the late 1980s.

4   Taxes, social security contributions and redistribution

The total rate of direct taxation (tax and social security) has fluctuated between 44 per cent and 45 per cent since 1984. This apparent stability is a clear departure from the rises recorded during the preceding decade. Between 1973 and 1984, the rate rose nearly 10 percentage points, mainly due to increases in social security contributions (table 11.7). Tax increases, on the other hand, were quite limited during this period. The relative weight of taxes raised for the benefit of the state has declined steadily since 1960. The slight rise in taxes actually came from the development of local taxes and the gradual increase of taxes for the EC.

Among developed countries, France is unique in that income tax makes

Table 11.7 *Taxes and social security contributions by origin*
(as per cent of GDP)

Year	Total	Social security contributions	Taxes Total	Taxes (of which state)
1960[a]	32.5	9.8	22.7	19.6
1970[a]	35.6	12.9	22.7	19.1
1970	35.1	12.7	22.4	18.6
1973	35.0	13.1	21.9	17.5
1979	40.2	17.0	23.2	17.5
1984	44.6	19.2	25.4	18.0
1990	43.8	19.4	24.4	16.6
Changes (percentage points)				
1970/60	+3.1	+3.1	–	−0.5
1984/70	+9.5	+6.5	+3.0	−0.6
1990/84	−0.8	+0.2	−1.0	−1.4
1990/60	+11.8	+9.8	+2.0	−2.5

Note:
[a] Old National Accounts system.
Source: INSEE, National Accounts.

up a comparatively low share of total revenue. Social security contributions
have to be taken into account when assessing the development of the tax
system. Apart from statistical problems, this question raises serious conceptual difficulties (Atkinson 1990). These mainly concern employer
contributions which are considerable in France and represent more than
twice the revenue from income taxes. Thus any measure of the progressivity of the tax and social security contributions system – or its evolution – is
sensitive to assumptions about these contributions. This is why we shall
look at two measures of progressivity.[9]

The first indicator is a ratio of total income taxes and employee social
security contributions to gross wages received by households. Between 1980
and 1988, this indicator rose across income levels, but the rise was greater
for the lowest incomes than for the highest incomes. In other words, the
progressivity of the tax and contributions system appears smaller at the end
of the period than at the start.

The second indicator that takes into account employer contributions
does not show exactly the same evolution according to the assumptions
made.[10] If we assume employer contributions are borne by labour, the
overall tax rate (all contributions plus income tax), which was almost independent of income for a single person and slightly decreasing with income

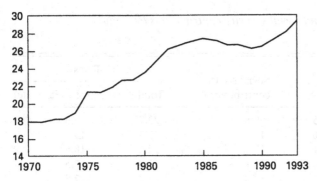

Figure 11.4 Social welfare expenditure (per cent of national income)

for a couple, became slightly progressive in 1988. If, on the other hand, we assume that employer contributions are in the end borne by consumers, i.e., distributed almost proportionally in consumption expenditure, we come to the same conclusion as the first indicator – that the progressivity of the tax and contributions system decreased in the 1980s.

Irrespective of which assumption is made, it should be noted that in the late 1980s the overall tax rate hardly depended on the level of income, and the changes that occurred in the beginning of the 1990s do not appear to have changed this situation significantly (Brion and Concialdi 1993). This finding matches Pechman's (1985), which showed that taxes and contributions were nearly proportional to income in the US. According to other estimates, the system of taxes and contributions in France today is less progressive than elsewhere, mainly due to the very low rate of progressive income tax (Malabouche 1991).

The levelling off of contributions since 1984 partly reflects a certain slowdown in the growth of public expenditure and particularly the public payroll. However, this change is especially a result of successive administrations, since 1983, tightening up social security expenditure. After increasing nearly 10 percentage points in 1970–83 (from 18.1 per cent up to 27.6 per cent), the share of social security benefits in GDP remained virtually unchanged until 1990 (figure 11.4).[11]

In a period where needs have continued to grow, largely because of the ageing of the population and the rise in unemployment, the slowdown seen in the 1980s is explained above all by the reduction of social security coverage and the stability or small increase of most other benefits. As shown in table 11.8, benefit-scale increases have not had any effect on the growth of aggregate benefit expenditure since 1983 (Neyret 1992; CERC-Association 1995).

Benefit entitlement conditions have also become more restrictive. The

Table 11.8 *The growth of social expenditure and the impact of benefit increases*

	1970–8 per cent	1978–82 per cent	1982–90 per cent	1990–3 per cent
Real annual growth of total social expenditure	6.4	4.1	2.8	3.6
Impact of benefit-scale increases (as per cent of overall growth)	46	31	5	10

Source: CERC-Association 1995.

unemployment insurance reforms of 1982 and 1984 drastically reduced the proportion of unemployed persons covered, while admission to certain kinds of early retirement packages (*'garanties de ressources'*) was ended. In health services, the share of expenditure covered by social security shrank (from 77.1 per cent in 1984 to 73.6 per cent in 1991), while tight controls on hospital expenses also contributed to slowing expenditure.

The deterioration of the economic situation and the rise of unemployment have revealed holes in the French social welfare system. Although 'solidarity benefits' already existed for special groups (the elderly, disabled, single parents), uncovered long-term unemployment brought poverty to the social groups most at risk. For example, the number of households with equivalent income below 40 per cent of the average grew twice as fast as the total number of households (1979–84). The need to reinforce social welfare protection became so acute that, in 1988, parliament instituted a safety net for society's have-nots: the minimum income (RMI). The data available on the population receiving this benefit show that most are jobless whose unemployment benefits have run out.[12] The amount of the RMI is far below other minimal social welfare benefits. For one person, it represents around 75 per cent of similar benefits currently available for special groups. In relation to the average standard of living in France, the RMI is very low (barely 25 per cent of the average equivalent disposable income). Since its creation, its purchasing power has stagnated like most other benefits.

5   Household income

During the 1980s real household disposable income grew 2 per cent annually, i.e., less than half the rate of the 1970s. The contributions of each type of income or transfer to growth in the last decade can be seen in table 11.9.

Four relatively homogeneous periods can be identified. Before 1978,

Table 11.9 *Household disposable income contributions to growth in purchasing power (percentage points of real annual growth in disposable income)*

	1970–8	1978–82	1982–5	1985–90
Net wages (a)	2.4	0.3	−0.6	0.8
Self-employment earned income (b)	0.2	−0.4	−0.3	0.2
Unearned income (c)	0.4	0.5	0.4	0.8
Social welfare benefits (d)	1.7	1.2	1.0	1.1
Current income and wealth taxes (e)	−0.4	−0.3	−0.3	−0.2
Total: Gross disposable income after taxes (a+b+c+d+e)	4.3	1.3	0.2	2.7
Population	0.6	0.5	0.4	0.4
Disposable income per inhabitant	3.7	0.8	−0.2	2.3

Note:
The figures for each type of income or transfer indicate the share of each component in the growth of this disposable income. Thus, net wages contributed 0.8 percentage points to this growth, earned income 0.2 percentage points, etc. The sum of these contributions equals total growth in disposable income.
Source: INSEE, National Accounts.

gains in household purchasing power came mainly from rises in earned income and, to a lesser extent, social welfare benefits. The second oil crisis marked the end of growth in household earned income. Between 1978 and 1982, social welfare benefits sustained purchasing power but at a lower rate. Between 1982 and 1985, a drop in total earned income in constant francs was marginally compensated for by an increase in social welfare benefits, and household purchasing power stagnated. Household income recovered 2.6 per cent a year in 1985–90. This arose in fairly equal measures from earned income, social welfare benefits and unearned income. Unearned income makes up a third of the increase in purchasing power, i.e., three times more than its share in the absolute value of total income.

What do these changes in the formation of household disposable income mean in terms of inequality in the income distribution? Information to answer that question is rather scarce in France, and results are published at five-year intervals. Thus, we need to examine long-time-series data to get an accurate view of changes in the income distribution.

First, we will look at the development of the relative welfare positions of various social groups over time. Such estimates are based on data from

Table 11.10 *Relative positions of social groups by status of head of household: France, 1962–1989*

	Group-specific average equivalent disposable income as a percentage of overall average					
	1962	1970	1975	1979	1984	1989
Farmers	98	100	92	92	101	114
Self-employed (without farmers)	200	187	177	178	152	143
Senior management	205	172	170	156	145	139
Middle/junior management	125	112	109	103	105	100
Clerical/technical staff	91	92	92	89	87	82
Manual workers	72	70	71	72	74	70
Inactive	71	83	92	97	98	103

Source: See appendix A.

National Accounts and other information gathered through periodic surveys (see appendix A). Due to a change in the definition of social groups, the figures for the years 1984 and after are not directly comparable with those of previous years. The data clearly indicate a long-term trend towards declining income inequality (table 11.10). From 1962 up to 1975, the relative position of all categories above the average showed a downward tendency, while the position of groups below the average remained unchanged (clerical and technical staff, manual workers) or improved substantially (inactive). Changes between 1975 and 1979 look much smaller. As a result, the ratio of the upper group to the lower one declined, from 2.9 in 1962 to 2.5 in 1975, and was still 2.5 in 1979.

Between 1984 and 1989, there was no tendency towards a decline in income inequality. With the exception of farmers, there has been virtually no change in the relative position of social groups with active heads of households. The relative position of the inactive group improved further, such that in 1989 the average standard of living for this group was slightly above average, compared with 30 per cent below average in 1962.

These aggregate figures relate to social groups whose relative size has changed over time. For instance, people living in farmers' households constituted 13.4 per cent of the total population in 1962 but only 3.6 per cent in 1989. On the other hand, the relative size of the population in 'senior management' households more than doubled during the same period. The first group was ageing, while the second one became younger and younger.

Table 11.11 *Dispersion of declared gross income per household: France, 1962–1984 (All households)*

	1962	1965	1970	1975	1979	1984
C90/C10	14.7	11.7	10.0	8.4	7.1	6.9
Gini coeff.	0.49	0.47	0.44	0.42	0.41	0.41

Source: See appendix A.

We therefore need to turn to microdata to better understand what happened in the distribution of income.

The microdata come mainly from household taxable income surveys carried out nearly every five years since 1956 (see appendix A). The resulting series of statistics will be referred to as ERF (*Enquêtes Revenus Fiscaux*). Results have been published by the national statistical office (INSEE) with the latest series ending in 1984.[13] In these publications, income inequality is measured for various concepts of income and for some specific populations. Consistent long-time series for all households are only available for the distribution of declared gross income per household (before redistribution and without adjustment for differences in family needs). These data show a sharp decline in income inequality from 1962 to 1979 (table 11.11). Together with aggregate figures published for various social groups, these statistics support the widespread view of a continuous long-term fall in income inequality in France.

However, the fall in income inequality does not seem to be very strong after 1979. Moreover, since we are ultimately interested in changes in the economic well-being of families, it would be better to look at the distribution of equivalent disposable income, i.e., gross income reduced by taxes and increased by transfers, after adjustment for differences in family needs. Although such statistics are not readily available, data on the distribution of per capita disposable income have been published and can be taken as good estimates of economic well-being. These results have been published for a sub-sample of the population excluding households where the head is self-employed.[14] They are shown in table 11.12 with data on the distribution of income per household (for gross and disposable incomes). The inequality measure is the C90/C10 ratio.

We shall first look at the largest population, i.e., all households except the self-employed. Between 1975 and 1979, the distribution of gross income per household became less unequal, but the trend reversed itself somewhat in 1979–84. Taking into account redistributive effects, we find income

Table 11.12 *Distribution of income: France, 1975–1984 (C90/C10 ratios)*

	1975	1979	1984
Households with head wage earner or inactive			
Gross income per household	6.8	5.8	5.9
Disposable income per household	6.2	4.9	4.7
Per capita disposable income	4.1	4.0	4.0
Households with head wage earner			
Gross income per household	4.4	4.2	4.5
Disposable income per household	3.8	3.6	3.8
Per capita disposable income	4.0	3.9	3.8

Source: See appendix A.

inequality continued to fall between 1979 and 1984. As pointed out by Canceill and Villeneuve (1990), the slight reduction of inequality in 1979–84 was only due to transfer income. Adjusting for differences in family needs (per capita disposable income), however, nearly offset all these changes. The C90/C10 ratio was 4.1 in 1975 and 4.0 in 1979 and 1984.

We find quite the same pattern for households where the head is a wage earner. It is worth noting that the slight fall in inequality in the distribution of per capita disposable income in 1979–84 (from a C90/C10 ratio of 3.9 in 1979 to 3.8 in 1984) was solely due to demographic changes. The dispersion of both gross incomes and disposable incomes per household, before adjusting for differences in family size, increased between 1979 and 1984.

More recent data based on the Family Expenditure Survey are shown in table 11.13 for the years 1984 and 1989. They relate to the distribution of equivalent disposable income for the population of employees. These data are shown together with results based on tax assessments (ERF) for the same population between 1975 and 1984.

The dispersion of equivalent disposable income increased slightly in 1984–9, mainly because of the rapid growth of the higher decile. Thus, this result is consistent with our knowledge of wage inequality during the same period (see section 3). Although the definition of income is not exactly the same, these data can be compared with those on per capita disposable income based on the ERF. One would then conclude that income inequality among employees virtually did not change between 1979 and 1989.

This 'quasi status quo' does not mean that all households experienced the same income variations. The inequality measure based on the C90/C10 ratio actually compares only two points of the distribution. By comparing

Table 11.13 *Distribution of income: France, 1975–1989 (employees)*

	Per capita disposable income			Equivalent disposable income	
	1975	1979	1984	1984	1989
C90/C10	4.05	3.94	3.82	3.38	3.48
C90/C50	2.16	2.02	1.96	1.79	1.88
C10/C50	0.53	0.51	0.51	0.53	0.54

Source: For per capita disposable income, *Enquêtes Revenus Fiscaux*; for equivalent disposable income, Family Expenditure Survey; see appendix A for details.

variations for each decile of the income distribution, we can get a better picture of changes in income inequality. Figure 11.5 shows the nominal growth for each decile of the income distribution for the periods 1975–9, 1979–84 and 1984–9.

For the period 1975–9, the lower middle part of the distribution experienced the most rapid growth. Changes at the bottom of the distribution were a bit lower and quite similar to those in the upper middle part. The upper end of the distribution experienced the slowest growth. Data for 1979–84 show a general levelling off. Increases were nearly the same at all levels except for the upper part of the distribution. Between 1984 and 1989, changes were quite symmetrical to those observed in 1975–9. The lower middle part of the distribution experienced the slowest growth, while increases were the highest at both ends of the distribution.[15]

To close this section, we look at qualitative studies that take a multi-dimensional approach with the help of a composite indicator using a variety of criteria related to five main variables: income and wealth, living conditions in a broad sense (housing, basic amenities, holidays and leisure, budget restrictions, etc.), work-force participation (unemployment, education), state of health and the interview subject's opinion of the development of his or her own standard of living (Hatchuel *et al.* 1990). Among the main conclusions of the survey, which covered the period 1979–88, we find growing inequality between the groups at either end. In addition, the group that has gained the most is retired couple households. In contrast, the situation has deteriorated for large families (not including executives), single women with children and unskilled manual labourers.

Periodic surveys have been conducted among French households asking them what they think inequality actually is (how large is it?) and their opinion about it. It is useful to compare these subjective views with the results of studies described above. According to French people, inequality

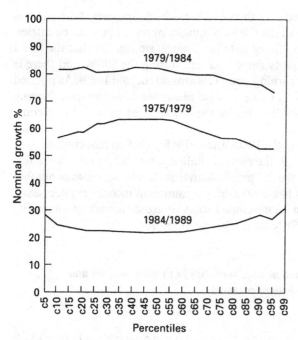

Figure 11.⌄ Changes in the income distribution
Source: See appendix A.

increased again in the 1980s after having declined in the 1970s. This result seems thus consistent with our statistical knowledge of inequality.

6   Summary and conclusions

The wage range, which continuously narrowed from the late 1960s, widened again in the 1980s, and job security declined for a growing proportion of employees, especially the youngest. Overall, the progressivity of taxes and social welfare contributions was reduced, and conditions for benefit entitlement became more restrictive. At the same time, the purchasing power of benefits has barely been maintained since 1984. These changes have resulted in a slight increase in income inequality between employees' households since the mid 1980s. Retired couples have succeeded the best in maintaining their standard of living, while the standard of living for young people and women with children has deteriorated.

However, the increase in measured inequality in the latter half of the 1980s was relatively modest. The increase was of about the same order of magnitude as the fall of 1979–84. Consequently, one cannot see any significant upward trend over the whole decade. At the same time, there is nothing comparable with the rise in inequality observed in other countries, such as the UK. From official data for France, we can say that the trend towards reduced inequality came to a halt during the 1980s, and there is some evidence that the turning point was around the mid 1980s. As pointed out by Atkinson (1994), France may be, like other countries, just 'lagging behind the US and the UK', and in the 1990s could see a rise in income inequality.

While public debate in the 1960s and 1970s focused on reducing inequality between social groups, the current challenge for society is to find effective means for battling the marginalisation that threatens a growing number of people. If measures like establishing a minimum income are necessary, preventive action must be developed so as to avoid the risk of increasing marginalisation, especially for the youngest groups.

Appendix A   Wages and income statistics in France: sources and methodological comments

1 Wages

The main source for measuring inequality is the analysis made by INSEE (the national statistical office) of a sample of declarations made by employers to the tax authorities. Since this information is provided by employers, it is thought to be a quite reliable source for measuring wages paid to employees. Today the resulting series of statistics are known as DADS (*Déclarations annuelles de données sociales*) but were previously referred to as DAS (*Déclarations annuelles de salaires*).

The wage concept is net earnings, i.e., gross pay less the employee's social contributions. Earnings are measured on an annual basis for full-time workers employed for a full year. The DADS source covers the private and 'semi-public' sectors. The field of inquiry excludes employees working in agriculture, domestic servants and all people working in public administrations. All sizes of establishments are covered.

This source of information was established in the early 1950s. Since then, the methodology of the survey has changed or been improved many times (especially in 1967, 1976 and the 1980s). Despite these changes, we have tried to build consistent series by using the following publications.

Baudelot, Christian, and Lebeaupin, Anne. 'Les salaires de 1950 à 1975'. Document rectangle INSEE. Also published in *Economie et Statistique*, no.113 (July–August 1979). Paris: INSEE.

INSEE. 1985. 'Les salaires dans l'industrie, le commerce et le services en 1980'. Collections de l'INSEE, série M, no. 113 (July). Paris: INSEE.

Girard, J. P., and Lhéritier J. L. 1992. 'Les salaires en 1990 – Tome 1: Le secteur privé'. Insee-Résultats, no. 292, série Emploi-Revenus, no. 34 (May). Paris: INSEE.
The above publications were used with more recent publications to construct figures 11.1 and 11.2. It should be noted that there was an important change in the concept of income during the 1980s. The series of statistics now relates to a newly introduced concept, *salaire offert*, whereas the concept of income used in the old series was *salaire déclaré*. Wage inequality measured on the new basis is 5–10 per cent lower than that based on the previous norm. Tables 11.1 and 11.6 show the wage dispersion according to the new concept of *salaire offert*. Data have been published in the following publications.
Bayet, A. 1994. 'L'évolution des salaires dans le secteur privé en 1993'. Insee Première, no. 321 (June). Paris: INSEE.
Girard, J. P. and Lheritier, J. L. 1993. 'L'évolution des salaires dans le secteur privé en 1992'. Insee Première, no. 275 (June). Paris: INSEE.
Data used for table 11.3 were released in:
Houriez, G. 1993. 'Les salaires en 1990 – Tome 2: La fonction publique d'Etat'. Insee-Resultats, no. 238, série Emploi-Revenus, no. 45 (May). Paris: INSEE.

2   Household income

There is no annual source on household income in France. The main source of information is the periodic analysis made by INSEE of a sample of declarations made by households to tax authorities. The surveys are referred to as *Enquête Revenus Fiscaux* and have been conducted by INSEE nearly every five years since 1956 (1956, 1962, 1965, 1970, 1975, 1979, 1984, 1990). Results are now available up to 1984.

The income concept is taxable income. These statistics based on tax assessments are sometimes regarded with suspicion, especially for self-employment income. For instance, declared self-employment income is 30 per cent lower than the estimated value of similar incomes in national accounts. Since households in which the head is self-employed have, on average, the highest incomes, this can be seen as a serious limitation of the data. Another limitation is that unearned income recorded in the survey only accounts for an estimated 40 per cent of overall unearned income. The main reason is that a big part of this income is not liable to progressive income tax (there are a variety of loopholes for that source of income). Since unearned income rose faster than income from other sources during the past decade, the change in income inequality as measured in the survey may have been affected.

Estimates shown in table 11.10 for various social groups have been computed from the following publications.

INSEE. 1981. 'Les ressources des ménages par catégorie socioprofessionnelle en 1975'. Collections de l'INSEE, série M, no. 87 (January). Paris: INSEE.

INSEE. 1985. 'Les ressources des ménages par catégorie socioprofessionnelle en 1979'. Collections de l'INSEE, série M, no. 116 (December). Paris: INSEE.

INSEE. 1992. 'Les comptes de revenu des ménages par catégorie socioprofessionnelle, 1984–1989'. Insee-Résultats, no. 226, série Emploi-Revenus, no. 42 (December). Paris: INSEE.

Up to 1984, the sources of figures shown in tables 11.11, 11.12 and 11.13 and figure 11.5 are the following.

INSEE. 1987. 'Les revenus fiscaux des ménages en 1979 (et principaux résultats pour 1975)'. Collections de l'INSEE, série M, no. 127 (December). Paris: INSEE.

INSEE. 1989. 'Les revenus fiscaux des ménages en 1984'. Collections de l'INSEE, série M, no. 139 (May). Paris: INSEE.

CERC. 1989. 'Les Français et leurs revenus : le tournant des années 80'. Documents du CERC, no. 94. Paris.

The source for the estimates of equivalent disposable income for 1984 and 1989 (table 11.13) is the Family Expenditure Survey. Figures have been computed for CERC by Bernard Legris (INSEE, Division Revenus).

Notes

1 See Canceill and Villeneuve 1990; Moutardier 1990; Atkinson 1993; Gottschalk 1993; Katz, Loveman and Blanchflower 1993.
2 Average wage net of social security contributions and before income tax.
3 Gottschalk looks at data based on the Income Tax Survey. For males aged 25–54, these data show an increase in wage inequality between 1979 and 1984.
4 The gap between the hourly rates of part-time and full-time employees mostly arises from the lower skill levels for part-time work. At a comparable skill level, the rates for the two job groups are very close. In other words, there does not seem to be specific wage discrimination connected with part-time work (CERC 1989).
5 Other minor limitations of these data are due to the fact that some fringe benefits, such as profit-sharing bonuses, are not included in the statistics. These benefits still only represent a small share of total pay, but they became increasingly common in the 1980s. In 1989, more than a million employees received profit-sharing bonuses, triple the 1984 figure and ten times more than in 1974.
6 Employees in this type of work are considered trainees and are not included in wage statistics.

7 According to an official report from the Ministry of Education in 1989 (the 'Decomps report'), the number of engineers trained in France meets slightly more than half the requirement.

8 CERC, *Constat de l'évolution récente des revenus en France*, various editions.

9 These indicators are applied to some standard household cases using calculations published by CERC on this subject. See CERC 1989, chapter V, 'Les prélèvements : moins d'impôts, plus de cotisations sociales'.

10 During the 1980s, the cap on employer contributions was lifted. As a percentage of the wage, the rate of employer contributions hardly changed for the lowest incomes but went up substantially for the highest incomes.

11 Sluggish growth in the early 1990s and the 1993 recession have boosted the ratio. In 1993, social welfare expenditure accounted for around 30 per cent of GDP.

12 This confirms the results of a previous study which, as early as 1985, pointed out the consequences of this absence of social welfare protection, particularly for young people and single parent families (Dupré, Pascaud and Simonin 1986).

13 Results for the year 1990 (the latest survey) are not yet available.

14 This is a limitation of the data since the self-employed have, as noted above, the highest incomes.

15 From a sociological point of view this result may be of some interest. Broadly speaking, one could thus say that in relation to the other groups the relative position of the lower middle class continuously deteriorated in the 1980s.

References

Atkinson, A. B. 1990. 'The Distribution of the Tax Burden: 30 Years after The Theory of Public Finance'. ST/ICERD Discussion Paper, WSP/51. London.
1993. 'What is Happening to the Distribution of Income in the UK?' ST/ICERD Discussion Paper, WSP/87. London.
1994. 'Seeking to Explain the Distribution of Income'. ST/ICERD Discussion Paper, WSP/106. London.
Bazen, S. and Martin, J-P. 1991. 'L'incidence du salaire minimum sur les gains et l'emploi en France'. *Revue Économique de l'OCDE*, no. 16 (spring). Paris.
Brion, P. and Concialdi, P. 1993. 'Les prélèvements obligatoires dépendent peu du niveau des revenus'. *Données Sociales 1993*. Paris.
Canceill, G. and Villeneuve, A. 1990. 'Les inégalités de revenus: quasi statu quo entre 1979 et 1984 pour les salariés et les inactifs'. *Economie et Statistique*, no. 230 (March). Paris.
CERC. 1989. 'Les Français et leurs revenus: le tournant des années 80'. Documents du CERC, no. 94, Paris.
Constat de l'évolution récente des revenus en France. Various editions. Paris.
CERC-Association. 1995. 'Les prestations sociales depuis 25 ans: croissance et maîtrise'. *La Note de CERC-Association*, no. 2 (February). Paris.
Chassard, Y. and Concialdi, P. 1989. *Les revenus en France*. Paris: Ed. La Découverte.

1990. 'Revenus et patrimoines'. In *Encyclopédie économique, X.*, eds. J. Greffe, J-L. Mairesse and Reiffers. Paris: Economica.

Concialdi P. 1990. 'Les revenus des activités indépendantes: des trajectoires qui divergent dans la crise'. *Données Sociales 1990.* Paris: INSEE.

Concialdi, P. and Guillaumat-Tailliet, F. 1993. 'Salaires et coûts de main-d'oeuvre dans les principaux pays industriels'. Documents du CERC, no. 106. Paris.

Concialdi, P. and Madinier, P. 1990. 'Formation, mobilité et disparités des salaires depuis quarante ans'. *Cerc-Notes et Graphiques*, no. 10. Paris.

Cornilleau, G., Marioni, P. and Roguet, B. 1990. 'Quinze ans de politique de l'emploi'. *Travail et Emploi*, no. 44. Paris.

Dupré, J. P., Pascaud, E. and Simonin, B. 1986. *La pauvreté-précarité en 1985: diversité des recours à l'aide sociale.* Paris: Crédoc.

Elbaum, M. and Marchand, O. 1993. 'Emploi et chômage des jeunes dans les pays industrialisés : la spécificité française'. Premières synthèses, no. 34, Ministère du Travail, de l'Emploi et de la Formation Professionnelle, October. Paris.

Gottschalk, P. 1993. 'Changes in Inequality of Family Income in Seven Industrialized Countries'. *American Economic Review*, May: 136–42.

Hatchuel, G., Payet-Thouvenot, V. and Poquet, G. 1990. 'Les inégalités en France et leur évolution depuis une dizaine d'années'. CREDOC, Collection des rapports, no. 83. Paris.

Katz, L. F., Loveman, G. and Blanchflower, D. 1993. 'A Comparison of Changes in the Structure of Wages in Four OECD Countries'. Discussion paper no. 144, Centre for Economic Performance. London.

Katz, L. F. and Murphy, K. M. 1992. 'Changes in Relative Wages, 1963–1987: Supply and Demand Factors'. *Quarterly Journal of Economics*, 107. MIT Press.

Levy, F. and Murnane, R. J. 1992. 'U.S. Earnings Levels and Earnings Inequality: A Review of Recent Trends and Proposed Explanations'. *Journal of Economic Literature*, 30, 3.

Malabouche, G. 1991. 'Le système de prélèvement est moins progressif en France qu'à l'étranger'. *Economie et Statistique*, no. 241 (March). Paris: INSEE.

Moutardier, M. 1990. 'Consommation en hausse, mais pas pour tous'. Insee Première, no. 62. Paris.

Neyret, G. 1992. 'Les tendances actuelles de la répartition'. *La Revue de l'Economie Sociale*, no. 23.

OECD. 1985. 'L'enseignement dans la société moderne'. Paris.

Pechman, J. A. 1985. 'Who paid the taxes, 1966–85'. *Studies of Government Finance.* Washington: Brookings Institution.

Rotbart, G. 1990. 'Salaires et restructuration du travail: une transformation massive et rapide'. *Données Sociales 1990.* Paris: INSEE.

12 The distribution of economic well-being in the Netherlands, its evolution in the 1980s and the role of demographic change

RUUD MUFFELS AND JAN NELISSEN

1 Introduction and outline

Evidence on income and poverty dynamics shows that in the second half of the 1980s, economic mobility, conceived as changes in income and poverty status, turned out to be relatively high in the Netherlands compared with other European countries (Muffels 1992a, 1992b, 1993; Duncan *et al.* 1993). At the same time, it appears that for some groups in society the likelihood of escaping low income or poverty declines rapidly during a spell of poverty. Thus, the persistence of low income and poverty emerged as an issue of concern for public policies even in the wealthy Dutch society, which is known for the generosity of its welfare arrangements and the strong redistributive impact of the social security system. On the basis of these findings, it was hypothesised that economic mobility is very low at the lower and upper tails of the income distribution but quite high in the income classes just below or just above the minimum income level. From this it follows that income earners in the low-income ranges will likely move upwards or downwards in the income distribution over time.

This study raises the issue of the extent of economic mobility and persistence of states of low income over time. Particular attention is given to the assessment of income mobility and stability for various population groups, to be examined through the estimation of 'fixed effects' panel regression models. The model utilised here is equivalent to the earnings dynamics model of Lillard and Willis (1978) and Moffitt and Gottschalk (1993) and the income dynamics model applied by Duncan and Rodgers (1991). The results corroborate those of American studies on the subject. On the one hand, it appears from Socio-Economic Panel Research (SEP) data that the year-to-year economic mobility at the lower tail of the income distribution is substantial but that this high mobility goes hand in hand with a high level of persistence of low incomes. In terms of poverty, it becomes apparent that about half of the single-year poor are 'persistently poor' over a longer period. Similar outcomes are observed for measures of inequality and poverty using the Income Panel data instead of the SEP data (Trimp 1992). Furthermore, it should be stressed that snapshot figures cannot provide insight into the structural causes of changes in poverty risk at the individual level over time, which can only be provided by panel data.

With respect to income inequality, measured by means of the Theil coefficient or by any other income inequality measure, there is ample evidence that in the second half of the 1980s income inequality rose (SCP 1990), whereas in the 1970s and early 1980s income inequality steadily declined. What are the causes of this change in the downward trend in inequality? Results from various studies show that structural shifts in the labour market situation and in household formation can be at the heart of this change (Sawhill 1988; Levy and Murnane 1992; Moffitt 1992; Muffels 1993; Duncan *et al.* 1993). In this study, the first issue concerning the impact of shifts in the labour market situation will be examined by studying the long-term evolution of income inequality. The latter issue of the impact of demographic changes on the evolution of economic well-being will be examined with dynamic microsimulation techniques.

2   The evolution of income inequality

2.1   *Income inequality between 1959 and 1990*

Evidence on the evolution of income inequality in the last three decades is found in the income statistics of the Netherlands Central Bureau of Statistics (NCBS). The figures are derived from a large sample of income earners, comprising about 100,000 couples and unmarried persons. The income concept used is disposable or 'net spendable' income. In figure 12.1, the evolution of income inequality from 1959 to 1990 is shown according to three income inequality measures: the relative interquartile distance (I), the ratio of the income share of the tenth and third (disposable) income deciles (R) and an entropy measure known as the Theil coefficient (T).

The relative interquartile distance (I) is defined as the ratio of the distance between the average income in the third quartile (25 per cent income earners) and the average income in the first quartile to the median income. The measure reflects the variation of income around the median and therefore represents a measure for income dispersion in the middle ranges of the income distribution. The ratio of the income shares of the tenth and third deciles (R) is a commonly used measure of income inequality. The third decile has been chosen as the reference category, because social security recipients with minimum welfare benefits and low unemployment benefits are mainly located in the first two deciles. If the ratio of the tenth to the first decile was chosen, the income dispersion measure would then reflect the

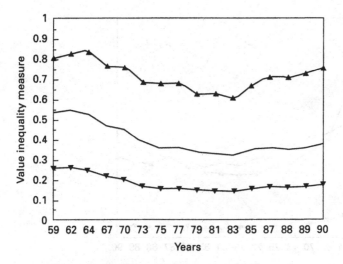

Income inequality measures

——— Ratio income share, 3 decile/10 decile (R)

—▲— Relative interquartile distance (I)

—▼— Theil coefficient (T)

Figure 12.1 The evolution of income inequality in the period, 1959–1990 by three income inequality measures (R, I, T)
Source: NCBS, Monthly Bulletin on Socio-Economic Statistics, 6, 1993.

income inequality between the top labour incomes and the lowest social security benefits. The choice of the measure R thus implies that the focus is on income inequality within the working population.

The entropy measure, known as the second Theil coefficient, is defined as follows:

$$T = \frac{1}{n\mu} \sum_{i=1}^{n} y_i \ln \frac{y_i}{\mu} \tag{1}$$

where n=number of observations, μ=population mean income and y_i the income of person or household i. The Theil coefficient has a zero value if the incomes are equally distributed. This measure appears to be more sensitive to changes affecting the higher end of the income distribution than the lower end. The advantage of this measure is that it can easily be decomposed into within- and between-group inequality. In figure 12.2, the results are given for the Theil coefficient only, but also broken down by the socio-economic status of the individual. The evolution of the between-group inequality is given as well.

Figure 12.1 indicates that until 1983 the level of income inequality

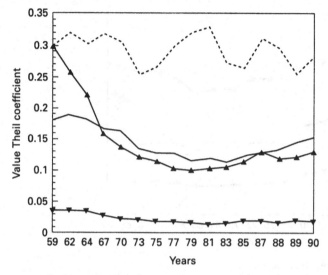

Figure 12.2 The evolution of income inequality in the period 1959–1990 by socio-economic status (Theil coefficients)
Source: NCBS, Monthly Bulletin on Socio-Economic Statistics, 6, 1993.

steadily declined according to all three measures applied here. However, after 1983 income inequality rose, although at a fairly moderate rate. This U-shaped pattern occurs regardless of the income inequality measure used.

Broken down according to socioeconomic characteristics of the population, it becomes apparent that income inequality is highest within the group of self-employed and lowest within the non-working population (excluding the unemployed). Income inequality within the self-employed seems to fluctuate strongly but at a rather stable level. Inequality within the group of employed and unemployed persons shows a steady decline until 1983 and a slightly rising trend thereafter. The largest decline in income inequality, at least until 1979, occurred within the group of the non-working population. This category consists of the elderly drawing benefits from pension schemes, disabled people, survivors and social assistance beneficiaries (excluding unemployed). The reason for the downward sloping trend until 1979 is the extension of existing and the introduction of new social security benefit schemes. After 1979, inequality within this non-working group shows a steady but fairly moderate rise. The increase in inequality within the non-working population can be attributed partly to the restrictive social security policies of the Dutch government in the 1980s, aimed at reducing social security expenditures and lowering the 'collective burden' (the burden of social security contributions and income taxes), and partly at encouraging structural change in the economy and the labour market. In the early 1980s, government policy was directed at tightening eligibility conditions, reducing minimum social security benefits (including the statutory minimum flat-rate old-age pension benefit, AOW) and levelling down benefits above the minimum by reducing the income replacement rates of unemployment and disability benefits; these replacement rates were reduced, in several stages, from 80 per cent to 70 per cent of previous earnings during 1984–5. From 1979 on, the index of social security benefits has been frozen, because the Benefit Adjustment Act (WAM), concerning annual adjustment of social security benefit levels to rises in the general wage level, was applied only once in the 1980s (in 1980). These policies led to a diminishing role for earnings-related benefits in favour of the role of minimum, means-tested flat-rate benefits.

With the reform of the social security system in 1987, the eligibility conditions for unemployment and disability benefits were tightened and the duration of employment benefits became dependent on work history. The duration of benefits was shortened for the young unemployed and school-leavers who had little or no work experience. The eligibility conditions of the Employee Disability Act (WAO) and the general disability scheme (AAW) were tightened through the abolition of the labour market consideration rule. According to this rule, the determination of the incapacity to work should take account of the labour market opportunities of the disabled person. Since 1987, the assessment of work incapacity is based primarily on the incapacity to perform a job which is perceived as 'commensurate employment' and not the incapacity to perform one's current work. The Disability Act of 1993 further tightened eligibility conditions for disability benefits, such that the duration of disability benefits became dependent on work history just as for unemployment benefits. These policy measures forced a steady decline over the 1980s in the purchasing power of net social security benefits, which lagged substantially behind the minimum wage in the private sector.

As stated earlier, part of the rising inequality must be attributed to autonomous and structural changes in the labour market. In the early 1980s, the proportion of people out of the labour force because of unemployment, disability or early retirement drastically increased in the Netherlands, to levels amongst the highest in Europe. It appears that elderly employees (aged 60–65 years) in particular paid the price for the economic recession, which resulted in extremely unfavourable job opportunities and low participation rates.

Rising non-participation in the 1980s has also reduced the level of benefits. After the recovery of the economy from 1984 on, it appeared that short-term labour market exits decreased, but long-term exits became more apparent. Employment growth was far too low in the late 1980s to absorb the large numbers of people who had acquired non-working status in preceding years. Because of this, long-term non-participation increased strongly. It created an autonomous impetus for a fall in the level of benefits due to the lower level of long-term benefits compared with short-term benefits. Long-term benefits granted by means-tested social assistance schemes or the minimum old-age benefit scheme (all of which are minimum, flat-rate benefits) are considerably lower than short-term benefits granted by earnings-related early retirement, unemployment or disability schemes. All in all, it appears that both the restrictive social security policies and the increase in long-term unemployment and disability led to increasing numbers of people drawing minimum benefits. This, together with the rising numbers of high earnings-related benefits for those retiring early or because of a disability, caused the inequality of people out of the labour force to rise.

The rise in inequality for the working population in the late 1980s can most likely be attributed to the increasing dispersion of primary earnings in the economic upswing from 1983 on. Between 1984 and 1990, the dispersion of contract wages, determined by collective agreements (CAO) increased. The lowest CAO scale earners saw their gross income rise 6.4 per cent a year between 1984 and 1990, while the highest CAO scales experienced an average rise of 10.2 per cent each year. The scales in between rose 9.2 per cent (Second Chamber 1990).

The inequality figures for the 1980s presented before show that according to the Theil coefficient, earnings and income inequality rose again after a steady decline in the 1960s and 1970s. If the figures are broken down by household composition, it appears that the rise in inequality was most striking for single households and one-parent families. Income inequality for couples without children decreased in the same period, which can be attributed to the increasing numbers of two-earner households in this category. The rising inequality figures are in part attributable to structural changes in the household formation process, particularly in a growing number of single households with low incomes. In this respect, the growing number of single elderly households seems particularly relevant.

So far we have focused on income distribution broken down by socio-economic status and household composition. The question of what impact changes in the tax and transfer system had remains unanswered. This issue

Table 12.1 *Per capita income, transfers and income taxes, 1983–1990* *(Index 1981 =100)*

	1983	1985	1987	1988	1989	1990
Per capita primary income	107	113	120	124	130	138
Received income transfers	115	117	124	128	131	142
Contributions	121	124	130	135	134	130
Income taxes	95	97	111	114	123	151
Direct taxes	90	98	99	93	97	105
Per capita disposable income	107	113	120	124	131	142

Source: van der Laan and Kriek 1992; NCBS 1992.

is addressed in the next section. Table 12.1 provides information on the changes in the incidence of income transfer and income tax systems over time.

From table 12.1 it is apparent that per capita disposable income rose between 1981 and 1990 at about the same rate (42 per cent) as primary per capita income (38 per cent).

Although government policies in the 1980s were aimed at reducing social security expenditures, the percentage growth of received income transfers, mainly consisting of social security benefits, appears to have been almost as great as the rise in primary income. Evidence from various sources (Muffels, Nelissen and Nuyens 1986 and 1988; Barr 1992; Nelissen 1993b) shows that the Dutch income transfer system has a strong redistributive impact on the distribution of primary income and reduces inequality in terms of the Theil coefficient by between 40 per cent and 50 per cent (particularly due to the AOW scheme). The small rise in income inequality for people drawing benefits from social security in the late 1980s hardly affected the strong redistributive impact of social security transfers (see figure 12.2). As Barr (1992) demonstrates, social security contributions and direct taxes have an unequalising effect on the primary income distribution. Table 12.1 shows that growth in contributions is generally higher and growth in direct taxes smaller than that of primary earnings and secondary income (income transfers). The joint impact of contributions and direct taxes on income inequality therefore hardly changed. On the other hand, it is apparent that the equalising impact of income taxes became slightly less because of the more modest growth of income taxes compared with primary income.

The situation in 1990 is different from that in 1989 because of the impact of the tax reform which came into force in 1990. The tax reform, known as the Oort tax law (after the president of the tax reform commission), broadened the tax base, abolished or restricted particular tax exemptions (general social insurance contributions, company cars, work-related expenses) and lowered the top marginal tax rates, from 70 per cent to 60 per cent. To prevent the net income distribution from being too strongly affected by these tax changes, gross wages were raised by a compensation allowance. For this reason, income tax liabilities rose more than 30 per cent from 1989 to 1990, simply as a result of changes in the tax structure. The income distribution effects of the Oort tax reform seem to have been moderate. The overall effect on the inequality of individual disposable income is slightly positive. In particular, single-earner households with lower incomes experienced the strongest negative income effects, though for the single elderly the effects were mitigated through compensating income measures. Multiple-earner households with high incomes appear to have profited most from the Oort tax reform measures. They saw net income rise because of lower marginal tax rates for high incomes (Second Chamber 1990).

3   Income inequality and income stability in the 1980s using Dutch panel data

3.1   Income inequality

The annual snapshot figures on the income distribution presented earlier cast some light on the evolution of income and income inequality over time. However, because of their static character they cannot tell us much about the income mobility patterns underlying these changes in income positions. Only longitudinal data can tell us more about the gross changes at the individual level that accompany these aggregate (net) changes. Changes at the individual level give us more insight into the stability of income positions over time and into the issue of economic mobility. On the other hand, a rise or fall in income over time can be evened out, which may have a levelling down effect on income inequality on a year-to-year basis.

There are two basic approaches to investigating longitudinal patterns of income changes. One approach is to use panel or cohort data to analyse real changes in income distribution. The disadvantage of this method is the rather short time period for which information is generally available, at least in the Dutch and most other European panel surveys. Another approach is to utilise microsimulation techniques. Since data covering a long time period are generally not available, this approach requires the creation of a hypothetical longitudinal data set on which changes in the income distribution can be assessed over the entire life cycle. This life-cycle approach gives much better insight into the

Table 12.2 *Income inequality (Theil coefficients) of the equivalent disposable household income by socioeconomic status of the head of household, Income Panel Survey (IPO), 1984–1988*

	One-year (1986)	Five-year (1984–8)
Socioeconomic status		
Self-employed	0.182	0.102
Civil servants	0.048	0.038
Employees	0.075	0.054
Unemployed/disabled	0.052	0.038
Pensioners	0.076	0.061
Others (e.g., on social assistance)	0.277	0.086
Total	0.106	0.066

Source: Trimp 1992.

redistributive effects of income transfer systems. Both approaches will be applied in the following.

Recently, some longitudinal figures have been published on the evolution of income inequality in the 1980s. The information is derived from the so-called Income Panel Survey (IPO) carried out at the end of 1989 by the NCBS based on about 75,000 households. On the basis of these figures, Trimp (1992) finds that the average five-year income inequality figure proves to be 38 per cent lower than the one-year figure (based on information for the year 1986). In table 12.2, Theil coefficients are given for the one- and five-year periods respectively, broken down by socioeconomic status. These figures show income inequality amongst heads of households measured in terms of equivalent disposable income. The results indicate that around two-thirds of the observed single-year inequalities are not evened out by income changes over five years. Apparently, changes in income over time are not equally spread over the entire range of the income distribution. It follows that income inequality on a year-to-year basis is only partly offset by changes in the persistent income level.

3.2   *Income mobility and poverty persistence – evidence from Dutch panel data*

In this section, we examine to what extent income positions tend to change over time or remain stable. For this purpose, several measures for assessing income mobility and income persistence can be applied. We have used two individual-based measures of income mobility and one model-based measure. The latter is derived from the estimation of a panel regression model as applied by Duncan and Rodgers (1991) on the PSID panel data. The data used here are the Dutch Socio-Economic Panel data. The first individual-based measure is the n-year income-to-needs ratio, which is a continuous measure for the ratio of aggregate income over n years of observation to aggregate minimum income needed to attain a minimum standard of living over n years. The minimum income levels in the numerator have been derived from the various poverty line definitions which have been applied in the study. For that reason, the income-to-needs ratio differs according to the poverty line definition used. The ratio reflects the mean income position of individuals and households over time relative to the mean income level needed to attain the bottom poverty line.

According to Sen (1983), the income-to-needs measure can be seen as a relative measure for income deprivation. This measure can easily be converted into a discrete poverty measure by defining a cut-off point at the ratio of 1.0, below which people are considered to live in permanent income poverty. By defining various cut-off points or income-to-needs classes, information can be presented on the distribution of n-year equivalent disposable income of the individual. The use of this permanent income-to-needs ratio refers to Friedman's notion of permanent income.

A second measure proposed by Bane and Ellwood (1986) departs from a spell approach, in which a spell is assumed to start after a transition has taken place from any other initial state in $t-1$ to the state of interest at time t. The approach is based on the standard life-table approach. Income mobility is defined here in terms of the exit rate out of poverty, conditional on experiencing a poverty spell during one year, two years, etc. The survival rates after n years of experiencing a spell provide estimates for the persistence of poverty over time. In both measures, income mobility is defined in terms of movements across certain 'needs' thresholds, which are derived from various poverty line definitions.

3.2.1   Needs thresholds

Various poverty lines or needs thresholds will be applied in this chapter to look at the sensitivity of outcomes for different definitions of poverty. There is much debate and little consensus in poverty literature about the most appropriate poverty line methodology. Hence, a 'multimethod' approach to poverty has arisen in which both absolute and relative definitions of poverty are employed. The standards used in this chapter are a subjective standard, the Subjective Poverty Line (Kapteyn, Kooreman and Willemse 1988), an absolute budget standard, i.e., the official US poverty threshold converted into Dutch guilders using OECD purchasing power parities (Orschansky 1969) and two completely relative standards, the 50 per cent of the mean standardised (i.e., equivalent) disposable income approach of O'Higgins and Jenkins (1989) used in various research projects commissioned by the EU (cf. Muffels 1993) and the National Social Minimum Income (NSMI) level, which by and large equals the amounts of social assistance benefits.

Table 12.3 reports the results using various measures of income mobility and income persistence. The results are given for the various poverty line methodologies just described. The population estimates of persistent poverty according to the spell-based measure of persistent poverty are not given in table 12.3 but can be found quite easily by multiplying the cumulative survival rates after two years with the average proportion of poor in the time period. The proportion persistently poor appears to be at a level of 5 per cent using the US standard, whereas for the SPL standard and the ESMI standard the percentages are 3 per cent and for the NSMI standard 1.75 per cent. These percentages are lower than the ones for the n-year income-to-needs measure – at least those based on the 100 per cent threshold level. The results of a higher threshold level (125 per cent) are a substantial rise in the proportion of persistent poor.

According to the spell-based measure, income mobility can be defined as the cumulative exit rate being the complement to the cumulative survival rate. The results indicate a high-income mobility particularly in the first year of a poverty spell. The drawback of the n-year income-to-needs measure is neglect of the issue of censoring, which creates biased probability estimates of the proportion of persistent poor.[1] The spell-based approach of persistent poverty is therefore obviously the most proper way to deal with the issue of measuring persistent poverty since it takes censoring into account. In the spell-based approach, left-censored observations are removed because the method only embodies observations for which the start of the poverty period is known. The issue of right censoring is solved through the specification of the 'hazard' function, describing the likelihood of exit out of poverty conditional on the duration of the previous spell.[2] However, one has to keep in mind that the accuracy of spell-based estimates is heavily influenced by the length of the observation period. The European data sets currently available cover a rather short period of time, so the spell-based measure of persistent poverty seems less appropriate for the relatively young European panels.

A comparison of the results for persistent poverty in table 12.3, based on the various poverty line definitions, reveals that the highest poverty persistence estimates are obtained for the US and SPL standards and the lowest for the European and national minimum-income standards. The former definitions show higher poverty line levels and on average higher

Table 12.3 *Individual-based measures of income mobility and persistent poverty for the Dutch population (proportion of poor) using four poverty thresholds, Socio-Economic Panel, 1985–1988*

Poverty standard	NSMI (per cent)	ESMI (per cent)	SPL (per cent)	US (per cent)
Ratio of four-year income to needs level				
<1.25	14.2	21.7	21.5	30.5
<1.00	3.2	6.0	7.5	9.4
<0.75	0.6	1.5	1.5	1.8
Spell-based measure of poverty. Cumulative survival rate or the fraction remaining poor after *n*th year in spell				
After 1st year	36.2	42.3	54.9	46.0
After 2nd year	21.7	27.3	40.2	31.3

Notes:
NSMI=National Social Minimum Income (based on amounts of social assistance benefits by household type).
ESMI=European Social Minimum Income (50 per cent of mean equivalent income).
SPL=Subjective Poverty Line (minimum income needed to make ends meet).
US=United States official poverty threshold (income equivalent of food basket times three).

'poverty gaps' (the income shortfall of the poor) than the latter. A recent comparative study (Duncan *et al.* 1993) finds an inverse relationship between the level of the poverty line, the distance to the poverty line and income mobility. The higher the poverty line level, the higher the distance to the poverty line (income shortfall of the poor) and the lower the income mobility of the poor in terms of the likelihood of moving out of poverty. Our results corroborate the results of Duncan *et al.* The US and SPL income thresholds appear to be at a high level compared with the European and national standards, whereas income mobility turns out to be relatively low, since estimates of poverty persistence are high for these standards compared with the others.

3.2.2   The empirical model

Our model-based measure of persistent poverty is based on the estimation of a random effect panel regression model. The dependent variable of the regression model is termed the log income-to-needs ratio, which is a continuous measure for the extent of relative deprivation (Sen 1983).

However, the income-to-needs ratio can easily be conceived as equivalent household income, where the equivalence scale is derived from the corresponding poverty standard. The model is given by

$$Y_{it} = Z_i \delta + X_{it} \gamma + \alpha_i + \mu_{it} \qquad (2)$$

where Y_{it} = the natural logarithm of the equivalent household income of the individual i in year t; Z_i = a vector of k_1 permanent characteristics of the individual and his household which are constant over time t for a given i; X_{it} is a vector of k_2 'non-permanent' characteristics that can vary over time, or other contextual variables, e.g., regional unemployment rates;[3] δ and γ are vectors of coefficients and $I_{\alpha i}$ is the permanent part of the income and is time invariant. This has been termed the permanent income-to-needs part of the residual variance by Duncan et al.

The framework for analysing this model is constituted by the random effect panel models. In this case, the individual random effect is treated as a constant fixed effect such that we have termed the model a fixed-effect model (cf. Hsiao 1986). This may be correlated with a number of observable and unobservable characteristics of the individual and the household, such as the regional employment situation, the current wage and reservation wage of the individual and the level of benefits guaranteed under the prevailing social security schemes.

As in Duncan and Rodgers (1991), a model without covariates is estimated (hence a model without X_{it} and Z_i effects). Thus, this represents variations in permanent income-to-needs positions which are not corrected for variations in observed time-varying characteristics. The model assumes that the error term of the log income-to-needs ratio can be decomposed into an autocorrelation term indicating how the income shocks in $t-1$ influence the residual incidental income at t and a random error term measuring the sum of all other incidental shocks that influence the log income-to-needs ratio at t. This is given by:

$$\mu_{it} = \rho_i \mu_{i,t-1} + \nu_{it} \qquad (3)$$

where ρ_i represents the autocorrelation term and ν_{it} the sum of incidental shocks to income. The simplest version of the model (without X_{it} and Z_i) assumes that the α_i and ν_{it} terms are uncorrelated. In the model including these covariates, the error term is assumed to be uncorrelated with the covariate terms. The variance of Y_{it}, conditional on X_{it} and Z_i, is therefore given by: $\sigma_y^2 = \sigma_\alpha^2 + \sigma_\nu^2$ a feature for which these models are often being called error components models. The variance of α is assumed to be constant, whereas the variance of ν is constant across individuals but varies over time.

The model allows the investigation of the transient or permanent nature of income changes over time. The model can be employed easily to investigate persistent poverty, if poverty is defined as a state in which the permanent standardised household income (income-to-needs ratio) is below a certain threshold level (a predefined poverty line). The use of various poverty lines which cut the income distribution at different levels, may then provide insight into the extent of mobility and persistent poverty according to different needs levels. That approach has been followed here.

To calculate the percentage of individuals living in persistent poverty based on the parameter estimates, it is assumed that the α_i are normally distributed with a mean equal to the mean of the observed t-year distribution of the natural logarithm of the income-to-needs ratio or the equivalent household income (M). Conditional on the estimated variance of α_i, the percentage of individuals living in persistent poverty can be estimated as the cumulative distribution function for the standard normal distribution for the value $(0-M)/o_\alpha$ (cf. Duncan and Rodgers 1991).[4] The model cannot identify individuals living in persistent poverty since it can only provide a population-wide estimate of the existence of persistent poverty in society. The idea behind the measure is that people have a rather permanent latent income-to-needs level from which occasional departures are possible because of temporary unemployment, employment, disability, illness or overtime work. As in the previous case, the model is inappropriate for monitoring changes in permanent income-to-needs positions due to the occurrence of certain life events such as the death of a partner, marital dissolution or the birth of a child.

3.2.3   The data

The data are from the Dutch Socio-Economic Panel covering four waves from 1985 to 1988. The analyses are carried out at the individual level taking into account the household situation. The needs measures or poverty lines are estimated first based on the household data sets for each year. In the second stage, the income thresholds of these poverty lines, calculated at the household level, are assigned to every person in the household. First, we applied the analysis to the entire population. Next, the analyses were disaggregated to various population categories. These categories included a group of children aged 13 years and under, in 1985, an age limit chosen to guarantee that none of the children was older than 16 (and having their own, regular earnings) at the end of the observation period in 1988. These children may have resided in different types of households at the start of the observation period, living in one-parent families, in families with other children, in multi-family households and so forth. During the observation period, they may have even moved to other households because of the divorce or separation of their parents. In the Dutch panel, children are followed when they move to other households but are lost when they become institutionalised.

Next, a group of women aged 25–44 years without children and a group of women in a similar age class with children were selected. The age category 25–44 was selected because it was assumed that persistent poverty is particularly associated with the occurrence of certain life events such as divorce or separation. It is well-known that events like divorce and separation particularly occur in this age class. Women with and without children were chosen to guarantee that lone mothers are included and that the income and poverty situation of women with and without children can be compared. These women may belong to single households with or without children, to families with or without children or to non-family households with at least one female member. The choice implies that single households with a male head and with or without children are excluded, as are non-family households with only male members. Except for single males, these groups appear to be relatively small. It was expected that the selection of these groups of children and women would encompass the most relevant groups with respect to the issue of persistent poverty.

Finally, to perform the analyses some preliminary cleaning procedures were employed to prevent extreme cases from colouring the results. Annual observations with a log income-to-needs ratio larger than 3.0 were excluded from the data set, as were individuals for whom the variance of the four-year log income-to-needs ratio was greater than 2.0. Observations with a log income-to-needs ratio less than −3 were truncated to −3.[5]

3.2.4   Results

Table 12.4 presents the results of the panel regression model-based estimate of income mobility and persistent poverty for the whole population and according to various poverty measures. The standard errors, given within parentheses, indicate that all parameter estimates are significant, particularly the estimates of fixed effect and shock variance parameters. The results differ considerably according to the poverty standard used. It appears that the US-standard persistent poverty estimates are the highest and, again, the NSMI estimates the lowest. The mean of the log income-to-needs levels which is lowest for the US standard indicates that the US standard seems to cut the income distribution at a higher level than the other standards. As was argued earlier, the lower the poverty threshold level is, the higher income mobility appears to be, which leads one to conclude that income mobility is apparently highest at the lower tail of the income distribution. This corroborates the findings of earlier studies (e.g., Muffels 1993) which find that a large fraction of people with low incomes have an income just below or just above the statutory minimum income. For these low incomes, any minor change in income due to a change in working hours or a change in family income through the occurrence of household formation events (a child leaving home, marriage, divorce, birth of a child) may lead to a change in benefits and/or family income, such that people enter or

Table 12.4 *A model-based measure of income mobility and persistent poverty for the Dutch population using four poverty thresholds, Socio-Economic Panel, 1985–1988.*

Model parameters	NSMI	ESMI	SPL	US
Number of observations	6,826	7,750	5,494	7,134
χ^2	41.18	56.52	60.45	58.17
df	2	2	2	2
Fixed effects variance	0.104	0.142	0.101	0.136
σ_α^2	(0.003)	(0.003)	(0.003)	(0.003)
Mean of autoregressive parameters	0.190	0.148	0.193	0.135
pt	(0.020)	(0.019)	(0.025)	(0.020)
Mean of variance of innovation	0.095	0.109	0.075	0.107
σ_{vt}^2	(0.002)	(0.003)	(0.002)	(0.003)
Mean ln income-to-needs ratio	0.561	0.496	0.454	0.416
Model-based estimate of proportion of persistently poor (per cent)	4.1	9.3	7.6	12.9

leave poverty. Duncan *et al.* (1993), mentioned earlier, reveals that particularly in the Netherlands factors such as getting a job or changing working hours can explain the high levels of economic mobility at the lower income ranges.

A closer look at table 12.4 reveals that the autoregressive parameter estimates are not very high. The autocorrelation for all poverty lines is less than 0.20, which means that incidental shocks to income over time appear to be correlated but less than one might expect. Table 12.4 also shows that the most stable poverty standards with the highest persistent poverty estimates (US, ESMI) exhibit the highest fixed effects variance, the lowest autoregressive shock variance and the highest random shock variance. This clearly suggests that at higher income levels changes in income are associated with changes in the permanent part of income rather than with incidental shocks to income. In the lower-income ranges, changes in income may be particularly related to incidental shocks to income, which also tend to persist over time. These results, again, indicate a higher income mobility within the lower-income classes.

Table 12.4 also shows a lower estimate of permanent poverty for the SPL standard compared with the European standard notwithstanding the lower log income-to-needs ratio. This must be attributed to the higher autoregressive variance and the lower fixed effects and shock variance in the SPL model which reflect the process of lagged adjustment of subjective perceptions of minimum income needs to actual changes in income. Income changes that manifest themselves in one period due to improved economic

Table 12.5 *Income mobility and persistent poverty in the Netherlands in the 1980s, according to the US poverty line, for various population groups, Dutch Socio-Economic Panel, 1985–1988*

	US poverty line		
Model parameters	Women	Women and children	Children
Number of observations	1,076	891	1,810
χ^2	13.2	11.3	4.4
df	2	2	2
Fixed effects variance	0.125	0.110	0.103
σ_α^2	(0.007)	(0.007)	(0.004)
Mean of autoregressive	0.116	0.129	0.143
parameters pt	(0.054)	(0.057)	(0.040)
Mean of variance of	0.088	0.083	0.076
innovation σ_{vt}^2	(0.006)	(0.006)	(0.004)
Mean ln income-to-needs ratio	0.419	0.381	0.320
Model-based estimate of proportion of persistently poor (per cent)	11.9	12.5	15.9

conditions and employment opportunities will increase earnings and actual income almost instantaneously, but perceived necessary income will lag actual.

In table 12.5 the results are reported for the US standard only but broken down into three population groups: women aged 25–44 years without children, women in the same age class with children and children below 14 years of age. The results show that for the children the estimated proportion of persistent poor is highest. The persistent poverty estimate is also significantly higher than for the whole population (see table 12.4). The conclusion must be that children if they become poor tend to stay poor longer. The fixed effects variance and the mean shock variance are substantially lower for children than for the whole population whereas the autoregressive variance is slightly higher. Hence, poverty amongst children tends to be more persistent since charges in income are less associated with changes in permanent income or changes in incidental income over time, compared with the whole population.

From the results presented in this section, we draw the following conclusions. The findings clearly show high-income mobility which, however, goes together with high persistence of poverty. High mobility was observed in particular in the low-income ranges, at incomes just below or just above the poverty thresholds. If we compare the findings across the various poverty lines, it appears that income mobility is higher and persistent poverty is lower for poverty thresholds at relatively low levels of income (the national minimum income standard), whereas income mobility is lower and persistent poverty is higher for poverty lines at high-income levels (US standard). The high mobility at low-income ranges in the mid and late 1980s is shown to be clearly associated with changes in working hours and employment status. Improved economic and employment conditions in the latter half of the 1980s seem to have created opportunities for low-income groups to escape from poverty.

4   The evolution of income inequality in the 1970s and 1980s and the role of demographic change – evidence from microsimulation

In section 3, we focused on the evolution of income inequality, income mobility and income persistence using Dutch panel data covering the period 1984 to 1988. Because of the short time period covered by existing panel surveys, we were unable to examine long-term trends in income inequality. However, there is much evidence that the distribution of economic well-being in a long-term perspective is affected by structural demographic shifts, such as the ageing of the population and changes in household formation through increasing divorce rates and changes in marriage patterns, and by structural labour market changes. Here the focus is on the impact of demographic trends. We will examine the effect of demographic changes between 1970 and 1989 on the income distribution in the Netherlands. To that end, we employ a microsimulation technique and use the dynamic microsimulation model NEDYMAS (Netherlands Dynamic Micro-Analytic Simulation Model).

NEDYMAS[6] has been expanded to study the impact of social security schemes on the distribution of lifetime income. An extensive description of the model can be found in Nelissen (1991, 1993a, 1993b and 1994). The model allows for the creation of an artificial panel of the Dutch population from 1947 on. The effect of demographic changes after 1970 on the income distribution for the year 1989 has been investigated by creating an artificial panel of the Dutch population starting in 1970. The results derived from this artificial panel are compared with actual developments. Hence, we compare an 'as-if' situation (in which the demographic transition rates do not change after 1970) with actual developments.

Instead of observed transition rates, the artificial panel is based on demographic transition rates observed for 1970. These transition rates are held constant during the period 1970–89. For example, for a woman 25 years old, the probability of giving birth to a child was 0.201 in 1970. It is assumed that the probability did not change between 1970 and 1989 and,

Table 12.6 *Simulated and actual demographic rates for 1989. Implications of a constant-demographic-ratio scenario (1970 rates) for some demo- graphic indicators*

Rates	Indicator	1989 simulated	1989 actual
Births			
Parity progression rates by	Total fertility rate	2.57	1.55
age, marital status	Number of births	371,000	189,000
Marriages	Number of marriages	140,000	90,000
Marriage rates by age, sex, marital status			
Divorces	Number of divorces	14,000	28,000
Divorce rates by age			
Deaths	Number of deaths	147,000	129,000
Death rates by age, sex and marital status			
Emigrants	Number of emigrants	72,000	60,000
Emigration rates by age, sex, marital status, family reunification and duration of residence since immigration			

consequently, in 1989 the probability of a woman of 25 having a child still equals 0.201. The actual probability was 0.089 in 1989. These transition probabilities result in a total fertility rate of 2.57 children in 1970, and the same total fertility rate holds in the artificial panel for all years between 1970 and 1989. The actual total fertility rate was 1.55 in 1989, so the number of births in the artificial panel is considerably larger than the actual outcome (see table 12.6).

One drawback of NEDYMAS is that it is not linked to a macromodel at the moment. Thus, the model is not capable of handling cyclical effects which may occur through alternative population growth scenarios. For example, if the evolution of the number of teenagers implies that consumption will grow at a higher rate, this will probably increase the demand for labour. If the growth path of unemployment results in low levels of unemployment, increased demand for labour would then lead to rising wages due to a shortage of labour. In view of the currently high unemployment rates in the Netherlands, one can hardly imagine the occurrence of accelerating wage rates, but increased demand for labour is not unthinkable.

Table 12.6 shows the consequences of assuming 1970 demographic

Table 12.7 *Simulated (mean and standard deviation) age
distribution for 1989 and actual for 1989 and 1970 (×1,000)*

Age group	Simulated 1989 (1970 rates)		Actual 1989	Actual 1970
	mean	s.d.		
0–4	1,745	20	927	1,186
5–9	1,659	28	887	1,218
10–14	1,590	8	900	1,161
15–19	1,473	21	1,108	1,112
20–24	1,240	9	1,264	1,204
25–29	1,265	12	1,291	927
30–34	1,159	11	1,211	825
35–39	1,119	7	1,146	773
40–44	1,154	10	1,176	759
45–49	880	2	899	751
50–54	759	3	779	662
55–59	729	2	728	627
60–64	674	4	670	571
65–69	616	4	633	485
70–74	440	3	468	370
75–79	346	4	381	257
80+	421	4	428	228
Total	17,269	64	14,896	13,116

Sources: NCBS 1971 and 1990; own calculations.

transition rates for the year 1989, compared with the actual figures in that year. The assumptions underlying the model calculations result in a demographic structure that strongly differs from the actual one in 1989. The simulated age distribution calculated on the basis of the actual transition probabilities is very close to the actual one and thus not reported (see Nelissen 1991 for a comparable exercise).

In table 12.7 the simulated age distribution in the constant demographic regime and the actual age distribution of the Dutch population in 1989 are given. The simulated distribution figures presented in table 12.7 refer to the average number of persons in the various age groups based on ten repeated simulations with different starting values for the random generator. These ten simulations start with about 13,000 persons in 1970. The constancy of transition rates results mainly in a larger number of persons in the age groups up to and including 15–19 years. This corroborates the results of table 12.6; the number of births is considerably larger in the constant-demographic-ratio scenario than the actual figures.

Table 12.8 *Population by marital status (thousands), number of households (thousands) and average household size*

	Simulated 1989		Actual 1989	Actual 1970
	mean	s.d.		
Males				
unmarried	4,413	28	3,451	3,215
married	3,856	15	3,485	3,142
divorced	96	2	271	46
widowed	217	4	151	146
Females				
unmarried	4,015	39	3,014	2,898
married	3,925	13	3,472	3,111
divorced	121	3	346	75
widowed	640	5	702	485
Number of households	6,356	7	6,026	4,056
Average household size	2.720	0.009	2.43	3.14

Sources: NCBS 1971; own calculations.

Only small differences are observed between the simulated and the actual numbers for the other age groups. Deviations are due to differences in death rates (in the higher age groups) and in emigration rates (particularly between the ages of 20 and 50 years). If the demographic transition rates had not changed after 1970, the Netherlands would have had more than 17 million inhabitants in 1989, instead of almost 15 million.

Since the difference in total numbers is chiefly a result of a higher birth rate, the simulated number of households hardly differs from the actual one (only 5 per cent higher), whereas the difference with respect to the average household size is larger. This is shown in table 12.8

It is further assumed that labour force participation rates between 1970 and 1989, under the hypothetical situation of constant demographic transition rates, do not differ from the actual ones in the period under investigation. This implies that the unemployment rate in the constant-demographic-ratio regime is assumed to equal the actual unemployment rate. The same holds for the distribution by age and for the demographic rates related to the labour market (unemployment, disability, private sector employee, civil servants and self-employed persons). This means that our results can be read as the direct (or second order) effects of demographic changes on income distribution. Another drawback of the simulation model is the impossibility of simulating non-labour income, because the model does not contain a module for private consumption. Hence, savings

Table 12.9 *The Theil coefficient for several income concepts and two income units for 1970 and under two demographic regimes for 1989*

	Demographic transition rates		
	Actual 1970	Actual 1989	Constant 1989
Income unit: individual			
Gross wages	0.279	0.269	0.265
Gross income	0.284	0.316	0.307
Before tax income	0.294	0.307	0.304
Net income	0.105	0.126	0.120
Income unit: household (equivalent income)			
Gross wages	0.244	0.241	0.231
Gross income	0.234	0.265	0.245
Before tax income	0.241	0.253	0.239
Net income	0.134	0.130	0.121

cannot be determined and, as a consequence, neither can wealth or income from wealth. Therefore, our analysis is confined to social security income and labour income.

Table 12.9 gives the results with respect to various microsimulated income distributions. First, we look at the Theil coefficients for the income distribution of individuals in the years 1970 and 1989, using the actual demographic transition rates (first two columns). According to several indicators, the income of individuals appears to be more unequally distributed in 1989 than in 1970. This is not true according to the gross wages indicator, however. For the gross wages indicator, the actual Theil coefficient in 1989 is insignificantly lower than the 1970 one. However, the differences between 1989 and 1970 for the other income indicators are significant. If the figures for the distribution of equivalent household income (where the household income is assigned to each household member) in both years are observed, a more equal distribution is found in the case of gross wages and of net income (but in both cases the difference is insignificant). The figures for the other two income indicators reveal a more unequal distribution in 1989, which differ significantly from 1970.

A comparison of the simulated income inequality with the actual income inequality in both years is not entirely possible, since capital income should have been included as well (cf. Trimp 1992a). Trimp has estimated the degree of income inequality for the year 1989 based on individual gross income (including gross wages, gross capital income and gross benefits) using the Theil coefficient. The Theil coefficient is 0.342 for that year. The corresponding NEDYMAS figure with exclusion of capital income (gross wages plus gross benefits) is 0.307 which is obviously lower because of the omission of the unequally distributed capital assets.

The last two columns of table 12.9 show that the direct effects of the demographic changes are rather limited. For the distribution of individual incomes, it appears that income inequality measured by the Theil coefficient under a constant-demographic-ratio regime is only a few per cent lower than the actual inequality figure. This finding is not surprising, since cyclical economic effects were not taken into account. The most important change in individual income is caused by the increase in family allowances resulting from the rise in the number of children (see table 12.6), although these family allowances are paid out to the parents.

If the equivalent household income is assigned to all individuals in the household (the lower panel of table 12.9), it becomes apparent that the difference between the two demographic regimes is somewhat greater. The constant-demographic-ratio regime shows a more equal income distribution irrespective of the income concept used. The difference is always significant and varies between 4.1 per cent and 7.5 per cent. The Theil coefficient for net income is 6.9 per cent smaller.

Briefly, the actual demographic changes of the 1970s and 1980s resulted in a more unequal income distribution compared with the constant-demographic-ratio scenario. The differences are rather small, but the analysis was aimed at the calculation of the direct effects only and did not take cyclical effects into account. These cyclical effects will probably enlarge the differences, since a lower unemployment rate would probably emerge. However, without further investigation, this remains a rather tentative conclusion.

5   Summary and conclusions

In the first part of the chapter, we discussed the evolution of income inequality in the Netherlands in the 1960s, 1970s and 1980s. It was concluded that after a steady decline in inequality in the 1960s and 1970s, in the second half of the 1980s income inequality began to rise again. The rising trend in income inequality occurs particularly within the non-working population, those who are out of the labour force, but also within the group of employed and unemployed workers. The rising trend in inequality for those out of the labour force must be attributed to an increasing number of people drawing minimum benefits in coexistence with a growing number of retired and disabled people with high earnings-related benefits. The higher share of minimum benefits also results from a shift of short-term earnings-related benefits to long-term means-tested flat-rate benefits. The core explanatory factor obviously appears to be the occurrence of structural imbalances in the labour market producing increasing rates of non-participation.

In the second part of the chapter, various measures were applied to calculate the incidence of economic mobility and stability of incomes over time. The results indicate that economic mobility is quite high, particularly amongst incomes just below or just above the minimum needs levels of income and hence at the lower tail of the income distribution. On the other hand, it appears that income stability is more common than change, particularly in the higher-income ranges but also in the very low-income ranges.

It is apparent that the various measures applied to calculate income mobility and income stability show quite different results in terms of the proportion of persistently poor people, i.e., those having a latent permanent income below the poverty threshold. The n-year income-to-needs measure provides higher estimates of persistent poverty (more than 9 per cent of the population according to the US standard) than the spell-based measure (which corresponding figure is 5 per cent). The latter seems more appropriate because it corrects for incomplete information due to censoring. On the other hand, it has to be kept in mind that the various measures stress different aspects of income mobility over time. The focus is either on permanent income, in which case the ratio of n-year income-to-needs level is most appropriate, or on duration of states of poverty, for which the spell-based measure would be appropriate.

The results also differ substantially across the various poverty standards. Poverty lines at a high-income level, like the US and SPL standards, show less mobility and more persistence than poverty lines at a relatively low level, such as the national minimum income standard. The reason for this can be found in the positive association between the level of the poverty line and the income shortfall of the poor. The higher the income shortfall, the less likely people will escape poverty and the less economic mobility will occur.

Next, model-based measures of income mobility and persistent poverty were examined. An error decomposition panel regression model was estimated, in which it was assumed that there exists a time-invariant persistent part of the income-to-needs level from which departures are occasionally possible because of particular events. The model-based estimates of persistently low-income positions are shown to be higher than the individual estimates of persistently low incomes. According to the US standard, almost 13 per cent of the population is at risk of being persistently poor. Changes in permanent income, which could lift people above a poverty threshold, occur more often at higher-income ranges. At lower levels of income, economic mobility appears to be more associated with incidental shocks in income due to changes in working hours or employment status. These changes occurred more often in the late 1980s because of improved economic conditions and employment opportunities. In addition to this, it appears that the estimates of persistent poverty differ considerably across the various poverty lines. Again, it was found that the highest estimates are obtained for the most generous poverty lines cutting the income distribution at a relatively high level. If the analysis is broken down into population groups, it emerges that children below 15 years of age tend to stay poor longer than the adult population. The results indicate that in this period changes in permanent or incidental income which could lift the household above the poverty threshold occurred less often in families with children.

In the third part of the chapter, a microsimulation technique was applied to examine long-term trends in income inequality. In particular, we looked at the impact of demographic changes on the evolution of income inequality. The approach was aimed at a comparison of the impact of the actual demographic trends and the impact on income inequality of a counter-factual demographic trend, in which the demographic transition rates of the year 1970 were held constant in the 20–year period to 1989. The outcomes reveal that actual inequality, as measured by the Theil coefficient, is higher than it would have been in the constant demographic scenario, although the differences are rather small. The inequality in primary earnings was approximately equal, whereas significant increases occurred in the case of gross income (wages plus benefits) and after-tax net income. The conclusion can be drawn that actual demographic trends in the 1970s and 1980s have led to a more unequal distribution of gross and after-tax income.

Notes

1 The issue of censoring refers to the problem that no information is available on how long the poor were already poor at the start of the observation period (left censoring) or how long they will remain poor at the end (right censoring).

2 Table 12.3 provides only estimates of the survival probabilities for the completed spell durations of one and two years. The reason for this relates to censoring. Observations in the first year of the four-year observation period are removed because of left censoring. Observations in the last year permit no estimation of survival probabilities as they are right censored.

3 The model assumes that income changes over time are codetermined by a number of variables which are either fixed over time (time-invariant) or vary

over time (time-variant). The former refer to variables such as gender, ethnicity or even education level, which can be assumed to be unchanging or fixed during the observation period, whereas the latter refer to variables which vary with time, such as unemployment benefits, the duration of unemployment and age.

4 This value can be calculated from the estimated mean and variances assuming that persistent poverty is defined as having a permanent income below the minimum needs income threshold, represented by any of various poverty lines. In that case, the income-to-needs ratio equals one, and the log of the ratio is equal to zero. The percentage of people with permanent incomes less than 125 per cent of the needs threshold can be estimated in a similar manner as the value $(0.223 - M)/\sigma_\alpha$. The same method can be applied for different levels of the income-to-needs ratio.

5 The number of cases affected by these truncations was quite small, so the analysis has not been distorted by these cleaning rules.

6 NEDYMAS is a dynamic cross-sectional model. The idea of dynamic micro-simulation was originally developed by Orcutt, Caldwell and Wertheimer (1976) and Orcutt, Merz and Quinke (1986). An overview of the ins and outs of the microsimulation approach, particularly with respect to social policy issues, can be found in Citro and Hanushek (1991). The dynamic approach implies that demographic processes are explicitly simulated, meaning that the size of the micro-database changes during the simulation period. The sample passes through time, year by year. Which personal characteristics change and to what extent each year are examined for each person in the database. The decision whether an individual will or will not undergo a potential transition is simulated with the aid of the Monte Carlo method. In view of this, the conditional probability of an individual undergoing the event has to be known. For example, for a 77–year old widow, the probability of dying was 6.75 per cent in 1968. We would then randomly draw a number from the uniform [0,1] distribution. If this number was smaller than or equal to 0.0675 (the probability of dying), the woman would be expected to die. If it was equal or greater, the woman would be expected to survive. Microsimulation creates an artificial database which reflects real developments in the sociodemographic and socioeconomic structure of the population. NEDYMAS is a recursive model. First, all demographic transitions are calculated. Second, educational transitions are forecast. Third, changes in economic activity with the resulting labour income are modelled, and fourth, changes in income, transfers and taxes. The model consists of four modules: a demographic module, a labour and income module, a social security module (premiums and benefits) and a tax module.

References

Bane, M. J. and Ellwood, D. 1986. 'Slipping Into and Out of Poverty: The Dynamics of Spells'. *Journal of Human Resources*, 21: 1–23.

Barr, N. 1992. 'Economic Theory and the Welfare State: A Survey and Interpretation'. *Journal of Economic Literature*, 30: 741–803.

Citro, C. F. and Hanushek, E. A. (eds.). 1991. *Improving Information for Social Policy Decisions. The Uses of Microsimulation Modelling*, Vols. I and II. Washington, DC: National Academy Press.

Duncan, G., Gustafsson, B., Hauser, R., Schmaus, G., Messinger, H., Muffels, R., Nolan, B. and Ray, J.-C. 1993. 'Poverty Dynamics in Eight Countries'. *Journal of Population Economics*, 6, 3: 215–34.

Duncan, G. and Rodgers, W. 1990. 'Has Poverty Become More Persistent?' University of Michigan. Mimeographed, p. 51.

1991. 'Has Children's Poverty Become More Persistent?' *American Sociological Review*, 56: 538–50.

Hsiao, C. 1986. 'Analysis of Panel Data'. *Econometric Society Monographs*, no. 11. Cambridge: Cambridge University Press.

Kapteyn, A., Kooreman, P. and Willemse, R. 1988. 'Some Methodological Issues in the Implementation of Subjective Poverty Definitions'. *Journal of Human Resources*, 23, 2: 222–42.

van der Laan, P. and Kriek, M. J. M. 1992. 'Sociale zekerheid en belastingen van huishoudens. Ontvangen uitkeringen en afgedragen premies en belastingen, 1981–1990'. *Statistisch Magazine*, 3: 39–52.

Levy, F. and Murnane, C. 1992. 'U.S. Earnings Levels and Earnings Inequality: A Review of Recent Trends and Proposed Explanations'. *Journal of Economic Literature*, 30: 133–8.

Lillard, Lee and Willis, Robert. 1978. "Dynamic Aspects of Earning Mobility'. *Econometrica*, 46: 985–1012.

Moffitt, R. 1992. 'Incentive Effects of the U.S. Welfare System: A Review'. *Journal of Economic Literature*, 30: 1–61.

Moffitt, R. and Gottschalk, P. 1993. 'Trends in the Covariance Structure of Earnings in the United States: 1969–1987'. Institute for Research on Poverty, Discussion Paper No. 1001–93. University of Wisconsin-Madison.

Muffels, R. 1992a. 'Dynamics of Poverty and Determinants of Poverty Transitions. Results from the Dutch Socio-Economic Panel'. Working Papers Series of the Scientific Network on Household Panel Studies of the European Science Foundation, Paper No. 48. University of Essex, ESRC-Research Centre on Micro-social Change.

1992b. 'A Multi-Method Approach to Monitor the Evolution of Poverty'. *Journal of European Social Policy*, 2, 3: 193–213.

1993. *Welfare Economic Effects of Social Security. Essays on Poverty, Social Security and Labour Market: Evidence from Panel Data*. Series on Social Security Science. Tilburg: Tilburg University.

Muffels, R., Nelissen, J. and Nuyens, W. 1986. *Social Security and Income Inequality; A Comparative Study*. Series on Social Security Science. Tilburg: Tilburg University.

1988. 'De inkomensherverdelende werking van sociale zekerheidsregelingen' (The Income Redistributive Impact of Social Security Schemes). *Sociaal Maandblad Arbeid*, 1: 35–48.

NCBS. 1992. *Personele Inkomensverdeling*. SDU-Uitgevery: S-Gravenhage.

Nelissen, J. H. M. 1991. 'Household and Education Projections by Means of a Micro Simulation Model'. *Economic Modelling*, 8: 480–511.

1993a. 'Labour Market, Income Formation and Social Security in the Microsimulation Model NEDYMAS'. *Economic Modelling*, 10: 225–72.

1993b. 'The Redistributive Impact of Social-Security Schemes on Lifetime Labour Income'. Tilburg Institute for Social Security Research, Series on Social Security Studies, no. 22: 285.

1994. *Income Redistribution and Social Security: An Application of Microsimulation*. London: Chapman & Hall.

Netherlands Central Bureau of Statistics. 1971. *Jaaroverzicht bevolking en volksge-zondheid 1970s*. The Hague: Staatsuitgeverij.

1990. 'Bevolking van Nederland naar burgerlijke staat, geslacht, leeftijd en land van nationaliteit, 1 januari 1990'. *Maandstatistiek Bevolking*, 90/9: 31–6.

1991. *Sociaal-Economisch Panelonderzoek, inhoud, opzet en organisatie* (Socio-Economic Panel Research, Content, Design and Organisation). Voorburg/Heerlen.

1993. *Sociaal-Economische Maandstatistiek* (Monthly Bulletin on Socio-Economic Statistics), 6: 40–53.

O'Higgins, M. and Jenkins, R. 1989. 'Poverty in Europe: estimates for the numbers in poverty in 1975, 1980, 1985'. European Programme to combat poverty, animation and dissemination service, evaluation unit. Centre for the Analysis of Social Policy, University of Bath. Bath. Mimeographed.

Orcutt, G. H., Caldwell, S. and Wertheimer, R., II. 1976. *Policy Explorations Through Microanalytic Simulation*. Washington, DC: Urban Institute.

Orcutt, G. H., Merz, J. and Quinke, H. (eds.). 1986. *Microanalytic Simulation Models to Support Social and Financial Policy*. Amsterdam: North-Holland.

Orschansky, Mollie. 1969. 'Counting the Poor: Another Look at Poverty'. *Social Security Bulletin*, 28: 3–29.

Sawhill, I. V. 1988. 'Poverty in the US: Why Is It So Persistent?' *Journal of Economic Literature*, 26: 1073–119.

Schiepers, J. 1988. 'Huishoudensequivalentiefactoren volgens de budget verdel-ingsmethode, NCBS'. *Supplement Sociaal-Economische Maandstatistiek*, 2: 28–36.

1990. 'Aspecten van Armoede; verbruikspatronen van arme huishoudens' (Aspects of Poverty: Consumption Patterns of Poor Households). CBS. *Supplement Sociaal-Economische Maandstatistiek*, 1: 4–15.

Second Chamber. 1990. *Nota Inkomensbeleid 1991* (Income Report 1991). Vergaderjaar 1990–1991, 2. The Hague: SDU Publisher.

Sen, A. K. 1983. 'Poor, Relatively Speaking'. *Oxford Economic Papers*, 35: 135–69.

Sociaal en Cultureel Planburau. 1990. *Social and Cultural Report 1990*. Rijswijk: SCP.

Trimp, L. 1992a. 'Inkomensverdeling 1989'. *Supplement Sociaal-Economische Maandstatistiek*, 92/5: 63–74.

1992b. 'Inkomens over meerdere jaren'. *Statistisch Magazine*, 3: 53–64.

13 Changes in Swedish inequality: a study of equivalent income, 1975–1991

BJÖRN GUSTAFSSON AND EDWARD PALMER

1 Introduction

Sweden stands out among industrial democracies for having pursued a unique socioeconomic course during the post-war period on at least four counts. All four operate in the direction of reduced inequality. The first is Sweden's solidaristic, i.e. strongly centralized, wage policy, a strategy promoted by the blue-collar unions. The second is a comprehensive system of universal social security for old age, sickness, disability and unemployment, complemented by extensive social policy measures. The latter include child, maternity and housing allowances. A third is the rapid increase in the participation of women in the labour force since the 1960s. A fourth is the extensive marketisation of previously non-market household activities, namely childcare and, to a larger extent than in many countries, care of the elderly. This has, in turn, tended to support the movement of women into the labour force.

Solidaristic wage policy has been pursued through the central negotiations of wages with the aim of reaching binding national agreements consistent with the development of overall productivity and competitor prices on foreign markets. Nevertheless, centrally negotiated wages have always been augmented by local wage drift, which tends to increase earnings in more productive firms and hence wage dispersion. Given the high degree of unionisation – 85–90 per cent – of the Swedish labour market, the reigning philosophy was that inflationary union wage competition could be avoided by centralising negotiations. In addition, it was argued, solidaristic wage policy would stimulate industrial growth by forcing less profitable enterprises out of the market by compelling them to accept wage increases consistent with the cost structure of more productive firms.

The risk of unemployment implicit in this policy has been counterbalanced with labour-market measures to facilitate labour mobility. Generally, the Swedish model has relied heavily on active labour-market policy, with public works and job training programs, to hold down unemployment.

Towards the end of the 1980s policy shifted towards holding down inflation to the OECD average or lower, and, with this shift in goals, unemployment was allowed to rise more freely. By the time the recession bottomed out in 1993, open unemployment had reached 'typical' European levels. Its consequences for the distribution of income for the next few years will depend on whether it signals a permanent rise in long-term open unemployment without benefit status.

The aim of the major social insurance reforms undertaken during the post-war period has been to ensure sick, injured and elderly workers a good standard of living. In the 1970s average pension benefits improved considerably, in part due to the maturation of the earnings-based old-age pension system and in part due to changes in rules.

Another major strand of social policy during the past three decades has focused on removing barriers to and providing incentives for women to enter the labour force. This has led to separate tax treatment of spouses since the early 1970s and large-scale construction of publicly financed childcare centres. In addition, social insurance covers income lost while caring for sick children and replaces income during time spent at home in the months immediately following childbirth, i.e., maternity leave. These benefits have been improved on several occasions. In addition, universal child allowances have been availed instead of tax deductions for families with children.

International comparisons show that Swedish women participate in the labour market to a greater extent than in any other industrial economy. From the 1960s, younger and middle-aged women entered the labour market in increasing numbers. By 1990, participation rates of men and women 55-years-old and younger differed only slightly. Much of the increase in female participation came hand-in-hand with the provision of care services outside the home and the expansion of the public sector as a provider of childcare, healthcare and care of the elderly.

The need to curb inflation and growth in public expenditure put the Swedish model under considerable stress during the 1980s. This brought into question, in particular, the viability of the inflationary 'solidaristic' wage model and the resilience of the vast tax-transfer system. Still, in the beginning of the 1990s the social-policy structure successively built since 1955 was almost completely intact.

There were two changes in political regime during the period covered by the study. The first was from a Social Democratic government to a right–centre coalition in 1977, and the second back to a Social Democratic regime in 1983, which remained until 1991, when a right-center coalition took over again, hence, an interesting question is what the consequences of the shift to the right were for the distribution of income.

The Swedish welfare system attained its present form during a period of annual growth of around 4 per cent, from the mid 1950s through the mid 1970s. It is an axiom that the welfare state manages best in a growth setting: It is easier to redistribute rapidly growing national income. From the mid 1970s, Sweden experienced a period of prolonged recession and then prolonged growth, followed in the early 1990s by deep recession.

In this study, we investigate the development of the distribution of economic well-being from the mid 1970s to the beginning of the 1990s. From the outset, we can state that the overall picture shows decreasing inequality from 1975 through 1982–3 and increasing inequality through 1991, the last year covered in this study. Here we are interested in uncovering the main forces behind this change.

The chapter proceeds as follows. In section 2 we discuss how economic well-being is measured in this study. In section 3 we provide a picture of how the distribution of income has changed. In section 4 we take a closer look at the development of earnings. In section 5 we examine the relation between unemployment and inflation and the distribution of income. The role of taxes and transfers is covered in section 6. In section 7, we apply an additively decomposable inequality index to examine how inequality has developed for various groups of the population. Our major findings are summarised in section 8.

2 Measuring distributional change

2.1 Earlier studies

The first work on the distribution of income in Sweden was based mainly on the tax returns of individuals, using data from a small number of selected years. Bentzel's (1953) investigation of tax units for the entire country for 1935, 1940, 1945 and 1948 and Järnek's (1971) study based on data for the city of Malmö from 1925, 1948 and 1964 indicate a long-term trend towards increased equality. Changes in inequality from the 1940s to the 1960s may have been relatively small, however. This is suggested by the work of Bergström (1967), who examined gross income for 1951, 1955, 1958, 1964 and 1966.

The 1960s were watershed years for the collection of income distributional data in Sweden. A Low-Income Commission was set up to gather information on the status of low-income households. This led to the establishment of Sweden's two major surveys used for analysis of the distribution of household income, the Level of Living Survey (LLS) and the Household Income Survey (HINK). Using LLS and early versions of HINK, Spånt (1981) reported decreases in inequality from 1967 to 1973.

Åberg, Selen and Tham (1984) compared the 1967 LLS survey with the second wave survey in 1980 and reported a decrease in inequality. Most work in this area during later years has been based on the HINK. Gustafsson (1987a), Jansson (1990), Gustafsson and Uusitalo (1990) and Jansson and Sandqvist (1993) all work with the concept of equivalent disposable income per person using the HINK data base. These studies taken together cover the period 1967–90. Also, Fritzell (1991) bases his comparison of LLS data for 1967 and 1980 on equivalent disposable income per person. Söderström (1988) and Björklund (1992), however, follow the older practice of studying the household as a unit of analysis.

The present study confirms the overall picture presented in these studies. A decrease in overall inequality continued from the mid 1970s into the early 1980s. By 1983, the trend had clearly reversed, and since then overall inequality has increased. Although the trend is well documented, the underlying causes are not so well known. In this study, we attempt to shed more light on the underlying reasons for the reversal of the trend. In addition, the study encompasses data at the end of the period that were not thoroughly examined in previous studies.

Finally, it is important to mention that Sweden participates in the Luxembourg Income Study (LIS) with data from LLS 1967, HINK 1981 and HINK 1987. Sweden has thus been examined together with other LIS participants in various international studies. These generally conclude that inequality and relative poverty were greater in 1987 than in 1981, falling in line with the studies cited above.

2.2   Data and the calculation of equivalent disposable income per person

Our study is based on the Household Income Survey (HINK). This is an annual survey covering about 10,000 households, conducted with comparable methodology since 1975. The survey encompasses all persons residing in Sweden at least half the calendar year, excluding persons living in institutions. A household consists of one or two adults and all children. A child becomes an adult, and hence a separate household, at the age of 18 in the survey, regardless of whether or not he or she still lives with his or her parents. No attempt is made in the survey to impute shared costs in families where two or more adult 'households' have the same domicile. Almost all information on income is obtained from tax records or registers. The extent of under-reporting is unknown, and, hence, no effort has been made to correct for this. General background information about households was obtained through questionnaires in the earlier years and is now collected using telephone interviews.

Our study is based on annual data for 1975–91 but excludes 1976, 1977 and 1979. The latter have been excluded due to definitional inconsistencies and other compatibility problems. A recent problem is the broadening of the tax base from 1991, which was an element of the 1991 tax reform. This led to an increase in household factor income of approximately 5 per cent, of which about half constituted earnings and half income from capital (Statistics Sweden 1993). Hence, data for 1991 are not comparable with data from previous years. In order to account for the effect of the definitional change we have worked with synthetic data sets for 1989 and 1990. With these an attempt has been made to apply the new definitional concepts, enabling the linkage of 1989–90 with 1991. The work was performed by Statistics Sweden (Statistics Sweden 1993).

Equivalent disposable income is obtained by dividing disposable income[1] with an equivalence scale. This scale follows social-assistance norms recommended by Socialstyrelsen (the National Board of Health and Welfare), including a regional adjustment for housing costs. The norm is based on the number of adults in the household and the number and ages of children (Gustafsson 1987a). Individuals are the unit of analysis in this study. This means each individual in a household is assigned the same value, based on the assumption that consumption opportunities are equally shared within the household.

3   The level and distribution of well-being since the mid 1970s

The level of well-being in Sweden increased considerably from the mid 1970s to the outset of the 1990s. Mean equivalent disposable income per person increased at an annual rate of around 1.6 per cent between 1975 and 1991. Growth was far from steady, however, as can be seen from figure 13.1. During the recession of 1980–3, the average economic well-being of households fell, and it took until 1985 for the mean to surpass the level reached in 1980. From then on, growth was rapid until the trend was broken in 1991.

Comparisons of inequality can be performed using both standard inequality indices and Lorenz curves. The appeal of inequality indices is that they provide unique orderings of distribution. Different indices can vary in magnitude, however, and may even give different rankings of a distribution. It is therefore important to examine several indices when possible.

The development of inequality in equivalent disposable income in Sweden as measured by the Gini coefficient, the mean logarithmic deviation (MLD) and Theil's index of inequality is shown in figure 13.2. Inequality decreased from 1975 through 1982 and then increased from

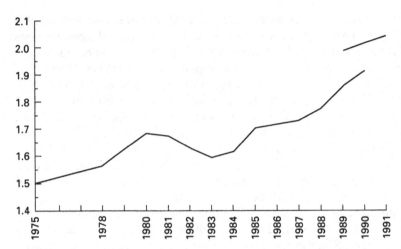

Figure 13.1 The development of equivalent disposable income in Sweden, 1975–1991

1983, rising substantially in 1990 and 1991. Inequality was greater at the end of the period than at the beginning.

As long as the Lorenz curves do not intersect, the measures of inequality examined here will all provide the same qualitative conclusions about the direction of inequality change. However, if the Lorenz curves intersect, the inequality indices can lead to different conclusions. Hence, as is well-known, it is important to confirm statements about the development of inequality by examining the underlying Lorenz curves. As it turns out, the conclusion that overall inequality decreased through 1980 and then increased from 1983 through 1991 is confirmed by analysis of the Lorenz curves.[2]

The broadening of the tax base in 1991 meant that previously untaxed benefits of earners in the upper deciles had to be declared as earned, taxable income. Because income was measured in two different ways in 1989 and 1990, the importance of the definitional change can be shown. The Lorenz curve for the new income concept is located entirely below the Lorenz curve for the older concept, meaning that inequality is greater for the broader base. Given the nature of the reform, this is not surprising. While the Gini coefficient in 1989 was 21.0 per cent according to the older definition, it climbed to 23.0 per cent for the new definition. For the other indices, the increase in inequality is even more pronounced.

Another way to examine what has happened with the distribution of income is to show the development of mean values for the various deciles. Table 13.1 gives this information for sub-periods as well as the entire

Table 13.1 *Relative change in equivalent disposable income by decile*

Decile	Change 1975–91	Change 1975–83	Change 1983–91
1	9.7	6.9	2.6
2	28.9	13.7	13.4
3	29.4	13.3	14.3
4	29.1	11.5	15.8
5	26.9	8.5	17.0
6	25.8	6.6	18.0
7	25.2	5.0	19.3
8	26.9	3.7	22.4
9	28.2	3.7	23.6
10	37.5	1.6	35.3
All	28.3	6.1	21.0

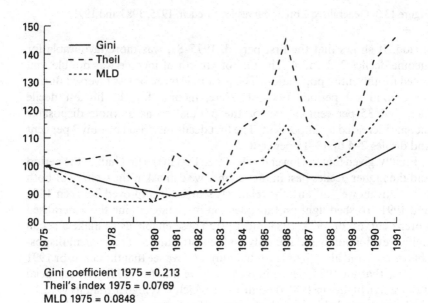

Gini coefficient 1975 = 0.213
Theil's index 1975 = 0.0769
MLD 1975 = 0.0848

Figure 13.2 The development of inequality in disposable income in Sweden, 1975–1991

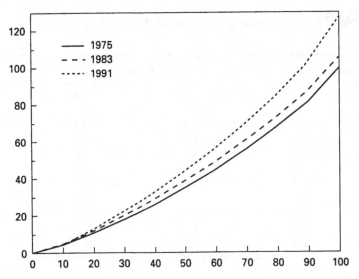

Figure 13.3 Generalised Lorenz curves for Sweden, 1975, 1983 and 1991

period. It shows that the first period, 1975–83, was more favourable for income deciles 2, 3 and 4. The rate of growth of income was double that noted for the entire population. The pattern is more or less reversed during the second sub-period, 1983–91. Here, income for the highest decile increased 35 per cent, while for the population as a whole disposable income increased by 21 per cent. The first decile increased by only 3 per cent and deciles 2–4 by 13–16 per cent.

Finally, given that the lower deciles fared best in the first half of the period and the higher deciles best in the second, we can ask if the welfare of both the relatively well-off and the relatively worse-off improved between 1975 and 1991. To shed light on this question, we can examine the generalised Lorenz curves for 1975, 1983 and 1991. These enable us to make a social welfare evaluation based not only on the distribution of equivalent disposable income, but also on its level. In figure 13.3 we see that the curve for 1991 is above that for 1983, which in turn is above that for 1975.[3] Hence, social welfare was higher in 1991 than in 1983, which was higher than in 1975.[4]

The processes behind the changes in welfare in the two sub-periods differ, however, as we have already seen. During the first sub-period, weak growth combined with less inequality, while in the second period increased inequality was more than offset by high growth.

In sum, between 1975 and 1983, when Sweden was governed by parties to the right of the Social Democratic Party, inequality decreased. From 1983 to 1991, with the Social Democratic Party in power, inequality increased. Taken at face value, the political ideology of governments and the distributional outcome did not go hand in hand during the period studied. It is important to note, however, that no significant changes in either social or economic policy were introduced during 1975–83. The non-socialist governments of this period resorted to traditional Social Democratic labour-market policy to hold down unemployment during recession and left social policy untouched on the whole. Even the following period saw little change in social legislation. The more dramatic changes in inequality originated from other sources, as we will see below.

4   Unemployment and inflation and the distribution of disposable income

Earlier studies (Metcalf 1969; Thurow 1970; Meier 1973a and 1973b; Gramlich 1974) addressing the issue of changes in the distribution of income over the business cycle owing to changes in unemployment and inflation, indicated that income equality in the United States increases during recessions and decreases during expansions. The question is: Is there evidence of this for Sweden?

During the period covered, unemployment insurance provided up to 90 per cent income replacement for low-income earners but less for persons in higher-income brackets. Due to the relatively small fluctuations in the unemployment rate and the countercyclical design of non-insurance support programmes, one would not expect unemployment to have a strong effect on the distribution of income during the period examined. We examine this conjecture below.

One mechanism by which inflation can affect the distribution of income is the redistribution of resources away from persons with fixed nominal incomes. In Sweden, practically all social security benefits are linked to inflation, and those that are not, i.e., child and housing allowances, have been periodically raised with inflation. Thus, this redistributional mechanism ought to be of little importance. Inflation might also redistribute income via the tax tables. With progressive taxes defined in nominal terms, inflation pushes higher-income earners into higher tax brackets, leading to less inequality.

We examine this using a framework first applied by Blinder and Esaki (1978) to study US data and then again by Blank and Blinder (1986) and Jäntti (1994). Weil (1984) and Nolan (1986) employ the same procedure to study the United Kingdom, and Buse (1982) applies it to Canadian data. Generally, the results from these studies suggest that unemployment has an adverse distributional effect while inflation effects are difficult to find.

The model explains changes in disposable equivalent income per person

Table 13.2 *The share of equivalent disposable income of the quintiles*
(*t*-statistics in parentheses)

Quintile	Intercept	Unemploy ment	Inflation	Dummy for broadened income measure	R² (adj.)	Durbin– Watson statistic
1	10.6778	0.0973	0.0183	−0.8191	0.5960	2.173
	(31.23)	(0.94)	(0.70)	(−4.51)		
2	15.4107	0.1924	0.0061	−0.7150	0.6345	1.258
	(49.35)	(2.04)	(0.25)	(−4.31)		
3	18.5842	0.0484	0.0328	−0.5952	0.8362	2.406
	(131.15)	(1.13)	(3.01)	(−7.91)		
4	22.4252	−0.0700	0.0486	−0.3542	0.5306	1.090
	(109.51)	(−1.13)	(3.09)	(−3.26)		
5	32.9269	−0.2735	−0.1070	2.4766	0.7723	2.160
	(46.00)	(−1.26)	(−1.95)	(6.51)		

per year, i.e., where the dependent variable Y_{itd} is the income share for quintile i (i=1,2,3,4,5) in year t (1975, 1978, 1980, 1981, . . . ,1991) per thousand and according to two definitions of income d (old, new). The explanatory variables are the unemployment rate (per thousand) according to the labour force survey, the change in the consumer price index, a dummy variable (new=1, old=0) for the definitional change in income and a trend (assuming a value of 0 for year 1975, 1 for year 1976, etc.).

The OLS estimates are presented in table 13.2. Coefficients for the new definition of income all have high t values and indicate a higher share for the fifth quintile and smaller shares for all other quintiles.

The t values for the unemployment rate are low, with the exception of that for the second quintile. The latter indicates that rising unemployment may have slightly increased the share of income at the lower end of the distribution. Nevertheless, the overall weakness of the unemployment variable indicates that changes in the level of unemployment was not a major driving force behind the development of inequality in Sweden. This result confirms the results of earlier studies of Swedish data (Gustafsson 1987b; Björklund 1991,1992).

The regression results indicate, on the other hand, that the inflation rate affected the income share of the third and fourth quintiles positively and the fifth negatively. The size of the effect, however, is moderate: A change in the inflation rate of 10 per cent yields a change in the relative share of 0.5 per cent. The negative inflation effect in the highest quintile suggests that inflation pushes high-income earners into higher marginal tax brackets. This process was, in fact, one of the reasons for the 1991 tax reform.

Why is the unemployment effect so weak? One explanation is that open unemployment has not varied enough to generate a significant effect. During the period studied the average duration of unemployment was short, while most unemployed persons were covered by insurance with replacement rates that are high for those more likely to become unemployed.

5   Earnings inequality

Income from work is the major source of income for most adults of working age and their families. To what extent has the changing wage dispersion driven changes in inequality in Sweden? To examine this, we analysed the homogeneous group of full-time employed males and females, excluding the self-employed and persons who have not worked the full year. Here, employment income includes wages, salaries and work-related transfers. Important examples of the latter are compensated leave because of illness and for care of sick children and maternal/paternal leave during the first year after childbirth.

Previous studies of changes in the wage dispersion point in the direction of decreasing dispersion through the early 1980s, followed by increasing dispersion. The development of wage dispersion in the Swedish context can be understood from the background of trade union action – the solidaristic wage policy described in the introduction (Hibbs 1990) – but can also be explained in terms of the supply of persons with different levels of education (Edin and Holmlund 1992). Our analysis differs from earlier work in various ways. We look at earnings for the entire labour force, not just blue-collar and white-collar workers separately (Hibbs 1990) or only males (Green et al. 1992). We use data for all the years since 1975, except 1976, 1977 and 1979, while Green et al. (1992) use only two years. Edin and Holmlund (1992) also limit their description to fewer years based on a smaller data base and covering only the 1980s.

Average full-time earnings in Sweden have developed much less favourably than equivalent disposable income (figure 13.4). A major reason for this during the period 1975–82 was the steep increase in employer contributions in the mid 1970s, together with a 'normal' process in which 80–90 per cent of these fees were passed on to wages over a period of 5–7 years (Palmer and Palme 1989). Earnings of full-time workers have increased at an annual rate of 1 per cent compared with the average growth rate of 1.6 per cent for equivalent disposable income. The level of earnings reached at the end of the economic boom in 1975–6 steadily declined during the recession of 1977–83. Between 1978 and 1980, average full-time earnings

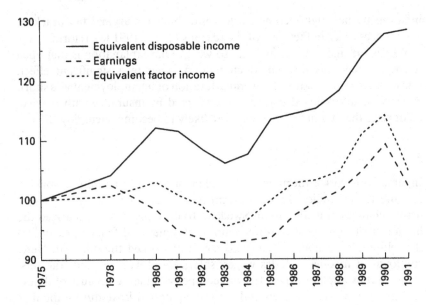

Figure 13.4 The development of different income measures for Sweden, 1975–1991

declined markedly, while disposable income actually increased by about 6 per cent. The curves map out the same general trend from 1980 until 1990. Note that it took until 1987 to return to the 1975 level of average earnings. Finally, mean earnings fell again with the onset of the most recent recession in 1991, while equivalent disposable income remained unchanged, increasing the gap between these even more.

What does an examination of the data tell us about the dispersion of earnings and the development of inequality in earnings? The development of inequality as measured by various inequality indices is shown in figure 13.5. Table 13.3 shows changes for the various deciles over the entire period. The general picture mirrors to a large extent the development of equivalent disposable income. Inequality decreased between 1975 and 1983, then increased through 1991, with a spike in 1986.[5] In contrast to equivalent disposable income, however, equality of full-time earnings is greater at the end of the period than at the beginning. In sum, as average full-time earnings decreased from the end of the boom in 1975, equality increased. However, the subsequent increase in average earnings from 1983 was accompanied by an increase in inequality.

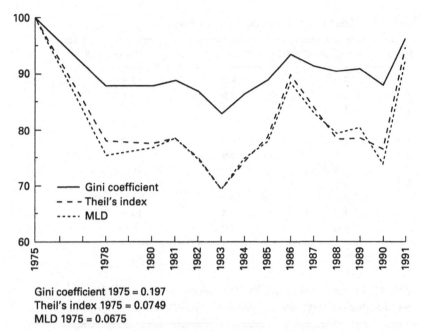

Gini coefficient 1975 = 0.197
Theil's index 1975 = 0.0749
MLD 1975 = 0.0675

Figure 13.5 The development of earnings inequality for Sweden, 1975–1991

Changes in the distribution of full-time earnings have clearly been one of the forces behind changes in inequality in equivalent disposable income, as is evident from a comparison of figures 13.2 and 13.5. Although their variation follows the same pattern, the decrease in inequality in equivalent disposable income during 1975–83 and the subsequent increase in 1983–91 were much more pronounced than the underlying changes in earnings, as is evident from the summary in table 13.4.

6 Taxes, transfers and inequality in equivalent disposable income

An overriding goal of Swedish post-war policy has been to improve the income standard of the elderly, the disabled and low-income families. In addition, family policy concentrated on compensated maternity leave and income replacement for days off for care of sick children. Social security transfers have increased strikingly during the period covered, as have contributions and direct taxes. In fact, almost half the increase in national income during the period 1970–89 was channelled into social-security contributions.[6]

By far the most significant increase in transfers since 1975 was that accruing to old-age pensioners. Social security provides both a universal non-

Table 13.3 *Relative change in earnings by decile*

Decile	Change 1975–91	Change 1975–83	Change 1983–91
1	9.9	8.0	1.8
2	3.7	0.6	3.1
3	1.2	−3.3	4.6
4	1.5	−4.5	6.3
5	1.8	−5.3	7.5
6	2.4	−5.9	8.9
7	2.4	−7.0	10.1
8	1.2	−8.6	10.8
9	−0.1	−10.3	11.4
10	1.3	−15.4	19.8
All	2.0	−7.2	9.9

Table 13.4 *Changes in inequality for equivalent disposable income and full-time earnings, 1975–1983 and 1983–1991*

	Theil	MLD	Gini
1975–83			
Equivalent			
disposable income (per cent)	−7	−8	−9
Earnings (per cent)	−31	−31	−17
1983–91			
Equivalent			
disposable income (per cent)	56	36	17
Earnings (per cent)	37	34	16

income-related basic pension and, since 1963, an income-related supplementary pension.[7] The amount of the inflation-indexed flat-rate basic pension was increased successively between 1975 and 1984 for persons not eligible for an income-related pension. The income-related system has also provided successively better pensions for new age cohorts of pensioners, and beginning in 1980 the first cohort could obtain an unreduced benefit. Hence, the average standard of pensioners increased throughout the period.

To a large extent, changes in the income tax system during the late 1970s and 1980s constituted inflation adjustments of nominally defined tax brackets. Changes during the first half of the 1980s nevertheless also

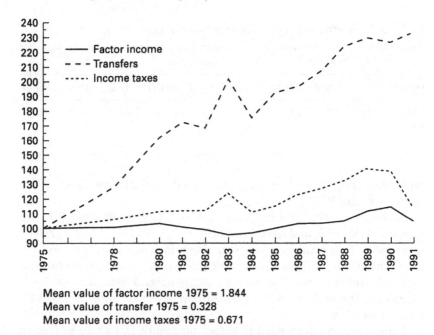

Mean value of factor income 1975 = 1.844
Mean value of transfer 1975 = 0.328
Mean value of income taxes 1975 = 0.671

Figure 13.6 The development of mean values of factor income, transfers and income taxes in Sweden, 1975–1991

reduced marginal tax rates at the high end of the scale, which by the early 1980s had reached 80 per cent for a not negligible number of full-time earners. With new legislation which went into effect in 1991, the tax base was broadened, and the highest marginal rate was decreased to 50 per cent.

We analysed the effects of changing transfers and taxes on inequality by looking at the redistributive effects calculated from equivalent factor income, equivalent gross income and equivalent disposable income. The difference between the first two indicates a transfer effect and that between the second two indicates a tax effect. The limitation of this approach is that we did not take into account behavioural responses to changes in taxes and transfers.[8]

Figure 13.6 shows the development of factor income, transfers and taxes. Mean factor income changed little in 1975–83 on the whole. It increased in 1979–80, subsequently falling during the recession to 1983. The subsequent increase in 1983–90 pushed mean factor income to about 20 per cent before income began declining in 1991 at the onset of the deep recession. Direct taxes followed the general trend in the tax base but tended to rise faster. With the introduction of the tax reform of 1990–1, tax revenues dropped faster than the tax base. On the other hand, transfers increased practically

Table 13.5 *Redistributive effects of transfers and taxes*

	Transfers			Income taxes			Both		
Index	Gini	Theil	MLD	Gini	Theil	MLD	Gini	Theil	MLD
1975	32.0	47.7	65.1	23.9	42.6	40.3	48.3	70.0	79.2
1983	40.6	62.4	76.3	23.0	35.2	34.0	54.2	75.6	84.4
1991	41.9	61.4	78.5	15.7	26.3	25.9	51.0	71.6	84.0

unabated during the entire period, although the rate of increase was lower starting around 1988.

The results for the three inequality indices for 1975, 1983 and 1991 are shown in table 13.5, and the overall development in 1975–91 of transfers, taxes and then the combined effects are shown in figures 13.7, 13.8 and 13.9. Given the massive expansion of transfer payments, it comes as no surprise that their redistributive effect shows a strong upward trend through 1983. Thereafter, the increase in the redistributive effect of transfers becomes much more modest.

While transfers have tended to reduce inequality, taxes have worked in the opposite direction. This is illustrated in figure 13.8. According to all three indices, the redistributive effect of taxes was only two-thirds as great in 1991 as in 1975. What can be said about the redistributive effects of the 1990–91 tax reform? According to our results, the redistributive effects of taxes decreased substantially in 1991 but were offset by the increasing redistributive effects of transfers.[9]

The redistributive effects of transfers and income taxes have thus moved in opposite directions. The net results are shown in figure 13.9, which indicates a trend towards increased equality into the early 1980s followed by an extended period of more or less no change through 1991. As a result, the net overall redistributive effect of taxes and transfers was larger in 1991 than in 1975.

This analysis indicates that the development of transfers is a major cause of the decrease in inequality from the mid 1970s to the early 1980s and was instrumental in offsetting the tendency of direct taxes to work in the direction of increased inequality. Changes in income taxes have for the entire period moved in the direction of increased inequality.

7   Sub-group inequality and changes in composition

The development over time of inequality of equivalent disposable income can be investigated further by disaggregating the population into sub-groups. We can then look for reasons for these changes in the changed

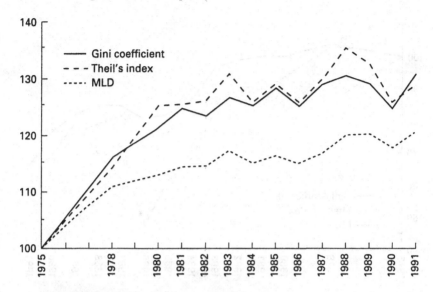

Gini coefficient for factor income 1975 = 0.412
Theil's index for factor income 1975 = 0.2560
MLD for factor income 1975 = 0.4070

Gini coefficient for gross income 1975 = 0.280
Theil's index for gross income 1975 = 0.1340
MLD for gross income 1975 = 0.1420

Figure 13.7 Redistributive effects of transfers in Sweden according to various measures, 1975–1991

composition of the population and in changes in means for sub-groups. Here we examine inequality between and within groups using an additively decomposable inequality index.

An additively decomposable inequality index is one which can be expressed as a weighted sum of inequality values calculated for population sub-groups plus the contribution from differences between sub-group means. Shorrocks (1980) derives the entire class of indices which are additively decomposable under relatively weak restrictions on the form of the index. He shows that the sub-class of mean independent measures turns out to be a single parameter family. To preserve independence between the intragroup and intergroup terms, there are only two methods: the Theil index and the mean logarithmic deviation (MLD). Since, in our analysis both provide rather similar results, we report results only for the latter.

We classified the population in terms of six different factors: the age of the individual, the degree of employment for a household's adults together, the household composition, the socioeconomic classification of the head of

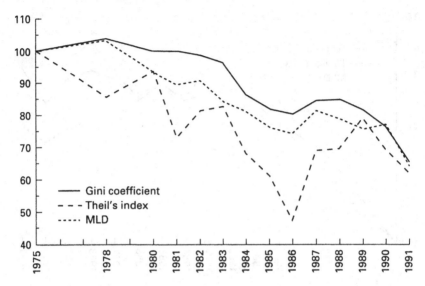

Gini coefficient for gross income 1975 = 0.280
Theil's index for gross income 1975 = 0.1340
MLD for gross income 1975 = 0.1420

Gini coefficient for disposable income 1975 = 0.213
Theil's index for disposable income 1975 = 0.0769
MLD for disposable income 1975 = 0.0848

Figure 13.8 Redistributive effects of income taxes in Sweden according to various measures, 1975–1991

the household, the region of residence and the nationality of the head of the household. The results for 1975, 1983 and 1991 are shown in table 13.6. This table provides information on the population shares, group means and inequality according to the MLD index. Figures in brackets indicate the proportion of total inequality in the relevant year. Table 13.7 shows how the changes in the various sub-groups influenced aggregate inequality.[10]

Table 13.6 shows an improvement in equivalent disposable income for practically all sub-groups during the period 1975–83, dominated by recession, and the strong growth period 1983–91. The improvement in mean income during the first period was relatively small but was coupled with a general decrease in inequality. Similarly, strong growth in mean income for most groups in the second period was coupled with a general picture of increasing inequality. During the first sub-period, both inequality within and between groups was generally non-increasing. In table 13.6, we see that inequality between groups was less for all the cross-sectional breakdowns except for decomposition by age, which was unchanged in 1975 and 1983.

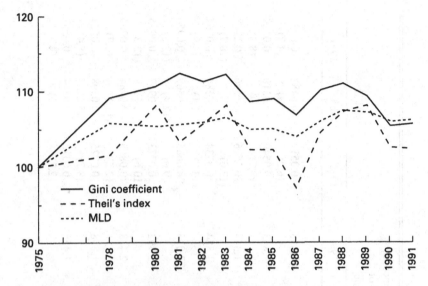

Gini coefficient for factor income 1975 = 0.412
Theil's index for factor income 1975 = 0.2560
MLD for factor income 1975 = 0.4070

Gini coefficient for disposable income 1975 = 0.213
Theil's index for disposable income 1975 = 0.0769
MLD for disposable income 1975 = 0.0848

Figure 13.9 Redistributive effects of income taxes and transfers in Sweden according to various measures, 1975–1991

Nevertheless, the overall picture is one of moderate change in this period, with a sub-group of pensioners, i.e., persons 65–74 years of age, emerging as the clear winners among all specific groups.

The improvement in mean income was considerable in the second period, as we have already shown. Table 13.6 reveals the extent to which different groups benefited from the increase. Although there were no losers, relative gains varied considerably between groups, as we will discuss in greater depth below. The most noteworthy general feature emerging for the growth period 1983–91 is that the increase in inequality occurred predominantly within, rather than between sub-groups. What is more, this conclusion holds regardless of the type of decomposition examined. Furthermore, as table 13.7 shows, increasing inequality had almost nothing to do with the changing weights of different groups. Instead, this table confirms that the increasing dispersion of incomes within groups is the single most important determinant of the overall increase in inequality in 1983–91.

The following is a summary of the main features in tables 13.6 and 13.7.

Table 13.6 Cross-sectional decomposition of inequality

Characteristic of person or household head	Population share (per cent)			Group mean income (proportions of the poverty line)			MLD		
	1975	1983	1991	1975	1983	1991	1975	1983	1991
Age of person									
0–7 years	10.35	8.70	10.30	1.352	1.419	1.658	0.0510 (6.2)	0.0482 (5.4)	0.0482 (4.7)
8–17 years	13.69	13.58	12.18	1.386	1.479	1.843	0.0540 (8.7)	0.0510 (8.9)	0.0720 (8.3)
18–24 years	9.50	8.74	9.00	1.342	1.236	1.343	0.1516 (17.0)	0.1556 (17.5)	0.2208 (18.7)
25–34 years	15.81	14.81	13.72	1.637	1.647	1.884	0.0734 (13.7)	0.0584 (11.1)	0.0764 (9.9)
35–44 years	11.16	14.49	13.99	1.572	1.676	2.033	0.0685 (9.0)	0.0669 (12.4)	0.0950 (12.5)
45–54 years	11.60	10.85	13.40	1.827	1.940	2.492	0.0773 (10.6)	0.0957 (13.3)	0.0975 (12.3)
55–64 years	12.22	11.02	9.61	1.705	1.904	2.438	0.0865 (12.5)	0.0784 (11.1)	0.0960 (8.7)
65–74 years	9.58	9.99	9.78	1.306	1.557	1.858	0.0725 (8.2)	0.0398 (5.1)	0.0584 (5.4)
Over 74 years	6.04	7.78	7.98	1.043	1.243	1.456	0.0312 (2.2)	0.0214 (2.1)	0.0567 (4.3)

Table 13.6 (*cont.*)

Characteristic of person or household head	Population share (per cent)			Group mean income (proportions of the poverty line)			MLD		
	1975	1983	1991	1975	1983	1991	1975	1983	1991
1–2 children	33.84	31.32	27.77	1.496	1.588	2.024	0.0454 (18.1)	0.0476 (19.2)	0.0618 (16.1)
3 children	10.51	8.35	10.36	1.172	1.257	1.531	0.0496 (6.2)	0.0451 (4.8)	0.0421 (4.1)
Single parents	4.87	5.97	6.70	1.344	1.338	1.434	0.0576 (3.3)	0.0439 (3.4)	0.0474 (3.0)
Without children	16.53	19.27	19.48	1.526	1.505	1.718	0.1514 (29.5)	0.1408 (34.9)	0.1941 (35.6)
'Within-groups' component of inequality							0.0695 (82.0)	0.0653 (83.9)	0.0880 (82.8)
'Between-groups' component of inequality							0.0152 (18.0)	0.0125 (16.1)	0.0183 (17.2)
Socioeconomic classification of household head									
Blue-collar	36.97	30.58	27.71	1.497	1.573	1.839	0.0439 (19.2)	0.0393 (15.4)	0.0401 (10.4)

	(1)	(2)	(3)	(4)	(5)	(6)	(7)	(8)	(9)
'Within-groups' component of inequality							0.0746 (88.0)	0.0678 (87.0)	0.0899 (84.6)
'Between-groups' component of inequality							0.0101 (12.0)	0.0101 (13.0)	0.0164 (15.4)
Degree of employment of household head									
0–24 per cent	21.84	25.28	25.29	1.075	1.280	1.429	0.0976 (25.1)	0.1081 (35.1)	0.1233 (29.3)
25–74 per cent	35.49	24.27	18.39	1.353	1.467	1.872	0.0523 (21.9)	0.0609 (19.0)	0.0927 (16.0)
75–100 per cent	42.66	50.43	56.31	1.840	1.809	2.167	0.0533 (26.8)	0.0498 (32.3)	0.0779 (41.3)
'Within-groups' component of inequality							0.0626 (73.8)	0.0672 (86.3)	0.0921 (86.6)
'Between-groups' component of inequality							0.0222 (26.2)	0.0106 (13.7)	0.0142 (13.4)
Household composition									
Over 64 years old	16.66	18.45	18.14	1.205	1.427	1.686	0.0623 (12.3)	0.0397 (9.4)	0.0692 (11.8)
Couples 0 children	17.56	16.62	17.53	2.007	2.145	2.674	0.0619 (12.8)	0.0575 (12.3)	0.0736 (12.1)

White-collar	30.73	30.32	32.09	1.818	1.879	2.340	0.0550 (20.0)	0.0469 (18.3)	0.0638 (19.3)
Pensioners	17.84	21.35	21.72	1.158	1.437	1.674	0.0525 (11.1)	0.0444 (12.2)	0.0666 (13.6)
Self-employed	7.52	6.46	4.99	1.389	1.331	1.556	0.1283 (11.4)	0.1345 (11.2)	0.2266 (10.6)
Others	6.92	11.26	13.46	1.109	1.316	1.668	0.2658 (21.7)	0.2225 (32.2)	0.2897 (36.7)
'Within-groups' component of inequality							0.0702 (82.8)	0.0695 (89.2)	0.0964 (90.7)
'Between-groups' component of inequality							0.0145 (17.2)	0.0084 (10.8)	0.0099 (9.3)
Region of residence of household head									
Stockholm	17.07	17.96	18.49	1.691	1.727	2.217	0.0894 (18.0)	0.0909 (21.0)	0.1529 (26.6)
Gothenburg and Malmö	14.05	14.15	15.11	1.556	1.643	1.976	0.0885 (14.7)	0.0818 (14.9)	0.1221 (17.4)
Medium-sized cities	29.81	30.93	35.14	1.477	1.590	1.889	0.0777 (27.3)	0.0709 (28.2)	0.0861 (28.5)
Southern Sweden	21.59	22.49	19.40	1.401	1.501	1.794	0.0773 (19.7)	0.0709 (20.5)	0.0875 (16.0)
Densely pop. northern areas	7.22	7.59	5.75	1.406	1.545	1.780	0.1036 (8.8)	0.0846 (8.2)	0.0896 (4.8)

Table 13.6 (cont.)

Characteristic of person or household head	Population share (per cent)			Group mean income (proportions of the poverty line)			MLD		
	1975	1983	1991	1975	1983	1991	1975	1983	1991
Sparsely pop. northern areas	6.54	6.84	6.09	1.315	1.497	1.697	0.0701 (5.4)	0.0653 (5.7)	0.0772 (4.4)
Unclassified	3.70	–	–	1.702	–	–	0.0614 (2.7)	–	–
'Within-groups' component of inequality							0.0819 (96.6)	0.0767 (98.4)	0.1038 (97.6)
'Between-groups' component of inequality							0.0028 (3.4)	0.0012 (1.6)	0.0025 (2.4)
Citizenship of household head									
Swedish	–	96.11	95.28	–	1.597	1.941	–	0.0784 (96.7)	0.1029 (92.2)
Foreign	–	3.88	4.71	–	1.482	1.625	–	0.0637 (3.2)	0.1616 (7.2)
'Within-groups' component of inequality							–	0.0778 (99.9)	0.1056 (99.4)
'Between-groups' component of inequality							–	0.0001 (0.1)	0.0007 (0.6)
Sweden	100.00	100.00	100.00	1.501	1.592	1.926	0.0848	0.0779	0.1063

Table 13.7 Decomposition of the change in aggregate inequality

Characteristic of person or household head	1975–91				1975–83				1983–91			
	1	2	3	4	1	2	3	4	1	2	3	4
Age of person	0.0162 (70.7)	−0.0010 (−4.3)	0.0009 (3.8)	0.0068 (29.9)	−0.0056 (−80.9)	−0.0014 (−20.3)	0.0003 (4.8)	−0.0002 (−3.6)	0.0217 (73.7)	0.0005 (1.6)	0.0007 (2.3)	0.0066 (22.4)
Degree of employment of household head	0.0291 (126.9)	0.0004 (1.6)	0.0030 (13.0)	−0.0095 (−41.5)	0.0034 (48.6)	0.0012 (17.0)	0.0017 (24.6)	−0.0134 (−190.1)	0.0256 (88.8)	−0.0008 (−2.6)	0.0005 (1.7)	0.0035 (12.1)
Household composition	0.0146 (63.5)	0.0037 (16.0)	0.0006 (2.8)	0.0041 (17.7)	−0.0071 (−102.8)	0.0027 (39.5)	−0.0006 (−8.7)	−0.0019 (−28.0)	0.0226 (77.3)	0.0000 (0.2)	0.0012 (4.0)	0.0054 (18.5)
Socioeconomic classification of household head	0.0129 (60.6)	0.0129 (60.6)	0.0019 (8.8)	−0.0064 (−30.0)	−0.0091 (−119.9)	0.0080 (105.7)	0.0014 (19.0)	−0.0080 (−104.8)	0.0239 (80.5)	0.0030 (10.2)	0.0003 (1.1)	0.0024 (8.1)
Region of residence of household head[a]	0.0308 (93.9)	0.0006 (1.9)	0.0001 (0.4)	0.0012 (3.8)	0.0043 (122.4)	−0.0000 (−1.3)	0.0000 (0.7)	−0.0008 (−21.7)	0.0268 (91.5)	0.0003 (1.2)	0.0001 (0.4)	0.0020 (6.9)
Citizenship of household head[b]	0.0317 (98.7)	−0.0002 (−0.5)	0.0000 (−0.1)	0.0006 (1.9)	0.0039 (102.3)	−0.0001 (−2.6)	−0.0000 (−0.7)	0.0000 (0.9)	0.0276 (91.8)	0.0002 (0.6)	0.0001 (0.2)	0.0022 (7.4)

Notes:

[a] Changes between 1980–91 and 1980–3 instead of 1975–91 and 1975–83.

[b] Changes between 1978–91 and 1978–83 instead of 1975–91 and 1975–83.

Sources: 1 Change due to changes in 'within-groups' inequality.

2 Change due to the effect of changes in population shares on the 'within-groups' component of inequality.

3 Change due to the effect of changes in population shares on the relative mean income.

4 Change due to changes in the relative mean income.

Age composition. Although the Swedish population has been aging, changes in composition during the period examined in this study were dominated by the relatively small birth-cohorts from the 1930s and the relatively large cohorts born during the 1940s. Mean disposable income improved for all groups between 1975 and 1991 with one exception: persons 18–24 years old, a group comprised of a large number of students in single households. The increase was also considerable throughout the period, with the greatest change during the growth years 1983–91. In this period, with the exception of persons 74 and older, the overall picture is one in which persons in relatively older households did better than those in younger age groups, as is indicated by the relative increases in mean income with increasing age. The mean income of the oldest group also increased but by less than that of persons 65–74 years old.

The increase in mean equivalent disposable income was accompanied by a significant increase in inequality of income for the majority of specific age groups, as can be seen by examining the MLD index in table 13.6. In addition to persons 18 to 24 years of age, mentioned above, persons 25–34 and 0–7 years of age stand out because they experienced practically no change in inequality between 1975 and 1991. There is, of course, an obvious connection between these two age groups, as the younger group consists chiefly of the children of the older group. Likewise, the increase in inequality among persons 8–17 years of age must be connected with the increase in inequality for persons 35–44 and 45–54 years of age.

In spite of the strong influence of the 1930 and 1940 birth-cohorts, very little of the total change in inequality can be attributed to changing population shares, as can be seen in table 13.7. According to the same table, the principal change during the entire period 1975–91 was the increase in inequality that occurred during 1983–91. This increase is associated with increased income dispersion within groups, although about one-fifth of the increase is the result of changes in means.

Degree of employment. Here we classified households according to the proportion of full-time employment the household's adults worked. Table 13.6 reveals very large changes in population shares. There is a strong trend away from the middle group and towards the two extremes of close to full-time (75 per cent) employment or none to little employment (0–24 per cent). The latter reflects an increase in the share of pensioners and 'others' (mainly students).

The differences in mean equivalent disposable income between the three sub-groups narrowed greatly during 1975–83. This reflects in part the less favourable development of full-time earnings (after deducting contributions for social security) discussed above and the improvement in pension benefits for the elderly. After 1983, both part-time and full-time earnings increased strongly. The former probably reflects a general tendency to work more hours during the 1980s. Inequality in these two groups increased along with the increase in mean income. As we have already seen, increased inequality in earnings cannot explain the entire change. In addition, a number of small changes in the tax system during the 1980s (inflation adjustment of tax brackets) ought to have been to the relative advantage of persons with full-time earnings.

Household composition. Changes in differences in means for various household types worked in the direction of decreased inequality until 1983 and towards increased inequality thereafter. Seen over the entire period, intra-group inequality for persons over 64 years of age changed little. Furthermore, intragroup inequality for families with three or more children and single-parent families actually decreased during the entire period 1975–91. What all three of these groups have in common is a greater relative share of transfers from the public sector, suggesting that transfers may have helped to even out income in these groups. On the other hand, during the second sub-period, intragroup inequality increased notably in the remaining groups, for which earnings are normally a more dominant source of total disposable income.

Socioeconomic groups. The socioeconomic classification distinguishes households in accordance with the type of income of the head of the household (the person with the highest income). There are three classifications for households whose head is employed: the self-employed, blue-collar and white-collar workers.[11] Pensioners – both disability and old-age pensioners – form a separate category. Some persons (for example, students and the long-term unemployed) do not belong to any of these four groups and are classified with 'others'. As table 13.6 shows, this group increased relatively strongly during the period examined. Its mean is on a level with that of pensioners, but income inequality is considerably greater. Table 13.6 also shows that the relative share of self-employed and blue-collar workers has decreased.

The disaggregation into socioeconomic groups provides a good overall picture of what happened with the distribution of income during the initial period, 1975–83. Changes in the composition of the population moved sharply in the direction of inequality with strong increases in the number of pensioners and 'others'. This effect was more than offset, however, by the decrease in the difference between the mean incomes of these two groups and the three employed groups.

Poor growth and decreases in earnings equality held back the development of the working population's income, while at the same time rising

320   Björn Gustafsson and Edward Palmer

social-security pensions bolstered the disposable income of disability and old-age pensioners. Intragroup inequality decreased for both blue-collar and white-collar workers during the first period and increased within most groups after 1983.

Regions of Sweden. We divided the country up into six regions. The Stockholm region is the largest in Sweden. Gothenburg and Malmö, located in southern Sweden, are the next two largest regions. Southern Sweden is more densely populated than northern Sweden. Northern Sweden – north of the Stockholm area – is divided into more and less densely populated areas.[12] Stockholm has the highest average equivalent disposable income, and the sparsely populated northern region the lowest. Over the years, there has been an increase in the relative proportion of the population in the three regions with the highest mean income, and a decrease in the others. However, these changes had only a marginal effect on changes in total inequality. Changes in intragroup inequality played the most important role, rather than changes directly attributable to regional association.

Citizenship. Mean equivalent disposable income is considerably lower for persons living in households with foreign heads than in those with heads who are Swedish citizens. Furthermore, mean income has increased by less for households with foreign heads. Households with foreign heads are relatively small in number, and, even though they are increasing in relative importance, their weight is too small to have had any noticeable impact per se on the development of total inequality.

8   Conclusions

Using Statistics Sweden's Household Income Survey (HINK) we have analysed changes in inequality for equivalent disposable income per person from 1975 to 1991. Our data set has the advantage of giving us a series of many points in time. However, at the end of the period, a major tax reform reduced the comparability of 1991 with earlier years, making it necessary for us to link older and newer figures.

Inequality in equivalent income was found to decrease from the beginning of the period, but around 1983 the direction of change reversed and inequality increased. In our data, a spike indicating a much higher level of inequality is observed for 1986, and we are inclined to interpret it as caused by data problems, probably in one of the extreme deciles. Inequality increased markedly in 1990 and 1991.

While inequality moved in different directions during the 17–year period studied, there was a long-term rising trend in average equivalent disposable income. As a result, the generalised Lorenz curve at the end of the period is located above the one for 1983, which in turn is above the one for 1975. Hence, we can conclude that, in spite of the trend towards inequality during the second half of the period, persons in all deciles were unequivocally better off in 1991 than in 1983 and 1975. It is worth mentioning, though, that persons in the first decile benefited very little from growth from 1983 onwards.

Curiously, the overall picture of the development of equality was the opposite from what one would expect from the ideological backgrounds of governments in power during the two sub-periods. This may be attributed to the fact that the major legislative changes in benefits were already in place by 1960. Changes thereafter were only marginal. More importantly, the non-Social Democratic government in 1977–82 pursued more or less traditional Social Democratic labour-market policy, whereas the Social Democratic government in 1988–9 pursued a traditional liberal–conservative growth policy.

Several reasons for the changes in equality were investigated. One of these could be largely dismissed. Changes in the distribution of equivalent disposable income seem not to have been driven by unemployment, although inflation may have caused a redistribution away from high-income earners through a tax-bracket effect.

For the first sub-period, two major forces contributed to decreased inequality: decreased earnings dispersion and the increased redistributive effect of public transfers. The latter meant a more favourable development for pensioners (and the partially overlapping category of families with low employment intensity). Counteracting this was the fact that categories having lower income became relatively more numerous, reducing the redistributive effects of income taxes.

Several, possibly interlinked, reasons for the increase in inequality during the second sub-period were found. The dominant forces were increased wage dispersion and a continued decreased redistributive effect of income taxes. These two forces resulted in considerably larger intragroup inequality for a large number of cross-sectional views of the Swedish population. This is also confirmed by the fact that inequality within households with high employment intensity became comparatively large. Increasing differences in the mean income of different groups was much less important in generating greater inequality.

Finally, the analysis showed that pensioners aged 65–74 fared best of all groups and that not all groups have fared so well. Young adults – persons 18–24 years of age – had about the same standard of living in 1991 as their counterparts had in 1975. The development of the well-being of two partially overlapping categories with 18–24-year-olds, i.e., non-aged single persons and single parents, was also less favourable than for other categories of the population.

Notes

We are grateful to Statistics Sweden, and in particular Bengt-Olof Gert, for excellent work providing us with basic calculations for this study and Mats Johansson for computational help and other assistance. The authors are, needless to say, responsible for any errors of omission or commission. The authors gratefully acknowledge financial support from the Swedish Council of Social Research and the National Social Insurance Board.

1 Disposable income can be defined in various ways. The most controversial definitional issue is the question of how to treat imputed rents for owner-occupied homes. In this study, imputed rents are computed as 2.5 per cent of the net asset value of a home, based on the tax value adjusted for average changes in market values between assessment dates.

2 All three indices reveal a spike in 1986. The spike also appears in other reports using the same data (Jansson 1990; Jansson and Sandqvist 1993). It is tempting to attribute it to data problems, although we have no evidence either confirming or refuting this conjecture. The spike vividly illustrates the possible pitfalls in selecting specific years for study, as opposed to examining the trend over an entire period.

3 As can be seen in table 13.1, however, the change from 1983 to 1991 for the first decile is very small.

4 Social Welfare must be a non-decreasing function of income to make this statement. See Shorrocks 1983 for a theoretical discussion.

5 Note that the 1986 spike does not appear that obvious in the development of income average (figure 13.4) but is pronounced in the inequality indices. The fact that it is particularly so in the MLD and Theil index suggests that it may be due to extreme income observations in the tails of the 1986 distribution.

6 For more detail, see Gustafsson and Klevmarken 1993.

7 For a more comprehensive discussion of the development of the social security pension system, see Eriksen and Palmer 1994.

8 The redistributive effect of public sector transfers (RP) is defined as one minus the ratio of the inequality index for gross equivalent income to the inequality index for equivalent factor income (multiplied by 100). The redistributive effect of income taxes (RT) is defined as one minus the ratio of the inequality index for equivalent disposable income to the inequality index for equivalent gross income (multiplied by 100). The redistributive effect of taxes and transfers combined (RPT) is defined as one minus the ratio of the inequality index for equivalent disposable income to the inequality index for equivalent factor income (multiplied by 100). Because the redistributive effects are defined as relative changes, the following relationship between the effects exists:

$$RPT = 1 - (1 - RP)(1 - RS).$$

9 This is in line with distributional effects simulated in a study prior to the reform (Schwarz and Gustafsson 1991) and found in Klevmarken and Olovsson 1993, which also include behavioural responses.

10 In constructing the different terms, we have followed the work of Mookherjee and Shorrocks 1982.

11 Employment income includes sick pay, maternal benefits and income replacement for care of sick children but not unemployment benefits. Self-employed persons who also have pension income but are working full time are classified as self-employed even if their pension income is greater than their income from self-employment.

12 In 1975, there is a residual group to catch other regions which is labelled 'unclassified'.

References

Åberg, R., Selén, J. and Tham, H. 1984. 'Ekonomiska resurser' (Economic resources) (pages 140–83), in Erikson, R. and Åberg, R. (eds.), *Välfärd i förändring. Levnadsvilkor i Sverige 1968–1981.* Arlöv: Prisma.

Bentzel, R. 1953. *Inkomstfördelningen i Sverige* (The Distribution of Income in Sweden). Uppsala: Almqvist & Wiksell.

Bergström, V. 1967. 'Inkomstfördelningen under efterkrigstiden' (The Distribution of Income Since World War II), in *Välståndsklyftor och standardhöjning.* Stockholm: Prisma.

Björklund, A. 1991. 'Unemployment and Income Distribution: Time-Series Evidence from Sweden'. *Scandinavian Journal of Economics,* 93: 457–65.

1992. 'Långsiktiga perspektiv på inkomstfördelningen' (Long-run Perspectives on the Distribution of Income), in *Inkomstfördelningens utveckling.* Bilaga 8 till LU 92. Stockholm.

Blank, R. and Blinder, A. 1986. 'Macroeconomics, Income Distribution, and Poverty', in Danziger, S. and Weinberg, D. H. (eds.), *Fighting Poverty: What Works and What Doesn't,* Cambridge, Mass.: Harvard University Press.

Blinder, A. and Esaki, H. 1978. 'Macroeconomic Activity and Income Distribution in the Postwar United States'. *Review of Economics and Statistics,* 60: 604–8.

Buse, A. 1982. 'The Cyclical Behaviour of the Size Distribution of Income in Canada'. *Canadian Journal of Economics,* 40: 189–204.

Edin, P. A. and Holmlund, B. 1992. 'The Swedish Wage Structure: The Rise and Fall of Solidarity Policy?' Uppsala: Department of Economics, Working Paper 13.

Eriksen, T. and Palmer, E. 1994. 'The Deterioration of the Swedish Pension System', in Ditch, J., Glennerster, H. and Hills, J. (eds.), *Beveridge and Social Security 50 Years On.* Oxford: Oxford University Press.

Fritzell, J. 1991. 'Icke av marknaden allena: Inkomstfördelningen i Sverige' (Not by the Market Alone: The Distribution of Income in Sweden). Stockholm: Institutet för social forskning, Avhandlingsserie, p. 16.

Gramlich, E. 1974. 'The Distributional Effects of Higher Unemployment'. *Brookings Papers on Economic Activity,* 2: 293–342.

Green, G., Coder, J. and Ryscavage, P. 1992. 'International Comparisons of Earnings Inequality for Men in the 1980s'. *Review of Income and Wealth*, 38: 1–15.

Gustafsson, B. 1984. *Transfereringar och inkomstskatt samt hushållens materiella standard* (Transfers and Income Taxes as well as the Economic Well-being of Households). Stockholm: Ds Fi. 1984: 17.

1987a. *Ett decennium av stagnerande realinkomster* (A Decade of Stagnating Real Income). Levnadsförhållanden, Rapport 54. Stockholm: Statistiska Centralbyrån.

1987b. *Den offentliga sektorn – fördelningsaspekter* (The Public Sector – Distributional Aspects). Bilaga 20 till LU 87. Stockholm.

Gustafsson, B. and Klevmarken, A. 1993. 'Taxes and Transfers in Sweden: Incentive Effects on Labour Supply', in Atkinson, A. and Mogensen-Viby, G. (eds.), *Work and Welfare: A North European Perspective*. Oxford: Oxford University Press.

Gustafsson, B. and Uusitalo, H. 1990. 'Income Distribution and Redistribution During Two Decades', in Perssen, I. (ed.), *Generating Equality in the Welfare State*. Oslo: Norwegian University Press.

Hibbs, D. 1990. 'Wage Dispersion and Trade Union Action in Sweden', in Perssen, I. (ed.), *Generating Equality in the Welfare State*. Oslo: Norwegian University Press.

Jansson, K. 1990. *Inkomst- och förmögenhetsfördelningen 1967–1987* (The Distribution of Income and Wealth 1967–1987). Bilaga 19 till LU 90. Stockholm.

Jansson, K. and Sandqvist, A. 1993. *Inkomstfördelningen under 1980-talet* (The Income Distribution During the 1980s). Bilaga 19 till LU 92. Stockholm.

Jäntti, M. 1994. 'A More Efficient Estimate of the Effects of Macroeconomic Activity on the Distribution of Income'. *Review of Economics and statistics*, 76: 372–8.

Järnek, M. 1971. *Hushållens inkomstförhållanden 1925–1965* (The Income Situation of Households 1925–1964). Skrifter utgivna av Ekonomisk-Historiska föreningen i Lund X. Lund.

Klevmarken, A. and Olovsson, P. 1993. 'Direct and Behavioral Effects of Income Tax Changes – Simulations with the Swedish Model MICROHUS'. Department of Economics, University of Göteborg, Working paper.

Meier, T. 1973a. 'The Distributional Impact of the 1970 Recession'. *Review of Economics and Statistics*, 55: 214–24.

1973b. 'The Effects of Macroeconomic Fluctuations on the Distribution of Income'. *Review of Income and Wealth*, 21: 385–405.

Metcalf, C. 1969. 'The Size Distribution of Personal Income During the Business Cycle'. *American Economic Review*, 59: 657–68.

Mookherjee, D. and Shorrocks, A. F. 1982. 'A Decomposition of the Trend in U.K. Income Inequality'. *Economic Journal*, 92: 886–902.

Nolan, B. 1986. 'Comments on "Cyclical and Secular Influences on the Size Distribution of Personal Income in the U.K.: Some Econometric Tests" by C. Weil'. *Applied Economics*, 18: 1103–7.

Palmer, E. and Palme, M. 1989. 'A Macroeconomic Analysis of Employer-Contribution Financed Social Security', in Gustafsson, B. and Klevmarken, A. (eds.), *The Political Economy of Social Security*. Amsterdam: North-Holland.

Schwarz, B. and Gustafsson, B. 1991. 'Income Redistribution Effects of Tax Reforms in Sweden'. *Journal of Policy Modeling*, 13: 551–70.

Shorrocks, A. F. 1980. 'A Class of Additively Decomposable Inequality Measures'. *Econometrica*, 48: 613–25.

1983. 'Ranking Income Distributions'. *Economica*, 50: 1–17.

Söderström, L. 1988. *Inkomstfördelning och fördelningspolitik* (Income Distribution and Distributional Policy). Kristianstad: SNS.

Spånt, R. 1981. 'The Distribution of Income in Sweden, 1920–76', in Klevmarken, N. A. and Lybeck, J. A. (eds.), *The Statics and Dynamics of Income*. Clavedon: Tieto.

Statistics Sweden. 1993. *Inkomstfördelningsundersökningen 1991*. Stockholm (Be 21 SM 9301).

Thurow, L. 1970. 'Analysing the American Income Distribution'. *American Economic Review*, 60: 261–9.

Weil, G. 1984. 'Cyclical and Secular Influences on the Size Distribution of Personal Incomes in the UK: Some Econometric Tests'. *Applied Economics*, 16: 749–55.

14 Income inequality and poverty in Finland in the 1980s

MARKUS JÄNTTI AND VELI-MATTI
RITAKALLIO

1 Introduction

Equalising economic inequality and defeating poverty, or at least alleviating its worst aspects, are two of the fundamental functions of the welfare
state (Ringen 1987; Gustafsson and Uusitalo 1990b). At the same time, the
welfare state is an elusive concept. There are almost as many definitions of
the welfare state as there are analysts. Definitions vary according to the
purpose of the analysis, but there is some kind of general agreement on
what the concept includes. The 'welfare state' can be thought of as short-
hand for 'the public sector's social insurance, welfare and social service
activities in industrialised democracies'.

Ringen (1987) distinguishes between regulative and redistributive
welfare state policies. State intervention in wage settlements or fiscal policies aimed at achieving full employment are typical examples of regulative
welfare state policies. Redistributive public policies typically aim at
redistributing resources after the market process, although in reality the
market process itself is likely to be affected by welfare policies. Public transfers, public services and progressive income taxation are typical examples
of redistributive public policies. We adopt a view of the welfare state as a
collection of services and policies involving the public sector, and focus on
the part of the welfare state that is involved in redistribution of income
(Barr 1992).

Different countries have chosen different types of welfare states. The
development of social expenditure, institutions and social rights in Finland
has been extensively analysed in several cross-national studies (Alestalo
and Uusitalo 1986, 1992; Kangas 1991). Finland is found to be a latecomer
to what Esping-Andersen (1990) calls the group of social-democratic or
Nordic welfare states. This type is characterised by universal coverage of
benefits and dependence of the level of benefits on earnings (and employment). In comparative studies of income inequality and poverty, Sweden
has normally represented the Nordic model. The effects of Finnish social

policy on income distribution and poverty have only infrequently been studied in a cross-national context (Uusitalo 1989; Gustafsson and Uusitalo 1990a, 1990b). It is commonly thought that Finland can be characterised as a Nordic welfare state only from the early 1980s on. The present study is an investigation of the results of Finnish social policy, of how far Finnish social policy succeeded in equalising incomes and alleviating poverty during the 1980s. We explore trends in income inequality and poverty in the 1980s and how far income transfer systems succeeded in alleviating poverty and equalising incomes during that period. There are no official poverty statistics in Finland and there is no officially defined poverty line. How one conceptualises poverty is therefore open to debate. We will settle on a common definition of a poverty line – half of median disposable income – but discuss and use other methods as well.

Income inequality and poverty increased in many industrialised countries during the 1980s. Most commonly these increases are attributed to increased inequality of earnings (Coder, Rainwater and Smeeding 1989). There is reason to expect that the trend towards increased inequality in many industrialised countries also prevailed in Finland. For instance, Finland's industrial structure and trading partners are very similar to those of Sweden. One would expect that the causal factors of increasing inequality in Sweden would also be active in Finland.

We have two major findings to report. The first is that the inequality of equivalent disposable income did not change in Finland between 1980 and 1990. The second major finding is that, although inequality of income did not change, poverty decreased substantially during the 1980s.

The chapter is organised as follows. We briefly review the macroeconomic conditions and changes in public policy during the 1980s in section 2. In the third section, we briefly review previous studies of poverty and income inequality in Finland and present the data and methods used in those analyses. In sections 4 and 5, we present trends in income inequality and poverty, and a final section presents our conclusions.

2   Macroeconomic conditions and public policy

2.1   Growth and unemployment

The Finnish economy was fairly stable throughout the 1980s. The international recession in the early 1980s was not particularly severe in Finland. A commonly cited reason for this relative stability was barter trade with the Soviet Union. Imports from the Soviet Union consisted mainly of crude oil. Price increases in crude oil, which hit most other countries, led to increased exports because of the balanced-trade requirement, and hence greater demand for Finnish goods, cushioning the adverse effects of oil price increases.[1] The rate of GNP growth declined, from 7–8 per cent during the late 1970s, to around 1.5 per cent. After 1982, real GNP growth (figure 14.1) picked up, to reach 3 per cent most of the decade (Pekkarinen and Vartiainen 1993, pp. 126–7). The last few years of the 1980s were a period of especially rapid growth, with annual GNP growth of 4–6 per cent.

Corporatism in the Finnish labour market reached a peak in the 1980s. Wage settlements varied from completely centralised to partially decentralised (on the union level). Governments participated actively by mediating in wage bargaining and by making promises on social and fiscal policy associated with the settlements reached by unions and employers' organisations. At the end of the decade, there was a tendency among white-collar workers' unions to abandon solidaristic wage policies in favour of improving the relative position of their members. These unions also voiced demands for lower income tax progression, a demand that was met by the government.

By the end of the decade, completely centralised wage settlements were unpopular among employers' organisations and white-collar workers. There is no consensus as to what level of wage bargaining will have the largest effect on decreasing inequality. However, it seems plausible that completely centralised wage bargaining would produce the smallest dispersion in earnings (Rowthorn 1989). The overall unemployment rate fluctuated around 5 per cent until 1989, when it declined to roughly 3.4 per cent. Throughout the decade, the unemployment rate for men was slightly higher than that for women.

2.2   Changes in social policy

The evolution of Finnish social policy since World War II has frequently been described as a shift from marginal to institutional welfare. Marginal (or residual) social policy is characterised by the discretionary award of a low level of benefits and is often described as relief for the poor. The characteristics of institutional social policy, on the other hand, are a reasonable minimum standard of benefits, the central role of the state in providing welfare and the principle of universality: all citizens are covered by statutory entitlement to welfare benefits. In institutional social policy, the definition of a reasonable level of benefits is based on minimum subsistence standards, on the one hand, and income-related coverage on the other. The purpose of minimum subsistence provision is to ensure all citizens, irrespective of their previous employment history, an acceptable standard of living, while the purpose of income-related benefits is to guarantee individuals a standard of consumption, with the discontinuation of active employment (Esping-Andersen and Korpi 1987, pp. 39–74) that is closely related to their previous level.

Using growth in social expenditure, Uusitalo (1989, p. 15) identifies five phases in the development of the Finnish welfare state: (1) beginning 1945–9, (2) relative stagnation (1950–60), (3) expansion (1961–76), (4) decelerating development (1977–81) and (5) accelerating development (1982–1990).

The basic legislation establishing the present income transfer system in Finland was passed during the 1950s and 1960s, starting with the National Pensions Act of 1956 and proceeding through the following decade with the establishment of income-related pensions and health insurance systems. The evolution of subsistence levels for minimum pensions and the gradual maturing of the income-related pensions system since the 1960s have moved Finland towards an institutional, Nordic social policy model.

By the 1980s, Finnish social policy met the high quality standards of Nordic welfare in terms of the level of social benefits and the breadth of coverage, yet the model had been implemented with significantly lower relative welfare costs than in Sweden (Kangas 1993, pp. 237–8). The general tendency since then has been to raise the minimum levels of support as well as to expand the principle that the level of benefits should depend positively on previous earnings. Several minor reforms of the social welfare system were legislated in the 1980s. Small changes were implemented for income-related and national (flat-rate) pensions, health and maternity insurance, income-related and flat-rate unemployment compensation, family support and social assistance. The general tendency in all these cases was to raise the minimum benefit, raise the maximum limit (or abolish it altogether) and decrease the extent of means testing while strengthening the (positive) dependence of benefits on the level of previous incomes and including all benefits in taxable income. In spite of several minor reforms, the development of the welfare state during the 1980s can be described as fine-tuning a widespread welfare system.

The expansion of social security legislation in the 1980s resulted in a steady increase in social security expenditure. However, the share of social security expenditure in Finland's GNP (figure 14.1) has been at a level considerably lower than that of other Nordic countries even at the end of the decade. It is perhaps noteworthy that the general direction of social policy reform was much the same throughout the 1980s, although traditional Finnish politics changed during the decade. In the first half of the 1980s, the government was led by a traditional coalition of the Social Democratic Party and the Center Party (formerly Agrarians). After the parliamentary elections of 1987, a new coalition was formed by the Social Democrats and the National Coalition Party (Conservatives).

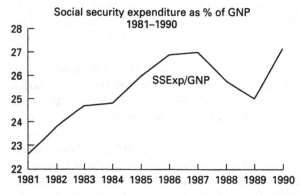

Figure 14.1 GNP growth, unemployment and social expenditure in Finland, 1981–1990

3 Measurement issues

3.1 Earlier studies

According to a review of studies on long-term income inequality in Finland (Hjerppe and Lefgren 1974), inequality increased during the early stages of industrialisation then began declining at the start of the twentieth century. There was little change in inequality during the 1920s and 1930s, but during World War II inequality decreased and generally remained, even after the war, lower than in the 1930s. The 1950s and 1960s seem to have been a fairly stable period. Hjerppe and Lefgren (1974, pp. 110–11) find that during the period they study, income inequality changed significantly only during periods of high inflation, when inequality decreased. Gustafsson and Uusitalo (1990a) find a declining trend in the inequality of equivalent disposable income from 1966 to 1985, with large declines occurring in the 1970s. Methodologically, our study is quite similar to Gustafsson and Uusitalo (1990a). Apart from similar research units and income concepts, both studies use Lorenz curve comparisons. Hjerppe and Lefgren (1974) summarise studies done before 1967. These are all based on tax records and generally use the tax unit (which varies over time) as the research unit and taxable income (which changes with tax regulations) as the income concept. Gustafsson and Uusitalo (1990a), on the other hand, use data from the household budget surveys of 1966, 1971, 1976, 1981 and 1985, study the individual and use disposable equivalent income as the income concept.

Gustafsson and Uusitalo (1990b) explore trends in poverty in Finland using the same data as above. Little work on economic poverty in Finland was done earlier, and most other studies, apart from Ritakallio (1994), are either only cross-sectional (covering only one point in time) or cover only a part of the time period in Gustafsson and Uusitalo (1990b). Gustafsson and Uusitalo (1990b) tell a story of poverty similar to that of inequality. Poverty dropped from quite high levels in 1966 to much lower levels in 1976. Taking 50 per cent of median income as the poverty line, poverty dropped from around 13 per cent in 1966 to less than 5 per cent in 1976. Between 1976 and 1985, the poverty rate dropped further to 3.5 per cent. Thus, as with inequality, the major decline in poverty occurred in the late 1960s and the first half of the 1970s with some further reduction in the 1980s.

3.2 Data and method

We use income data from the Household Budget Surveys (HBS), collected by the Central Bureau of Statistics in 1981, 1985 and 1990. We assign the equivalent household income to each individual in the household and use sampling weights, corrected for non-response, to estimate population level statistics. The sample sizes after non-response are 7,368, 8,200 and 8,258, with non-response rates of about 25 per cent, 32 per cent and 30 per cent, respectively. The income variables have been collected from tax and various other registers, augmented with interview data and are generally considered to be of fairly high quality.

There was very little cyclical variation during the 1980s. The data used in this study, HBS for 1981, 1985 and 1990 have been collected near or at cyclical troughs (the current depression started in 1990, from which time growth has been negative). Overall unemployment rates varied very little during the 1980s, but 1981, 1985 and 1990 are years of lower unemployment than the immediately preceding or succeeding years, as can be seen in figure 14.1. However, the fact that unemployment is at locally low levels in each sample year suggests that differences in unemployment rates will not predetermine our results. Thus, we should have little systematic bias in our results due to cyclical variation. The exception to this is that the lower unemployment rate for 1990 might lead us to expect a reduction in the inequality of and incidence of low labour income.

In our analysis, we concentrate on four income concepts: labour income, factor income, gross income (factor income + income transfers) and disposable income (gross income – direct taxes). We use the OECD equivalence scale in which the first adult has the unit weight, all other adults are weighted by 0.7 and all children by 0.5. As far as we can tell from experimentation, the results are not greatly affected by this particular choice of equivalence scale. An important limitation of the method we employ is that we do not consider possible behavioural responses of persons or households to government transfers or taxes. That is, when we measure the effect of transfers and taxes on factor income in reducing inequality, for example, we do not take into account the possibility that households adjust their market behaviour in response to the public sector. If the actual distribution of factor income would have been very different in the absence of net transfers or under some different tax/transfer schedule, we risk overstating the effect of the public sector on the distribution of income. However, modelling the whole income-formation process and taking into account all possible behavioural responses are well beyond the scope of the present chapter.

To study changes in income inequality over time, we use paired Lorenz curve comparisons rather than relying on a particular index of income inequality. As is well-known, if Lorenz curves do not intersect, all relative income inequality indices that satisfy the Dalton transfer principle will result in the same ranking of two income distributions. On the other hand, for intersecting Lorenz curves, the direction of the ranking depends on the inequality index chosen. There is a risk, as always when sample data are used to draw inferences regarding whole populations, that we could conclude that inequality has changed when the difference in two estimated Lorenz curves is really only due to sampling error. Thus, in comparing Lorenz curves for two different years, we test for the equality of the two Lorenz curves, i.e., we take into account the fact that the curves are estimated subject to random error.[2]

To study poverty, we need to specify both the relevant space in which to measure poverty (e.g., income or consumption) and a particular cutoff point, a poverty line. In this study, we mainly use income rather than consumption and define the poverty line to be 50 per cent of the median equivalent disposable income in the total population in each survey year (the relative income method). However, Heikkilä (1990) finds that the group of income poor in 1987 overlapped only partly with groups identified to be poor by other measures. To ascertain that our results are not unique to this particular way of defining poverty, based on Ritakallio (1994), we explore trends in poverty using three other methods as well: (1) the relative expenditure method, i.e., individuals whose equivalent consumption expenditure is below half of the median equivalent consumption expenditure; (2) politico-administrative method 1, i.e., individuals whose annual equivalent income is less than the current guaranteed minimum pension; and (3) politico-administrative method 2, i.e., individuals who are clients of last-resort social welfare during the year.

There are also several methods of aggregation or poverty indices from which to choose (Sen 1979). Ritakallio (1994) makes use of the poverty rate and the poverty gap measures. The poverty rate refers to the proportion of the total population below the poverty line, and the poverty gap is the sum of all individual poverty gaps (i.e., the difference between the individual's income and the poverty line). Ritakallio (1994) reports that trends in poverty are very similar regardless of which of the two indices is used. Therefore, we only use the proportion of poor to measure poverty.

4 Inequality

4.1 Trends in inequality

The most striking feature of income inequality in Finland during the 1980s is that there was little or no change. Figure 14.2 shows the Lorenz curves for each year for the four income concepts. Neither of the Lorenz curves for

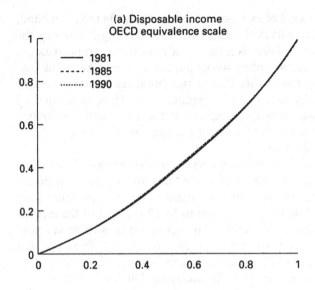

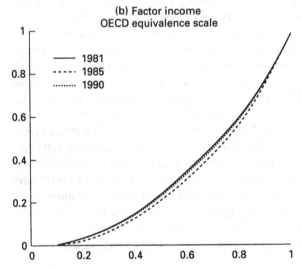

Figure 14.2 Lorenz curves for different income concepts in Finland, 1981, 1985 and 1990

equivalent disposable income in 1981, 1985 or 1990, shown in figure 14.2, dominates the other. In other words, inequality cannot be said to have changed in the 1980s.[3]

Does this conclusion hold also for the components of disposable income. Figure 14.2 contains the Lorenz curves of equivalent labour income for

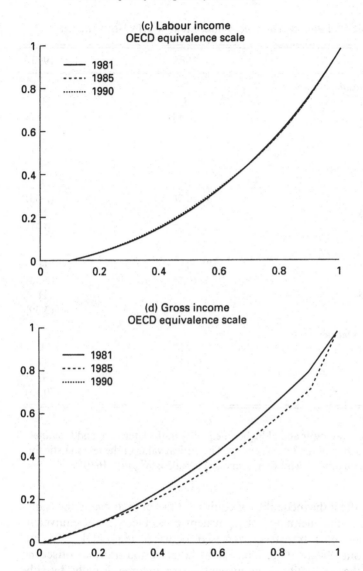

(c) Labour income
OECD equivalence scale

—— 1981
----- 1985
········ 1990

(d) Gross income
OECD equivalence scale

—— 1981
----- 1985
········ 1990

1981, 1985 and 1990. The Lorenz curves for 1981 and 1985 intersect, while that for 1990 is completely below those for the other two years, although the differences are negligible. Hence inequality of equivalent labour income increased in the late 1980s, albeit only slightly.[4] Inequality of equivalent factor income, i.e., labour plus capital income, increased throughout the 1980s. The Lorenz curve for equivalent factor income in 1981 dominates that in 1985, which in turn dominates the curve in 1990. Two income

Table 14.1 *Lorenz curve dominance and X^2$_{.95}$(9)-test statistics*

	1985	1990
Disposable income		
1981	I	I
	(1.44)	(5.62)
1985		I
		(2.95)
Labour income		
1981	I	I
	(0.96)	(2.33)
1985		H
		(0.91)
Factor income		
1981	H	H
	(0.55)	(5.30)
1985		H
		(3.30)
Gross income		
1981	H	I
	(94.85)	(3.43)
1985		L
		(70.13)

Note:
L denotes lower and H higher inequality in the later year, and I denotes
a crossing of the Lorenz curves. The critical value of the test statistic for
the equality of two Lorenz curves at a =.05 is $X^2_{.95}(9)=16.919$.

sources can affect the inequality of equivalent factor income: public transfers and taxes. The inequality of equivalent gross income, i.e., equivalent
factor income plus transfers, increased between 1981 and 1985 but
decreased from 1985 to 1990. Thus, in the latter period transfers offset the
increase in the inequality of equivalent factor income. Finally, by subtracting taxes we derive equivalent disposable income, the inequality of
which did not change over the period.

In table 14.1 we show whether inequality was lower or higher in the
second year as well as the X^2-test statistics associated with the test for the
equality of the Lorenz curves in every paired comparison (Beach and
Davidson 1983; Beach and Kaliski 1986). These results are only indicative,
in that we conduct every test as if it were independent of the comparisons

for other years (which, by and large, they are) and other income concepts (which they are not).

Only in the case of equivalent gross income are the differences so large that the hypothesis of equal Lorenz curves can be discarded. That is to say the observed increase in equivalent gross income inequality from 1981 to 1985 and the observed decrease from 1985 to 1990 are statistically significant. All other changes are not strong enough to be significant.

4.2   Inequality effects of taxes and transfers

In studies of trends in inequality, it is customary to study the magnitude of the inequality-reducing effect of taxes and transfers. In figure 14.3, we illustrate the difference in the inequality of different income concepts in each year using Lorenz curves and the size of the area between the Lorenz curves, i.e., the absolute reduction in the Gini coefficients on moving from one income concept to another.[5]

The figures make apparent a somewhat surprising result. Namely, in 1981 and 1990 a large reduction in inequality occurs on moving from equivalent factor income to equivalent gross income, i.e., by adding public transfers to equivalent factor income. The move from gross to equivalent disposable income, i.e., subtracting direct taxes, only leads to an additional small decline in inequality. The effect of taxes in reducing inequality is virtually the same in 1981 and 1990, with transfers accounting for a greater part of the reduction in inequality in 1990. The year 1985 seems to be an outlier, in that the Lorenz curve for gross income in that year intersects the curve for equivalent factor income. Interestingly, gross income seems to be more unequally distributed in the higher-income groups (above the eighth decile) while equivalent factor income, as one would expect, is more unequally distributed in the lower deciles.

4.3   Differences in relative income

In principle, it is possible that relative incomes shifted between various population groups, though little happened to overall inequality. Table 14.2 shows the relative incomes of selected demographic groups. The first thing to note is that real disposable income per equivalent adult, shown in the first row in table 14.2, increased at an average annual rate of 3.7 per cent during the 1980s. Further, the growth rates by population sub-group varied very little relative to the average growth rates (not shown here), a notable exception being single-parent households.

Single-person households tend to have the highest relative income, followed by elderly households. Childless couples generally have the lowest

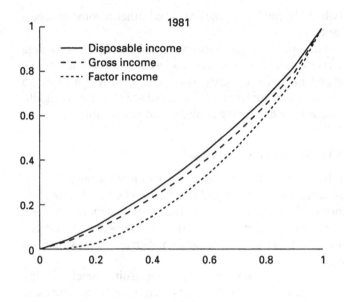

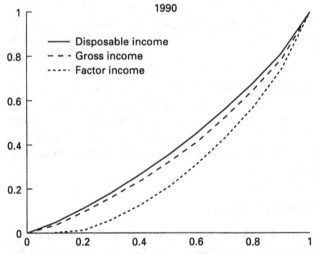

Figure 14.3 Effect of social transfers and taxes on income inequality, 1981, 1985 and 1990

incomes, with single parents being next. Households headed by a single parent are relatively less wealthy than other households. Apart from that, the relative incomes contain few surprises. Households are ranked in relative income strictly by the number of children: the more children, the lower the relative income. Households with heads younger than 30 and older than 64

1985

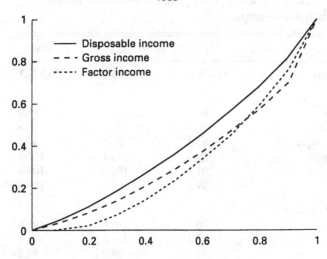

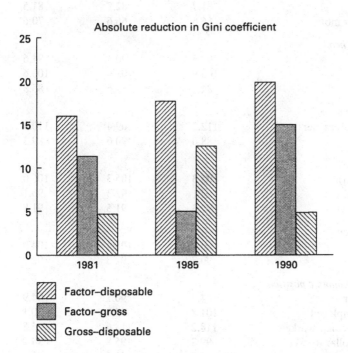

Table 14.2 *Relative differences in equivalent disposable income among selected sub-groups*

Partition	1981	1985	1990
Overall mean	51,736.8	57,913.1	70,872.1
Household type			
Single-parent	90.1	88.4	83.0
Two-parent	96.4	96.2	95.6
Childless couple	83.3	85.6	84.3
Single-person	120.4	119.1	122.4
Elderly	103.7	100.5	104.6
Other	99.9	101.4	100.3
Number of children			
None	106.4	105.6	105.6
One	103.3	103.6	104.1
Two	94.5	94.2	95.2
Three	81.7	82.3	81.5
Four or more	66.6	66.6	70.6
Age of head			
<30	92.5	90.7	94.6
30–64	103.9	103.6	103.6
64>	84.3	87.6	85.3
Adult earners			
All adult earners	112.2	109.4	110.4
Other	88.0	90.6	89.3
Region			
Southern	105.3	105.3	106.0
Central	92.1	92.3	90.1
Northern	92.3	91.5	91.8
Location			
Urban	106.3	105.4	104.9
Rural	90.7	92.0	92.3
Socioeconomic position			
Farmer	84.4	90.1	94.9
Self-employed	101.8	94.0	100.1
White-collar worker	118.2	118.6	115.8
Blue-collar worker	99.2	95.8	94.2
Non-worker	78.3	81.6	83.1
Education			
High school	90.9	91.7	90.0

Table 14.2 (*cont.*)

Partition	1981	1985	1990
Lower vocational	99.0	95.2	92.9
Higher vocational	111.4	106.3	105.2
University	130.4	134.3	133.5

Note:
Mean equivalent disposable incomes relative to the overall mean.
Source: Authors' calculations from HBS.

are less well-off than those with heads in between. Mean incomes are above average in the south of Finland and below average in northern and central Finland. White-collar workers rank above the self-employed and blue-collar workers; farmers and non-workers are last. The higher the educational level of the head, the higher the relative position of the household.

5   Poverty

5.1   Trends in poverty

As measured by the relative income method, poverty fell steadily throughout the 1980s (table 14.3). The proportion of the population below the poverty line was 4.9 per cent in 1981 (corresponding to 233,000 persons), whereas ten years later the corresponding figure had fallen to 2.5 per cent (126,000 persons). These figures are difficult to match in national or international history. Nor is the trend they describe in the poverty rate dependent upon the level of the poverty line used. Regardless of whether the line is drawn at 40 per cent, 50 per cent or 60 per cent of median income, the poverty rate fell throughout the 1980s. Measured in terms of minimum pension levels, the official poverty rate fell even more sharply during the last decade than poverty measured by the relative income method. By 1991, the poverty rate as defined by minimum pension levels was no more than 1 per cent. On the other hand, poverty as measured by low consumption is revealed by the HBS to be somewhat more widespread than low incomes, and the downward trend in low-consumption poverty is less marked than that in low-income poverty: from approximately 6 per cent at the beginning of the decade, to 5 per cent by 1990 (246,000 persons).

At the same time, the trend during the 1980s in the number of persons receiving last-resort social assistance contradicts the poverty trends measured by other indicators, as clientele virtually doubled during the decade,

Table 14.3. *Trend in poverty, 1981–1990*

Method	Poverty line	1981	1985	1990
Disposable income	40 per cent of median	2.4	1.6	1.1
	50 per cent	4.9	3.5	2.5
	60 per cent	9.8	8.3	6.7
Consumption expenditure	40 per cent of median	2.2	2.2	1.5
	50 per cent	6.0	6.3	5.0
	60 per cent	12.6	12.6	10.6
Minimum pension		4.4	2.6	1.0
Social assistance recipients		3.0	4.9	6.3

Source: Ritakallio (1994).

to 6.3 per cent of the total population by 1990. Moreover, this growth in last-resort social assistance is in conflict with the principles of Finnish welfare policy since the 1960s, the aim having been to organise social security in such a way as to eliminate the need for discretionary support to individuals. This situation is explained by the fact that the minimum unemployment benefit did not rise during the 1980s as fast as that for social assistance. Nonetheless, this situation does not represent a rise in overall welfare dependency, in the sense that in 1990 many clients of social assistance were not in poverty as measured by relative annual income.

Long-term social assistance dependency, however, would in general mean decline into poverty, since social assistance levels are below the poverty line as defined by the relative income method. The overall correlation between findings based on the various poverty indicators is in fact surprisingly weak, since the relative income method, the relative consumption method, and the last-resort criterion identify three quite distinct populations as being in poverty. The consumption indicator emphasises poverty in elderly households. The last-resort indicator, in contrast to the other criteria, highlights poverty among single parents and young people. Despite these disagreements, the overall observation is that by 1990 poverty as traditionally measured (whether by low income or in relation to minimum pension levels) had been effectively alleviated in Finland and that income differences had been significantly reduced.

5.2   Poverty effects of income transfers and taxes

We examine the impact of income transfer systems in reducing poverty usually by the difference in poverty rates before and after income transfers

Table 14.4 *Poverty effects of transfers and taxes, equivalent disposable income*

Poor	1981	1985	1990
40 per cent of median			
Factor income	17.6	18.3	21.2
Disposable income	2.4	1.6	1.1
Reduction	−15.2	−16.7	−20.1
50 per cent of median			
Factor income	20.6	21.4	24.2
Disposable income	4.9	3.5	2.5
Reduction	−15.7	−17.9	−21.7
60 per cent of median			
Factor income	24.4	25.2	27.7
Disposable income	9.8	8.3	6.7
Reduction	−14.6	−16.9	−21.0

Source: Ritakallio (1994).

and taxes. Increasing poverty as measured by equivalent factor income during the 1980s would have required increasing income transfers just to keep the poverty rate constant. As we report in table 14.4, income transfers reduced pre-transfer poverty by 15.7 percentage points in 1981 (with the poverty line at half of median income). In 1990, the corresponding reduction amounted to 21.7 percentage points. The finding that the welfare state's poverty-reducing effect increased over time is robust with respect to variations in the level of the poverty line. In 1990, the 21.7 percentage point reduction in poverty means that income transfer systems lifted approximately one million persons (a fifth of the population) above the poverty line and very nearly eliminated poverty. These figures are evidence of the large impact of the welfare system and provide justification for the statement that by 1990 the Finnish welfare state had practically eliminated income poverty. Moreover, it is possible that while income transfers remove households from poverty, taxes would at the same time push some households into poverty. Analyses conducted by Ritakallio (1994) show that this was not the case. Poverty alleviation was not reversed by this type of 'horizontal inequality'.

5.3   Differences in poverty risk between population groups

Changes in the poverty rate within various population groups were, with few exceptions, similar in tendency to those for the population as a whole

Table 14.5 *Poverty rate by population sub-group, 1981 and 1990*

	Income		Consumption	
Partition	1981	1990	1981	1990
Household type				
Single-parent	9.8	1.9	7.2	2.7
Two-parent	4.7	2.7	4.6	2.7
Childless couple	2.6	1.6	3.0	1.6
Single-person	10.8	6.1	5.8	6.1
Elderly	5.3	1.8	16.0	12.5
Other	3.9	1.7	6.7	4.9
Number of children				
None	4.8	2.3	7.1	6.0
One	3.2	1.7	3.7	2.2
Two	3.9	2.7	3.9	1.8
Three	8.8	3.5	7.9	4.5
Four or more	17.4	6.0	18.7	8.6
Age of head				
<30	7.5	4.1	4.9	3.4
30–64	4.3	2.3	4.8	3.3
64>	5.6	2.0	15.8	12.1
Adult earners				
All adult earners	2.3	1.5	2.4	1.7
Other	7.5	3.5	9.6	7.3
Region				
Southern	4.0	1.9	4.7	3.6
Central	5.9	3.7	8.2	5.9
Northern	7.2	2.8	7.8	5.6
Location				
Urban	3.3	1.9	3.6	3.7
Rural	7.3	3.3	9.6	5.6
Socioeconomic position				
Farmer	10.1	5.9	12.7	4.7
Self-employed	8.2	9.0	4.1	1.6
White-collar worker	1.3	0.5	1.3	1.0
Blue-collar worker	2.5	0.9	4.4	4.4
Non-worker	12.0	4.9	14.1	11.1
Education				
High school	5.8	3.1	9.2	7.2
Lower vocational	4.9	2.4	4.3	4.0

Table 14.5 (cont.)

	Income		Consumption	
Partition	1981	1990	1981	1990
Higher vocational	4.2	2.9	1.9	2.2
University	1.8	0.5	0.6	0.4

Source: Ritakallio (1994).

(table 14.5). Measured in terms of annual income, poverty fell during the 1980s for all groups except the self-employed (small businesses), where it remained approximately constant. Relatively speaking, the poverty risk fell most sharply among single parents, large families and the elderly. For single parents, the poverty risk fell in the course of the decade to one-fifth of its previous level, and for families with many children and for the elderly, to one-third. By 1990, the overall risk of low-income poverty was extremely low, and the risk differentials between various groups in the population had been sharply reduced. In that year, poverty risk levels of 6 per cent or greater applied only to persons living alone (6.1 per cent), families with four or more children (6.0 per cent) and the self-employed (9.0 per cent). The best defence against poverty was provided by salaried employment and a high level of education. For persons in families, poverty has traditionally been closely correlated with labour market participation. In Finland, the labour force participation rate of women is very high. During the period under investigation, for example, between 85 per cent and 90 per cent of single parents were employed. In 1981, 50 per cent of jobless single parents were living in poverty; by 1990, this figure had fallen to 5.1 per cent. Correspondingly, the poverty rate among employed single parents fell, from 3.7 per cent in 1981, to 1.4 per cent ten years later. During the 1980s, the link between poverty and employment also fell for two-parent families with children. In families with only one parent in employment, the poverty rate in 1981 was 9.2 per cent, whereas by the end of the decade it had fallen to 4.1 per cent. Non-participation in the labour force is a factor increasing poverty risk, but in the course of the decade this link was weakened. These findings suggest that family-targeted social policy, emphasised in the 1980s, was successful in alleviating poverty.

These analyses demonstrate that differences between population groups in the incidence of poverty (as measured by the conventional poverty line) had almost been eliminated by 1990. As poverty risks are equalised, the demographic composition of those in poverty will automatically come to match increasingly that of the overall population. Accordingly, irrespective of the poverty indicator applied, the majority of those in poverty live in households supported by a middle-aged person. Another important correlate of poverty is the joblessness of one or several adults in poor households. All forms of poverty also characteristically affect persons with insufficient education. Although changes in the composition of poverty have been minor, they match the observations made for poverty risk. If the poverty line applied is raised, however, the traditional ranking of groups in terms of mean income levels quickly becomes apparent. In terms of their equivalent disposable income, a large proportion of the elderly, young people, single parents and families with many children are found in the income bracket immediately above the poverty line.

Although the different ways of identifying the poor result in partially non-overlapping populations, there were in 1990 five categories which displayed a higher-than-average incidence of poverty on all indicators. These are those with low education, those living alone, people in northern Finland, families with three or more children and those not in employment. On the other hand, six categories with below-average poverty risk also emerged. These categories are couples with no children, households dependent upon a middle-aged provider, households in which all the adult members were in employment, people in southern Finland, administrative and clerical workers and persons with at least some education after the compulsory grades. Households economically dependent upon a middle-aged provider are thus not at greater risk on these grounds. Since this is the largest group in the population, the numerically largest group among people in poverty live in such households.

6   Concluding comments

The inequality of equivalent disposable income did not change in Finland during the 1980s. By 1990, traditional poverty, i.e., long-term subsistence on very low income, had been extensively alleviated in Finnish society. For those not active in the labour market, traditional poverty had been reduced through income transfer systems, especially the pensions system, while for the active population, it was the result of effective action taken against long-term unemployment. In the early 1980s, the alleviation of poverty through the income transfer system affected different population groups very unevenly. The pensions system was already functioning smoothly and effectively, but for the active population the poverty-alleviating effect of income transfers was still relatively weak. By 1990, the income transfer system treated different groups within the population in a much more even manner than it had done ten years earlier. The emphasis placed on family policy during the 1980s can also be shown to have produced results (poverty among the elderly had effectively been addressed earlier). It is also important to note that by international standards these good results were achieved at low cost. With a healthy economy, Finland did not need to fund social security by borrowing abroad; the Finnish foreign debt remained fairly steady throughout the period under investigation, at between 10 per cent and 15 per cent of GNP.

In Finland, Norway and Sweden, one of the cornerstones of social policies during recent decades has been the achievement of steady economic development and high levels of employment. During the period under investigation here, 1981–90, these conditions were met, whereas the economic situation prevailing at the time of writing (1994) is drastically different. The rosy scenario of low unemployment and high growth, in the late 1980s in particular, changed quite abruptly in 1990, when GNP started to decline. In 1991, it declined more than it had during the depression in the 1930s. The unemployment rate in Finland in 1995 was still around 20 per cent, long-term unemployment was rising rapidly and welfare had been subjected to many cuts, with further reductions planned. In many respects, the present investigation offers a history of the achievements of the Finnish welfare state during the 1980s and a benchmark for future studies examining the effects for welfare (or illfare) of societal changes and cuts in social security in the 1990s.

The very high levels of unemployment are likely to endanger the fairly equal distribution of income. The combination of earnings-related income transfers with some universal benefits can under many circumstances equalise differences in equivalent factor income. This is especially the case if unemployment spells are fairly short and most of the unemployed receive unemployment insurance. But once long-term unemployment becomes persistent and a larger proportion of the unemployed have exhausted their earnings-related unemployment insurance (after 500 days of unemployment), the effect of the flat-rate unemployment benefits will increase the differences in equivalent disposable income. Since items such as sick pay and pensions, in particular, depend on earlier earnings, with time the move to mass unemployment can have extremely detrimental effects on the income distribution.

It is to the credit of the Finnish social security system, which stands up well in international comparison, that the current severe economic recession has not generated serious social suffering (Jäntti 1993). Indeed, income inequality did not increase during the first few years of the crisis (Uusitalo 1993; Central Office of Statistics 1994). It is well established that unemployment becomes a poverty problem in the traditional sense only when it becomes persistent. Since 1990, the situation has changed radically, especially in terms of manpower policy. The mechanisms for the prevention of long-term unemployment have been dismantled, and the priority formerly accorded avoiding unemployment more generally has been overshadowed by other objectives in public policy. The daily allowance from the basic unemployment benefit is currently set at only about 75 per cent of the poverty line level. It is likely that the numbers of long-term unemployed persons grew rapidly in 1994 and 1995, as the number of those entitled to income-related unemployment insurance (payable for 500 days) will fall, reducing their benefit levels to the social assistance level. All the evidence suggests that during the next few years, the dominant factor in Finnish poverty will be long-term unemployment. It remains to be seen how seriously the fundamental mission of the welfare state – the alleviation of poverty – will be taken. The only means by which this can be achieved is through statutory measures to combat long-term unemployment and/or by raising the minimum levels of unemployment benefit.

Under current regulations, long-term unemployment automatically leads to long-term dependence on social assistance, since the minimum unemployment benefit is set below the assistance threshold. However, the assistance threshold is defined by reference to the minimum pension level, which serves as an administrative, 'semi-official' poverty line. Finland therefore faces the threat of a large group of the population being forced into dependence upon welfare and subsistence in permanent poverty. Such a development would be a major setback for Finland's welfare society and would reinforce a division of the Finnish people into the haves and the have-nots.

Notes

This research was supported in part by a grant from the Yrjö Jahnsson Foundation. The authors can be reached via e-mail at mjantti@aton.abo.fi and vemari@sara.cc.utu.fi.

1 See Andersson, Kosonen and Vartiainen 1993 for a thorough survey and discussion of the Finnish socioeconomic model.
2 See Beach and Davidson 1983 and Beach and Kaliski 1986 for details.
3 Gustafsson and Uusitalo 1990a find that the distribution in 1985 dominates that in 1981. They do not give the Lorenz curve ordinates. In our data, however, there is only one slight crossing of the Lorenz curves at the ninth decile. The difference in the results could be due to a different treatment of the imputed income from housing, which we subtract from equivalent disposable income. However, we suspect that the dominance they find is not significant. The results reported in Uusitalo 1993, p. 5, are very similar to ours. There the Lorenz curves cross at the ninth decile.

4 See also Eriksson and Jäntti 1993.
5 We do not test for the significance of these differences, though in principle that would be possible (but laborious). The reason is that in each year the Lorenz curves for different income concepts are correlated (since the incomes on which they are calculated are correlated). However, the covariance matrix for two income concepts is likely to be very complicated to derive analytically and would be the subject of a separate paper. Note also that we give the inequality reduction due to, say, transfers (equivalent factor >> equivalent gross income) as the absolute reduction in the Gini coefficient rather than the relative reduction in the same. This is because the Gini is twice the area between the diagonal and the Lorenz curve, which is basically a percentage. Percentage changes of percentages are difficult to interpret.

References

Alestalo, M. and Uusitalo, H. 1986. 'Finland', in Flora, P. (ed.), *Growth to Limits. The Western European Welfare States since World War II*, vol. 1. Berlin: De Gruyter and Aldine and Mouton, pp. 198–292.
1992. 'Social Expenditure: A Decompositional Approach', in Kolberg, J. E. (ed.), *The Study of Welfare State Regimes*. Armonk: M. E. Sharpe Inc., pp. 37–68.
Andersson, J. O., Kosonen, P. and Vartiainen, J. 1993. 'The Finnish Model of Economic and Social Policy – from Emulation to Crash'. Technical Report 401, Nationalekonomiska institutionen, Meddelanden från Ekonomisk-Statsvetenskapliga fakulteten vid Åbo Akademi.
Barr, N. 1992. 'Economic Theory and the Welfare State'. *Journal of Economic Literature*, 30: 741–803.
Beach, C. M. and Davidson, R. 1983. 'Distribution-Free Statistical Inference with Lorenz Curves and Income Shares'. *The Review of Economic Studies*, 50: 723–35.
Beach, C. M. and Kaliski, S. 1986. 'Lorenz Curve Inference with Sample Weights: An Application to the Distribution of Unemployment Experience'. *Applied Statistics*, 35 (1): 28–45.
Central Office of Statistics. 1994. 'Income Distribution Statistics 1992'. Technical Report, Central Office of Statistics.
Coder, J., Rainwater, L. and Smeeding, T. 1989. 'Inequality among Children in Ten Modern Nations: The United States in an International Context'. *American Economic Review*, 79: 320–4.
Erikson, R., Hansen, J. E., Ringen, S. and Uusitalo, H. (eds.). 1987. *The Scandinavian Model. Welfare States and Welfare Research*. Armonk: M. E. Sharpe, Inc.
Eriksson, T. and Jäntti, M. 1993. *The Distribution of Earnings in Finland 1970–1990*. Åbo Akademi University.
Esping-Andersen, G. 1990. *Three Worlds of Welfare State Capitalism*. Cambridge: Polity.
Esping-Andersen, G. and Korpi, W. 1987. 'From Poor Relief to Institutional

Welfare States: The Development of Scandinavian Welfare Policy', in Eriksson, R. *et al.* (eds.), *The Scandinavian Model. Welfare States and Welfare Research.* Armonk: M. E. Sharpe, Inc., pp. 39–74.

Gustafsson, B. and Uusitalo, H. 1990a. 'Income Distribution and Redistribution During Two Decades – Experiences from Finland and Sweden', in Persson, I. (ed.), *Generating Equality in the Welfare State.* Oslo: Oslo University Press.

1990b. 'The Welfare State and Poverty in Finland and Sweden from the Mid-1960s to the Mid-1980s'. *Review of Income and Wealth*, 36 (3): 249–66.

Heikkilä, M. 1990. *Köyhyys ja huono-osaisuus hyvinvointivaltiossa* (Poverty and Deprivation in a Welfare State). Helsinki: Ministry of Social Affairs.

Hjerppe, R. and Lefgren, J. 1974. 'Longterm Trends in Finland's Income Distribution 1881–1967'. *Kansantaloudellinen Aikakauskirja*, 5: 117–19.

Jäntti, M. 1993. 'Behov och inkomstfördelning – Finland 1989 och 1991' (Needs and the Distribution of Income – Finland 1989 and 1991). *Ekonomiska Samfundets Tidskrift*, 93(4): 213–18.

Kangas, O. 1991. *The Politics of Social Rights: Studies on the Dimensions of Sickness Insurance in OECD Countries.* Stockholm: Swedish Institute for Social Research, Stockholm University.

1993. 'The Merging of the Welfare State Models? Past and Present Trends in Finnish and Swedish Social Policy'. *Journal of European Social Policy*, 4 (2): 79–94.

Pekkarinen, J. and Vartiainen, J. 1993. *Suomen talouspolitiikan pitkä linja* (Finnish Economic Policy in the Long Run). Helsinki: WSOY.

Ringen, S. 1987. *The Possibility of Politics.* Oxford: Clarendon Press.

Ritakallio, V.-M. 1994. *Köyhyys Suomessa 1981–1990: Tutkimus tulonsiirtojen köyhyyttä poistavista vaikutuksista* (Poverty in Finland 1981–1990: A Study of Effects of Income Transfers). Helsinki: STAKES.

Rowthorn, B. 1989. 'Corporatism and Labor Market Performance'. Työväen Taloudellinen Tutkimuslaitos. Tutkimusselosteita.

Sen, A. K. 1979. 'Issues in the Measurement of Poverty'. *Scandinavian Journal of Economics*, 81: 285–307.

Uusitalo, H. 1989. *Income Distribution in Finland.* Central Statistical Office of Finland, Helsinki.

1993. 'Tulonjaon muutokset Suomessa 1966–1991: Ensimmäisen lamavuoden vaikutukset' (Changes in Income Distribution 1966–1991: The Effects of the First Year of Recession), in *Hyvinvoinnin päätepysäkillä.* STAKES, raportteja 128, Helsinki.

15 Disparities in the economic well-being of Hungarian society from the late 1970s to the 1980s

ÖDÖN ÉLTETÖ

1   Introduction

This study concentrates on changes in and factors contributing to income inequality in the late 1970s and the 1980s, in some cases also touching upon earlier periods. To provide some background and a broader context to the main object of the study, it seems expedient to begin by sketching briefly a few essential features of the Hungarian economy in the period considered.

Until 1990, Hungary was a so-called socialist country. Although its economic and social policies were far more liberal than those in other socialist countries of the time – expressed by the saying of that time that Hungary was the merriest barrack in the socialist camp – its economy was a centrally planned economy differing basically from a market one and with all the essential characteristics of the former. One of these was the relatively high level of employment: in 1989 the activity rate was 53 per cent (nearly 57 per cent for men and 50 per cent for women), higher than in most EC countries and then especially for women (Kollányi 1993). Because there was practically no registered unemployment in Hungary until the end of the 1980s (the rate was a mere 0.3 per cent in 1989), the activity rate also expresses the level of employment. For decades the labour market was highly inelastic, in practice the number of people in employment changing only on account of demographic factors. As a result, labour productivity declined in periods of economic stagnation and improved somewhat in line with economic prosperity. Moreover, the small changes in the rate of employment had almost no real effect on disparities in earnings or in household income.

In the second half of the 1970s, it became increasingly evident that the Hungarian economy had severe troubles, for it was clearly, fundamentally malfunctioning. The government at that time tried to protect the domestic economy from the effects of repeated oil price shocks, but considering that a rather large part of Hungarian GDP was, and still is, realised through foreign trade, the government's attempts could not succeed. Thus, in spite of borrowing more funds abroad and thereby incurring heavy debts for the country, the government could not avoid exposing Hungarian society to the much-abused phenomenon of capitalism, inflation. Inflation in Hungary lagged in time and in extent most European market economies. After several decades of the yearly consumer price index (CPI) totalling at most a few per cent, in 1979 and 1980 the CPI reached about 9 per cent and in 1988 and 1989 exceeded 10 per cent, ending at 16 per cent and 12.5 per cent, respectively. The grave problems of the economy forced the government to introduce a restrictive economic policy towards the end of the 1970s which continued, with respite for a few years, through the following decade. Because the level of and changes in wages were centrally regulated, one of the consequences of the restrictive economic policy was that wages generally increased at a slower pace than the CPI, resulting in a decrease in real wages, except for three years in the 1980s. In 1989, the level of wages was only about 80 per cent of that in 1978. The real value (purchasing power) of pensions and other social income also decreased in that period.

However, most households did not want to lower their living standards and therefore pursued activities to supplement their earnings from wages at their main employment or from social benefits in cash. In the 1980s, particularly from 1982 when certain private and semi-private enterprises and other initiatives were legally accepted or at least tolerated, there were quite a number of opportunities for earning supplementary income. Thanks primarily to these increased opportunities for supplementary incomes, the real value of all incomes from work did not decrease until 1988, despite decreasing real wages, and in 1987 per capita real disposable income of the population exceeded that in 1977 by 12 per cent. During this decade, disposable income grew somewhat more slowly in the first five-year period than in the second (4.7 per cent compared with 6.7 per cent).

Another characteristic feature of centrally planned economies was the generally minor role played by the private sector in the economy. Consequently, income from self-employment outside agriculture and particularly from capital accounted for only a small portion of the disposable income of the population. Although Hungary was not typical of socialist countries in this respect, especially from the mid 1980s on, in 1989 gross incomes from small private enterprise outside agriculture constituted only 7.1 per cent of all gross income of households and a similar proportion, 7.5 per cent, originated from small private farms. Incomes from capital were practically confined to interest on savings, and only the balance of interest received and paid by households was accounted for as income.

2   Data sources

More than 30 years ago, the Hungarian Central Statistical Office (HCSO) began its series of quinquennial Household Income Surveys (HIS). The HIS were carried out during the first three months in each year ending in 3 or 8 to collect income data referring to the preceding 12 months. They were large-scale surveys, the sample size ranging from 15,000 to 27,000 households and covering the entire population living in private households, including, for most of the surveys, the households of professional members of the armed forces.

As most of the statements in the present study are based on the data of the HIS, it seems expedient to outline briefly their major characteristics.

One of the most essential characteristics of the HIS is that for employed and cooperative member earners, earnings and some other data collected through interviewing selected households were complemented by more precise and quite reliable equivalent data supplied by employers. Having reliable data on earnings enriched greatly the possibilities of analysis, partly for earning distributions, partly for investigating the correlation between earnings and family incomes.

A further characteristic of the HIS is worth mentioning. In addition to asking households about their income from all possible sources, the HCSO asked questions about the utilisation of educational, health care, recreational, cultural and social facilities rendered free of charge or at reduced prices, as well as about the possible fees households may have paid for such use. Using the corresponding macrostatistical amounts and the so-called impact-incident approach,[1] it was possible to estimate the value of such in-kind social benefits obtained by each household in the sample. Thus, income differences could be analysed not only on the basis of disposable income but also for total income including the value of in-kind social benefits.

HIS have of course been voluntary. Nevertheless, we experienced rather favourable response rates; even in 1988 the refusal rate was less than 5 per cent.

Finally, it must be noted that, for many reasons, the type of income surveys described briefly above could not be continued without essential modifications after the fundamental changes in Hungary's economic and social system. Thus, the circumstances for the HIS carried out in 1992 were quite different and required new methodology, such as no longer collecting data on earnings from employers. Although the final results of this most recent HIS are not yet available, we know that total non-response increased to 20 per cent, including a 12 per cent rate of refusal, and that agreement between macro- and microstatistical income levels is far from being as good as previously.

As in any normal economy, in Hungary wages and salaries constitute the bulk of household income. Moreover, the distribution of household incomes is substantially affected by that of earnings. Concerning gross earnings, the HCSO commands rather detailed and reliable information covering more than three decades based on the biennial Earnings Surveys (ES) carried out in September. Unlike the HIS, these surveys have been enterprise-type surveys, i.e., enterprises and cooperatives (all of them until 1990) supplied data on the number of their employees (from 1978, full-time employees) classified by sex falling into the given size categories of gross earnings paid in the reference month.

Atkinson and Micklewright (1992) analyse the characteristics of the earnings distribution in Hungary, together with those of some other former socialist countries, in detail. Here I will only touch upon those aspects relevant to the topic of the study.

In the following, disposable household income refers to income essentially as defined in United Nations recommendations (United Nations 1977), except in section 6 where the notion of total income is also used. As in most household surveys, HIS disposable income does not include employers' contributions to social security schemes or the value of imputed rent of owner-occupied dwellings. The income unit in most Hungarian income studies is the individual, i.e., distributions and disparities in per capita income are shown and compared. However, the publications of the HCSO containing the results of the HIS always show income differentials on a household equivalent unit basis, too.[2] It must be noted, however, that many authors around the world use per capita income in their analyses of income differentials (e.g., Atkinson and Micklewright 1992; Podder 1993). Furthermore, I share the opinion of authors claiming household income, i.e., considering the household as the income unit, is inappropriate for characterising the economic well-being of households of different sizes.

To characterise the inequality of an income or earnings distribution in addition to the corresponding decile distribution, certain inequality measures are used in this study. These are the Hungarian Inequality Measure (HIM), which is the ratio of the average income of those above the mean to the average income of those below the mean (Atkinson and Micklewright 1992, p. 112; Éltető and Frigyes 1968); E, the so-called maximum equalisation percentage; v, the coefficient of variation in per cent; and T, the income-weighted Theil inequality measure. E represents that percentage of total income which, if transferred from decile groups with shares exceeding 10 per cent to those with shares less than 10 per cent, would achieve complete equality.

3   Trends in earnings and income inequality in the 1970s and 1980s

Economic policy in Hungary affected not only the general standard of living of the population but also earnings and income differentials. After the introduction of the New Economic Mechanism in 1968, earnings and incomes became less equal. However, this was not tolerated for long by certain leftist party leaders. Thus, a counteroffensive took place in the early 1970s. As a result, egalitarian tendencies revived, and after 1972 inequalities in earnings and income began to decrease again, reaching their lowest point around 1980. Considering the fact that the correlation between the earnings of an earner and the per capita income of his/her household was rather loose in this period according to HIS data (the value of the correlation coefficient between the two variables was only 0.35 in 1977 and 1982), it is rather interesting that the inequalities tended to change similarly: a decrease in the 1970s and an increase in the 1980s.

The trend in disparities of earnings is clearly shown in figure 15.1. The figure shows changes in the coefficient of variation of gross earnings in the period 1972–90 on the basis of ES data, as well as those from the HIS for the years 1972, 1977, 1982 and 1987. From 1977 on, the concept of gross earnings and the reference group (full-time employees and cooperative member earners) are more or less identical in the two types of surveys. It must be noted, however, that the dispersions of gross earnings in 1988 and 1990 are not directly comparable with those for earlier years. Until 1988, earnings of employees and members of cooperatives were not taxed but had a contribution to pension funds deducted. The rate of this contribution varied in a rather narrow range: first between 3 per cent and 10 per cent, then in the 1980s from 3 per cent to 15 per cent. Consequently, there was not too much difference between the dispersions of gross and net earnings. In the 1987 HIS, for example, the coefficient of variation was 0.443 for both types of earnings.

The situation changed fundamentally in 1988 when the personal income tax (PIT) system was introduced. The contribution to pension funds was then standardised at 10 per cent. On the other hand, marginal tax rates varied between 0 per cent and 60 per cent. In January 1988, wages and salaries from main employment were increased – grossed up – to compensate for tax deductions, i.e., in such a way that net earnings remained as before. That explains mostly the jump in the coefficient of variation of gross earnings in 1988 from previous years.

As mentioned earlier, income inequality changed in a manner similar to earnings disparities in the period under study.

Similar to earnings, disparities in incomes were markedly higher in 1972 than in 1967 but began to decrease again in the mid 1970s, reaching a low point in 1982. The economic stagnation of the 1980s combined with much wider opportunities for extra earnings in the legal and shadow economies led again to more greatly dispersed incomes. Hence, income differentials in 1987 considerably exceeded even those of 1972.

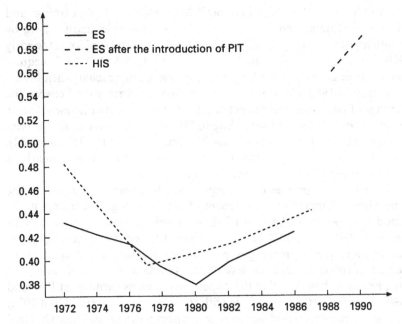

Figure 15.1 Trends in the coefficient of variation of gross earnings

These tendencies can clearly be seen in table 15.1, which includes the quintile distributions of per capita disposable incomes in four different years, household equivalent disposable incomes in three years, the share of the extreme deciles and the upper 5 per cent as well as some inequality measures.

Two further, major conclusions can be drawn from the figures above. First, although the decrease in inequality from 1977 to 1982 was slight and appears primarily in the greater shares of the bottom two deciles, the increase during the next five years is more remarkable, when chiefly the upper part of the distribution became more unequal. This can be attributed partly to increased differentials in earnings from main employment but, perhaps to an even greater extent, is also owing to the highly unequal opportunities for income from secondary activities. Data clearly show that in the mid 1980s, the number and proportion of persons (primarily men) performing extra work on auxiliary farms and outside agriculture increased considerably. Moreover, not only did the number of those performing income-supplementing work increase, but the average time devoted to such work also rose. According to the data of two time budget surveys carried out in 1976 and 1986, between those two years the time devoted by men to income-supplementing work increased nearly 25 per cent, and for certain

Table 15.1 *Shares of quintile (decile) groups of persons ordered according to household per capita and equivalent unit income from total disposable income*

	Household						
	Per capita income				Equivalent unit income		
	1972	1977	1982	1987	1977	1982	1987
1st decile	4.0	4.5	4.9	4.5	4.7	5.3	4.6
1st quintile	9.9	10.8	11.3	10.5	11.2	12.2	10.7
2nd quintile	14.9	15.4	15.4	14.6	15.7	16.3	14.7
3rd quintile	18.6	18.7	18.4	17.9	18.8	19.1	17.9
4th quintile	22.9	22.7	22.6	22.3	22.6	22.4	22.2
5th quintile	33.7	32.3	32.3	34.7	31.7	30.2	34.4
10th decile	19.7	18.6	18.6	20.9	18.2	17.1	20.7
Top 5 per cent	11.5	10.6	10.6	12.5	9.5	9.6	12.3
HIM	1.96	1.84	1.82	1.99	1.68	1.66	2.00
E	16.6	15.0	14.9	17.0	14.3	12.6	16.6
v	47.4	41.5	40.2	48.1	36.5	36.5	47.4
T	0.0967	0.0772	0.0731	0.1029	0.0570	0.0540	0.0870

Sources: Hungarian Central Statistical Office 1980, 1985 and 1990.

social groups (e.g., skilled and semi-skilled workers), the increase was almost 250 per cent (Babarczy, Harcsa and Pääkkönen 1991).

Furthermore, it is worth noting that the introduction of the personal income tax system in 1988 resulted in a decrease in net income from secondary jobs, at least in the observable economy, partly because the marginal tax rate on such incomes fell in the highest category for the persons concerned, and partly because many persons gave up performing extra work in such income-supplementing jobs or switched to the shadow economy, thus entirely evading taxes on such income.

There is further support for the argument that the remarkable increase in income inequality between 1982 and 1987 was primarily attributable to increased dispersions of earnings from main employment and secondary earning activities. Among inactive households, i.e., households without an active earner and thus in which earnings play but a minor role in income, income disparities increased only slightly during this period, while income disparities increased among active households to a greater extent than among all households. The data of table 15.2 below corroborate this statement.

The tendency of greater income disparities in the second half of the 1980s

Table 15.2 *Quintile distributions of per capita disposable income in households with and without an active earner*

	Households with active earners		Household without active earner	
	1982	1987	1982	1987
1st decile	4.9	4.4	4.9	5.0
1st quintile	11.3	10.3	11.4	11.4
2nd quintile	15.4	14.4	15.4	15.2
3rd quintile	18.6	17.9	18.4	18.2
4th quintile	22.6	22.3	22.6	22.1
5th quintile	32.1	35.1	32.2	33.1
top decile	18.5	21.1	18.6	19.5
top 5 per cent	10.5	12.7	10.6	11.4
HIM	1.81	2.01	1.81	1.85
v	39.9	49.0	40.0	43.5

Sources: Hungarian Central Statistical Office, 1985 and 1990.

appears in increased dispersion in income distributions as well as in larger relative income differences between various social groups. For example, the difference between the income levels of two extreme groups, households of leaders and of unskilled workers, increased from 66 per cent in 1982 to 85 per cent in 1987. Similarly, the income level of households of skilled workers exceeded that of unskilled workers by 10 percentage points more in 1987 than in 1982 (27 per cent compared with 17 per cent).

4   Sources of differences in income

When investigating sources of income differences in Hungary during the period under review, it should be pointed out that income inequality was brought about only to a rather limited extent by differentials in earnings from main employment.

Before quantifying the contributions of various sources of income inequality, I will present a few characteristics of the decile groups and what changes took place in these characteristics, because these data also throw light on the sources of income inequality. Characteristics of the deciles of per capita disposable income are shown in tables 15.3–15.5.

Comparing the figures in table 15.1 and table 15.3, we can conclude that in all three years inequality in earnings was smaller than inequality in household income. While the ratio of the average income of the top decile

Table 15.3 *Average earnings from the main job as a percentage of the average*[a]

Deciles of per capita disposable income	1977	1982	1987
1	76.7	74.8	71.5
2	86.8	83.2	79.6
3	89.6	87.8	84.6
4	93.0	90.6	87.6
5	93.4	92.7	92.2
6	96.1	96.2	93.7
7	96.1	98.8	98.6
8	100.6	102.6	103.9
9	104.1	105.3	111.3
10	123.7	127.3	139.0

Note:
[a] Average earnings from main employment for employees and cooperative members who are active earners in each respective decile group.
Sources: Hungarian Central Statistical Office, 1980, 1985 and 1990; some unpublished tables from each respective HIS.

to that of the bottom decile was 3.4, 3.1 and 4.0 in the three years, the corresponding ratio of average earnings was only 1.6, 1.7 and 1.9, respectively. These data also show that earnings differentials were not the most important source of dispersion in incomes during the period under review, although their importance surely grew somewhat from 1977 to 1987.

The figures in table 15.4 exhibit much greater differences between low- and high-income households with respect to the number of dependants per 100 households, especially in 1977 and 1982 and when taking into account only dependants under 15 years of age. In 1982, for example, 124 children under 15 lived in 100 households in the bottom decile group, while the figure was only ten for the top decile. Even considering all dependants, the difference in the average number of dependants in a household between the two extreme deciles was a multiple of 6.7 in 1977, 8.9 in 1982 and 4.2 in 1987. The completely different demographic composition of households in the bottom and top deciles is reflected even more markedly by the so-called earner–dependant ratio, i.e., the number of dependants per 100 active earners. In the bottom decile, 100 active earners were responsible for 283 dependants in 1977, in the top decile 100 earners were only responsible for 13 dependants. Thus, in this respect the difference between the extreme deciles was almost 22-fold. Still, in 1987 the relative difference in the

Table 15.4 *Household composition and size in decile groups*

	Average household size			Active earners			Inactive earners			Other household members		
Deciles	1977	1982	1987	1977	1982	1987	1977	1982	1987	1977	1982	1987
1	2.80	3.26	3.25	0.52	0.77	0.88	0.81	0.72	0.67	1.47	1.77	1.71
2	3.01	2.95	2.89	0.81	0.86	0.93	0.86	0.81	0.76	1.34	1.29	1.19
3	3.15	3.13	2.90	1.07	1.10	1.04	0.79	0.72	0.79	1.28	1.31	1.07
4	3.23	3.14	2.92	1.27	1.21	1.18	0.68	0.72	0.78	1.28	1.23	0.96
5	3.16	3.12	2.87	1.39	1.34	1.25	0.67	0.68	0.78	1.10	1.10	0.84
6	3.16	3.08	2.84	1.56	1.42	1.35	0.59	0.71	0.76	1.01	0.96	0.73
7	3.00	2.92	2.79	1.61	1.47	1.45	0.59	0.66	0.68	0.80	0.78	0.66
8	2.90	2.89	2.67	1.76	1.59	1.44	0.50	0.65	0.70	0.65	0.65	0.52
9	2.64	2.56	2.56	1.80	1.63	1.56	0.43	0.54	0.54	0.42	0.37	0.46
10	2.23	2.19	2.39	1.69	1.59	1.54	0.32	0.40	0.43	0.22	0.20	0.41
All	2.89	2.89	2.79	1.36	1.32	1.28	0.61	0.65	0.68	0.92	0.91	0.83

Sources: See table 15.3.

earner–dependant ratio between the two extreme deciles was more than sevenfold.

Throughout the period, the bottom decile consisted predominantly of families with three or more children (or one-parent families with children) and of pensioner households, while the top decile consisted mostly of active households without dependent children or at most with one child. This situation is also naturally reflected in the structure of incomes by major source. As shown in table 15.5, for the bottom decile only 51–56 per cent of income originated from work, but a very high proportion, 44–48 per cent, consisted of social income in cash (pensions, family allowances, etc.). In the top decile, on the other hand, the bulk of income (84–88 per cent) was related to work, and only 11–13 per cent to social income in cash.

The rapid decrease in the number of dependants per 100 active earners over decile groups points to one of the most characteristic features of the income distribution in Hungary in past decades, namely that the lion's share of income inequality was brought about by differences in the demographic composition of households. Before quantifying the contribution of such differences to income inequality, it seems expedient to present an important aspect of the topic: relative income differences between groups of households classified by the number of dependent children under 19. It is preferable to express these differences on the basis of equivalent unit income, i.e., using the equivalence scale mentioned earlier, because here

Table 15.5 *The structure of incomes in the deciles*

	Per cent of total disposable income from								
	Employment			Other income from work			Social benefits in cash		
Deciles	1977	1982	1987	1977	1982	1987	1977	1982	1987
1	32.2	35.8	37.9	19.1	18.3	17.8	47.5	44.5	44.2
2	42.5	42.1	41.6	19.1	18.2	18.0	37.1	38.1	38.7
3	47.7	47.0	44.5	20.5	20.6	19.6	30.5	31.2	34.7
4	53.2	48.5	47.0	21.1	21.9	20.4	24.7	28.4	31.5
5	54.3	51.4	49.1	21.6	22.2	21.5	22.9	25.4	28.3
6	58.2	51.8	50.7	21.2	23.6	22.4	19.5	23.7	26.1
7	57.6	53.5	53.0	23.5	23.8	23.7	18.1	22.0	22.3
8	61.4	53.3	52.3	23.0	26.0	25.1	14.7	20.1	22.0
9	62.7	57.8	54.4	25.1	24.6	28.1	13.5	17.2	16.6
10	59.7	56.7	45.3	28.0	27.0	42.2	11.1	13.3	11.0
All	55.7	51.9	48.5	22.9	24.0	26.9	20.3	23.3	23.5

Sources: See table 15.3.

income per person clearly exaggerates differences in economic well-being. Moreover, relative differences are shown within active households, i.e., households with at least one active earner, since only a few per cent of dependent children under 19 live in pensioners' households. Table 15.6 shows these relative income differences expressed as a percentage of the mean income of households without dependent children together with the weights of the various groups.

As can be seen in table 15.6, the disadvantage of households with up to three children increased somewhat from 1977 to 1982, while in the following period their relative income positions improved slightly.

5   Major factors contributing to income inequality

It has always been a challenge for researchers of income distributions to investigate and try to quantify the major factors giving rise to income inequality and how the role of these factors in bringing about inequality changes over time and is affected by various economic circumstances. One possible means of investigation consists in the decomposition of the inequality measure into between-group and within-group inequality. This can be done most conveniently (Bourguignon 1979) using Theil's income or population-weighted entropy inequality coefficients T and L, respectively.

Table 15.6 *Relative income differences between and weight of active households grouped by the number of dependent children under 19 years of age*

Number of dependent children under 19	Average household equivalent income in per cent of the average of childless households			Percentage share of the groups in the population of all households with active earner		
	1977	1982	1987	1977	1982	1987
0	100.0	100.0	100.0	32.9	29.4	30.8
1	85.3	83.1	86.5	28.3	26.8	26.8
2	78.5	75.7	80.5	29.0	33.2	32.7
3	67.5	65.9	67.7	6.6	7.5	7.3
4 and more	49.1	51.3	51.3	3.2	3.1	2.4
All active households	86.9	83.2	87.4	100.0	100.0	100.0

Sources: Hungarian Statistical Office 1980, 1985 and 1990.

Using $T(G)$ to denote the between-group part of T $100T(G)/T$ can be considered as the contribution in per cent of characteristics used for the classification of total inequality.

We used quite a number of characteristics to classify and cross-classify households and calculated the decomposition of the inequality T. Unfortunately, the calculations were not performed for exactly the same factors or cross-classifications in the three years considered. Hence, table 15.7 only shows those results which proved, either in themselves or in cross-classification, rather relevant and were available for at least two of the three years. The number of groups is indicated in parentheses, because the contribution of a given factor to inequality is also affected by the number of groups into which the households were classified. The various factors are denoted by capital letters, thus AB denotes cross-classification by factors A and B, and so on.

Classification characteristics

A: average net earnings of active earners in the household from the main job (11)
B: number of household members (6)
C: number of active earners in the household (4)
D: type of activity of the head of household (12)

F: number of dependants under 19 (5)
H: type of household by size and composition (22)
I: age of the head of household (12)

Although the decomposition calculations were carried out for all households, it turned out that income inequality for inactive households is brought about mostly by different factors than for active households. Thus, we gain a clearer understanding and the results are easier to interpret if we deal with these two basic population groups separately. Consequently, table 15.7 presents some selected results for active households. For 1977 and 1982, only the decomposition of the inequality of per capita income is available. For 1987, though, both per capita and equivalent unit income inequalities were decomposed. The maxima of contributions of single factors, double factors, etc. to inequality are enhanced in the table.

Table 15.7 shows the contribution to inequality of all single factors considered, although in certain cases they were not too significant. The number of active earners (factor C), for example, differentiates to a small and decreasing extent the per capita (or equivalent unit) income level of the households only contributing a few per cent to inequality. However, cross-classifying households by their size (B), too, considerably increases the income differentiating effect of both single factors, because the number of members and active earners in the household determines its earner–dependant ratio, which in turn proved to be one of the most important factors inducing income inequality during the period or at least until the mid 1980s (as pointed out in connection with table 15.4).

Studying the results of the inequality decomposition presented in table 15.7, it is remarkable that factors representing various aspects of the demographic composition of the households, namely F, H and BC, seem to have been rather decisive in bringing about income disparities in 1977 and 1982. It is especially conspicuous that income differences between only five groups formed by the number of dependent children under 19 explained almost 40 per cent of total per capita income inequality in 1977 and 1982.

On further examination of table 15.7, perhaps the changes from 1982 to 1987 are most striking. In 1982, almost two-fifths of income inequality could be attributed to differences in the average incomes of groups formed by one single factor (F or H), nearly three-fifths to differences in group averages formed by two factors (AF), almost two-thirds by three factors (ACF) and nearly three-quarters of the inequality could be explained by income differences between groups formed by four out of the six factors considered (ABCD). In 1987, though, proportions of the inequality explained by single or joint factors are considerably lower. This can be accounted for partly by the considerable increase in income inequality from

Table 15.7 *Per cent contribution of certain single and joint factors to the inequality of per capita (equivalent unit) disposable income – economically active households*

	Per capita income			Equivalent unit income 1987
Factors	1977	1982	1987	
A	11.6	17.7	**21.9**	**25.7**
B	24.5	24.6	15.0	6.7
C	5.3	3.5	1.3	0.8
D	9.3	10.4	9.3	10.5
F	**38.1**	**39.2**	20.8	9.2
H	–	39.2	21.9	9.9
I	14.8	18.0	9.2	3.9
AB	37.4	41.3	35.8	31.5
AF	**53.3**	**57.1**	**43.8**	**35.6**
BC	43.6	41.7	23.5	–
DF	47.5	48.5	31.0	20.2
ABD	44.3	49.0	41.4	37.6
ACF	**61.0**	**65.0**	**48.3**	39.1
ADF	58.0	61.8	47.9	**40.2**
AFI	–	62.4	47.4	38.9
CDF	51.5	52.7	–	–
ABCD	–	**73.3**	55.7	46.9
ACDF	**65.7**	70.8	53.6	45.6
ADFI	–	70.9	**56.6**	**49.6**

1982 to 1987 but perhaps even more by the previously mentioned fact that in the second half of the 1980s there were many opportunities to supplement earnings from main employment with income from secondary jobs or various earning activities in the shadow economy. These supplementary earnings surely contributed to the higher dispersion of incomes but are not represented directly by any of the factors considered (factor A reflects differences in earnings from the main job only).

Nevertheless, the dispersion of earnings from the main job was also distinctly greater in 1987 than previously, resulting in a considerably more significant contribution to income inequality than in 1982 and especially in 1977. As can be seen from table 15.7, among the single factors taken into consideration in 1987 differences in per capita incomes of groups of households classified by the average level of earnings (from the main job) – together with those between types of households – contributed most to the inequality of per capita income and by far the most to that of equivalent unit income, though still not as much as demographic factors had in the previous two sample years. These results greatly agree, by the way, with the inferences drawn from the information in tables 15.3 and 15.4.

6   The effect of in-kind social benefits on the income distribution

As mentioned earlier, in the HIS households are also asked about the use of various educational, health care and other facilities rendered free of charge or at reduced prices, so income differences could be investigated on the basis not only of disposable income, but also of total income including the value of in-kind benefits utilised. There is no doubt that total income is a better approximation than disposable income of the economic well-being of a household or group of households, especially if the former considerably exceeds the latter. During the period investigated, total income exceeded disposable income 13–15 per cent in Hungary.

The bulk of these benefits consisted of educational and health care services. For the total population, free-of-charge educational services accounted for 41–42 per cent of the value of all in-kind benefits during the period, while health services represented 29–31 per cent.

It is characteristic that the value of health services is distributed rather evenly over income groups while the value share of educational services utilised decreased with increasing income level in 1987, after first slightly increasing then rapidly decreasing in the previous years. This behaviour of in-kind educational benefits is connected with the previously mentioned fact that better-off households have fewer dependent children than do low- or medium-income households.

Within the total population there are significant differences between economically active and inactive households with respect to the importance of educational and health services utilised and the effect of all social benefits on the income distribution. Quite understandably, for inactive households educational services represent but a small part of in-kind social benefits, between 9 per cent and 12 per cent during the period considered. Such benefits amounted to 45–48 per cent of the total value of social benefits for active households. On the other hand, the use of health care facilities presents quite a different picture. The average value of health care services for inactive households was more than double that of active ones. Consequently, the share of health care services in all in-kind benefits varied between 57 per cent and 66 per cent in the case of inactive households but was only around 26 per cent for active households.

Overall, benefits play a levelling role in the income distribution. However, this equalising effect is rather restricted in the case of inactive households, since it is more or less the result of adding a constant (the value of health services) to disposable income. In-kind social benefits are more effective in reducing income inequality among active households, because here primarily the value of educational services exhibits a rather strong negative correlation with disposable income. Even for the whole population, though, total income is considerably more evenly distributed than disposable income.

7   Present situation

In 1990, the transition from a centrally planned to a market economy began with remarkable growth of the private sector, restructuring of the entire economy and increasing unemployment. Moreover, a personal income tax system was introduced in 1988, almost all price subsidies were gradually abolished and the rather high CPI has made living conditions hard for the majority of the population. The decline of average economic well-being is well illustrated by the figures below, showing the trend in the real value of per capita disposable income in the population since 1987.

1987	1988	1989	1990	1991	1992	1993	1994	1995
100.0	99.1	101.8	100.8	97.6	95.6	89.9	93.7	88.2

The various factors mentioned above had distinct rearranging effects on the income distribution of households. To estimate these effects, microsimulation methods were applied to the individual records of the 1987 HIS in an attempt to update its income data for subsequent years. However, because of fundamental changes in a great number of factors affecting the income distribution,[3] changes in income differentials could not be followed up after 1990. Thus, although there is general agreement that the inequality of incomes must have increased considerably from 1987, in the absence of reliable data on the present situation we can only guess the extent of the increase.

In 1992, the Social Research Informatics Center on cooperation with the Sociological Department of the Economic University of Budapest initiated a Panel Household Survey on a sample of 2,000 households. Although with respect to the income distribution for a given year the results of this survey are not sufficiently reliable and are not directly comparable with data of former HIS done by the HCSO, the dynamics in the income disparities obtained from successive rounds of the survey can be considered rather well founded. According to the results of the 1992–1995 rounds, income inequality stopped increasing in 1993, but increased again afterwards.

However, the main concern is not the growing dispersion of incomes but the spread of poverty. According to data from the 1988 income survey, less than 10 per cent of the population lived below the official poverty line in 1987. For some years, the HCSO regularly (recently as often as monthly) calculates and publishes the poverty line – the so-called subsistence level – for quite a number of types of households living in Budapest, country towns and villages.[4] The published poverty lines are more or less accepted, but there is hot debate concerning the number of people living below or around the subsistence level. The number is certainly larger than in 1987, but a more exact answer can only be obtained based on reliable data on the present income distribution. Because such data are currently unavailable, we can only make estimates. According to statistical estimates, by mid 1992 the number of people living below the poverty line could have increased to 1.6 million (15.6 per cent of the total population), and in 1993 this number was likely to have been roughly 2 million.

In the light of the findings on the sources of income inequality it is not so surprising that there is a rather strong relationship between the number of children in the household and the proportion of those living below the poverty line. While in 1992 this proportion was only 9 per cent in the case of childless households and 15–16 per cent of those bringing up one child only, it amounted to 21 per cent from the population of households with two children, to 35 per cent of those with three children and nearly half of the population of households with four or more children.

One further problem is to be mentioned in this connection. Presently a rather huge amount of income of the households originates from the shadow economy and tax evasion (primarily through over-reporting production costs). These incomes cannot be observed in statistical surveys should they use any kind of sophisticated method. Consequently only if tax morals as well as the willingness of the society to co-operate in household surveys improves considerably can we hope to obtain reliable data again on the real income differences through income surveys.

Appendix Equivalence scales used in Hungarian HIS

1977 and 1982		1987	
Child under 4	0.4	Child under 3	0.45
Child aged 4–6	0.5	Child aged 3–5	0.5
Child at school, aged 7–10	0.6	Child aged 6–10	0.6
Child not at school, aged 7–13	0.7	Child aged 11–14	0.7
Dependant above retirement age	0.7	Child aged 15–18	0.95
Child at school, aged 11–13	0.8	Economically active person	1
Retired person	0.8	Inactive person below retirement age	0.9
Any other persons	1	Inactive person above retirement age	0.8
Addition for head of household	0.4	Addition for head of household	0.2

Notes

1 The macrostatistical amount corresponding to the sample is distributed among the households according to the reported extent (frequency) of utilisation.
2 The equivalence scales used in 1977, 1982 and 1987 are shown in the appendix.
3 Such fundamental changes include the introduction of personal income tax in 1988; the rapid rise in the rate of unemployment from 1990 on, varying greatly by region, branch of industry, age and occupation; and considerable changes in various income sources, with wages and salaries decreasing and income from self-employment and property increasing.
4 The HCSO poverty lines represent the cost of a prescribed subsistence food basket plus allowances for housing costs and other non-food expenses. Subsistence food expenditure is based on a weekly menu for each season meeting the different dietary intake level requirements of active adults, children and pensioners established by the National Research Institute of Dietetics. These various baskets were valued at average national 1989 quarterly prices and aggregated to get minimum annual food expenditure. Next, the 1989 Household Budget Survey was used to identify a group of households with food expenditures in the range of 20 per cent below and above the subsistence food expenditures. These households were then differentiated into various groups according to activity, location of residence and demographic characteristics. Allowances for housing and other expenses were then calculated for each household group based on their actual expenditure. Differentiated monthly CPIs are used to update these 1989 poverty lines.

Because the disposable income of the population increased at a slower pace than the CPI in recent years, each year the average poverty line, which in 1989 amounted to 54 per cent of the mean income, represents a higher percentage of the latter.

References

Atkinson, A. B. and Micklewright, J. 1992. *Economic Transformation in Eastern Europe and the Distribution of Income*. Cambridge: Cambridge University Press.

Babarczy, Á., Harcsa, I. and Pääkkönen, Hannu. 1991. *Time Use Trends in Finland and in Hungary*. Helsinki: Central Statistical Office of Finland.

Bourguignon, F. 1979. Decomposable Income Inequality Measures. *Econometrica*, 47, no. 4: 901–20.

Bruinooge, G., Éltetö, Ö., Fajth, G. and Grubben, B. 1990. 'Income Distributions in an International Perspective – The Case of Hungary and the Netherlands'. *Statistical Journal of the UN ECE*, 7: 39–53.

Éltetö, Ö. 1992. 'The Unified System of Household Surveys in Hungary'. Paper presented at the TES Seminar, International Comparison of Survey Methodologies, 30 March–1 April, Athens.

Éltetö, Ö. and Frigyes, E. 1968. 'New Income Inequality Measures as Efficient Tools for Causal Analysis and Planning'. *Econometrica*, 36, 2: 383–96.

Hungarian Central Statistical Office. 1980. 'The Level and Distribution of House-hold Incomes in 1977' (in Hungarian).
    1985. 'The Level and Distribution of Household Incomes in 1982' (in Hungarian).
    1990. 'Income Distribution in Hungary' (in Hungarian).
Kollányi, M. 1993. 'Employment, Unemployment, Labour Productivity'. *Statistical Review* (Periodical of the Hungarian CSO), 71, 8–9: 638–50.
Podder, Nripesh. 1993. 'The Disaggregation of the Gini Coefficient by Factor Component and its Application to Australia'. *The Review of Income and Wealth,* 39, 1: 51–62.
United Nations. 1977. 'Provisional Guidelines on Statistics of the Distribution of Income, Consumption and Accumulation of Households'. Studies in Methods M, no. 61. New York.

16 The emergence of the labour market and earnings distribution: the case of the Czech Republic

JIŘÍ VEČERNÍK

1 Introduction

The re-introduction of labour markets in east-central Europe has created a new set of problems. On the demand side, harsh budgetary constraints have reappeared. On the supply side, skills acquired under the Communist regime are being transformed into marketable skills. On both sides, however, the drive towards market behaviour is burdened by many remnants of the past. 'Social employment' continues, even following formal privatisation. Lack of skills and adaptability, poor work habits and resistance to change are evident throughout the labour force.

The independence granted the Czechoslovak Republic in 1918 stressed values that strengthened the Czech economy and placed the new state among the 20 most advanced countries in the world. This legacy, however, was heavily undermined by the Communist regime, which reoriented manufacturing sectors from light to heavy industry and undermined the level of qualifications of the labour force. Fortunately, traditions and work commitment were not fully destroyed during that time. The return of capitalism to the Czech economy was facilitated by combining this legacy with the skilful implementation of economic reform and the maintenance of social peace.

In this contribution, I shall examine labour markets from the micro-perspective of individuals and households. First, I focus on the changing aspects of labour market participation and the vulnerability of the emerging market economy to unemployment. Second, I look at changes in human capital production and utilisation. Third, I examine changes in earnings distribution. And fourth, I present some attitudes reflecting the changing tolerance towards inequality in earnings. By exploring all these aspects, I seek to combine 'objective' and 'subjective' indicators by stressing the effects of institutions and values.

2   Work perspectives and unemployment

Under the Communist regime, the state bureaucracy kept the labour force under strict control, which began with the educational planning of future workers and ended with worker placement and detailed wage tariffs. The strict labour administration had several long-term consequences. On the one hand, the large supply of cheap labour sustained the technological backwardness and expansion of a large bureaucratic system. On the other hand, the utilisation of labour capacity was low as workers adapted to the lower requirements.

A characteristic feature of labour allocation in the command economies was a permanent shortage of labour resulting from the inefficient or even wasteful use of labour. There was generally a high employment rate in the Communist countries, especially the former Czechoslovakia, which boasted the highest employment rate for women in the world. Similarly, the private sector was virtually non-existent in the former Czechoslovakia, and the informal economy not nearly as important as that of Hungary or Poland. This served to increase the population's dependence on centrally administered work and job allocation.

With the introduction of market criteria, artificial overemployment, low qualification levels and the inefficient use of labour inevitably turned into unemployment. Thus, in the early 1990s unemployment appeared or increased across east-central Europe, although the unemployment rates and changes over time are extremely uneven among individual countries due to their varied economic background and pace of economic reform. The Czech Republic continues to have the lowest unemployment rate, which peaked at 4 per cent at the end of 1991 and then dropped to below 3 per cent.

Unemployment is influenced by various factors: the macroeconomic stability of the system, the ability to maintain export capacity, the absorption potential of new private businesses (especially in the tertiary sector) and the paternalistic behaviour of formerly state-owned companies. In the Czech Republic, economic reform was implemented relatively slowly and has thus far avoided bankruptcies. Private firms expanded suddenly, and a huge transfer from the secondary to the tertiary sector occurred. Despite the privatisation process, all big firms continue to hoard labour and practise 'capitalist paternalism' (Možný 1992).

The impending unemployment problem can be seen by examining employees' attitudes towards job security and towards their firms (table 16.1). At the end of 1991, a mere 20 per cent of economically active respondents in the Czech Republic regarded their firms as having good economic

Table 16.1 Expectations of respondent's employment perspectives (per cent)

	Perspective of			Fear of	Willingness to work for wage:	
	occupation 1	firm 2	qualifications 3	unemployment 4	lower 5	minimum 6
December 1991						
definitely yes	25.7	19.5	19.7	17.3	23.7	17.1
rather yes	36.3	35.1	37.5	25.6	45.0	30.8
rather no	26.2	28.8	29.3	34.8	18.1	23.9
definitely no	11.9	16.5	13.5	22.3	13.2	28.2
Total	100.0	100.0	100.0	100.0	100.0	100.0
January 1993						
definitely yes	27.7	22.4	22.4	14.0	17.3	7.4
rather yes	37.0	38.7	40.1	22.3	42.1	20.1
rather no	23.1	27.1	25.3	38.9	23.3	25.0
definitely no	12.2	11.8	12.2	24.8	17.3	47.5
Total	100.0	100.0	100.0	100.0	100.0	100.0
November 1993						
definitely yes	23.0	26.1	20.1	15.2		
rather yes	36.3	41.1	42.5	21.7		
rather no	27.8	23.2	25.7	40.6		
definitely no	13.0	9.7	11.6	22.5		
Total	100.0	100.0	100.0	100.0		

November 1994

definitely yes	33.6	26.1	33.3	9.8
rather yes	40.8	46.9	38.9	22.4
rather no	18.4	21.4	19.7	43.1
definitely no	7.3	5.6	8.0	24.7
Total	100.0	100.0	100.0	100.0

Notes:

Questions:

1 'Do you think the outlook for your occupation is good from the point of view of contemporary changes?'

2 'Do you think the outlook for your firm is good from the point of view of contemporary changes?'

3 'Do you think the outlook for your qualifications is good from the point of view of contemporary changes?'

4 'Do you fear unemployment?'

5 'If your job were in danger, would you be willing to work for a lower wage than you now have?'

6 'If your job were in danger, would you be willing to work for the minimum wage?'

Source: Economic Expectations and Attitudes, 1991–4 (population 25–60 years of age only).

prospects, and 26 per cent were optimistic about the prospects of their occupations. As a result, 17 per cent seriously feared the prospect of unemployment, and an additional 26 per cent feared it somewhat. Workers' confidence in keeping their jobs oscillated later, reaching the highest level at the end of 1994. This can be equated with the experience of steady demand for labour. More than 70 per cent of the Czech workforce is currently fairly optimistic about the future of their firms and occupations.

The flip side of the low unemployment rate and low fear of unemployment in the Czech Republic is pressure on wage growth and an unwillingness to work for a lesser wage. In December 1991, 24 per cent of Czech respondents were willing to work for a lower wage than they received to keep their jobs, and 17 per cent were even willing to accept the official minimum wage. These percentages have fallen significantly since then. The minimum wage has only changed slightly in nominal terms since then, thus lowering its real value considerably.

Future unemployment rates will be influenced by several contradictory tendencies. On the one hand, we might expect some increase in unemployment due to the ongoing privatisation of large state firms, which will probably be followed in some cases by bankruptcies, and 'social employment' will be considerably reduced. On the other hand, the ability and efforts of new private entrepreneurs to increase the number of jobs can be expected to rise. The number of firms involved in trade and services is still not sufficient, and the activities of large firms should be complemented by medium-sized firms that are more flexible in the consumer market.

3   The production and utilisation of human resources

Before World War II, Czechoslovakia had a highly qualified working class and creative intelligentsia. However, the population's high level of skill and education was considered a latent source of discontent and criticism of the Communist system. The pre-war system of differentiated schooling was therefore transformed into a unified one, and the emphasis on classical education was replaced by a mixture of ideology and pragmatic skills. Instead of the diploma, the working class's 'political sense' and 'university of life' were valued. Secondary education was emphasised as economically more practical and politically less dangerous than university training.

The heritage of a generally high cultural level, professionalism and the work ethic were systematically destroyed by the regime. Rather than the best workers, the most obedient and willing were rewarded, and respected professionals were replaced by freshly trained 'working class cadres'. Negative influences on human resources prevailed throughout three emigration waves (coming immediately after 1938, 1948 and 1968), because they affected the most qualified and committed people in particular. The general levels of culture, occupational skills and work ethic also diminished with the passing of time and natural demographic change.

Success in the competitive labour market requires certain dispositions and abilities suppressed under communism: competence, education, adaptability and aptness to mobility. The Communist system was based on pragmatic training and having one job for life. Professional occupations and intellectual work lost prestige, resulting in the divorce of school education and job rewards. Although education, ambition and hard work are now considered more important, the amount of utilisable human capital in market competition is seriously limited. This notwithstanding, measuring the current level of human capital is a task fraught with problems.

According to the original concept (Becker 1964; Mincer 1974), human capital can be increased by higher education and experience. However, most of the educational credentials in post-Communist societies did not impact marketable skills. Instead of schooling, people's views as to their qualifications' compatibility with the marketplace are more useful. In the Czech Republic, about one-third of the population is currently sure their skills meet the demands of new job opportunities. Detailed analysis has shown that younger and especially university-educated men are the most confident about their qualifications.

The Czech population seems quite receptive to being trained or working longer hours if the work will be better paid (table 16.2). The trend of this willingness is decreasing somewhat, a fact which corresponds to declining fears of unemployment. Towards the end of 1991, only 18 per cent of workers were resolute in taking managerial responsibilities, 45 per cent in working more and 38 per cent ready to undertake self-training. Whereas there is an increasing number of workers ready to assume managerial responsibility and a growing majority of people determined to work more, readiness to pursue new qualifications is declining slightly. Nevertheless, encouraging individual initiative might be considerably faster than reforming the educational system and awaiting the real change in educational levels of the population.

4   Work incentives and rewards

The range of earnings and income inequality in socialist countries has been small in comparison to Western countries (Atkinson and Micklewright 1992; Večerník 1991, 1995). The differences were extremely minimal in the former Czechoslovakia and have remained almost stable the past 30 years. Moreover, a levelling trend began during the Nazi occupation and continued after 1945, due to the post-war need for reconstruction and the

Table 16.2 *Willingness to work more and invest in one's own human capital (per cent) (non-retired employed and unemployed persons)*

	December 1991	January 1993	November 1993	November 1994
Manager				
definitely yes	18.2	26.7	25.1	27.5
probably yes	20.3	25.0	27.5	21.1
probably no	29.6	22.6	22.8	23.3
definitely no	31.9	25.7	24.6	28.2
Work more				
definitely yes	45.3	47.2	45.8	49.9
probably yes	30.6	33.0	34.2	30.0
probably no	13.6	10.3	12.2	11.2
definitely no	10.6	9.5	7.8	8.9
Self-training				
definitely yes	38.1	38.8	39.1	35.3
probably yes	31.9	35.1	37.0	36.8
probably no	19.2	13.9	13.7	15.9
definitely no	10.8	12.1	10.2	12.0
Learn language				
definitely yes	24.3	28.8	24.1	24.2
probably yes	27.7	29.8	31.0	25.7
probably no	24.2	24.2	24.8	23.9
definitely no	23.9	17.2	20.1	26.2
Count of number of activities (definitely yes)				
0	42.0	40.0	37.8	45.4
1	20.6	20.8	24.2	20.0
2	17.6	15.9	17.0	15.4
3	13.3	12.0	10.8	10.1
4	6.6	11.3	10.2	9.0

Notes:
Question:
If somebody were to offer you a job at twice the earnings, would you be willing to
(A) take a managerial position? (Manager)
(B) work 10 hours per day? (Work more)
(C) train for more than six months? (Self-training)
(D) learn a foreign language within one year? (Learn language)
Source: Economic Expectations and Attitudes, 1991–4.

overwhelming influence of socialist ideology. The most important changes, however, occurred during the Stalinist transformation of 1948–53, when restrictions on living standards were closely aligned with a militant stress on equalisation.

The first period of economic reform in the Czech Republic brought changes to the economic and social system that have both potentially equalising and de-equalising effects on earnings distribution. On the one hand, a minimum wage was introduced in 1991 and increased in 1992, representing 47 per cent of the average wage at the time. Moreover, in awarding cost-of-living-related wage increases, the common practice was to increase lower wages faster. Even now, wage growth is still regulated by the state establishing an actual ceiling. On the other hand, opportunities have multiplied for private entrepreneurship, employment with foreign firms and special managerial rewards.

East-central European countries shared a similar earnings distribution in the late 1980s, which was even more equalised in the former Czechoslovakia (table 16.3). The position of the top 10 per cent and 5 per cent of employees was highest in Hungary and lowest in Czechoslovakia. Recently, their relative positions have grown very fast in all the countries studied and reached their highest level again in Hungary. The most recent developments indicate that earnings differentials in the post-Communist societies are now nearly equal to the level of inequality visible in certain developed industrial countries in the West, such as Germany and Austria.

As data covering the period 1988–94 attest, the relative positions of the lowest categories were maintained while those of the highest categories have increased, with the highest 5 per cent increasing the most (table 16.4). It appears that the introduction of a minimum wage and a generous policy combating low wages has brought about a better relative position for the lowest income groups; at the same time, the possibility of higher earnings and wages offered by the private sector has induced a jump in the highest incomes and a general expansion of the income distribution range. The increase at the highest earnings levels is likely to reflect employees of foreign and international firms who have good knowledge of foreign languages and good managerial skills.

Returns to education systematically decreased in the former Czechoslovakia. As table 16.5 confirms, data from the most recent period have witnessed a certain valuation of human capital. Whereas in the late 1980s one year of schooling added only about 4 per cent to one's earnings in the former Czechoslovakia (less than in neighbouring countries), this figure increased to 5 per cent in the Czech Republic in 1992. In contrast, there was very little change in the returns to education in Slovakia.

Table 16.3 *Earnings distributions for east-central and western Europe, 1988–1992 (quantiles in percentage median and the decile ratio)*

	Percentile (per cent median)						Ratio 90/10
	5th	10th	25th	75th	90th	95th	
1988							
Czech R.[a]	53.8	60.0	74.4	118.9	143.8	162.5	2.40
Slovakia[a]	53.6	61.7	77.0	123.2	149.3	168.0	2.42
Hungary[b]	50.0	58.3	74.4	135.1	183.3	225.9	3.14
Poland[b]	55.4	62.7	78.2	126.3	163.3	191.6	2.60
E. Germany[d]		68.1	82.1	121.1	141.9		2.08
W. Germany[d]		62.5	78.3	129.7	173.1		2.77
Austria[f]		51			181		3.55
UK[b]	47.3	54.7	72.3	137.1	183.9	226.5	3.36
France[f]		65			194		2.98
1991/92							
Czech R.[a]	51.2	56.1	69.6	116.7	153.5	184.2	2.74
Slovakia[a]		68.1			170.5		2.50
Poland[c]		61.6	77.3	132.4	179.8	219.3	2.92
Hungary[e]	48.3	56.0	72.6	145.9	203.7	257.1	3.64
E. Germany[d]		69.6	82.9	123.8	159.4		2.29
Austria[f]		51			178		3.49
UK[b]	47.3	54.8	71.7	138.0	186.5	228.0	3.40
France[f]		65			196		3.02

Sources: [a] Microcensus 1989 and 1992.
[b] Atkinson and Micklewright 1992.
[c] Rutkowski 1994.
[d] Krueger and Pischke 1992.
[e] Personal communication from the Statistical Office.
[f] OECD *Employment Outlook* 1993.

Simultaneously, the effect of experience (years on the job) decreased considerably in both the Czech and Slovak Republics. Gender disparities, typical for former Czechoslovakia, also weakened considerably.

Industrial earnings differentials also changed during the 1989–93 period. As table 16.6 shows, earnings in the banking sector and other service branches improved substantially, while earnings in the material production branches increased very little. But whereas rapidly increasing incomes from trade attracted new workers, the education, state administration, health and social service sectors experienced a shortage of labour in response to

Table 16.4 *Earnings distributions 1988–1994 (coefficients and decile shares in percentages)*

	Year 1988 gross	Year 1992 gross	January 1993 net	November 1993 net	November 1994 net
Coeff. of variation	0.35	0.48	0.54	0.61	0.58
Gini coefficient	0.19	0.23	0.27	0.27	0.28
Decile shares					
1	5.3	5.0	4.5	4.5	4.5
2	6.6	6.1	5.6	5.7	5.1
3	7.4	6.9	6.4	6.5	6.4
4	8.3	7.7	7.2	7.1	7.2
5	9.2	8.5	8.1	7.9	8.1
6	10.0	9.4	9.0	8.8	8.9
7	10.9	10.4	10.5	10.1	10.3
8	12.0	11.7	12.1	11.7	11.8
9	13.3	13.8	14.1	13.9	14.2
10	17.0	20.5	22.6	23.8	23.5
Total	100.0	100.0	100.0	100.0	100.0
Robin Hood Index[a]	13.2	16.4	19.3	19.5	19.8

Note:
[a] The 'Robin Hood Index' (coined in Atkinson and Micklewright 1992) measures the share of incomes necessary to equalise the whole distribution.
Sources: Microcensus 1989 and 1992; Economic Expectations and Attitudes, 1993–4.

their declining relative earning potential. The cleavage between the public and private sector so far has been substantial in terms of whole industries and is now beginning to widen considerably in more specific areas.

Drawing together the broad spectrum of various earnings determinants, table 16.7 shows the results of estimating standard ln earnings equations. The demographic variables of gender and age continue to be the most important factors affecting earnings in 1993. Educational achievement has a lower but very significant explanatory power (with a contribution of 5 per cent of the explained variance). The importance of occupational and branch divisions in labour seems to be even lower (with contributions of only 4 per cent). Classification by ownership also reveals some considerable differences, with the cooperative and state sectors at the bottom and larger private firms at the top of the income hierarchy (contributing at least 6 per cent of the explained variance).

Table 16.5 *Returns to education in east-central Europe (multiple regression analysis, dep. variable=earnings)*

		gross/ net	years of school	experience	exp²/100	female	R²
Czech R.	1988[a]	gross	0.040	0.037	−0.064	−0.335	0.441
Slovak R.	1988[a]	gross	0.046	0.057	−0.034	−0.333	0.479
E. Germany	1988[c]	gross	0.077	0.020	−0.035	−0.234	0.414
W. Germany	1988[c]	gross	0.077	0.045	−0.077	−0.251	0.457
USA	1986[e]	gross	0.094	0.038	−0.062	−0.228	0.228
Czech R.	1992[b]	gross	0.050	0.023	−0.046	−0.274	0.302
E. Germany	1991[c]	gross	0.062	0.014	−0.020	−0.198	0.284
Czech R.	1992[d]	net	0.048	0.003	−0.048	−0.307	0.248
Hungary	1992[d]	net	0.054	0.004	0.002	−0.232	0.265
Poland	1992[d]	net	0.056	0.007	−0.001	−0.351	0.204
Slovakia	1992[d]	net	0.038	0.014	−0.005	−0.291	0.269

Sources: [a] Microcensus 1989.
[b] Microcensus 1992.
[c] Krueger and Pischke 1992.
[d] Social Stratification survey.
[e] Luxembourg Income Study database.

Table 16.6 *Earnings according to branch of employment 1988–1993 (percentages, total average gross earnings=100)*

	1988	1989	1990	1991	1992	1993
Manufacturing	104.5	104.4	103.8	103.6	103.5	101.3
Construction	111.3	111.2	109.9	106.6	108.2	112.3
Agriculture	106.5	108.2	109.6	97.7	91.8	87.7
Transport and communications	107.5	106.4	104.6	103.2	99.1	97.5
Trade and catering	82.5	83.8	85.0	86.2	90.1	88.6
Health and welfare	90.2	90.1	92.6	96.6	94.5	95.0
Education	90.4	89.8	88.1	90.3	90.6	90.3
Banking and insurance	97.1	98.3	102.0	136.9	169.6	177.7
Administration	101.8	101.3	100.4	105.3	114.6	117.8
Other services	90.6	91.1	90.6	89.8	94.4	96.3
Total	100.0	100.0	100.0	100.0	100.0	100.0

Source: Wage statistics of firms.

Table 16.7 *Determination of earnings by demographic and economic variables (multiple regression analysis, dep. variable = ln earnings, standardised regression coefficients)*

Variable	I	II	III	IV
SEX	−0.356***	−0.325***	−0.312***	−0.294***
A2 (Age)	0.124***	0.080**	0.091***	0.082***
A3	0.149***	0.142***	0.159***	0.165***
A4	−0.030	−0.012	.042	0.069*
A5	−0.332***	−0.246**	−0.119***	−0.047***
E2 (Education)		0.106***	0.073**	0.069**
E3		0.201***	0.194***	0.173***
E4		0.410***	0.409***	0.353***
Z1 (Occupation)			0.078*	0.036
Z2			0.021	0.000
Z3			0.037*	−0.021
Z5			0.064**	0.018
S2 (Sector)			0.126***	0.048
S3			0.105**	0.053
S4			0.264***	0.078**
S5			0.208**	0.126*
S6			0.138*	0.066*
S7			0.047***	−0.011
O1 (Ownership)				0.135***
O3				0.194***
O4				0.347***
O5				0.587***
R2	0.286	0.337	0.375	0.439

Notes:
*** significance on the level <0.001
  ** significance on the level <0.01
   * significance on the level <0.05
Source: Economic Expectations and Attitudes, January 1993.

Description of variables
SEX= Male–female
Age
A1 = 20–9 (omitted category)
A2 = 30–9
A3 = 40–9
A4 = 50–9
A5 = 60–

Annex to table 16.7 (*cont.*)
Education
E1 = elementary (omitted category)
E2 = vocational
E3 = secondary
E4 = university
Occupation
Z1 = professionals
Z2 = clerks and employees
Z3 = workers in business and services
Z4 = agricultural workers (omitted category)
Z5 = manual labourers in manufacturing industry, construction, etc.
Sector
S1 = agriculture, forestry (omitted category)
S2 = manufacturing industry, building
S3 = transport, communications
S4 = trade, services
S5 = banks, insurance
S6 = administration, social services
S7 = education, health care, research, cultural services
Ownership
O1 = state enterprise
O2 = cooperative organisation or firm (omitted category)
O3 = other state organisation
O4 = employee of a private firm or enterprise
O5 = owner of a firm or enterprise

5   Attitudes towards earnings inequality

For economic reforms to succeed, the creation and entrenchment of a competitive and anti-equalising climate is likely to be necessary, as opposed to the equalising climate under Communist rule. In the initial post-revolutionary period, enthusiasm is increasing, and people are ready to make sacrifices and accept large inequalities provided they are efficient. In contrast to early affinity, direct experience of the transformation has made people more cautious. They see that the Communist nomenklatura has survived and converted its political capital into economic capital; black marketeers enrich themselves with ease, speculation is more successful than fair-playing entrepreneurship and the creation of new firms is burdened by complicated procedures and subject to huge taxes. This makes for a rapid turnabout in attitudes.

Table 16.8 shows the change in several attitudes concerning earnings disparities. A considerable and stable percentage of the population is (at

Table 16.8 *Opinions on income inequality and wealth and poverty legitimacy (per cent)*

	May 1990	Dec. 1990	June 1991	Dec. 1991	June 1992	Jan. 1993	Nov. 1993	Nov. 1994
'It is right that capable and competent people have a lot of money, even millions.'								
	40.5	47.0	49.5	45.0	47.4	42.8	40.7	37.1
	67.9	77.0	81.6	76.5	82.5	78.6	78.8	78.0
'Differences in wages and salaries should increase.'								
	57.8	55.5		48.0	43.4	35.2	24.9	20.5
	89.4	87.7		84.3	81.7	74.2	66.7	62.2
'A competent and hard-working person can soon become wealthy.'								
			29.2		31.5	20.8		12.0
			56.5		67.0	39.3		48.2
'Each person is responsible for his/her own poverty.'								
					18.0	15.2	11.8	7.1
					59.0	54.2	44.1	37.0
'People get rich mostly by unfair means.'								
					31.7	34.4	40.4	38.6
					76.2	79.9	80.3	79.6

Notes:
For categories of answers see table 16.1.
First line = percentage answers 'definitely yes'
Second line = percentage answers 'definitely yes' plus 'rather yes'
Source: Economic Expectations and Attitudes, 1990–4 (population 25–60 years only).

least verbally) ready to accept salaries in the 'millions for competent people,' but the portion of the population convinced that differences in earnings should be greater is steadily decreasing. A majority of respondents – albeit decreasing – share the opinion that 'a competent and hard-working person can soon become wealthy'. Even more people are convinced that 'people get rich mostly by unfair means'. Whereas wealth is considered mostly illegitimate, the state is increasingly blamed before the poor themselves. Suspicion (largely legitimate) and jealousy (deeply rooted) of the new rich have arisen, while the equality/efficiency trade-off (Okun 1975) is apparently not yet functioning in people's minds.

To a lesser and greater extent, the same is true of all of east-central Europe. According to the 'Social Inequality' and 'The Dismantling of the Safety Net and its Political Consequences' surveys, there are considerable differences in the relative tolerance for income inequalities and expectations of state involvement in income distribution. The belief that enabling businessmen to make profits is the best strategy for all is most accepted in Poland (where there is also a large non-response rate) and in the Czech Republic. Similarly, considerable differences in earnings are tolerated most in Poland and the Czech Republic. Finally, the attitude that differences in incomes are too great is most prevalent in Slovakia and very strong in Hungary and Poland. Although also rooted in Communist egalitarianism and etatism, the Czech population seems to be the most market-oriented and the least demanding of etatist solutions.

For the near future, it is still an open question whether the difficulties inherent in the development of economic reform will maintain or even strengthen the old climate of equalisation and attitudes characteristic of the socialist system of 'social guarantees'. The balance between the welfare state and the market incentives, and between a functional and unjust inequality, are extremely precarious everywhere. They are even more shaky in post-Communist societies, where the old Communist structure of privileges transferred into personal wealth is trying to reproduce itself and enter the new stage of the market economy. The population's views are rather ambiguous in this sense because people simultaneously demand increased incentives for market behaviour and more social security. Nevertheless, people's attitudes are also crystallising insofar as the divisions between the more market-oriented and social-protection-oriented populations are becoming clearer.

6   Conclusions and discussion

The transformation period requires profound changes on both the demand and supply sides of the labour market. First, full employment, which served the Communist regime both for its publicity value and as an instrument of control, is being replaced by the interplay of market forces; as a result, unemployment is appearing and increasing. Second, jobs under market conditions pose new requirements for skills and new responsibilities for workers. Third, the state is withdrawing from labour administration before other institutions appear. This has led to a period of friction and confusion during the search for new ways of matching jobs and people. This is also a period in which increasing labour mobility is accompanied by the tensions and stresses produced by these changes.

In the intermediary period, the labour market is emerging not as a homogeneous whole but as various fragments and segments, depending on the kind of industry, type of ownership and regional character. In fact, modern economic and sociological theories have also shown that the market is not homogeneous but heterogeneous. According to the labour market segmentation theory, only the external market (or secondary sector) is characterised by the open play of supply and demand, whereas the internal market is treated as 'an administrative unit . . . within which the market functions of pricing, allocating, and often training are governed by a set of institutional rules and procedures' (Doeringer and Piore 1971, pp. 1–2). In the primary sector, working conditions are better, allocation principles clearer, returns to personal investments higher and promotion rules more advantageous.

In east-central Europe, the labour market will probably be divided, and the development of its individual parts uneven. Expansion of large foreign and multinational firms into the newly opened markets will introduce a situation akin to the primary sector. Further temporary boundaries and divisions are nevertheless now being created. The first is due to small private firms moving into the hitherto centralised system. In the initial period, small private firms were established on entrepreneurial courage and skills and on previously accumulated property (family, black market, Communist). The second is represented by the introduction of western firms and foreign capital. In both cases, the common relations and forms of reward are broken. Whereas the reward policy in state firms produces further equalisation (low wages rise faster than high wages to maintain the standard of living for lower-paid workers), small businesses and western firms introduce greater earnings inequality.

Despite the introduction and rise of minimum wages, overall earnings inequality has increased considerably in the Czech Republic since the Velvet Revolution of 1989. In addition, in other east-central European countries the range of earnings distribution has widened and reached – or even exceeded – that in neighbouring western countries. In concrete terms, some increases were due to higher returns to education. Lawyers, bank officials and managers were all winners in the transformation. On the other hand, teachers, physicians and educated people in social and cultural services have thus far been the losers. Unlike education, the branch differentials forced under the Communist regime are being attenuated under the transformation. Replacing them, differences in the ownership sector are appearing, with new foreign and domestic private firms faring better than the old state firms, however transformed they might be.

In the transformation period, workers' subjective potential, their human capital and their commitment and adaptability are at least as important as available financial capital and other objective conditions. Although there is a lower percentage of university-educated people in the Czech labour force than in neighbouring countries (including Slovakia), an increasing majority feels more or less ready to face the new requirements of the market order. This percentage has not decreased since the initial, some-times discouraging, experience. Most skills, jobs and firms are likely to survive. Most workers do not foresee big problems in the market-oriented future, and most people view the capitalist solution (through good profits for private business) as the best way to increase everyone's standard of living.

In contrast with this acceptance of the market, tolerance to earnings inequality is decreasing. After a short period of enthusiasm towards the widening range of income distribution (as a spontaneous reaction to the previous extreme equalisation of reward), most people are once again becoming suspicious of large inequalities. The percentage of people who believe that differences in salaries should increase is lessening, with most respondents believing that differences in income are already too great. Such a continuous change in attitudes is partly legitimated by recent expe-riences, which have generated a great deal of suspicion of the nouveaux riches. Simultaneously, however, this change reveals a return to previous values of levelling and social envy towards the establishment of middle and upper classes.

The greatest lesson we can learn from the study of recent changes in the labour market and earnings inequality in the Czech Republic and other east-central European countries is that there is a progressive differentia-tion of economic changes in countries experiencing social change, the dis-tinctive career paths of individuals and a crystallisation of people's attitudes. Instead of the east-central European region or populace consti-tuting one opaque whole, we face national specificities amongst the regions and emerging social differences amongst the countries, both of which affect the labour market's success or failure, increases or decreases in real earnings and loyalty to or contestation of the regime in very concrete terms.

Note

This paper is a reworking of an earlier paper using new data and completed during my stay at the Russell Sage Foundation in New York City, 1–15 December 1993. I express my sincerest thanks to Eric Wanner, President of the Foundation; Madge Spitaleri, Foundation Secretary; and to the Foundation staff for providing excellent research facilities. I gratefully extend my thanks to Professor Lee Rainwater, Harvard University, principal investigator of the project 'Labor Markets and Economic Well-Being,' and to Professor Peter Gottschalk, Boston College, a project participant, for their valuable comments and suggestions. I also thank Vivian Kaufman, of the Russell Sage Foundation, for editing this paper.

References

Atkinson, A. B. and Micklewright, J. 1992. *The Economic Transformation of Eastern Europe and the Distribution of Income.* Cambridge University Press.

Becker, G. S. 1964. *Human Capital.* New York: Columbia University Press.

Doeringer, P. B. and Piore, M. J. 1971. *Internal Labour Markets and Manpower Analysis.* Lexington, MA: Heath.

Krueger, A. B. and Pischke, J.-S. 1992. 'A Comparative Analysis of East and West German Labor Markets Before and After Unification'. Zentrum für Europäische Wirtschaftforschung Discussion Paper No. 92–11.

Microcensus 1989, conducted by the former Federal Statistical Office on a 2 per cent random sample of households ($N = 69912$) in March 1989 and including yearly incomes 1988.

Microcensus 1992, conducted by the Czech Statistical Office on a 0.5 per cent random sample of households ($N = 16234$) in March 1993 and including yearly incomes 1992.

Mincer, J. 1974. *Schooling, Experience and Earnings.* New York: National Bureau of Economic Research.

Možný, I. 1992. 'An Attempt at a Non-Economic Explanation of the Present Full Employment'. *Czech Sociological Review*, 1, 2: 199–210.

OECD. 1993. *OECD Employment Outlook 1993.* Paris: OECD.

Okun, A. M. 1975. *Equality and Efficiency, the Big Trade-Off.* Washington: Brookings Institution.

Rutkowski, J. 1994. 'Labor Market Transition and Changes in Wage Structure: The Case of Poland'. Center for International Studies, Princeton University.

Večerník, J. 1991. 'Earnings Distribution in Czechoslovakia: Intertemporal Changes and International Comparison'. *European Sociological Review*, 7, 3: 237–52.

    1995. 'Changing Earnings Distribution in the Czech Republic'. *Economics of Transition*, 3(3): 355–71.

Surveys used

'Economic Expectations and Attitudes'
Survey organised by the socioeconomics team of the Institute of Sociology of the Academy of Sciences. The quota-based samples include about 2,000 adults, 18 to 60 years of age. Surveys were conducted biannually between May 1990 and January 1993 and annually thereafter.

'The Dismantling of the Safety Net and its Political Consequences'
Survey conducted in October 1991. Coordinated and financed by the Institute of East–West Security Studies, New York. The international file includes: the Czech Republic (1187), Slovakia (817), Hungary (1500) and Poland (1491).

'Social Inequality – 1992'
Regular module of the ISSP (International Social Science Programme) series,

carried out in October 1992. Four national files were used here: the Czech Republic (687), Slovakia (423), Hungary (1250) and Poland (1647).

'Social Stratification – 1993'

International comparative research project 'Social Stratification in Eastern Europe after 1989' coordinated by the Institute for Social Science Research of the University of California, Los Angeles. The principal investigators are Donald J. Treiman and Ivan Szelenyi. Six former Communist countries participated in the project: the Czech Republic (5621), Slovakia (4920), Hungary (4997), Poland (3520), Russia (5002) and Bulgaria (4919).

Name index

Subject index